# Taiwan

## a travel survival kit

台灣

**Robert Storey**

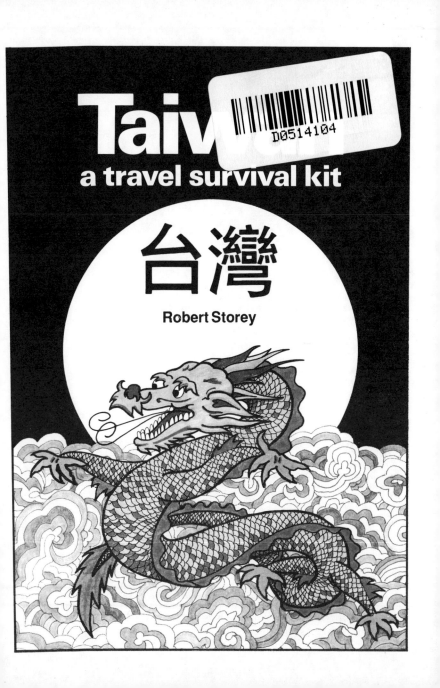

**Taiwan – a travel survival kit**
2nd edition

**Published by**
Lonely Planet Publications
Head Office: PO Box 617, Hawthorn, Vic 3122, Australia
US Office: PO Box 2001A, Berkeley, CA 94702, USA

**Printed by**
Colorcraft Ltd, Hong Kong

**Photographs by**
Robert Storey
Robert Strauss
Front cover: Aboriginal Women in Traditional Costume (Far East Trading Co)

**First Published**
November 1987

**This Edition**
December 1990

**Although the authors and publisher have tried to make the information as accurate as possible, they accept no responsibility for any loss, injury or inconvenience sustained by any person using this book.**

National Library of Australia Cataloguing in Publication Data

Storey, Robert.
Taiwan – a travel survival kit.

2nd ed.
Includes index.
ISBN 0 86442 100 1.

1. Taiwan – Description and travel – 1975 – Guide-books.
I. Title .

915.1249045

### Robert Storey

Robert Storey is an experienced budget traveller who has spent much of his life trekking all over the backwaters of the USA pursuing his favourite hobby, mountain climbing. Having explored all 50 states, he then ventured into neighbouring Canada and Mexico and then on to Australia, South-East Asia, China, Japan and Europe.

Robert has had a number of distinguished careers, including taking care of monkeys at a zoo and repairing slot machines in Las Vegas. Presently back in the USA, he often wanders around deserts and mountains carrying essential survival gear such as his camera and IBM portable computer. Robert has updated two other Lonely Planet travel survival kits: *Hong Kong, Macau & Canton* and *China*. He is also the author of a bestselling English textbook in Taiwan, *Creative Conversation*.

### From the Author

Special thanks go to Meimei for her diligent efforts at proofing and translating Chinese. In Tainan, special thanks to Pamela Hong for her tireless assistance. In Taipei, appreciation goes to Jason Gau, Derek Anderson, Sean Curtin and Phillip Deery for all the information they supplied. I am also indebted to Nick Voudouris, Daniel Matonic, Chen Longchen, George Lu, Jack Tsai, Wu Hsiuchueh, Hsieh Yuhsia, Shih Chuancheng, David Chen and Bill Slay for their help and suggestions. Thanks also to the Lonely Planet staff who worked on this book.

### Lonely Planet Credits

| Editor | Michelle de Kretser |
|---|---|
| Maps | Vicki Beale |
| | Peter Flavelle |
| Cover design | |
| & design | Trudi Canavan |
| Illustrations | Vicki Beale |
| | Ann Jeffree |

Special thanks to Chris Taylor for additional editing and proofing the Chinese script. Thanks also to Greg Alford for proofing and author corrections; to Sharon Wertheim for indexing; and to Sue Mitra for patient supervision.

### A Warning & a Request

Things change – prices go up, hotels go out of business and new ones open up, even government policies on visas can suddenly change. This is especially true in a rapidly changing place like Taiwan. If you come across some information in this book that you believe is outdated, please write to Lonely Planet and let us know.

Your letters will be used to help update future editions, and where possible important changes will also be included as a Stop Press section in reprints.

We love letters from out on the road and good letters are rewarded with a free copy of the next edition or another Lonely Planet guide if you prefer.

# Contents

# Introduction

On the world map, Taiwan looks very small when compared to the neighbouring giant landmass of Asia, the world's largest continent. With Hong Kong, mainland China and Japan drawing in most of the tourists to the region, Taiwan tends to be forgotten. But that 'small island', 395 km long with a population of 20 million, offers a great deal to those who take the time to visit it.

Taiwan has one of the world's most dynamic export-oriented economies and is a familiar destination for many business travellers. Just a few decades ago, Taiwan only produced low-technology goods like clothes and cheap toys. Today, Taiwan manufactures TV sets, cameras and computers. No longer considered in the Third World, Taiwan is classified as a 'newly industrialised country (NIC)'. Economists playfully refer to Taiwan, along with South Korea, Singapore and Hong Kong, as one of Asia's 'Little Dragons'.

One could say that Taiwan has two faces: one is the factories, container ships and crowded cities; but there's also the other, lesser known side of Taiwan – exotic Chinese culture, Taoist temples, wonderful food, friendly people, beaches, bamboo forests and spectacular mountain scenery. The Portuguese sailors called it Ihla Formosa, which literally means 'Island Beautiful', and the name is still appropriate.

Taiwan is a fast-changing, complex society that defies simple generalisations. Due to the rapid advances in health and an increase in the average life expectancy, Taiwan's population is among the most dense in the world. But the standard of living and level of education have also increased. Western pop music and clothing are in vogue, yet students still study traditional Chinese waterpainting and calligraphy. Hamburgers and disco are popular, but so are chopsticks and Chinese shadow boxing. In spite of the effects of Westernisation, Chinese culture remains alive and flourishing. To see Taiwan today is to see a society in transition.

When the Chinese travel abroad, it's usually with a tour group. A solo traveller so far away from home is a real oddity. People will be curious about you, but you will discover that the Chinese are amongst the most hospitable people in the world. Above all, the Chinese fear loneliness and they will go out of their way to make sure you are not lonely. The Chinese have an expression, rén qíng wèi, which means 'warm feelings' towards people. Perhaps the greatest pleasure of travelling in Taiwan is the hospitality you will receive everywhere you go.

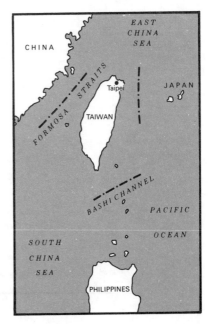

7

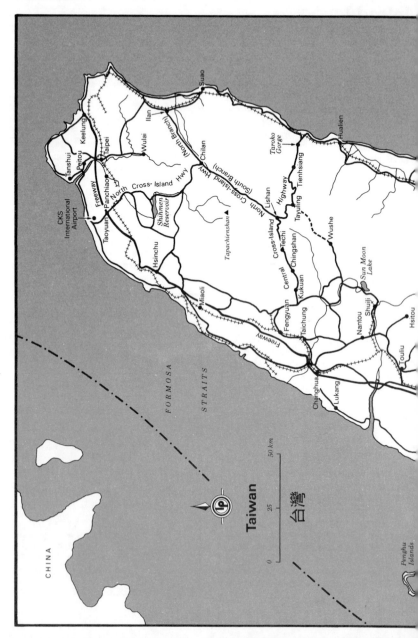

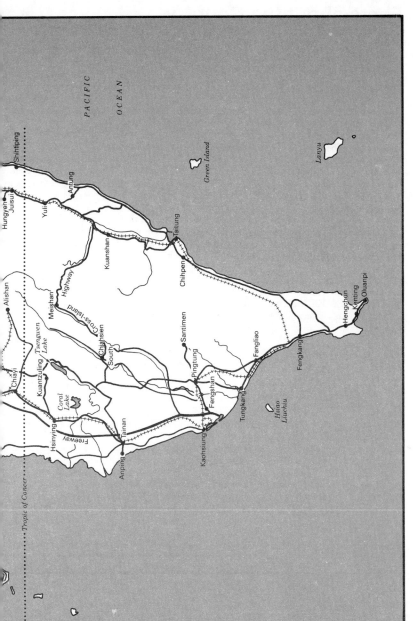

# Facts about the Country

## HISTORY
### The Aborigines
Little is known of Taiwan's earliest history, but with the results of radiocarbon dating of primitive utensils it has been estimated that people have inhabited Taiwan for at least 10,000 years. The Chinese were not the first inhabitants of Taiwan. In fact Taiwan has always been on the periphery of the Chinese Empire and, although Chinese history dates back more than 3000 years, there was no significant Chinese migration to Taiwan until the 17th century. Indeed, the earliest inhabitants probably migrated from the Pacific islands. The descendants of these aborigines live mostly in the mountains and eastern parts of Taiwan.

When the Chinese arrived in Taiwan, there were two distinct groups of aborigines. One lived on the rich plains of central and south-western Taiwan and the other group lived in the mountains.

### Arrival of the Chinese
The first Chinese emigrants to reach Taiwan were probably the Hakka. Coming from the Henan province in northern China, the Hakka people first moved to the Guangdong and Fujian provinces in the south to escape severe persecution in their homelands. The name Hakka means 'guests' and as guests in search of a home, they gradually trickled into Taiwan in small numbers. When the Hakkas began to settle in large numbers, they drove the aborigines living on the plains into the mountains. The Hakka speak their own dialect. Perhaps due to the persecution they have suffered and the severe conditions they once lived under, the Hakka have a reputation for being hard workers, especially the women.

Beginning in the 1400s and increasing thereafter, large numbers of Chinese from the Fujian province migrated to the island. Fujian is just across the straits from Taiwan so this doesn't seem surprising. The Fujian-ese have always been the keenest travellers among the Chinese, and today they can be found all over South-East Asia. The Fujian dialect is virtually the same as the Taiwanese dialect.

### European Imperialism
In 1517 the first Europeans – Portuguese sailors – landed on Taiwan's shores and were so impressed by the beautiful scenery that they named it Ihla Formosa, which literally means 'Island Beautiful'. The name Formosa has been used right up to the present, though nowadays it is considered proper to use the Chinese name Taiwan, which means 'Terraced Bay'.

Following the tradition of European imperialism in Asia, the Dutch decided to invade Taiwan in 1624. The Dutch established the first capital on Taiwan at what is now the city of Tainan in the south-west part of the island. Two years later the Spanish grabbed control of north Taiwan, but were expelled by the Dutch in 1641.

Meanwhile, blood was flowing on the mainland as the up-and-coming Ching (Manchu) Dynasty armies were destroying the Ming Dynasty supporters. Fleeing the victorious Manchu armies, Cheng Chengkung, also known as Koxinga, arrived in Taiwan with 30,000 troops in 8000 war junks. In 1661 he successfully expelled the Dutch from their stronghold in Tainan.

### The Manchu Period
Koxinga's forces hoped to launch an invasion to recapture the mainland from the Manchus, but instead the Manchu armies captured Taiwan in 1682. For the next 200 years there was substantial migration from the Fujian province across the Formosa Straits to Taiwan. These immigrants brought with them their culture and language, which are still in evidence today. Taiwan remained a county of the Fujian province from 1684 until 1887, when with a population of more

10

than 2½ million it became a province of China.

## Japanese Imperialism

In 1895 a dispute over Korea led to the Sino-Japanese War. China was defeated and as a result Japan went on to occupy Korea. Being a somewhat remote place, Taiwan managed to avoid most of the dislocations of war which took place on the mainland, but in 1895 Taiwan was ceded to Japan as one of the spoils of the Sino-Japanese War.

Although the Japanese brought law and order, they also brought harsh rule. Many of Taiwan's residents objected and rebelled, proclaiming an independent republic. The republic, the first in Asia, was short-lived as the Japanese quickly and brutally crushed it. For the next 50 years Taiwan remained part of Japan. The Japanese influence was quite extensive and even today many of the older people speak Japanese.

Although the Japanese ruled with an iron fist, they were efficient and contributed substantially to Taiwan's economic and educational development. During their rule Taiwan became more developed than mainland China. The Japanese built roads, railroads, schools, hospitals and also improved agricultural techniques. However, WW II created a great demand for men and raw materials to feed Japan's war machine. By the time the war had ended, Taiwan's economy, along with the rest of China and Japan, was in ruins.

## The Kuomintang Era

Events in mainland China were destined to affect Taiwan's future greatly. China's last dynasty – the Ching Dynasty – collapsed in 1911 following a nationwide rebellion led by Dr Sun Yatsen, who became the first president of the Republic of China (ROC). Dr Sun did not lust for power, but instead stepped down in favour of Yuan Shihkai. Unfortunately, Yuan did not share Dr Sun's vision of a democratic China and he attempted to install himself as a new emperor. He was unsuccessful and died in 1916.

A period of civil war ensued while various rival warlords and factions struggled for power. Unity was eventually restored when the Nationalist army, led by Generalissimo Chiang Kaishek, took power. However, the Nationalist Party (Kuomintang or KMT) soon found itself beleaguered by Japan's growing militancy and the communist rebellion. In 1931, Japanese forces occupied Manchuria. In 1937, the Japanese invaded the Chinese heartland.

Under the Yalta Agreement, China regained sovereignty over Taiwan with Japan's defeat in WW II. In 1949, as the communists wrested control of the Chinese mainland, the Kuomintang, led by Chiang Kaishek, fled to Taiwan. About 1½ million Chinese, including 600,000 soldiers, moved to Taiwan after the communists captured the mainland. As a result, the island's population grew from around 6 million in 1946 to 7½ million in 1950.

Kuomintang troops were able to hold the battle line at two small islands – Kinmen (Quemoy) and Matsu – just off the Chinese mainland, a position they still occupy. An invasion of Taiwan was fully expected, but the communist army became more bogged down in the Korean War and the USA sent its 7th Fleet into the Formosa Straits.

The Kuomintang maintained from the beginning that their stay in Taiwan was temporary – that they would retake mainland China from the communists very soon, and that in the meantime no political opposition could be permitted. Such policies did not necessarily endear the KMT to the native Taiwanese. Nevertheless, the KMT proved itself capable of repairing Taiwan's war-torn economy. An excellent land-reform programme was introduced in the 1950s which resulted in a far more equitable income distribution than is found in most Asian countries. Rapid industrialisation in the 1960s made Taiwan one of the wealthiest places in Asia.

In October 1971 the Kuomintang lost the China United Nations seat. A further blow came in January 1979, when the USA withdrew recognition of the ROC and recognised the communist regime on the mainland. Most countries have withdrawn their diplomatic recognition of the Republic of China. In spite of this, most of the noncommunist world maintains very strong unofficial economic ties with Taiwan.

Chiang Kaishek died in 1975 at the age of 87 from a heart attack. His son, Chiang Chingkuo, became president of the Republic of China in 1978 after an election was held. He was re-elected and served a second term.

In 1986, a major event occurred in Taiwan's political history with the formation of the Democratic Progressive Party (DPP). The DPP was formed in spite of a government ban on new political parties. After much debate, the KMT – under the specific orders of President Chiang Chingkuo – decided not to interfere with the DPP. A large number of DPP candidates were elected in 1986 and were permitted to take their seats in the legislature, thus creating Taiwan's first genuine opposition party. The first really free election for the legislature was in 1989. The Kuomintang took approximately 70% of the vote with the remainder going mostly to the DPP.

In 1987, 38 years of martial law ended. It was one of the last important acts of Chiang Chingkuo, who died in January 1988. He was succeeded by Lee Tenghui, the first native Taiwanese to hold the post of president.

## GEOGRAPHY

Shaped roughly like a tobacco leaf, Taiwan is an island just a mere 160 km from the Fujian province of mainland China. A flight to Hong Kong only takes an hour, while Japan and Korea require a 2 hour flight. The maximum length of the island is 395 km and its maximum width is 144 km. In spite of its small size, the mountains are extremely high. The highest mountain in Taiwan is Yushan (Jade Mountain) at 3950 metres, which makes it higher than Japan's Mt Fuji.

The mountains rise straight out of the sea on Taiwan's east coast, but the west side of the island is a flat and fertile plain. This geography makes the western side of the island much more hospitable for human habitation, and 90% of Taiwan's population

Mei blossom,
the national flower

resides there. This makes the mountainous eastern side far more scenic.

In addition to the island of Taiwan itself, there are a number of smaller offshore islands which can be visited by tourists. These include the Penghu Islands, Lanyu, Lutao and Hsiao Liuchiu. There are two other major islands controlled by the ROC, Kinmen and Matsu. Both these islands are within eyesight of mainland China and therefore serve as military bases.

Taipei, at the very northern end of the island, is the largest city and seat of the federal government. The provincial government has its headquarters in the village of Chunghsing, near Taichung in central Taiwan. Other large cities include Kaohsiung, Taichung and Tainan – all on the west side of the island.

## CLIMATE

Taiwan is a subtropical island with two – rather than four – seasons. For such a small island, there are considerable variations in climate. Winter is most noticeable in the northern and eastern parts of the island. Taipei has an unpleasantly cool, gloomy, damp winter, but it never freezes. The northeast is very wet, but the south-west is warmer and drier. Summer is uniformly hot and wet throughout the island, except for the mountains which are even wetter but definitely cooler.

From November through to March or the middle of April, the monsoonal winds from Central Asia often cause a sudden plunge in temperature. In the northern coastal area of Taiwan, it can get down to around 10°C and in the mountains it can snow.

Spring is warm and mild but there are frequent rains throughout the island known as the 'plum rain'. The rains can continue through to August but the wettest month is usually June.

Summer is the typhoon season. The brief autumn season (October and November) is the most delightful time to visit the island, though typhoons are possible in October. Autumn temperatures are ideal and it is the driest time of year, especially in the southwest.

## Typhoons

One should not be overly concerned about typhoons, but a few words of warning are in order. A typhoon is what we in the West normally call a hurricane or a cyclone. It's a large tropical storm – basically just a lot of wind and rain. Typhoons occur mostly in the summer, but some years can pass with no typhoons at all.

Some typhoons are weak and not much worse than a thunderstorm, but others are 'super-typhoons' which can level trees and houses. Typhoons are tricky – they can change course suddenly, wreaking havoc on the weather forecast. I've often cancelled a weekend trip due to the threat of a typhoon, only to have the storm change direction and move away from Taiwan. In Taiwan, the east coast gets the worst typhoons because they come in from the Pacific Ocean. The west coast is better protected by the mountains.

If a typhoon alert is issued while you are in Taiwan, be equipped to stay indoors for at least a day, maybe 2. Have some books and magazines, candles and matches, a flashlight, food (canned and dried goods) and water. Lastly, don't worry, a typhoon is just a bad storm and the worst that is likely to happen is that you'll get bored waiting for it to end.

## GOVERNMENT

Democracy has come recently to Taiwan. Martial law only ended in 1987, but since that time the political process has been thrown almost wide open. The Kuomintang is still in control, but the current president, Lee Tenghui, has shown himself to be a political moderate. He performs a delicate balancing act between the hardline conservatives who still plan to retake mainland China, and the younger generation, who are more interested in Taiwan's political and economic development.

The Democratic Progressive Party (DPP) is by far the largest opposition party. And no discussion of Taiwan's politics would be complete without also mentioning the tiny Labor Party, which is well known for colourful candidate Hsu Hsiaotan, a dancer with a propensity for stripping in public. So far, Ms Hsu has been unsuccessful in obtaining office, but her presence on the political scene shows just how liberal Taiwan's politics have become in an amazingly short time. There are also some independent legislators, the so-called 'nonpartisans'.

Power is distributed among five major branches of government which are called Yuan – the Legislative, Executive, Judicial, Examination and Control Yuan. The first three are self-explanatory. The Examination Yuan oversees Taiwan's formidable system of exams, which determines one's access to education, jobs, business licences, etc. The Control Yuan is a watchdog agency that tries to keep things honest.

Next to the president, the premier is the most powerful figure because he or she appoints the heads of Taiwan's many ministries which oversee the ubiquitous bureaucracy.

The Communist Party and Kuomintang agree on little, but one thing they do agree on is that Taiwan is still a province of China, not an independent country. Both the KMT and the Communist Party claim to be the sole legitimate government of China. Reunification of China remains a national goal, even though the two sides are far apart in their ideologies. In Taiwan the DPP is split on the issue: the radical New Tide faction advocates Taiwanese independence, while the Formosa faction is willing to settle for a vaguely defined 'self-determination'. Ideology aside, most Taiwanese are mindful of the fact that the communists have repeatedly threatened to launch a military invasion should Taiwan declare independence from the mainland.

Foreign visitors should not make the mistake of calling Taiwan a country. Taiwan is a province of China and the people are Chinese.

All over Taiwan you can see statues and monuments honouring Chiang Kaishek and also Dr Sun Yatsen, the founding father of the Republic of China. Their pictures appear on all ROC-issued coins and paper currency, and they are regarded as national heroes.

Those wishing to understand the political doctrine of the ruling Kuomintang might want to read Dr Sun Yatsen's *The Three Principles of the People*. Be forewarned that the book is not easy reading. The three principles – Nationalism, Livelihood and Civil Rights – are constantly promoted by the government. The book is required reading for all students in Taiwan. To get a government job, one must pass an exam in the three principles. The national anthem is entitled 'Three Principles of the People'. Every city in Taiwan has a Mintsu (Nationalism) Rd, a Minsheng (Livelihood) Rd and a Minchuan (Civil Rights) Rd, as well as a Chungshan (Sun Yatsen) Rd.

## ECONOMY

The business of Taiwan is business. Starting from an economy shattered by WW II, the island has experienced rapid economic growth. Annual per capita income in 1989 was over US$7500 and increasing rapidly. The engine behind this economic success story is largely foreign trade. The label 'Made in Taiwan' can be found on merchandise sold all over the world. Taiwan's exports in 1989 were valued at over US$60 billion, exceeding those of mainland China.

Indeed, one of Taiwan's biggest headaches is trying to find a solution to the foreign trade imbalance, which is heavily weighted in Taiwan's favour. Taiwan is believed to have the world's second-largest reserves of foreign currency, surpassed only by Japan. So much foreign currency is piling up in Taiwan's banks that it is causing inflationary pressure. With too much money and too many government regulations to invest it freely abroad, a lot of speculative money has poured into real estate and the stock market. As a result, real estate prices have doubled in about 2 years and the stock market has come to resemble a gambling casino. The government-owned banks lose money because they must pay interest on deposits but have trouble finding enough borrowers – everyone has enough money, so why borrow? It is a problem, but a problem that many other countries wish they had.

Although many foreigners assume that Taiwan has a thoroughly capitalist, free-market economy like Hong Kong, it is in fact regulated by a number of cumbersome bureaucratic controls and more social programmes than most foreigners realise. The state heavily subsidises education and transportation, even in remote rural areas. A lot of government money has gone into public health, family planning, agriculture and reforestation. Government workers, of which there are too many, enjoy numerous health insurance benefits and pensions. It's true that there are no welfare schemes of the type found in Sweden and many semisocialist countries, but no one in Taiwan appears to be starving.

Another role the government plays in the economy is seen in the many large government-owned monopolies controlling such industries as tobacco and liquor, sugar, telephones, bus and rail transportation, and banking. In this sense, Taiwan's economy is more socialist than most people think. The government has been talking a lot about privatising the banks, but so far it's been more talk than action. Nevertheless, private business flourishes and remains the backbone of the economy. Furthermore, the economy is undergoing a gradual process of deregulation and liberalisation.

In addition to the legitimate economy, there is an enormous black economy. The chief culprit is the licensing and tax bureaucracy. Complying with the law is so arduous that many businesses prefer to operate illegally. In most cases penalties are not severe, so it's cheaper to pay the fine than to become legally licensed. For example, it's extremely difficult to get a licence to operate a private language school (a business that many foreigners go into) so most of these schools simply operate illegally. As an additional benefit, they avoid paying taxes by remaining unlicensed. Ditto for dance halls, pubs, cable TV, investment houses, street vending and private bus companies.

Even licensed businesses often underreport their income. Accounting standards are low – 'double-bookkeeping' and other tax avoidance schemes are common. Taiwan is basically a cash economy and cheques are seldom used, which makes it even more difficult for the tax office to keep track of business transactions. No one knows for sure, but some sources estimate that up to 40% of Taiwan's economy operates outside the law and therefore doesn't show up in official statistics. This means that Taiwan's per capita income is considerably higher than the government realises, and that the government is considerably poorer than it could be.

## POPULATION

A combination of the postwar baby boom and an increase in the average life expectancy – largely due to better health conditions – has pushed the population of Taiwan past 20 million. Thanks to government-instituted family planning and increased financial security the population growth rate has slowed to about 1.5% annually, but Taiwan has a population density of 550 persons per square km, making it one of the most crowded places in the world.

## PEOPLE

At least 70% of the people are considered Taiwanese. For definition purposes, Taiwanese means someone of more or less Chinese background whose family was in Taiwan before the Kuomintang arrived en masse after WW II. Those who came after WW II are simply called 'mainlanders', but these days there is so much intermarriage between Taiwanese and mainlanders that not much difference is visible. The Hakka, who today comprise an estimated 5% of the population, have also intermarried to such an extent that they are no longer a visible minority.

Today, Taiwan's aborigines represent less than 2% of the population. Intermarriage between the aborigines and the Chinese majority certainly occurs, but is much less common than marriages between Taiwanese and mainlanders. The aborigines have darker skin and rounder eyes than the Chinese, and the vast majority have converted to Christianity. There are 10 tribes, each of which has its own language. The total aboriginal population is around 300,000 and the tribes are the Ami, Atayal, Bunun, Paiwan, Puyuma, Rukai, Shao, Saisiat, Tsou and Yami. Like elsewhere, the aborigines have been the victims of ridicule and scorn, but in recent years it has become very trendy to collect aboriginal art and to attend aboriginal song and dance shows.

## CULTURE

The Chinese have an intricate and fascinating culture which dates back at least 3000 years, making it one of the world's oldest surviving societies.

Culture is something that is learned – it is not natural behaviour or inborn. If you've never travelled in the Orient before, you may be surprised, even shocked, at the different notions of what is proper social behaviour. What is considered normal and polite in one country may be regarded as rude or even illegal in another.

People will judge you by your actions, even though they will make allowances for the peculiar ways of foreigners. If you unknowingly commit a faux pas, you'll have to live with the consequences. Avoid an embarrassing situation by learning as much as possible about the exotic land you are about to visit. Don't forget that people from the Orient encounter these same difficulties when travelling in Western countries.

Here's a checklist of some social situations you may encounter.

### Opening a Conversation

Chinese people will often strike up a conversation with a total stranger by asking questions such as: 'Are you married?', 'How many children do you have?', 'How much money do you make?', 'May I know your name, address and telephone number?' or 'What is your blood-type?'. To ask such questions in the West would be most unsettling, but it is quite normal in Taiwan. Asking personal questions is considered friendly.

How do you respond if you don't wish to reveal your blood type, how much money you make or your personal family history to a complete stranger? Simply make up whatever answer you feel comfortable with. No need to say how much money you make, just make up a figure. But don't blow up and yell, 'None of your business!'. That would be a major faux pas on your part. The person asking the question was only being friendly, not nosey.

## Face

Having 'big face' is synonymous with prestige, and prestige is important in the Orient. All families, even poor ones, are expected to have big wedding parties and throw around money like water, in order to gain face.

Much of the Chinese obsession with materialism is really to do with gaining face, not material wealth. Owning nice clothes, a big car (even if you can't drive), a piano (even if you can't play it), imported cigarettes and liquor (even if you don't smoke or drink), will all cause one to gain face. Therefore, when taking a gift to a Chinese friend, try to give something with snob appeal such as a bottle of imported liquor, perfume, cigarettes or chocolate. This will please your host and help win you points in the face game.

The whole concept of face seems very childish to Westerners and most never learn to understand it, but it is important in the Orient.

## Not Speaking too Frankly

In the Orient, people don't always say what they mean. They often say what they think the other person wants to hear – it is always necessary to preserve face. Getting straight to the point and being blunt is not appreciated in Taiwan. If a local asks you, 'Do you like my new car?' be sure to say you love it, even if it's a piece of junk.

If you are asked, 'Are you married?' never say 'I just got divorced last month'. Divorce is a taboo topic, a deep, dark, secret. If a Chinese friend asks for something of yours as a souvenir of your friendship, let him down easily if you don't want to give it to him. Don't simply say 'No'. You could say something like, 'Sorry, this book belongs to my brother and I borrowed it from him so I must return it. But if you give me your address, I'll send you another one from home when I get back'. Whether or not you send another one from home is not the point; you have helped preserve his face and yours by not bluntly saying 'No!'.

Avoid direct criticisms of people. The Chinese stress polite manners and smooth social relations. It's better to make up a story or avoid the topic rather than confront someone with unpleasant facts that will cause embarrassment.

## Flowery Rhetoric

This is basically a corollary of the 'don't speak too frankly' rule. Form is more important than content. It has been said that the Chinese speak in circles, and there is some truth to this. Rather than saying exactly what is meant, a speaker or writer may beat around the bush with polite greetings, praise for your past deeds, hopes for more in the future, wishes for good health, inquiries about your family, and various other digressions, redundancies and superfluities.

One examination given to prospective employees involves taking a single meaningful sentence and rewriting it into a two page essay with no increase in content. Many people also talk this way.

Chinese literature contains many examples of such flowery rhetoric. One classic Chinese novel available in English translation, *The Red Chamber Dream*, is such a complex riot of plots, characters and digressions that diagrams are included to prevent the reader from getting lost.

## Name Cards

The Chinese love them. Get some printed before or immediately after you arrive in

Taiwan. Hand them out like confetti. Every professional needs a name card and never mind if you are a professional dishwasher. Your name card can say that you are a sanitary engineer.

In Taiwan, name cards can be printed cheaply with one side in English and the other side in Chinese characters. If you get name cards or anything printed in Taiwan, you must check the English carefully after it's typeset because misspellings are common.

Don't be caught without name cards if you are doing any business in Taiwan. You will almost certainly lose face if you mumble something about having run out of cards. Keep them in your wallet all the time.

## No Red Ink

Don't write a note in red ink. If you want to give someone your address or telephone, write in any colour but red. Red ink conveys a message of unfriendliness. If you're teaching in Taiwan it's OK to use red ink to correct students' papers, but if you write extensive comments or suggestions on the back of the paper, use some other colour besides red.

## Gift-Giving

This is a very complex and important part of Chinese culture. When visiting people it is important to bring a gift, perhaps a tin of biscuits, flowers, a cake or chocolate. As a visiting foreigner, people will want to give you gifts. While sitting in a restaurant or just walking on the street, I've had total strangers come up to me and hand me candy, cigarettes and chewing gum. The first time it happened to me, I thought the guy was just a pushy door-to-door salesman so I handed the goods back to him and said abruptly 'I don't want to buy it'. I'm afraid I insulted the poor gentleman – a good example of cultural misunderstanding.

The most fascinating part of gift-giving is when you visit somebody's home. You are expected to bring a gift for your host. Your host will invariably refuse it. You are expected to insist. The verbal volleyball can continue for quite some time. If the host accepts too readily, then he or she is considered to be too greedy. They must first refuse and you must insist.

*You* – I brought this gift for you.
*Host* – No, no, it's not necessary.
*You* – Oh please, I want you to have it.
*Host* – No, you shouldn't waste your money on me.
*You* – Never mind, I've already bought it. It's my honour to give it to you.
*Host* – No, you should keep it for yourself.
*You* – Oh, but I insist that you take it.
*Host* – But I am not worthy of such a gift...ad infinitum, ad nauseam, ad exhaustium.

When receiving a gift, never open it in front of the person who gave it to you. That makes you look greedy. Express your deep thanks, then put it aside and open it later.

## Guanxi

The closest English word to this would be 'relationship'. However, *guanxi* has a stronger meaning, sort of like the English expression 'You scratch my back and I'll scratch yours'. To build up good guanxi, you have to do things for people, give them gifts, take them to dinner, grant favours, etc.

Once this is done, an unspoken obligation exists. It is perhaps because of this unspoken debt that people automatically try to refuse gifts. They may not wish to establish guanxi with someone, because sooner or later they may have to repay the obligation. Even after it is 'repaid', guanxi is rarely terminated. It is a continuing process of mutual gift-giving, back-scratching and favouritism that may last a lifetime.

I don't mean to make it sound all bad either. Knowing the right people can often dispense with a lot of red tape and can be mutually beneficial to all the parties involved – very important in Taiwanese society, where stifling bureaucracy can make it difficult to accomplish anything.

Of course guanxi exists everywhere, but in Taiwan it is particularly strong. Those doing business with local people should pay particular attention to this.

## Asking Favours

The longer you stay in Taiwan, the more you will encounter people asking favours. Of course this happens everywhere, but in Taiwan it can reach irritating proportions. For example, having established guanxi by bribing you with a gift of Chinese moon cakes, you may then be asked to do some translating work – again and again. If you speak fluent English, you may soon find yourself in great demand to give lectures to English clubs, judge speech contests, correct term papers, proofread business faxes and write letters of recommendation for students who want to study abroad. All of this would be fine if anyone wanted to pay for these services, but that usually isn't the case.

What to do? First, try not to lose your temper – a big no-no in Chinese society – but politely make excuses. If that doesn't work, the last resort is to say you'll try to do it and then fail to complete the job. You will not be asked again.

## Removing Shoes

One thing that the Chinese detest is a dirty floor. They usually mop the floor daily, maybe even twice a day, and they won't appreciate you tramping dirt all over it. There are usually slippers by the entrance door, and if so, remove your shoes and wear the slippers. Your hosts may say, 'Never mind, just wear your shoes inside', but they aren't speaking frankly, they're being polite. You should take your shoes off.

When using the bathroom, there is usually another set of slippers especially for bathroom use because the floor is often wet. Most foreigners don't seem to mind this custom because it feels good to take your shoes off on a hot day. Unfortunately, the slippers provided are often too small for Western feet.

## Dust

Besides a dirty floor, another thing the Chinese detest is dust. You will often see motorcyclists and bicyclists wearing surgical masks to protect themselves from dust, even though they don't usually care about chemical pollutants from motor vehicle exhaust.

Students will often not want to sit in the front of the classroom because they fear the dust from the chalk board – as well as being afraid of the teacher.

## Smiling

A smile in the Orient doesn't always mean the person is happy. Smiling is a proper response in an embarrassing situation. The waitress who smiles at you after she poured tea all over your lap isn't laughing at you. The smile is offered as an apology. If you get angry, she may smile more. I can assure you she doesn't think it's funny. If you jump up and yell, 'What are you smiling at, you idiot! Do you think it's funny?', then you have committed a major social error. Losing your temper is a big no-no. Smile.

## Not Showing Anger

Venting your rage in public is bad form. Screaming and yelling will draw an instant crowd and some may regard you as being uncivilised. Rather than solving your problem, you may create more trouble for yourself. Smile. A lot of Westerners really blow it on this point. Maybe you want to say 'This food isn't what I ordered!' but if you need to complain about something, then do so in a polite, almost apologetic tone.

The Chinese are very successful at controlling their emotions in public. Even when greatly distressed, they try to look cheerful. Harmonious social relations are greatly stressed in Taiwan. Even when people disagree with what you are saying, they often pretend to agree or just smile rather than confronting you.

Westerners, on the other hand, tend to be argumentative and quick to complain when things don't go right. In the eyes of many Asians, this makes us appear rough-mannered or rude. Try to envision a scenario with a Western tourist in a hotel, screaming and yelling with much righteous indignation at the hotel clerk because the bed wasn't made and the hot water isn't turned on. The clerk just smiles and politely agrees, even though he thinks the tourist is a lunatic.

## Touching in Public

Not long ago, touching a member of the opposite sex in public was scandalous behaviour. Today, many young lovers do walk around hand in hand, but don't let it get any further than that in public. Also, members of the same sex may walk hand in hand or arm in arm, especially classmates. This is nothing sexual, just a simple display of friendship, a common sight in Asia.

## Handing Paper to Somebody

Always hand a piece of paper to somebody using both hands. This shows respect. This is especially true if that person is somebody important, like a public official, your landlord or a business associate. If you only use one hand, you will be considered rude.

## Renao

It's hard to translate *rènào* into English. It means something like 'lively', 'festive', 'happy' and 'noisy' – especially 'noisy'. Many Chinese seem immune to noise. You'll notice that in restaurants and department stores, the background music is often kept up at around 100 decibels. This is done to attract customers, whereas in Western countries it would surely drive them away. Lighting firecrackers is also very renao.

Many people in Taiwan have asked me why Americans like to live in the suburbs and commute to the city for work. 'The city is so much more exciting (renao),' they say, 'so why would anyone want to live out in the lonely countryside?' I have met a number of people in Taiwan who must work in the country, but they live in the city where housing is much more expensive and they commute every day to the country. 'Why?' I ask. 'Because,' they say, 'the city is a good place to raise children.'

## Your Age?

Do you know how old you are? Many Chinese say you are already 1 year old on the day you are born. And they don't necessarily think that your second birthday comes a year later. You gain another year when the lunar new year begins. So a child born a week before the New Year is already 2 years old when Westerners would say that he or she was only a week old.

## Family & Children

The family is the basic foundation of Chinese society and children are highly prized. If you travel with children in Taiwan, everywhere you go someone will want to play with your kids. Avoid punishing your kids in public. If you spank your child publicly you will quickly draw a crowd of indignant onlookers. If you need to discipline them, do it in private.

Chinese parents are very indulgent with their children and tend to baby them right into adulthood. It is not unusual to meet people in their late 20s still living at home. Chinese parents are appalled that Westerners leave teenage children at home while the parents go away for the weekend or that Western children can move out of the family home at the age of 18. The Chinese are also shocked that Western teenagers in high school and college often work part-time and use the money to pay for their education, rent an apartment or buy a car.

Chinese teenagers never baby-sit their younger brothers and sisters because a teenager is still considered a child. Chinese children are sheltered from most adult responsibilities until after they finish school. Perhaps as a result, most Chinese are overly dependent on their parents by Western standards.

The parent-child relationship is very strong in Taiwan throughout a person's lifetime and trouble within the family is never discussed publicly. When the parents get old and can no longer care for themselves, they usually live with their children rather than being packed off to rest homes as in many Western countries. In my opinion, the strong family ties are one of the best characteristics of Chinese society.

Taiwan is a patriarchal society, in line with Confucian tradition. When a woman marries, her ties with her family are partially severed and she joins her husband's family – though, interestingly, she doesn't usually give up her maiden name. If the couple still live at home after marriage, it will be with the husband's family, never the wife's family. If they get divorced, the father gets custody of the children if he wants them.

A divorce is considered the ultimate catastrophe. Never tell people in Taiwan that you are divorced. It would be a major social blunder. You would be better off saying that your former spouse died.

## Staring

Get used to it. In Taipei, where Westerners are common, few people stare, but in rural areas where Westerners are scarce, you'll be the best show in town. Staring back doesn't have any effect. Indeed, the crowd may love it. There's no point in getting upset about it, just smile. Westerners with hairy arms and legs may find that little children will pull their body hair. They seem to want to test it to make sure it is real.

## Flattery

Flatter your host and guests. Give them big face. Words of praise like 'You're so intelligent and humorous (or beautiful, etc)' will go down well. If you speak three words of Chinese someone will surely say 'You speak Chinese very well'. The proper response should be self-deprecating: 'Oh no, my Chinese is very bad' (probably true). Boasting is a real faux pas. Remaining humble is very much a part of the Confucian tradition. The Chinese are famous for their humility. 'Oh, I'm so ugly and stupid!' is the kind of self-deprecating comment one often hears in Taiwan. Be sure you don't agree with such comments, even to be funny.

## Left-Handedness

Conformity is valued over individualism in the Orient and being left-handed makes one 'odd'. Children who are naturally left-handed are discouraged from using their left hand. If you are left-handed, you may draw comments when you sign your name or write a letter. However, the left hand is not unclean as in many parts of Asia so it is OK to touch people with it.

## Geomancy

This word doesn't even appear in many English dictionaries and it's not easy to define. Known to the Chinese as 'wind-water' (fēngshǔi), to be in correct geomancy is to be in proper physical harmony with the universe. This not only includes the living, but the spiritual world as well. If a Chinese person finds that their business is failing, they may well consult a geomancer. Sometimes the solution will be to move the door of the business establishment, at other times the solution may be to relocate an ancestor's grave.

Many Chinese worship their departed ancestors and build elaborate tombs for them. A geomancer should be consulted when this is done. If he is not and misfortune does strike, then a geomancer may be called and the tomb moved. There is even a holiday in Taiwan known as Tomb Sweep Day, when you must clean the grave site of your ancestors. Of course, not all Chinese take geomancy and ancestor worship seriously, but many do. Like astrology and fortune telling, they are an intricate part of Chinese culture which has been passed down through the generations.

## Taboos & Omens

Certain things are considered to be bad omens, such as leaving chopsticks sticking vertically into the bowl. This resembles incense sticks in a bowl of ashes, a sure death sign. Many Chinese are afraid to receive a clock as a gift because this is another death sign. The Chinese are very sensitive to death signs, so don't talk about accidents and death as if they might really occur. For example, never say to anyone, 'Be careful on that ladder, or you'll break your neck'. That implies it will happen. Chinese people almost never leave a will, because to write a will indicates the person will die soon. If you write a will, it would be virtually impossible to find a local to witness your signature for you. They will not want anything to do with it.

The number four sounds just like the Chinese word for death. As a result, hospitals never put patients on the 4th floor and you never give anyone a gift of NT$400 or NT$4000. If you give someone flowers, you always give red flowers, not white. In Chinese symbolism white – not black – is the colour associated with death. The Chinese are really into longevity and death is a taboo topic. Sellers of life insurance have a very bleak future in Taiwan.

The belief in omens probably explains why Chinese geographical names always mean something wonderful like 'Paradise Valley', 'Heaven's Gateway' or 'Happiness Rd'. The Chinese would never consider going to one of America's most famous national parks, Death Valley.

The lunar (Chinese) New Year has its special taboos and omens which are associated with your fortune in the coming year. You shouldn't wash clothes on this day or you will have to work hard in the coming year. On New Year's Day, don't sweep dirt out of the house or you will sweep your wealth away. Be sure you don't argue during the New Year, or you will face a year of bickering.

Young people are far less likely to pay heed to taboos and omens than the older generation. Similarly, urban residents care less about these things than rural people.

## Weddings

If you spend any length of time in Taiwan, you're likely to be invited to a wedding. The wedding invitation is invariably red – a happy colour – and it usually brings with it the obligation to present money to the newly-weds. Therefore, it is often referred to as a 'red bomb'.

Should you receive a red bomb from a Chinese friend, you'll be happy to know that the money you are expected to give is really to pay for the fabulous 10 course meal that will be served at the wedding party. You needn't bring any other gifts, just the money. The money should be cash – not a cheque – and *must* be placed in a red envelope. It must be red because a white envelope is a death sign. As mentioned previously, never give NT$400 or NT$4000 as the number four is

also taboo. The typical amount expected these days is about NT$600 to NT$1000 per person. It's OK to bring an uninvited friend with you, but put an extra NT$600 in the envelope for each guest and let the host know in advance so enough food will be ordered. Be sure to write your name on the envelope so they know who it's from. Red envelopes should be used any time you give money to somebody, such as for a birthday, a gift or if you just owe money to somebody.

Wedding parties do not last very long, usually just a little more than an hour. Everyone just tends to eat and run, and there's very little time for talking and socialising. Guests are permitted to take home extra food in plastic bags which the restaurant will provide.

## Funerals

Hopefully, you won't be attending many of these. However, if someone you know dies there are certain formalities that must be observed. If you receive a card informing you of the death of a friend or business associate, you are expected to send money, just as if you had received a wedding invitation. About NT$500 is typical. Of course you don't have to, but if you value the relationship with the deceased's family you'd better pay up. In return, you will probably receive a cheap gift. I once received a towel (worth about NT$30) for my NT$500.

You aren't expected to attend funerals unless specifically invited, and if you just send money, you can be excused. If you do go, you'll find it very different from a funeral in the West. As at a Chinese wedding, you must bring an envelope stuffed with cash, but it *must* be in a white envelope for funerals. Dress somewhat formally and be ready for anything – I say that because there are different types of funerals. A conservative, traditional Chinese funeral is a solemn affair, just as a funeral is in the West. However, the ceremony is very different. Children draped in white robes and with white hoods over their heads surround the casket. They also hold a white rope to keep out any bad spirits.

So much for the traditional funeral. Some

people prefer a more festive occasion. They may employ the services of an 'electric organ flower car' (*diànzǐqín huachē*), which is a very brightly decorated truck containing an organ in the back. Beautiful young girls clad in the scantiest bikinis will sing songs, and sometimes they remove the bikinis, supposedly to entertain the spirits. Afterwards, a big feast is usually held.

It is perfectly acceptable to bring flowers to a funeral. Again, bring white flowers, not red.

## CULTURE SHOCK

When travelling, the physical differences can be a source of endless delight. The exotic language, the interesting food, the strange but charming social customs, all make foreign travel fascinating and exciting.

Perhaps you've never thought of this but what we see as so exotic in the Orient is in fact very ordinary to Orientals. They consider us Westerners to be very exotic.

But not everything you encounter overseas will be charming. Many travellers come prepared to deal with such conditions as jet lag, diarrhoea and athlete's foot, but few recognise the hazards of culture shock.

Tourists who only go abroad for a few days or weeks have little to fear, but those who are abroad for months or years are certain to suffer from some culture shock. Culture shock has been extensively studied by numerous psychologists, sociologists, anthropologists and various government organisations. The symptoms and stages of culture shock are well documented and highly predictable. Culture shock can be serious, in some cases leading to severe depression.

Some people are more susceptible than others, and much depends on which countries you are visiting. As a general rule, the more alike the two cultures are, the less problem there will be in adapting.

If you stay in Asia for a long time, you can expect to encounter the first two and possibly the third stages of culture shock. Ironically, you may experience reverse culture shock when returning to your home country after a long stay overseas. The three stages of culture shock are:

### Enrapture

On arrival, most people are totally dazzled with the charming, exotic surroundings. 'Wow, I'm in Taiwan!' (or India or wherever) is a common reaction. Everything is new, interesting and exciting. Just riding an ordinary city bus is an experience. Eating dinner can be a real adventure and there is so much to see and do. It's all so much fun. You've discovered a new paradise, and many newcomers will even say things like: 'This country is more civilised than mine. There's a lot we can learn from this country.' Which may or may not be true, but it's doubtful that you really understand the country and its problems after just a few days or weeks. If you stay for a long time though, you will almost certainly reach stage two, which is:

### Disillusionment

Paradise lost. This feeling can come suddenly, gradually, very soon or very late, but it will come. The happiness bubble bursts. If you travel to a very poor country, disillusionment is liable to come sooner than if you visit a clean, prosperous, well-managed country. Yet even in a prosperous country, things will irritate you – maybe the food, language, climate, or people's ideas and attitudes.

Travellers will often get annoyed and start complaining about some minor cultural difference. How many times have people had rotten things to say about 'those Americans' and 'those British' and 'those French'. Yet, in spite of all the whining and complaining you may hear from travellers in Europe and the USA over petty issues, the cultural differences between these countries are trivial compared to what you will encounter in an Asian country.

In Asia, everything is different. Many things are 'illogical' according to Western ways. If you visit some of the poorest countries of Asia, Latin America and Africa, you are really going to have to tolerate a lot – an army of beggars, thieves, traveller's diarrhoea, amoebic dysentery, corrupt and brutal police, unbelievably dirty restaurants, etc.

Of course, conditions are much better than that in Taiwan, but you will get plenty of opportunities to experience culture shock. Typical complaints include: 'Why can't people stand in line?', 'Why don't they Romanise the street signs?', 'The taxi drivers are crazy', 'How can anyone eat seaweed and watery rice for breakfast?', and 'Why does everyone stare at me?'. Finally, 'Why are these people so illogical?'.

All the petty but irritating hassles pile up until the foreign visitor ends up wishing for nothing but a plane ticket home, back to a 'sensible country'. Many do indeed leave, reducing the length of their intended stay. Others, both tourists and foreign residents, withdraw from the local culture entirely and seek out the refuge of their fellow expatriates. I should point out that Chinese living abroad also do this, which is why there are Chinatowns in many Western cities. The tendency is to look for something familiar in a foreign land. Expatriates in the Orient often choose to live in 'foreigners' ghettos', eat nothing but hamburgers, peanut butter sandwiches, Coca-Cola and imported canned goods, and usually fail to learn the local language.

People who are suffering from culture shock tend to complain a great deal. Many develop the 'superman complex' ('We are superior to these natives'). They constantly write letters 'home' and always seem to be checking their mailbox. They search relentlessly for magazines and newspapers from their home country, and have no interest in local news. Some just bottle themselves up indoors with books or music tapes, or simply sleep all day, afraid to go out of the door. Chronic fatigue, a bad temper and frequent complaining are all signs of emotional depression. And that is the ultimate result of culture shock...depression.

The traveller can simply go home or at least to another country. An expatriate working overseas on a contract may not have this option. Married couples 'stuck overseas' are likely to take out their frustrations on each other, and divorce is sometimes the result. The best solution, of course, is to try to reach the third stage:

### Adaptation

Asian people often ask a foreigner, 'So, how do you like my country?'. And the reply that they often get is, 'First of all, it's too hot, secondly I can't understand what people are saying, thirdly it's chaotic and no one obeys the traffic rules and...'

Face it. You cannot change the foreign society you are living in. You must adapt to it. It's hard to say how long it takes to adapt. Maybe 3 months, maybe 6 months, maybe a year, maybe never. Casual travellers of course doesn't have time to reach this stage. They must simply accept whatever comes and move on to a new country if the local culture becomes too frustrating. Foreign residents, on the other hand, must adapt or else suffer the consequences of isolation from the society they live in.

An important factor is learning the local language. Communication is everything when it comes to social relations. Unfortunately, Chinese is not an easy language to learn for most Westerners. It takes several years of persistent effort to master the language, but you can get by with it in 2 years or so. I have known some foreigners to live in Taiwan for 30 years and never learn more than a couple of dozen words. Since Chinese is such a difficult language to write, it's probably best to concentrate on the spoken language at first and not worry about reading and writing until later. It takes a good 5 years to master the written language, but learning to speak can take less than half that amount of time.

Study everything you can about the country you are visiting or living in. There are many books written about Chinese culture and they apply as well to Taiwan as they do to the rest of China. Mix with the people and be sure to eat the local food. It may take some getting used to but it's good. Don't head straight for McDonald's and Kentucky Fried Chicken every day. Try to avoid those 'foreigners' ghettos', where everything is 'just like home'.

This advice sounds easy to follow, but actually it's not. Only a small number of Westerners ever gain a true understanding of Asia. For most, a trip to Asia is a love-hate experience. But there are some who adapt very well.

There is also the opposite danger. Some foreigners are heavily influenced by the local culture, 'going native' in a sense. This is not necessarily a good adaptation. If it reaches the point of thoroughly rejecting your native culture and disparaging your home country, to the point that you don't want anything to do with your country or its people, then you are suffering from another form of culture shock. For lack of a better term, I'll call it the 'rejection syndrome'. It's not a healthy sign at all.

The rejection syndrome is a common ailment among wandering Westerners who are drifting through Asia 'in search of themselves' and who think they've discovered 'true enlightenment' by adopting Eastern cult religions and rejecting all things Western. Indeed, they come to believe that they now possess some exclusive wisdom that makes them superior to other Westerners. To put it more simply, they suffer from an inflated ego. What these 'enlightened' individuals fail to see is that Western culture, for all its faults, has many strong points, which is why it's so pervasive in the world today. While many Westerners go to China and India seeking knowledge and enlightenment, so do many Asians go to the West seeking the same thing. Just as the Chinese have contributed to the world's knowledge of science, literature, music, fashion and philosophy, so has the West. Living abroad for many years has made me recognise the strengths of Western culture, as well as its weaknesses. My advice would be to borrow the strong points of all the cultures you encounter and adapt them to your own needs. Very few manage to do so.

If you find yourself with the traveller's blues, be aware that you are in good company. Even Marco Polo had traveller's diarrhoea. Travel may not always be fun and games, but it is an enriching experience. To my mind, Asia is the world's most fascinating continent.

## ARTS

Traditional Chinese arts and culture have been well preserved in Taiwan – indeed, far more so than in mainland China.

### Chinese Opera
*(píngjù)* 平劇

The traditional Chinese opera, and the closely related Taiwanese opera, are an integral part of Chinese culture that every visitor to Taiwan should see at least once. The dialogue is all in Mandarin Chinese, or Taiwanese for Taiwanese opera. The acting, colourful costumes, music and the entire atmosphere is thrilling to watch even if you can't understand what is being said. In a few operas put on for foreigners, an English translation of the dialogue is flashed on a screen near the stage. But in most cases, no translation is available.

These operas are beautiful and well worth photographing. It is advisable to use a high-speed film, at least ASA 400, as the operas are often at night and you may have to watch from a distance. A telephoto or zoom lens would also be helpful.

Chinese opera is used to preach virtue. The operas are now shown on TV and this is gradually displacing the live performances. The opera is usually played near a temple to entertain the gods. Sometimes men play female roles and women play male ones, but the make-up is so good that it's hard to tell. Old people particularly love the opera, but young people are increasingly becoming more interested in other things like disco music and home video games.

### Taichichuan
*(tàijíquán)* 太極拳

*Taichichuan*, or slow motion shadow boxing, has in recent years become quite trendy in Western countries. It has been popular in China for centuries. It is basically a form of exercise, but it's also an art and is a form of

Taichichuan symbol

Chinese martial arts. Kung fu (*gōngfū*) differs from taichichuan in that the former is performed at much higher speed and with the intention of doing bodily harm. Kung fu also often employs weapons. Taichichuan is not a form of self-defence but the movements are similar to kung fu. There are different styles of taichichuan, such as *chen* and *yang*.

Taichichuan is very popular among old people, and also with young women who believe it will help keep their bodies beautiful. The movements are supposed to develop the breathing muscles, promote digestion and improve muscle tone.

A modern innovation is to perform taichichuan movements to the thump of disco music. Westerners find it remarkable to see a large group performing their slow motion movements in the park at the crack of dawn to the steady beat of disco music supplied by a portable cassette tape player.

Taichichuan, dancing in the park and all manner of exercises are customarily done just as the sun rises, which means that if you want to see or participate in them, you have to get up early. In Taipei the best places to see taichichuan are the Chiang Kaishek Memorial Hall, the Sun Yatsen Memorial Hall, Taipei New Park and the hills around the Grand Hotel and Yangmingshan Park just north of the city. Some people, for lack of a better place, just perform their taichichuan on the footpath or on the roof of their homes. There are organised taichi classes and Westerners are usually welcome to participate in these activities.

There is a Taichichuan Association (tel (02) 7056743) on the 12th floor at 157

Fuhsing S Rd, Section 2, Taipei. No one there seems to speak English, so if you're not fluent in Chinese you must supply an interpreter.

## Martial Arts
### (*wǔshù*) 武術

While kung fu is the only martial art that is truly Chinese, you can find several imported varieties in Taiwan, borrowed from Japan and Korea. There are a number of associations in Taipei that practise martial arts. All are Chinese speaking, but if you're really interested, give them a call and see if you can participate in their activities. Some places to contact include: Aikido Association (*héqìdào xiéhùi*) (tel (02) 7121490); Judo Association (*róudào xiéhùi*) (tel (02) 7213115); Karate Association (*kōngshǒudào xiéhùi*) (tel (02) 5210131); Taekwondo Association (*táiqúandào xiéhùi*) (tel (02) 7024911); and the Martial Arts Association (*gúoshù hùi*) (tel (02) 7213115, 8820083).

## Chikung
### (*qìgōng*) 氣功

As much an art form as a traditional Chinese medicine, *chikung* cannot easily be described in Western terms, but it's rather like faith healing. *Chi* represents life's vital energy, and *kung* comes from kung fu – Chinese martial arts. Chikung can be thought of as energy management and healing. Practitioners try to project their chi to heal others.

It's interesting to watch them do it. Typically, they place their hands above or next to the patient's body without actually making physical contact. To many foreigners this looks like a circus act, and indeed even many Chinese suspect that it's nothing but quackery. However, there are many who claim that they have been cured of serious illness without any other treatment but chikung, even after more conventional doctors have told them that their condition is hopeless.

Chikung is not extremely popular in Taiwan, although it's experienced a recent revival in mainland China. It was denounced as another superstitious link to the bourgeois past by rampaging Red Guards, who nearly obliterated chikung and its practitioners during the Cultural Revolution. It's only recently that chikung has made a comeback in China, but many of the highly skilled practitioners are no longer alive. In Taiwan, you are most likely to see chikung in the ever-popular kung fu movies, where mortally wounded heroes are miraculously revived with a few waves of the hands.

Does chikung work? It isn't easy to say, but there is a theory in medicine that all doctors can cure a third of their patients regardless of what method is used. So perhaps chikung too gets its 33% cure rate.

## Musical Instruments

These days people in Taiwan are more into disco and rock videos than traditional Chinese music. Nevertheless, traditional musical instruments are still studied in Taiwan. Courses are normally taught in the Chinese departments of various universities around the island, and a number of the students are foreigners. Probably the best place to study this is at the Chinese Cultural University in Yangmingshan, Taipei. Most of the instruments are string and flutelike instruments that have a pleasant, melodious sound. However, the instruments you are most likely to encounter while travelling are the awful-sounding gongs and trumpets used at temple worship ceremonies and funerals.

A brief rundown of the most common traditional instruments includes the following:

two-stringed fiddle
    *èrhú* 二胡
three-stringed flute
    *sānxúan* 三絃
four-stringed banjo
    *yùeqín* 月琴
two-stringed viola
    *húqín* 胡琴
flute (vertical)
    *dòngxiāo* 洞簫
flute (horizontal)
    *dízi* 笛子
piccolo
    *bāngdí* 梆笛
four-stringed lute
    *pípá* 琵琶

zither
    *gǔzhēng* 古箏
trumpet (for ceremonies)
    *sǔonà* 嗩吶
gongs (for ceremonies)
    *dàlúo* 大鑼

## RELIGION
### Buddhism

One of the world's great religions, Buddhism originally developed in India from where it spread all over East and South-East Asia. With this spread of influence, the form and concepts of Buddhism have been changed significantly. Buddhism today has developed into numerous sects or schools of thought, but these sects are not mutually exclusive or antagonistic towards one another.

The religion was founded in India in the 6th century BC by Siddhartha Gautama partly as a reaction against Brahmanism. Of noble birth, he lived from 563 BC to 483 BC. Dissatisfied with the cruel realities of life, he left his home at the age of 29 and became an ascetic in search of a solution. At the age of 35 Siddhartha attained enlightenment, to become the Buddha. Buddha means 'The Enlightened One'.

There are four noble truths which form the core of Buddhism. These are:

1. The truth of suffering, which all living beings must endure.
2. The origin of suffering, which is craving and causes one to be reborn.
3. That craving and thereby suffering can be destroyed by attaining enlightenment.
4. There are right views, right intentions, right speech, right livelihood, right action, right concentration, right effort and right ecstasy.

Most Westerners misunderstand certain key aspects of Buddhism. First of all, it should be understood that the Buddha is not a god but a human being who claims no divine powers. In Buddhist philosophy, human beings are considered their own master and gods are irrelevant. There has been more than one Buddha, and there will be more in the future.

Reincarnation is also widely misunderstood. It is not considered desirable in Buddhism to be reborn into the world. Since all life (existence) is suffering, one does not wish to return to this world. One hopes to escape the endless cycle of rebirths by reaching nirvana, a state of blissful 'extinction and perfection'. Whether or not a person will be reborn and at what level of existence is determined by their karma, the net total of their good and bad deeds in life. When enlightenment is attained, one can reach nirvana and find true bliss.

Buddhism had reached its height in India by the 3rd century BC, when it was declared the state religion of India by King Ashoka. However, it declined after that, partly due to factionalism and persecution by the Brahmans.

Numerous sects of Buddhism have evolved in different parts of the world. Classical Buddhists will not kill any creature and are therefore strict vegetarians. They further believe that attempting to escape from life's sufferings by committing suicide will only generate more bad karma and force one to be reborn at a lower level. Yet there are other Buddhist sects that hold opposite views – during the 1960s, Vietnamese Buddhists made world headlines by publicly burning themselves to death to protest against the war. Somehow, the various sects of Buddhism manage not to clash with each other. One outstanding fact of Chinese history is that the Chinese have never engaged in religious wars. This is very different from European history, which has witnessed many religious wars.

**Buddhism in China** Buddhism reached China around the 1st century AD and became prominent by the 3rd century. Ironically, while Buddhism expanded rapidly throughout East Asia, it declined in India.

Buddhism in China mixed with other Chinese philosophies such as Confucianism and Taoism. The Chinese in particular had a hard time accepting 'extinction' as something good, as they believe in longevity. As many as 13 schools of thought evolved in China, the most famous perhaps being Chan, which is usually known in the West by its Japanese name, Zen.

Chan, which can be thought of as a hybrid of Indian Buddhism and Taoism, has had a great influence on Chinese behaviour, attitudes, art and literature. Chan emphasises finding the truth, and to do this the mind must be kept clear of distractions. Meditation is seen as the vehicle to help you along the road in search of truth.

When you finally succeed in finding the basic truth of the universe, you have achieved Buddhahood or nirvana. Nirvana to Chinese Buddhists differs somewhat from the Indian concept of nirvana, having rejected extinction but accepted perfection as a goal.

## Taoism

Originally a philosophy, Taoism has evolved into a religion. Unlike Buddhism, which was imported from India, Taoism is indigenous to China and second only to Confucianism in its influence on Chinese culture.

The philosophy of Taoism is believed to have originated with Laotse (which literally means 'The Old One'), who lived in the 6th century BC. Relatively little is known about Laotse, and some question whether or not he really existed. He is believed to have been the custodian of the imperial archives for the Chinese government and Confucius is supposed to have consulted him.

Understanding Taoism is not simple. The word *tao* (pronounced 'dào') means 'the Way'. It is considered indescribable, but signifies something like the 'guiding path', the 'truth', or the 'guiding principle'. It is not a god, saviour, statue or object of any kind.

A major principle of Taoism is the concept of *wuwei* or 'doing nothing'. A quote attributed to Laotse, 'Do nothing, and nothing will not be done', emphasises this principle. The idea is to remain humble, passive, nonassertive and nonaggressive.

Chien Szuma, a Chinese historian who lived from 145 BC to 90 BC, warned 'Do not take the lead in planning affairs, or you may be held responsible'. Nonintervention, or live and let live, is the keystone of the Tao. Harmony and patience are needed, action is obtained through inaction. Taoists like to note that water, the softest substance, will wear away stone, the hardest substance. Thus, eternal patience and tolerance will eventually produce the desired result.

Westerners have a hard time accepting this. The Western notion of getting things done quickly and efficiently conflicts with this aspect of the Tao. Westerners note that the Chinese are like spectators, afraid to get involved. The Chinese say that Westerners like to complain and are impatient. Taoists are baffled at the willingness of Westerners to fight and die for abstract causes, such as a religious ideal.

It is doubtful that Laotse ever intended his philosophy to become a religion. Chang Ling has been credited with establishing the religion in 143 BC. Taoism later split into two divisions, the 'Cult of the Immortals' and 'The Way of the Heavenly Teacher'.

The Cult of the Immortals offered immortality through meditation, exercise, alchemy and various other techniques. The Way of the Heavenly Teacher had many gods, ceremonies, saints, special diets to prolong life and offerings to the ghosts. As time passed, Taoism increasingly became wrapped up in the supernatural, self-mutilation, witchcraft, fortune telling, magic and ritualism. This is very evident today, as you will see if you visit a Taoist temple in Taiwan during a worship ceremony.

## Confucianism

Without a doubt, Confucius is regarded as China's greatest philosopher and teacher. The philosophy of Confucius has been borrowed by Japan, Korea, Vietnam and other countries neighbouring China. Confucius never claimed to be a religious leader, prophet or god, but his influence has been so great in China that Confucianism has come to be regarded as a religion by many.

Confucius (551 BC to 479 BC) lived

through a time of great chaos and feudal rivalry known as the Warring States Period. He emphasised devotion to parents and family, loyalty to friends, justice, peace, education, reform and humanitarianism. He also emphasised respect and deference to those in positions of authority, a philosophy later heavily exploited by emperors and warlords. However, not everything said by Confucius has been universally praised – it seems that he was a male chauvinist who firmly believed that men are superior to women.

Confucius preached the virtues of good government, but his philosophy helped create China's horrifying bureaucracy which exists to this day. On a more positive note, his ideas led to the system of civil service and university entrance examinations, where one gained position through ability and merit, rather than from noble birth and connections. Confucius preached against practices such as corruption, war, torture and excessive taxation. He was the first teacher to open his school to all students on the basis of their eagerness to learn rather than their noble birth and ability to pay for tuition.

The philosophy of Confucius is most easily found in the *Lunyu* or the *Analects of Confucius*. Many quotes have been taken from these works, the most famous perhaps being the Golden Rule. Westerners have translated this rule as 'Do unto others as you would have them do unto you'. Actually, it was written in the negative – 'Do not do unto others what you would not have them do unto you'. The Chinese, who are influenced by Confucius and the Tao, are not so aggressive as to wish to 'do unto' anybody.

No matter what his virtues, Confucius received little recognition during his lifetime. It was only after his death that he was canonised. Emperors, warlords and mandarins found it convenient to preach the Confucian ethic, particularly the part about deference to those in authority. Thus, with official support, Confucianism gained in influence as a philosophy and has attained almost religious status.

Although Confucius died some 2500 years ago, his influence remains strong in

China today. The Chinese remain solidly loyal to friends, family and teachers. The bureaucracy and examination systems still thrive and it is also true that a son is almost universally favoured over a daughter. It can be said that much of Confucian thought has become Chinese culture as we know it today. As Confucius was the greatest teacher in China, his birthday, 28 September, is celebrated as Teacher's Day in Taiwan.

## Today's Religions

Depending on who's counting, about 2% to 5% of the population are Christian. The vast majority of the people in Taiwan today consider themselves Buddhist or Taoist with Confucian influence. It should be pointed out that most people make no sharp distinction between Buddhism and Taoism in Taiwan, and the majority practise a blend of these two major religious philosophies.

Confucianism is not truly regarded as a religion by most Chinese, although you may see statues of Confucius in Buddhist and Taoist temples next to the other major deities. However, in Confucian temples there are no statues or images of the gods. Confucian temples are simple and quiet. There are no monks or nuns in residence, just a temple caretaker.

Confucian temples hold only one ceremony per year and that is to celebrate the birthday of Confucius on 28 September. This ceremony begins about 4 am and lasts for 2 hours. It is a solemn affair with many dignitaries in attendance. An ox, goat or pig is sacrificed and those in attendance always hope to acquire some of the animal's fur, as it is believed to impart wisdom. Incense is never burnt in Confucian temples nor do they let off firecrackers.

Far more elaborate than the Confucian temples are the Buddhist and Taoist temples. The Buddhist temples are the quieter of the two. The most common deities you will see in a Buddhist temple are Kuanyin (*gūanyīn*), the goddess of mercy, and Shihchia (*shìjiā*), from the Indian Sakyamuni, who represents the Buddha, Siddhartha Gautama. One can often see large, fierce-looking statues of warriors brandishing swords placed near the temple doors. These are the temple guards, not deities. In Buddhist temples there are normally nuns and monks in residence; they are strict vegetarians and pass their time working in well-tended gardens.

Taoist temples are among the most colourful in the world, with lots of activity, burning of incense, parades, firecrackers, crashing of cymbals, ceremonies, exorcisms and offerings to the ghosts. Of all the Chinese religions, Taoism is the most steeped in mysticism and ritual. Among the better known Taoist deities are Matsu, goddess of the sea, and the red-faced Kuankung (*gūangōng*), also known as Kuanti and Kuanyu. Fishermen often pray to Matsu for a safe journey, while Kuankung is believed to offer protection against war. Kuankung is based on an historical figure, a soldier of the 3rd century. If you are interested in learning more about him you can read the Chinese classic *The Romance of the Three Kingdoms*.

Although Confucian temples are readily distinguished from other types, Taoist and Buddhist temples have partially merged, with the deities of both religions prominently displayed side by side in the same temple. Sometimes a statue of Confucius is displayed as well.

There are a few temples in Taiwan which are not Buddhist, Taoist or Confucian, but were simply built to honour a great hero. Many Chinese also worship their ancestors, building elaborate altars and tombs for their departed relatives.

The government in Taiwan is tolerant of Christian missionaries and they have arrived en masse; there are representatives of nearly every denomination, including Baptists, Catholics, Presbyterians, Mormons, Jehovah's Witnesses and Seventh Day Adventists. Muslims are also represented in Taiwan and have built a mosque in Taipei. In addition, there are a very small number of people who practise what might be termed folk religions – 'Duck-Egg Religion' is practised in the Kaohsiung area by one such group.

## Temples

All over Taiwan one can find interesting and colourful temples ranging in size from a back alley hut to a monumental, multistoreyed structure that would dwarf some of the cathedrals of Europe. Although Taipei has some impressive temples, the best city for temple viewing is Tainan in the south of Taiwan.

One great thing about visiting temples in Taiwan is that they are free. Although they certainly welcome contributions, nobody in Taiwan will hustle you to pay. I find this an interesting contrast to Japan, where at nearly every temple you are greeted by a monk selling admission tickets. Having visited literally hundreds of temples throughout Taiwan, I have yet to find a single one charging admission.

You are free to photograph temples, art objects and even religious ceremonies, but Chinese people don't appreciate having a camera poked in their face any more than Westerners do. It's best to photograph worshippers from a distance with a long telephoto lens and no flash. Monks and nuns are usually camera-shy, so respect their wishes. Inside temples avoid loud talk and romantic displays like kissing, hugging or whatever with your partner. Dress neatly, and be quiet and respectful so that travellers who come after you will continue to be welcomed. I have seen foreigners do some quite outrageous things in temples, such as ridiculing the deities, taking some 'souvenirs', or climbing up onto a Buddha's lap to have a photograph taken. I know of at least one place where foreigners carved their initials into a wooden temple image. Such rude behaviour is certainly unnecessary and will undoubtedly generate ill will towards foreigners.

In most temples you do not have to take off your shoes unless the floor is carpeted, but look to see what others do. If everyone piles their shoes outside the door, you should follow their lead.

Monks and nuns usually welcome visitors who show a genuine interest in their temple. Most are happy to answer questions about the temple's history but few speak English.

## Religious Ceremonies

Many forms of worship exist in Taiwan. Some worship takes place at home. Many people have altars in their homes and you can frequently see people performing a worship ceremony known as *bàibài* in front of their homes. A worship ceremony can take many forms as they're performed for different reasons. Most often, you will see somebody burning pieces of paper, which in fact represents money. If the money has a silver square in the middle it is 'ghost money'; if it has a gold square it's 'god money'. The money is usually burned to satisfy a 'hungry ghost' from the underworld (hell) so that it will not bother you or members of your family. The money could also be for a departed relative who needs some cash in heaven. Truck

Ghost money furnace

drivers often throw ghost money out of the window of their vehicles to appease the 'road ghosts' so that they don't have an accident. Some people place the ashes of ghost money in water and drink the resulting mixture as a cure for disease.

Another custom is for people to burn paper models of cars and motorcycles so the dearly departed may have a means of transport in heaven. Incense is frequently burned; often placed on a table with some delicious-looking food which is meant for the ghosts. However, after the ghost has had a few nibbles, the living will sit down to a feast of the leftovers. It is also possible for people to rent or borrow carved images of the deities to take home from the temple for home worship ceremonies.

If you go to a temple in Taiwan, you will probably encounter some strange objects that you have never seen before. One such object is a box full of wooden rods (*qiān*). Before praying for something you desire, such as health, wealth or a good spouse, select a rod. Then pick up two kidney-shaped objects called *shimbui* ('shimbui' is a Taiwanese word, not a Mandarin one). Drop them on the ground three times. If two out of three times they land with one round surface up and one flat surface up, then your wish may be granted. If both flat sides are down, then your wish might not be granted. If both flat sides are up, god is laughing at you.

Many festivals are held throughout the year in accordance with the lunar calendar. Some festivals only occur every 12 years at the end of every cycle of the 12 lunar animals, which are the rat, ox, tiger, rabbit, dragon, snake, horse, sheep, monkey, rooster, dog and pig. Some festivals occur only once in 60 years. This is because each of the 12 animals is associated with five elements: metal, wood, earth, water and fire. The full cycle takes 60 years (5 x 12) and at the end of this time there is a super-worship festival.

I had the good fortune to attend one of these once-in-60-years festivals. Over 300,000 people were there, having come from all over Taiwan, and the firecrackers and feasting provided a sight I will never forget.

You can frequently see a Taoist street parade in Taiwan. The purpose is usually to celebrate a god's birthday.

Look closely at the temples in Taiwan and you will see some Chinese characters inscribed on every stone, engraving, painting and statue. These characters are not those of the artist, but rather the names of the people who have donated money to purchase that particular temple ornament. Judging by the number of new temples being constructed in Taiwan through private donations, there is no shortage of believers who are willing to give a little cash to assure that they stay on the good side of the gods. Should you donate some money to a temple, you may also have your name engraved in stone.

It must be said that although religion is alive and well in Taiwan, many elders complain that the young people don't care about it. Of course, the older generation always tends to say that. People somehow seem to get more religious as they get older and approach death. Yet it is true that some religious traditions are beginning to fade as the people of Taiwan get more exposure to the outside world.

Other than monks and nuns, practically nobody in Taiwan receives any formal religious education. Thus, the majority of the population understands little of the history and philosophy behind Buddhism and Taoism.

## CHINESE ZODIAC

As in the Western system of astrology, there are 12 signs of the zodiac. Unlike in the Western system, your sign is based on which year rather than which month you were born, though the exact day and time of your birth are also carefully considered in charting your astrological path.

Fortune tellers are common in Taiwan. Making use of astrology, palm reading and face reading, fortune tellers claim they can accurately predict the future. If you are so inclined, you can try out this service,

| Rat | 1912 | 1924 | 1936 | 1948 | 1960 | 1972 | 1984 |
| Ox/Cow | 1913 | 1925 | 1937 | 1949 | 1961 | 1973 | 1985 |
| Tiger | 1914 | 1926 | 1938 | 1950 | 1962 | 1974 | 1986 |
| Rabbit | 1915 | 1927 | 1939 | 1951 | 1963 | 1975 | 1987 |
| Dragon | 1916 | 1928 | 1940 | 1952 | 1964 | 1976 | 1988 |
| Snake | 1917 | 1929 | 1941 | 1953 | 1965 | 1977 | 1989 |
| Horse | 1918 | 1930 | 1942 | 1954 | 1966 | 1978 | 1990 |
| Sheep | 1919 | 1931 | 1943 | 1955 | 1967 | 1979 | 1991 |
| Monkey | 1920 | 1932 | 1944 | 1956 | 1968 | 1980 | 1992 |
| Rooster | 1921 | 1933 | 1945 | 1957 | 1969 | 1981 | 1993 |
| Dog | 1922 | 1934 | 1946 | 1958 | 1970 | 1982 | 1994 |
| Pig | 1923 | 1935 | 1947 | 1959 | 1971 | 1983 | 1995 |

though you are almost certain to need an interpreter since few fortune tellers in Taiwan can speak English.

## Lunar Calendar

There are two calendars in use in Taiwan. One is the Gregorian (solar) calendar which Westerners are familiar with, while the other is the Chinese lunar calendar. The two calendars do not correspond with each other because a lunar month is slightly shorter than a solar month. To keep the two calendars from becoming totally out of harmony, the Chinese add an extra month every 30 months to the lunar calendar. Thus, the Chinese lunar New Year – the most important holiday – can fall anywhere between 21 January and 28 February on the Gregorian calendar.

You can easily buy calendars in Taiwan showing all the holidays for the current year. These calendars look just like the ones Westerners are familiar with, but the lunar dates are shown in smaller numbers.

## HOLIDAYS & FESTIVALS

The most interesting holidays are determined according to the lunar calendar, but the majority of the public holidays are based on the Gregorian (solar) calendar.

## Solar Calendar Holidays

**Founding Day** (*yúandàn*) The founding day of the Republic of China falls on 1 January of the Gregorian calendar. Many businesses and schools remain closed on 2 January as well.

**Youth Day** (*qīngnián jié*) Youth Day falls on 29 March of the Gregorian calendar. Of course, all schools are closed on this day.

**Tomb Sweep Day** (*qīng míng jié*) A day for worshipping ancestors; people visit the graves of their departed relatives and clean the site. They often place flowers on the tomb and burn ghost money for the departed. Falls on 5 April in the Gregorian calendar in most years, 4 April in leap years.

**Teacher's Day** (*jiàoshī jié*) The birthday of Confucius is celebrated as Teacher's Day. It occurs on 28 September of the Gregorian calendar. There is a very interesting ceremony held at every Confucius Temple in Taiwan on this day, beginning at about 4 am. However, tickets are needed to attend this ceremony and they are not sold at the temple gate. The tickets can sometimes be purchased from universities, hotels or tour agencies, but generally are not easy to obtain.

**National Day** (*shūangshí jié*) As it falls on 10 October – the 10th day of the 10th month – National Day is usually called 'Double 10th Day'. Big military parades are held in Taipei near the Presidential Building. There is a huge fireworks display at night by the Tanshui River. Overall, it's an interesting time to visit Taipei.

**Restoration Day** (*gūangfù jié*) Taiwan Restoration Day celebrates Taiwan's return to the Republic of China after 50 years of Japanese occupation. It is celebrated on 25 October.

Top: Hsimending district, Taipei (Storey)
Left: Guard at the Martyrs Shrine, Taipei (Storey)
Right: Furnace for burning 'ghost money' (Storey)

Top: Funeral hearse (Storey)
Left: Wufengchi Waterfall, Chiaohsi Hot Springs (Storey)
Right: Statue of Chiang Kaishek (Storey)

**Chiang Kaishek's Birthday** (*jiǎnggōng dànchén jìniàn rì*) Chiang Kaishek's birthday falls on 31 October.

**Sun Yatsen's Birthday** (*gúofù dànchén jìniàn rì*) Sun Yatsen is regarded as the father of his country. His birthday is celebrated on 12 November.

**Constitution Day** (*xíngxiàn jìniàn rì*) Most Westerners and many Chinese consider this to be a Christmas (*shèngdàn jié*) holiday since it falls on 25 December, but this isn't a Christian nation and the official designation is Constitution Day.

### Lunar Calendar Holidays

There are only three lunar public holidays: the Chinese lunar New Year; the Dragon Boat Festival; and the Mid-Autumn Festival. All government offices and most private businesses are closed on these holidays. However, many of the 'unofficial' holidays are the most fascinating.

**Lunar New Year** (*chūn jié*) The 1st day of the 1st moon. Actually, the holiday lasts 3 days and many people take a full week off from work. It is very difficult to book tickets during this time and all forms of transport and hotels are filled to capacity – not a good time to travel. Workers demand double wages during the New Year and hotel rooms triple in price. Your best bet is to stay home and read a book until the chaos ends.

**Lantern Day** (*yúanxiāo jié*) Also known as Tourism Day, this is not a public holiday, but it's very colourful. It falls on the 15th day of the 1st moon. Hundreds of thousands of people use this time to descend on the towns of Yenshui, Luerhmen and Peikang to ignite fireworks – making them good places to visit or to avoid, depending on how you feel about fireworks and crowds.

**Kuanyin's Birthday** (*gūanshìyīn shēngrì*) The birthday of Kuanyin, the goddess of mercy, is on the 19th day of the 2nd moon

and is a good time for seeing temple worship festivals.

**Matsu's Birthday** (*māzǔ shēngrì*) Matsu, goddess of the sea, is the friend of all fishermen. Her birthday is widely celebrated at temples throughout Taiwan. Matsu's birthday is on the 23rd day of the 3rd moon.

**Dragon Boat Festival** (*dūanwǔ jié*) On the 5th day of the 5th moon, colourful dragon boat races are held in Taipei and in a few other cities – they're shown on TV. It's the traditional day to eat steamed rice dumplings (*zòngzi*).

**Ghost Month** (*gǔi yùe*) The Ghost Month is the 7th lunar month. The devout believe that during this time the ghosts from hell walk the earth and it is a dangerous time to travel, go swimming, get married or move to a new house. If someone dies during this month, the body will be preserved and the funeral and burial will be performed the following month. As Chinese people tend not to travel during this time, it is very convenient for foreign tourists to travel around the island and avoid crowds. It is also a good time to see temple worship. On the 1st and 15th day of the Ghost Month, people will be burning both ghost money and incense and will also place offerings of food on tables outside their homes. The 15th day is usually most exciting. Definitely try to get to a Taoist temple during that time.

**Mid-Autumn Festival** (*zhōngqiū jié*) Also known as the Moon Festival, this takes place on the 15th day of the 8th moon. Gazing at the moon and lighting fireworks are very popular at this time. This is the time to eat tasty moon cakes, which are available from every bakery. Of course, you can buy moon cakes much more cheaply on sale the next day.

## LANGUAGE

Mandarin Chinese is the official language of Taiwan; it's spoken on TV and radio and taught in the schools. However, more than half the people speak Taiwanese at home, especially in the south and in the countryside. Taiwanese is nearly identical to the Fujian dialect spoken on the Chinese mainland. Taiwanese and Mandarin are similar in many respects, but they are still two different languages and not mutually intelligible. Taiwanese has no written script and therefore no literature, unless you count a Romanised version of the Bible used by missionaries. While virtually all the young people can speak Mandarin, many of the older people don't speak it at all. However, many older people know Japanese as a result of the 50 year occupation by Japan.

The study of English is required in Taiwan from junior high school on, but actually few students learn to speak it at all. They generally read and write English much better than they can speak it, so if you need to communicate, try writing it down. The reason for this is that students learn English by rote memory of textbooks, without having any opportunity for conversation. For tourists the language barrier can be formidable at times, but try to overcome it with a smile and sign language. Don't get frustrated and angry – Chinese people are very friendly and will do their best to try to overcome the language gap.

Another dialect found in Taiwan is Hakka. The Hakka people currently comprise some 5% of the total population of Taiwan and are believed to be the earliest immigrants from the Chinese mainland. The Hakkas fled to southern China to escape severe persecution and then later migrated to Taiwan. They have been largely assimilated and are not a highly visible minority today, but you can still hear the Hakka language being spoken occasionally.

It's not a very widely known fact that Taiwan has 10 aboriginal tribes, each of which has its own language. Their language, like those of the aboriginal tribes of the Philippines, is not related to Chinese but is believed to be related to the languages of the Pacific Islands. These languages may die out with time as the aboriginal people become assimilated into mainstream Taiwanese society.

Mandarin Chinese, Taiwanese and Hakka are all tonal languages – by changing the tone of a word the meaning is completely changed. Mandarin has four tones, while other dialects can have as many as nine. For example, in Mandarin Chinese the word *ma* can have four distinct meanings depending on which tone is used:

| high tone | *mā* | means 'mother' |
| rising tone | *má* | means 'hemp' or 'numb' |
| falling-rising tone | *mǎ* | means 'horse' |
| falling tone | *mà* | means 'to scold' or 'to swear' |

In some words, the tone is not important. This so-called neutral tone is usually not indicated at all. Mastering tones is tricky for the untrained Western ear, but with practice it can be done.

Foreigners often make fools of themselves with botched attempts to speak the Chinese language. A subtle difference in pronunciation can radically alter the meaning of a word. For example, the verbs *wèn* (to ask) and *wén* (to kiss) are only differentiated by the tone. I can only guess how many times I have said to my Chinese teacher 'I want to kiss you', when I meant to say 'I want to ask you'. Similarly, it's easy to forget the difference between *pifu* (skin) and *pigu* (buttocks). After a long day at the beach, I meant to tell one of my friends that his skin was red, but instead I told him...well, you get the idea.

So, try to be understanding when the Chinese err in their attempts to speak English. I met a nice gentleman on the train who told me that he was an 'executor' in Taipei. After further discussion, I determined that he meant 'executive'. My neighbour claimed he was a 'taxi diver'. On the bus, I sat next to a charming Chinese woman who asked me 'What is your obsession?'. I almost told her, but she probably meant 'profession'. Then there was the now famous case of a Taiwanese manufacturer who tried to market towel racks that attach to the bathroom wall with suction cup feet. The name of his product was Suck-All. Another manufacturer tried his luck at exporting paint mixers that mix the paint by shaking and vibrating the container – his Jiggling Vibrators were an instant hit. Many Chinese seem to be confused about the difference between the bathroom and the toilet – which explains why one of my English students told me that he washed his hair in the toilet. And even after many years in Taiwan, it still brings a grin to my face when I check into a hotel and there is a sign on the front desk proclaiming 'We are happy to service you'.

## Characters

It is estimated that about 50,000 Chinese characters exist, but only about 5000 are used today and only 2000 are needed to read a newspaper.

Chinese characters are very complex and it takes many years of study to achieve complete literacy. Ironically, the spoken language is not very difficult to master, apart from the problems with tones. From my experience, it only takes about a month to learn 200 characters, but it's also very easy to forget them quickly if you don't practise reading and writing constantly. In mainland China, a system of simplified characters was introduced to improve literacy. There is little doubt that the simplified characters are easier to learn and about twice as fast to write. However, traditions die hard – in Taiwan, Hong Kong and in most Chinese communities outside mainland China, the older complex characters are still used. In this book we will stick with the older characters, since these are the only kind you will encounter in Taiwan.

It is often said that Chinese is a monosyllabic language – that is, every word is claimed to be just one syllable long. Although I have seen this claim made in some academic texts, I dispute it. It's true that each character represents a single syllable and it's true that each character has a meaning of its own, but most modern Chinese words require more than one character to be written. The Chinese word for

massage is composed of three characters, *mǎ shā jī*, which mean 'horse kill chicken' if you translate them as three separate words. It's as if we took the English word 'carpet' and claimed it was two separate words, 'car' and 'pet'. We could then write English using the Chinese characters for 'car' and 'pet', but this would radically alter our perceptions of the English language. Perhaps we can say that Chinese has a monosyllabic writing system, but it is no more a monosyllabic spoken language than English is. Japanese, a language noted for very long words, uses a slightly modified version of Chinese characters. The Koreans also used to write with Chinese characters, but abandoned them in favour of an alphabetic system.

If you are going to be in Taiwan for a while, it's a good place to learn Mandarin. There are a number of good government-approved language institutes in Taipei and other major cities.

## Romanisation Systems

Chinese can be written in Romanised form. Unfortunately, there are three competing Romanisation systems in common use, which causes great confusion. These are Yale, Pinyin and Wade-Giles. The three systems are similar, especially for vowels, but there are some significant differences in the way Chinese consonants are represented.

Yale is the easiest system for untrained Westerners to learn. It was developed by Yale University some years ago as a teaching aid, and at one time most Chinese textbooks for foreigners used it. Nowadays, Yale University has dropped this system in favour of Pinyin.

Pinyin takes more time to learn than Yale. A number of Pinyin letters are confusing, as they are not pronounced the same as in English. On the other hand, Pinyin is the most accurate system of Romanisation yet devised for Chinese. Unfortunately, Pinyin is not used in Taiwan, except in some Chinese textbooks written for foreigners. It is used much more extensively in mainland China.

Wade-Giles is the oldest of the three systems, dating back to the early days of

European contact with China. In Taiwan, Wade-Giles is still the official system used for street signs, maps, books, newspapers and name cards. The system is accurate if written correctly. Unfortunately, Romanisation is not taught in Taiwan's schools. Therefore most locals are unfamiliar with it and misspellings are common. For example, one street in Taipei alternately appears on maps as Tehui St and Tehhwei St; in Kaohsiung, Jeouru Rd and Chiuju Rd are the same place; a fashionable neighbourhood in east Taipei is variously spelled Dinghao, Dinghow and Tinghao. Most Taiwanese cannot even Romanise their own names.

A more serious problem with the Wade-Giles system is the use of the apostrophe. For example, the city of Taipei should be written with an apostrophe: T'aipei. Without the apostrophe, the initial t would be pronounced as a **d** – Daipei. But the apostrophes are almost always omitted, thus undermining the accuracy of the Wade-Giles system. As a result, the letter **ch'** is confused with **j**; **k'** with **g**; **p'** with **b** and so on. Without the apostrophe, the pronunciation radically changes, and the result is most confusing even for native speakers.

The presence of various conflicting systems of Romanisation poses a dilemma. Since maps, street signs and all official publications in Taiwan use the Wade-Giles system, I have decided to stick with convention and use the Wade-Giles system for all official geographical names and names of persons. Also in line with accepted practice in Taiwan, this book will ignore the apostrophes used in the Wade-Giles system. So we will write Taipei and Taiwan, not T'aipei and T'aiwan.

However, with the need for an accurate and easily learnt Romanisation scheme to assist foreign visitors in pronouncing Chinese words, the Wade-Giles name will be followed with the Pinyin Romanisation in italics and parentheses wherever necessary for clarification. For example, 'the second largest city in Taiwan is Kaohsiung (*gāoxióng*)'. When Pinyin is used in this text, it will always be in italics with tones shown.

Other Romanised words will be written in the Wade-Giles system. Note that no tone marks will be shown with Romanised names on maps.

In line with the theory that Chinese is not a monosyllabic language, Romanisation shows multicharacter words as multisyllable words. Thus, the four character expression for 'messy' is written *luànqībāzāo* rather than *luàn qī bā zāo*.

## Pronunciation

The following is a description of the sounds produced in spoken Mandarin Chinese. The letter **v** is not used in Chinese. The trickiest sounds in Pinyin are **c**, **q** and **x**. Most letters are pronounced as in English, except for the following:

### Vowels

| | |
|---|---|
| a | like the 'a' in 'father' |
| ai | like the 'i' in 'I' |
| ao | like the 'ow' in 'cow' |
| e | like the 'u' in 'blur' |
| ei | like the 'ei' in 'weigh' |
| i | like the 'ee' in 'meet' or like the 'oo' in 'book'* |
| ian | like in 'yen' |
| ie | like the English word 'yeah' |
| o | like the 'o' in 'or' |
| ou | like the 'oa' in 'boat' |
| u | like the 'u' in 'flute' |
| ui | like 'way' |
| uo | like 'w' in 'wear' followed by 'o' like in 'or' |
| yu | like German umlaut 'ü' or French 'u' in '*union* ' – purse your lips and then try saying 'ee' |
| ü | like German umlaut 'ü' |

### Consonants

| | |
|---|---|
| c | like the 'ts' in 'bits' |
| ch | like in English, but with the tongue curled back |
| h | like in English, but articulated from the throat |
| q | like the 'ch' in 'cheese' |

| r | like the 's' in 'pleasure' |
| sh | like in English, but with the tongue curled back |
| x | like the 'sh' in 'ship' |
| z | like the 'ds' in 'suds' |
| zh | like the 'j' in 'judge' but with the tongue curled back |

*The letter **i** is pronounced like the 'oo' in 'book' when it occurs after **c**, **ch**, **r**, **s**, **sh**, **z** or **zh**.

Consonants can never appear at the end of a syllable except for **n**, **ng**, and **r**.

## Tones

| 1st tone | high | ē |
| 2nd tone | rising | é |
| 3rd tone | falling-rising | ě |
| 4th tone | falling | è |

In Pinyin, apostrophes are occasionally used to separate syllables. So, you can write (*ping'an*) to prevent the word being pronounced as (*pin'gan*).

## Major Differences between Wade-Giles & Pinyin

| Pinyin | Wade-Giles |
|--------|------------|
| b | p |
| c | ts' |
| c | ch' |
| d | t |
| g | k |
| p | p' |
| q | ch' |
| r | j |
| t | t' |
| x | hs |
| z | ts, tz |
| zh | ch |

## Pronouns

I
   *wǒ* 我
you
   *nǐ* 你
he, she, it
   *tā* 他
we, us
   *wǒmen* 我們

you (plural)
   *nǐmen* 你們
they, them
   *tāmen* 他們

## Greetings & Civilities

hello
   *nǐ hǎo* 你好
goodbye
   *zàijiàn* 再見
thank you
   *xièxie* 謝謝
you're welcome
   *búkèqì* 不客氣
I'm sorry/excuse me
   *dùibùqǐ* 對不起

## Some Useful Words & Phrases

How much does it cost?
   *dūoshǎo qián?* 多少錢
too expensive
   *tài gùi* 太貴
no/don't have
   *méiyǒu* 沒有
I want...
   *wǒ yào...* 我要
No, I don't want it.
   *búyào* 不要
to eat/let's eat
   *chī fàn* 吃飯
toilet (restroom)
   *cèsǔo* 廁所
toilet paper
   *wèishēng zhǐ* 衛生紙
bathroom (washroom)
   *xǐshǒujiān* 洗手間
I don't understand.
   *wǒ tīng bùdǒng* 我聽不懂
I do understand.
   *wǒ tīngde dǒng* 我聽得懂
Do you understand?
   *dǒng bùdǒng?* 懂不懂
Wait a moment.
   *děng yī xià* 等一下
laundromat (laundry service)
   *xǐyī zhōngxīn* 洗衣中心

## Getting Around

railway station
   *hǔochē zhàn* 火車站

bus station
  *gōngchē zhàn* 公車站
airport
  *fēijīchǎng* 飛機場
taxi
  *jìchéngchē* 計程車
local bus
  *gōnggòng qìchē* 公共汽車
highway bus
  *bāshì* 巴士
train
  *hǔochē* 火車
motorcycle
  *jīchē* 機車
car
  *qìchē* 汽車
I want to get off. (bus/taxi)
  *xià chē* 下車
Which platform?
  *dì jǐ yùetái?* 第幾月台
number...
  *...hào* 號
upgrade ticket (on train)
  *bǔ piào* 補票
luggage
  *xínglǐ* 行李
luggage storage room
  *xínglǐ shì* 行李室

## Directions
Where is the...?
  *...zài nǎlǐ?* 在那裡
I'm lost.
  *wǒ mí lù* 我迷路
Turn right.
  *yòu zhǔan* 右轉
Turn left.
  *zǔo zhǔan* 左轉
Go straight.
  *yìzhí zǒu* 一直走
Turn around.
  *zhǔan gewān* 轉個彎

## Accommodation
hotel name card
  *míngpiàn* 名片
hotel
  *lügǔan* 旅館
small cheap hotel
  *lüshè* 旅社

big hotel
  *dàfàndiàn* 大飯店
big youth hostel
  *húodòng zhōngxīn* 活動中心
mountain hostel
  *shān zhuāng* 山莊
room
  *fángjiān* 房間
dormitory
  *tuántǐfáng* 團體房
tatami
  *tātāmǐ* 榻榻米
cheap room (shared bath)
  *pǔtōngfáng* 普通房
room with private bath
  *tàofáng* 套房
suite
  *gāojífáng* 高級房

## Post & Communications
telephone
  *diànhùa* 電話
telephone company office
  *diànxìn jú* 電信局
post office
  *yóujú* 郵局
GPO
  *zǒng yóujú* 總郵局
stamp
  *yóupiào* 郵票
aerogram
  *yóujiǎn* 郵簡
fax
  *chúanzhēn* 傳真
telex
  *diànchúan* 電傳
telegram
  *diànbào* 電報

## Emergencies
I'm sick.
  *wǒ shēng bìng* 我生病
I'm injured.
  *wǒ shòushāng* 我受傷
hospital
  *yīyùan* 醫院
police
  *jǐngchá* 警察
Fire!
  *hǔo zāi!* 火災

Help!
  *jiùmìng a!* 救命啊
Thief!
  *xiǎo tōu!* 小偷

## Numbers

| 0 | *líng* |
| 1 | *yī* 一 |
| 2 | *èr, liǎng* 二 |
| 3 | *sān* 三 |
| 4 | *sì* 四 |
| 5 | *wǔ* 五 |
| 6 | *liù* 六 |
| 7 | *qī* 七 |
| 8 | *bā* 八 |
| 9 | *jiǔ* 九 |
| 10 | *shí* 十 |
| 11 | *shíyī* |
| 12 | *shí'èr* |
| 20 | *èrshí* |
| 21 | *èrshíyī* |
| 100 | *yìbǎi* |
| 200 | *liǎngbǎi* |
| 1000 | *yìqiān* |
| 2000 | *liǎngqiān* |
| 10,000 | *yíwàn* |
| 20,000 | *liǎngwàn* |
| 100,000 | *shíwàn* |
| 200,000 | *èrshíwàn* |

## Time

What is the time?
  *jǐ diǎn?* 幾點
hour
  *diǎn* 點
minute
  *fēn* 分
now
  *xiànzài* 現在
today
  *jīntiān* 今天
tomorrow
  *míngtiān* 明天
yesterday
  *zúotiān* 昨天

## Geographical Terms

alley
  *nòng* 弄
cave
  *dòng* 洞
cliff
  *dùanyái* 斷崖
hot spring
  *wēnqúan* 溫泉
lake
  *hú* 湖
lane
  *xiàng* 巷

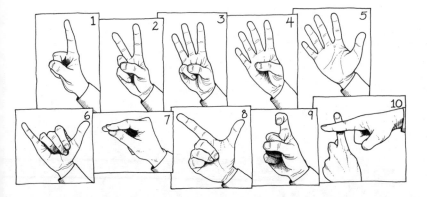

Finger counting

mountain
*shān* 山
river
*hé, xī* 河，溪
road, trail
*lù* 路
section
*dùan* 段
street
*jiē* 街
valley
*gǔ* 谷
waterfall
*pùbù* 瀑布

## Studying Chinese

There are a number of centres in Taipei and other cities where you can study Chinese, and some private schools teach Taiwanese as well. There are both government and privately run centres. The government places are good but tend to be advanced and will really push you; so if you study at these places you'd better be willing to really apply yourself. The private ones will allow you to progress at a more leisurely pace.

Mandarin Daily News
11-1 Fuchou St, Taipei (tel (02) 3915134)
Taiwan Normal University Mandarin Training Center
129-1 Hoping E Rd, Section 1, Taipei (tel (02) 3639123)

National Taiwan University
Roosevelt Rd, Section 4, Taipei
Taipei Language Institute (TLI)
7th floor, 104 Hsinyi Rd, Section 2, Taipei (tel (02) 3410022, 3938805)
Shihlin Branch, 2nd floor, 684 Chungshan N Rd, Section 5, Shihlin, Taipei (tel (02) 8360480/1)
Taichung Center (tel (04) 2318842)
Kaohsiung Center (tel (07) 2513638)
Cathay Language Center
2nd floor, 8 Lane 190, Chungshan N Rd, Section 7, Tienmu, Taipei (tel (02) 8729165)
Language Testing & Training Center
170 Hsinhai Rd, Section 2, Taipei (tel (02) 3216385)
My Language School
2nd floor, 126-8 Hsinsheng S Rd, Section 1, Taipei (tel (02) 3945400)

## Body Language

One of the most important things to learn is how to beckon to someone. This is done with the hand waved, palm down and it looks remarkably like the Western body sign to 'go away'. This same body sign is used throughout most of Asia. The typical Western form of beckoning, with the index finger hooked up, will draw a blank stare from an Asian.

The number 10 is indicated by using the index fingers on both hands to form a cross. If you hold up all 10 fingers to indicate 10, no one will understand what you're doing.

# Facts for the Visitor

As the Chinese say, 'A journey of 1000 miles begins with a single step'. This is as true today as it was in the time of Confucius.

## VISAS

A visa is definitely required for visiting Taiwan. No airline will even allow you to check in for your flight if you don't have a visa. If you somehow arrive in Taiwan without a visa, you will be politely put back on the plane. There has been talk for years about permitting a short visa-free stay, but so far it has not materialised. The tourist industry has been lobbying for such a visa-free policy so perhaps things will change, but don't hold your breath waiting.

Visas are usually obtained from the embassy of the country you wish to visit, but in the case of Taiwan there are only a few countries which maintain diplomatic relations with the Republic of China. As there are so few ROC embassies in the world, Taiwan's government gets around this by maintaining a number of 'nongovernmental offices' in many countries. Besides issuing visas, these offices are important links in Taiwan's vital international trade.

To apply for a visa, you need your passport and three passport-type photos. They will usually accept cheapie machine prints. Sometimes you need to show your plane ticket to prove that you have booked an onward flight from Taiwan. Any destination will do – it needn't be a return ticket to your home country.

It normally takes only a day to receive your visa if all the papers are in order. You must leave your passport with the office processing your visa. They'll give you a receipt for your passport. Since a passport is normally needed to cash travellers' cheques, make sure you have enough cash on hand.

Most travellers from Europe will not usually be given a visa when they apply for one, but will be issued a letter which can be exchanged for a visa in the airport on arrival in Taiwan. Travellers entering Taiwan with such a letter in lieu of a visa must arrive at one of the two international airports, Taipei or Kaohsiung.

### Visa-Issuing Offices

You can get a visa for Taiwan at any of the following offices.

Australia
> Far East Trading Co Pty Ltd, D401, International House, World Trade Centre, Melbourne (tel (03) 6112988)
> Suite 1902, MLC Centre, King St, Sydney (tel (02) 2233207)

Austria
> Institute of Chinese Culture, Stubenring, 4/III/18, A-1010, Vienna (tel 524681)

Belgium
> Centre Culturel Sun Yatsen, Rue de la Loi 24, 1000-Bruxelles (tel (02) 5110687)

Canada
> Far East Trade Service Inc, Suite 3315, 2 Bloor St East, Toronto, Ontario M4W 1A8 (tel (416) 9222412)

France
> ASPECT, 9 Ave Matignon, 75008 Paris (tel 42991688)

Greece
> Far East Trade Centre, 4th floor, 54 Queen Sophia Ave, GR 115 28 Athens (tel 7243107)

Hong Kong
> Chung Hwa Travel Service, 4th floor, East Tower, Bond Centre, Queensway, Hong Kong Island (tel 5-258315)

Indonesia
> Chinese Chamber of Commerce to Jakarta, No 4 Jalan Banyumas, Jakarta (tel 351212)

Italy
> Centro Commerciale per L'Estremo Oriente, Via Errico Petrella 2, 201124 Milan (tel (02) 2853083)

Japan
> Association of East Asian Relations, 8-7, Higashi-Azabu 1-Chome, Minato-Ku, Tokyo 106 (tel 5832171)
> Association of East Asian Relations, 3rd floor, Sun Life Building III, 5-19, 2-Chome, Hakataeki, Higashi Hakata-Ku, Fukuoka (tel 092-4736655)

Malaysia
> Far East Trading & Tourism Centre, SDN, BHD,

LOT 202, Wisma Equity 150, Jalan Ampang, 50450 Kuala Lumpur (tel 2425549)

**The Netherlands**

Far East Trade Office, Javastraat 56, 2585 AR, The Hague (tel (070) 469438)

**New Zealand**

East Asia Trade Centre, Level 21, Marac House,105-109 The Terrace, Wellington (tel (04) 736474)

3rd floor, Norwich Union Building, corner Queen and Durhan streets, Auckland (tel (09) 33903)

**Norway**

Taipei Trade Centre, Eilertsundtsgate 4/2 Etg, 0209 Oslo 2 (tel 555471)

**The Philippines**

Pacific Economic & Cultural Center, 8th floor, BF Homes Condominium Building, Aduana St, Intramuros, Manila (tel 472261)

**Singapore**

Trade Mission of the Republic of China, 460 Alexandra Rd, 23-00 PSA Building, Singapore 0511 (tel 2786511)

**South Africa**

Embassy of the ROC, 1147 Schoeman St, Hatfield, Pretoria 0083 (tel (012) 436071)

**South Korea**

Embassy of the Republic of China, 83, 2Ka, Myung-Dong, Chung-Gu, Seoul (tel 7762721)

**Spain**

Centro Sun Yatsen, Paseo de la Habana 12-4, 28036 Madrid (tel 4113463)

**Sweden**

Taipei Trade Tourism & Information Office, Wenner-Gren Center, 4tr, Sveavagen 166, S-113 46 Stockholm (tel 08-7288533)

**Switzerland**

Centre Sun Yatsen, 54 Ave de Bethusy, 1012 Lausanne (tel (21) 335005)

**Thailand**

The Far East Trade Office, 10th floor, Kian Gwan Building, 140 Wit Thayu Rd, Bangkok (tel 2519274)

**UK**

Free Chinese Centre, 4th floor, Dorland House, 14-16 Regent St, London, SW1Y 4PH (tel (071) 9305767)

**USA**

Head Office, Coordination Council for North America Affairs (CCNAA), 4201 Wisconsin Ave NW, Washington, DC 20016-2137 (tel (202) 8951800)

CCNAA, Suite 1290, 2 Midtown Plaza, 1349 W Peachtree St NE, Atlanta, GA 30309 (tel (404) 8720123)

CCNAA, Suite 801, 99 Summer St, Boston, MA 02110 (tel (617) 7372050)

CCNAA, 19th floor, 20 North Clark St, Chicago IL 60602 (tel (312) 3721213)

CCNAA, 2746 Pali Highway, Honolulu, HI 96827 (tel (808) 5956347)

CCNAA, Suite 2006, 11 Green Way Plaza, Houston, TX 77046 (tel (713) 6267445)

CCNAA, Suite 1001, 3100 Broadway, Kansas City, MO 64111 (tel (816) 5311298)

CCNAA, Suite 700, 3731 Wilshire Blvd, Los Angeles, CA 90010 (tel (213) 3891215)

CCNAA, Suite 610, 2333 Ponce de Leon Blvd, Coral Gables, FL 33134 (tel (305) 4438917)

CCNAA, 6th floor, 801 Second Ave, New York, NY 10017 (tel (212) 3706600)

CCNAA, Suite 501, 555 Montgomery St, San Francisco, CA 94111 (tel (415) 3627680)

CCNAA, 24th floor, Westin Building, 2001 6th Ave, Seattle, WA 98121 (tel (206) 4414586)

**West Germany**

Asia Trade Centre Tourism Bureau, Dreieichstrasse, Frankfurt/Main 70 (tel (069) 610743)

Fernost Informationen Hamburg, Mittelweg 144, 2000 Hamburg 13 (tel (040) 447788)

Fernost Informationen Munchen, Ottostrasse 5/II, 8000 Munchen 2 (tel (089) 592534)

## Visitor Visas

There are two types of visitor visa: single-entry and multiple-entry. Both of these permit a stay for 60 days. Under some circumstances it is possible to extend a visitor visa twice for a total stay of 180 days.

Single-entry visas are easily obtained, but a multiple-entry visitor visa is usually only issued in your native country and is very hard to get while travelling in nearby Asian countries such as Hong Kong, Singapore or South Korea. Sometimes it is possible to exchange a single-entry visa for a multiple-entry visa after arrival in Taipei. See the Changing a Visa section further on in this chapter.

## Resident Visas

These are the most difficult visas to get. They are usually issued only to people coming to Taiwan to work for a foreign company, to full-time students at a university, to spouses of ROC citizens, and to certain missionaries, researchers and big-time investors. To get this kind of visa, supporting documentation is required. Those with resident visas may be required to apply for an Alien Resident Certificate after arriving in Taiwan. Such certificates permit one to live and work in Taiwan for a specified period. The certificate must be renewed each year at a cost of NT$1000. Regular tourists and part-time students will not be given a resident visa.

Alien residents must apply for an exit and re-entry visa in advance every time they wish to leave the country. Failure to do this will result in loss of resident status.

## Visa Extensions

A visitor visa is valid for 60 days and can only be extended if the visa holder has some special reason to stay longer in Taiwan. Among the special reasons considered valid are study at a government-approved school, visiting close relatives, medical treatment, doing business or technical assistance. Supporting documentation is required. In general, the authorities don't consider sightseeing to be a valid reason for extending a visa beyond 60 days. In some cases, you will be requested to get a tax clearance form from the tax office, especially if you extend more than once. Some of the youth hostels in Taipei offer 'visa services'. For a fee, they will handle the paperwork for you. Usually this only works for the first visa extension. I can't swear by the reliability of such services, so you'll have to make your own inquiries at the hostels. Ask other travellers and see if it's worked out for them. These visa services are advertised in the local newspapers, the *China Post* and *China News*.

When applying for an extension, you must go to the Foreign Affairs Police. There are a total of 21 Foreign Affairs Police offices in Taiwan, one in each county seat and also one in each of the five special municipalities – Taipei, Keelung, Taichung, Tainan and Kaohsiung. You need to bring your passport of course, but no photos. Don't go during or near the lunch hour (hours!) – about 11.30 am to 2 pm.

All Foreign Affairs Police can speak English and can provide assistance to travellers in emergencies. I have found them to be very helpful, so the telephone numbers of all the Foreign Affairs Police offices are included here:

Changhua
    Changhua County (tel (047) 222101)
Chiayi
    Chiayi County (tel (05) 2274454)
Fengshan
    Kaohsiung County (tel (07) 7460105)
Fengyuan
    Taichung County (tel (045) 263304)
Hsinchu
    Hsinchu County (tel (035) 224168)
Hsinying
    Tainan County (tel (06) 2229704)
Hualien
    Hualien County (tel (038) 324144)
Ilan
    Ilan County (tel (039) 325147)
Kaohsiung City
    (tel (07) 2215796)
Keelung City
    (tel (032) 268181, 241991)
Makung
    Penghu County (tel (06) 9272105)
Miaoli
    Miaoli County (tel (037) 211302)
Nantou
    Nantou County (tel (049) 222111)
Panchiao
    Taipei County (tel (02) 9614809)
Pingtung
    Pingtung County (tel (08) 7322156)
Taichung City
    (tel (04) 2241141)
Tainan City
    (tel (06) 2229704)
Taipei City
    (tel (02) 3817475)
Taitung
    Taitung County (tel (089) 322034)
Taoyuan
    Taoyuan County (tel (03) 3327106)
Touliu
    Yunlin County (tel (055) 322042)

**Warning** Many privately run language schools claim that they are government approved and therefore can get you visa extensions. Don't take their word for it! Once you hand over the tuition fee, don't expect a refund even if it turns out that the school is not government approved. Some travellers have been ripped off this way. To be sure, always first ask at the Foreign Affairs Police if a certain school is government approved and if enrolling at it will guarantee you a visa extension.

### Changing a Visa

Under some circumstances it is possible to exchange one type of visa for another kind after arrival in Taipei. For example, it is possible to exchange a single-entry visitor visa for a multiple-entry visitor or resident visa. However, it is not easy. You will need a good reason for requesting such a change and supporting documentation is required. Study at a government-approved school will usually get you a multiple-entry visa but will not be sufficient to get a resident visa. A legal teaching job at a government-approved school will usually *not* gain you a resident visa unless it's a full-time job. Illegal employment, such as teaching English at one of Taipei's numerous private 'cram schools', will not endear you to the immigration authorities. For reasons I've been unable to determine, missionaries are heartily welcomed and granted resident visas.

The only city in Taiwan where you can change your visa is Taipei. It is possible to do it by post, though this requires mailing your passport to Taipei, which means you have to trust the post office not to lose it. Use registered mail, which is very reliable in Taiwan. If your application is approved, it will still take several days to complete the procedure. The place to contact for changing your visa is the Ministry of Foreign Affairs (tel (02) 3617785) (*wàijiāo bù*), 2 Chiehshou Rd, Taipei.

### Overstaying a Visa

If you overstay your visa by even 1 day you won't be able to leave the country until you clear up the matter. If you overstay by only a few days, you won't get into any serious trouble if you can give a valid reason, such as illness or missing your flight. If this happens to you, report as soon as possible to the Foreign Affairs Police at the main police station in whatever city you are in. You will have to pay a fine of around NT$600 – the exact amount will be determined by such factors as how long you overstayed and the reason why. The amount of paperwork you'll have to do is more of a punishment than the fine, so try to avoid overstaying.

### CUSTOMS

Taiwan's customs agents have a reputation for being thorough and strict, but they are also fair and honest and will not solicit bribes. First-time travellers to Taiwan should not encounter any special difficulty as long as you don't try to bring in prohibited items. However, if you are an overseas Chinese or a returning foreign resident, expect to be searched more thoroughly than tourists.

Items for normal personal use can be brought in duty-free with no trouble. This includes such things as a camera, tape recorder, radio, portable typewriter, video camera, clock and calculator. If you're bringing a dutiable item out of Taiwan, register it with customs before you depart if you intend to bring it back in duty-free at some future date.

Travellers arriving from Hong Kong, Australia or Japan are allowed a duty-free limit of US$1500 in goods. Those arriving from elsewhere are permitted a duty-free allowance of US$3000. The limit for children is half that of adults. These limits are not applicable to gold, liquor and cigarettes.

If you are carrying such items but only intend to stay a short time, you can place your dutiable items in bonded baggage and take them out again on departure. If you do this you won't be required to pay duty. If you want or need the dutiable item for use during your stay in Taiwan, it is possible to pay the duty and have the money returned to you on departure. This is a hassle, but some people do it.

Customs rules regarding gold, silver and foreign currency are strict. Any amount of foreign currency can be brought in but must be declared on arrival. Otherwise, only US$5000 in cash or the equivalent amount in another foreign currency can be taken out on departure. No more than NT$8000 can be brought in or taken out. Travellers' cheques and personal cheques do not have to be declared.

Any gold or silver brought in must be declared on arrival or else it can be confiscated. Gold imports are subject to tax. Be warned that if you bring gold or silver into

the country you cannot take it out again. However, if you arrive in Taiwan carrying gold or silver you may place it in storage under the custody of customs and a receipt will be issued. Don't lose it. On departure the gold or silver will be returned on presentation of the receipt. Of course, you must depart from the same place that you arrived.

Everyone aged 20 and over can bring in a litre of liquor and either a carton of cigarettes, 25 cigars or 500 grams of tobacco duty-free.

Any literature deemed pro-communist or subversive may be confiscated. This may include regular Hong Kong newspapers. Pornography, which includes *Playboy* magazine, is not permitted.

Needless to say, narcotic drugs are prohibited. Travellers caught smuggling in drugs could face many years of imprisonment. The Chinese suffered a long plague of opium addiction in the last century and they haven't forgotten it. Other Asian countries have similarly harsh penalties for possession of drugs, including the death penalty. Foreigners should not consider themselves above the law in Asia.

## MONEY

The official unit of currency is the New Taiwan dollar (NT$), which totals 100 cents. Coins in circulation come in denominations of 50 cents, NT$1, NT$5 and NT$10; notes come in denominations of NT$50, NT$100, NT$500 and NT$1000.

| | | |
|---|---|---|
| US$1 | = | NT$32 |
| A$1 | = | NT$23 |
| UK£1 | = | NT$53 |
| DM 1 | = | NT$19 |
| FFr 1 | = | NT$5 |
| Y100 | = | NT$21 |

When you change money, it is essential to save your receipts if you wish to reconvert your excess NT$ when you depart. To reconvert your NT$ into US$ on departure, you must take the receipts to the bank at the airport, *not* the city bank. If you stay in Taiwan for more than 6 months you cannot reconvert excess NT$ on departure. At least that is what the rules say – in practice, they will convert small amounts without the receipt.

US$ and other major currencies are *not* widely accepted in shops and hotels. Though some people may exchange them for you, it's illegal to do so. The NT$ is a controlled currency – not freely traded – so you will have difficulty exchanging it outside Taiwan. An exception is Hong Kong, where it can be freely exchanged, but at a slightly lower rate than in Taiwan.

Perhaps it will change by the time you read this, but as of now you *cannot* change Korean currency in Taiwan even though the Korean Tourist Bureau says you can. If you arrive in Taiwan with Korean money, your only hope is to exchange with other travellers at some of the youth hostels, or wait until you get to Hong Kong if you're headed that way. Most Western European currencies, except Danish money, can be exchanged at Taiwanese banks.

### Where to Change Money

Foreign currency and travellers' cheques can be changed at the two international airports and at large banks. Some major international hotels will cash travellers' cheques, but they usually only do it if you're staying there. It can be difficult or even impossible to cash travellers' cheques in rural areas, so take care of this in the cities.

Almost any bank will change US$ cash, but travellers' cheques can be a problem. Banks which are permitted to change travellers' cheques include the Bank of Taiwan, International Commercial Bank of China (ICBC), Changhua Commercial Bank, Hua Nan Commercial Bank and First Commercial Bank. ICBC is the best because you can cash travellers' cheques at all their branches. With the other banks you cannot be certain that they will cash travellers' cheques except at their major branches.

Many banks charge a small fee for each cheque cashed, so those with small denomination cheques get burned. Large denominations are better. The exchange rate given at banks is very good and you will not gain any benefit by seeking out black market moneychangers.

Taiwan does not have private moneychangers like you find in Hong Kong. Normal banking hours are 9 am to 3.30 pm, Monday to Friday, and from 9 am to noon on Saturday. The bank at CKS Airport is supposed to remain open whenever there are international flights departing or arriving. However, in my experience you'd better not count on this if you arrive or depart very late at night. The bank at Kaohsiung International Airport is only open during regular banking hours, which is useless if you arrive or depart on weekends, holidays or in the evening.

It is also possible to change money at some jewellery stores. You have to make inquiries to find out which stores will do it. This whole business is illegal, so they will not advertise. They only handle cash, not travellers' cheques, and they only want major currencies like US$ or Japanese yen. A small commission of around 2% is charged and is included in the quoted exchange rate.

### Bank Accounts
Silly as it may seem, the bureaucracy has deemed that foreigners are not permitted to open bank accounts in Taiwan unless they have resident visas. Since most foreigners living, studying and working in Taiwan do not have resident status, this is a major inconvenience. It wasn't always like this. The

restriction was slapped on in 1987 to prevent 'currency speculation by foreigners'. At the same time, Taiwan has declared its intention to replace Hong Kong as East Asia's financial centre – perhaps another case of the right hand not knowing what the left hand is doing.

If you need a place to stash money while in Taiwan, you'll be happy to know that foreigners are still permitted to have safe-deposit boxes. Hopefully, this won't lead to safe-deposit box speculation by foreigners and, thus, new restrictions.

Taiwan's Central Bank, which oversees banking policy, has received literally thousands of complaints from foreigners about the restrictions. So far, this hasn't resulted in any loosening of the rules, but perhaps things will have changed by the time you read this.

### COSTS
At one time, Taiwan was a very cheap place to visit but this is no longer the case. Prices have almost reached the level of many European countries, but Taiwan is still much cheaper than Japan...for now. The problem is that the strength of Taiwan's economy has rapidly pushed up the value of the NT$ making it expensive for foreign visitors. On the other hand, the strong NT$ has been a boon to travellers working (usually illegally) in Taiwan.

How much does it cost to visit Taiwan? Excluding airfare, you can probably manage on NT$500 per day if you stay in youth hostels, buy food from noodle vendors, take buses rather than taxis and resist the urge to go shopping. If you require a higher standard of living, it could easily cost several thousand NT$ daily. Expenses in Taipei are noticeably higher than elsewhere in Taiwan.

### TIPPING
Good news for the budget-minded: tipping is not customary in restaurants, taxis or in most other places in Taiwan. The Chinese almost never tip. The only time when you must definitely tip is when you are helped by a hotel bellhop or a porter at the airport. The usual tip is NT$25 per bag. Most of the bigger hotels or restaurants will automati-

cally add a 10% service charge to your bill, plus a 5% value-added tax (VAT). The smaller places almost never do that.

## TOURIST INFORMATION
The Taiwan Tourism Bureau publishes all sorts of helpful maps, booklets and brochures which are available free to tourists. The most convenient place to pick up these free goodies is at the information desk at the airport when you arrive.

### Local Tourist Offices
**Taipei** You can visit the Tourism Bureau at their main office near the Sun Yatsen Memorial. It's not too hard to find, but there is no sign outside the building to indicate that the Tourism Bureau is inside. From the central area you get there on bus Nos 27, 212, 240, 259, 261, 281 or 504.

There are other sources of tourist information in Taipei. The most useful is the China External Trade Development Council (CETRA), which has a good international library and will assist people coming to Taiwan on business.

Tourism Bureau
9th floor, 280 Chunghsiao E Rd, Section 4 (tel (02) 7218541)
Tourist Information Hot Line
daily from 8 am to 8 pm (tel (02) 7173737)
China External Trade Development Council (CETRA)
5 Hsinyi Rd, Section 5 (tel (02) 7251111)
Consumers' Foundation ROC
11th floor, 28 Jenai Rd, Section 3 (tel (02) 7001234)
Government Information Office ROC
3 Chunghsiao E Rd, Section 1 (tel (02) 3419211)
Taiwan Visitors' Association
5th floor, 111 Minchuan E Rd (tel (02) 5943261)
Travel Information Service Center
Sungshan Domestic Airport (tel (02) 7121212, extension 471)

**Branch Offices** The Tourism Bureau maintains branch offices in Taoyuan, Hsinchu, Taichung, Changhua, Tainan and Kaohsiung. A few smaller cities, such as Taitung, maintain local tourist information offices. They can provide you with some information

about local attractions, but don't expect too much from them. The level of service is not as high as it is in Taipei. On the other hand, I have found them very useful for providing information about local buses, restaurants, theatres, etc. They will try their best, though the level of spoken English varies. The addresses of these branch offices is as follows:

Changhua Branch
3rd floor, 39 Kuangfu Rd (tel (047) 232111)
Hsinchu Branch
3rd floor, 115 Chungcheng Rd (tel (035) 217171)
Kaohsiung Branch
5th floor, 253 Chungcheng 4th Rd (tel (07) 2811513)
Kaohsiung-Hsinhsing Branch
3rd floor, 308 Chungshan 1st Rd (tel (07) 2013001)
Taichung Branch
4th floor, 216 Minchuan Rd (tel (04) 2270421)
Tainan Branch
2nd floor, 90 Chungshan Rd (tel (06) 2265681)
Taoyuan Branch
2nd floor, 2 Chengkung Rd, Section 2 (tel (033) 376611)

### Pseudo-Embassies
Because Taiwan has diplomatic relations with only a handful of countries, the following offices in Taipei are not true embassies (South Korea is an exception). These 'unofficial organisations' can issue visas and replace lost passports, but the paperwork must be sent elsewhere, usually Hong Kong, so it normally takes about 3 weeks. However, that can vary – the Japan office can process a visa application in 3 days.

American Institute in Taiwan (AIT)
1 Lane 134, Hsinyi Rd, Section 3 (tel (02) 7092000)
Anglo-Taiwan Trade Committee
11th floor, West Wing China Building, 36 Nanking E Rd, Section 2 (tel (02) 5214116)
Australian Commerce Office
4th floor, Hsiang Tang Building, 148 Sungchiang Rd (tel (02) 5427950)
Austrian Trade Delegation
Suite 806, Bank Tower, 205 Tunhua N Rd (tel (02) 7155220)

Belgian Trade Association
Suite 901, 685 Minsheng E Rd (tel (02) 7151215)
Canadian Trade Office
Suite 707, Bank Tower, 205 Tunhua N Rd (tel
(02) 7137268)
Danish Trade Organisation
4th floor, 12 Lane 21, Anho Rd (tel (02) 7213386)
France Asia Trade Association
Suite 602, Bank Tower, 205 Tunhua N Rd (tel
(02) 7138216)
German Trade Office
15th floor, 87 Sungchiang Rd (tel (02) 5069028)
Hellenic Organisation for Promotion of Exports
(Greece)
Room 2, 6th floor, 125 Roosevelt Rd, Section 3
(tel (02) 3910597)
Indonesian Chamber of Commerce
46-1 Chungcheng Rd, Section 2 (tel (02)
8310451)
Japan Interchange Association
43 Chinan Rd, Section 2 (tel (02) 3517250)
Korean Embassy
345 Chunghsiao E Rd, Section 4 (tel (02)
7619361)
Malaysian Friendship Center
8th floor, 102 Tunhua N Rd (tel (02) 7132626)
Netherlands Council
Room B, 5th floor, 687 Minsheng E Rd (tel (02)
7135760)
The Philippines
Asian Exchange Center, Suite 902, 112
Chunghsiao E Rd, Section 1 (tel (02) 3413125)
Singapore Trade Representative
9th floor, 85 Jenai Rd, Section 4 (tel (02)
7721940)
South African Embassy
13th floor, 205 Tunhua N Rd (tel (02) 7153250)
Spanish Chamber of Commerce
Room C, 5th floor, 122-4 Chunghsiao E Rd,
Section 4 (tel (02) 7112402)
Swedish Trade Representative
1st floor, Chiahsin Building, 96 Chungshan N
Rd, Section 2 (tel (02) 5627602)
Swiss Trade Office
12th floor, 50 Hsinsheng S Rd (tel (02) 3931610)
Thai Airways International Ltd
6th floor, 150 Fuhsing N Rd (tel (02) 7121882)

## GENERAL INFORMATION
### Post

Of all the government agencies in Taiwan, the post office deserves mention for being one of the fastest, most reliable, inexpensive and efficient. For domestic letters, you can count on delivery within 2 days to almost any place on the island. International mail is also

fast – about 7 days to the USA or Europe, fewer to Hong Kong or Japan.

Post offices are open from 8 am to 5 pm Monday to Saturday; they're closed on Sunday and holidays.

**Postal Rates** Domestic express letters arrive within 24 hours. Rates are just NT$3 for letters and NT$8 for express mail.

Aerograms are much cheaper to send than international letters, but there are different rates depending on the destination. Aerograms destined for Hong Kong are the cheapest, followed by Asia, Australia and New Zealand. The next level up in price is the USA and Africa. Mail to Europe is the most expensive. You'd better tell them where you're sending it to or you will most likely be sold the most expensive aerogram whether you need it or not.

Printed matter, including photographs, can be sent at a much cheaper rate than letters. If you want to send some photos home it will be much cheaper to send them in a separate envelope stamped 'printed matter'. Be sure to write 'airmail' on the envelope as well. You cannot seal the envelope with glue but it can be stapled closed. This is so the postal inspectors can open it and check that you didn't slip a letter inside. If you do hide a letter inside, it will be returned or sent by surface mail, and will probably take several months to arrive.

**Sending Mail** When mailing a letter overseas, use the red mailboxes. The left slot on the box is for international airmail and the right slot is for domestic express. Green mailboxes are for domestic surface mail; the right slot is for local letters and the left slot is for 'out of town'. Should you mistakenly put the letter in the wrong box or slot, don't panic. It will be delivered but may be delayed a couple of days at the most.

Most large post offices offer a very convenient packing service if you want to send a parcel. They'll box it up and seal it for a nominal charge, saving you the time and trouble of hunting for a cardboard box. Unfortunately, they don't keep any padding at the post office, so bring some old newspaper with you if your goods are fragile. If you pack your own, you can seal the box with tape but it must also have a heavy string around it – the post office will not accept parcels that are not well tied. Stationery, grocery and hardware stores sell a very strong plastic string for just this purpose.

**Receiving Mail** You can receive letters poste restante (general delivery) at any post office.

### Freight Forwarders

Most travellers aren't going to need this service, but if you're shipping something too large or heavy to be handled by the post office, you need the services of a freight forwarder. There are many, and they usually advertise in the pages of *This Month in Taiwan*. One that I recommend is Jacky Maeder (tel (02) 5624225), 4th floor, 21-1 Lane 45, Chungshan N Rd, Taipei. They handle both sea and air freight.

You may also want to contact United Parcel Service (tel (02) 7170580), 5th floor, 689 Minsheng E Rd.

### Telephones

Taiwan's government-owned monopoly International Telecommunications Administration (ITA) operates all over the island and also offers generally good service on international calls. I have called the USA from Taiwan and the line is (usually) as clear as calling the house next door. However, this isn't true for all countries, and many travellers calling to Europe have complained about noisy phone lines.

Within Taiwan the service is mostly OK, but there are problems. Most annoying is that you'll often get a busy signal when in fact the line isn't busy at all. At other times, you'll dial and nothing happens – the line just goes dead. This problem has actually become worse in recent years as demand for new lines has outstripped supply. There are plans to install new high-speed digital lines, but so far they're just plans.

Public pay phones can be another source of frustration. Many of the older models seem to be perpetually out of order. Additionally, the older phones will only allow you to talk for 3 minutes, after which the line will suddenly go dead without warning. The newer phones will also go dead after 3 minutes, but they will warn you first by beeping, thus giving you a chance to feed in NT$1 so you can talk for another 3 minutes.

For long-distance calls, you're better off using the newer digital display phones. These phones have a digital display meter that tells you how much money you have put into the phone. You can clearly see how much money remains. When the meter reads zero, you get disconnected. There are two types of digital display phones. One kind allows you to put in coins, while the other type requires a special magnetic card that you insert into a slot when you want to make a call. These cards cost NT$100 and can be

Telephone card

bought in some grocery stores, bakeries, or other locations where you see the phones that accept these cards. Most 7 Eleven stores sell these cards, and they are also available at major railway stations. Of course, you can always buy the cards from any telephone company branch office. Hand the clerk NT$100 and say (*diànhùa kǎ*) 電話卡. These cards are very convenient.

Local calls all cost NT$1 for 3 minutes. Domestic long-distance rates are as follows: full rate – 7 am to 6 pm; 40% discount – weekdays 6 to 11 pm, Saturday 1 to 11 pm, Sunday and holidays 7 am to 11 pm; 70% discount – every day from 11 pm to 7 am.

Reduced rates are in effect for all calls to Hong Kong from 9 pm to 7 am on weekdays and for 24 hours on Sunday. Discount rates apply for all calls to the USA from 4 to 9 pm, but the cheapest rate is from 1 to 7 am. For all other countries, reduced rates are in effect from 1 to 7 am.

To make an overseas call from a private phone, first dial 100 to reach the overseas operator. Person to person calls can be booked for the same price, but anytime you use the overseas operator it's going to cost you big money. Direct dialling is *much* cheaper. Direct dialling overseas is possible from private phones and from ISD (international subscriber dialling) phones at the telephone company. Many hotels charge a large fee to make a collect call on top of the fee that the phone company charges, so you're better off going to the phone company.

To dial direct, the international prefix is 002, followed by the country code, area code and the number you want to dial. If you don't know the country code, contact ITA (tel (02) 3212535).

If you want to call Taiwan from abroad, the country code is 886. All Taiwanese area codes begin with zero – eg, Taipei is 02. However, when calling from abroad you must omit the zero.

Privately owned red or green pay phones found in some hotels (especially youth hostels) are for local calls only. Furthermore, when you are connected, you must push a button on the phone so the money goes down. If you fail to push the button, you will be able to hear the other party but they will not be able to hear you.

Numbers starting with the prefix 080 are toll-free numbers. There are very few of these in Taiwan, but some large companies have them.

**Useful Telephone Numbers** Some useful phone numbers are as follows:

English directory assistance – (02) 3116796
Chinese local directory assistance – 104
Chinese long-distance directory assistance – 105
Overseas operator – 100
Fire – 119
Police (Chinese-speaking) – 110
Taipei Foreign Affairs Police – (02) 3817475

### Fax, Telex & Telegraph

Telex and telegram service is available at large hotels and the ITA main office. Faxes are very popular with the Chinese, since they're the only fast way to transmit documents written in Chinese characters. Fax service is available from the ITA main office and from major hotels.

### Electricity

Americans will be pleased to learn that Taiwan uses the same standards for electric power as the USA – AC 60 cycles, 110 volts. People from Europe, Australia and South-East Asia will not be able to use their appliances in Taiwan unless they have a transformer.

### Time

Taiwan Standard Time is 8 hours ahead of Greenwich Mean Time. Taiwan does not have daylight-saving time.

When it is noon in Taiwan it is also noon in Singapore, Hong Kong and Perth; 2 pm in Sydney; 8 pm the previous day in Los Angeles; 11 pm the previous day in New York; and 4 am in London.

### Calendar

All official documents in Taiwan use the

founding of the Republic of China (1911) as a reference point in establishing the date. Thus the year 1990 is 79 (1990 minus 1911) – ie, the 79th year of the founding of the republic.

In Taiwan the date is written in the order year, month, day. So 20 October 1990 would be written 79/10/20.

## Business Hours

Almost the same as in Western countries – weekdays, from 8 or 8.30 am to 5 or 5.30 pm. On Saturday, most people work a half-day until noon.

Chinese people take lunch *very* seriously. Most businesses and all government offices close for the 'Chinese siesta'. Known to the Chinese as a *xiūxí*, the afternoon nap lasts from about noon to 1.30 or 2 pm. Don't expect to get anything done during this time. If you walk into an office during the lunch break, don't be surprised to find the whole staff asleep. Not being aware of this, on my 2nd day in Taiwan I walked into a travel agency at 1 pm, only to find all the office workers slumped over their desks. My first thought was that there must be a gas leak! I was in a near state of panic until somebody woke up and asked me why I was there during the siesta.

Many small shops keep long hours, typically from 6 am to 11 pm. This is especially true of small, family-owned restaurants. You'll have no trouble in Taiwan getting something to eat at the crack of dawn or at midnight. The Chinese like nightlife and normally stay up very late, so there is always some store or restaurant open late at night. They make up for the lack of sleep with the siesta.

Department stores open somewhat late, at either 10 or 11 am, but they usually close at 10 pm. They keep the same hours 7 days a week and they are open on most holidays. Banks are open from 9 am to 3.30 pm Monday to Friday and from 9 am to noon on Saturday.

Most workers have a holiday on Sunday, but plenty of small businesses are still open. Buses and trains can be packed to overflow-ing on Sunday, so if you have a choice, try to avoid travelling on a Sunday.

## Notary Service

It is not local custom to notarise a document. Consequently, public notarys are few and far between in Taiwan. They can only be found in the county or city courthouse. Most foreigners will probably prefer the notary service offered by the American Institute in Taiwan (AIT), at both the Taipei and Kaohsiung offices.

## Weights & Measures

Officially Taiwan subscribes to the international metric system. However, ancient Chinese weights and measures still persist. The most likely ones that tourists will encounter are the *tael* (*liǎng*) and the *catty* (*jīn*).

One catty is 0.6 kg (1.32 pounds). There are 16 taels to the catty, so one tael is 37.5 grams (1.32 ounces). Most fruits and vegetables in Taiwan are sold by the catty, while tea and herbal medicine are sold by the tael.

The other unit of measure that you might encounter is the *ping*. Pings are used to measure area, and one ping is approximately 1.82 square meters (5.97 square feet). When you buy cloth or carpet, the price will be determined by the number of pings. Ditto for renting an apartment or buying land.

## Laundry

Overall, doing their laundry is a big headache for travellers in Taiwan. Some of the youth hostels offer laundry service and others have a machine (often broken) for your use. There are plenty of laundry services in Taiwan, but most are slow, expensive and geared towards ironing and dry cleaning. Fortunately, there are fast and cheap laundry services around the universities catering to the student population. They charge by the weight of the clothes and some have a 4 kg minimum. Of course, student laundry services don't do ironing or dry cleaning.

Many travellers wind up doing their own laundry in the sink – a hassle, but it's better than smelling bad. If you're going to take this approach, light and thin stretch nylon is best for underwear and socks because it dries quickly. Wash everything as soon as you check into a hotel room so it has time to dry before you depart.

## Public Toilets

Toilet paper is seldom provided in the toilets at bus and train stations or in other public buildings. You'd be wise to keep a stash of your own with you at all times. In train stations, women must pay NT$3 to NT$5 to use the toilet, while for men it is free. Women should keep some change handy for this. In a few resort areas, men may be charged to use the toilet too, but this is rare. To avoid embarrassment, try to remember:

Men          Women

The issue of what to do with used toilet paper can be confusing. As one traveller wrote:

We are still not sure about the Chinese toilet paper...in two hotels they have been angry with us for flushing down the paper in the toilet (one was Hotel Jui Chung in Kaohsiung). In other places it seems quite OK though.

In general, if you see a wastebasket with a plastic bag liner next to the toilet, that is where you should throw the toilet paper. But don't throw used toilet paper in the basket if it is not lined with a plastic bag. The problem is that in many hotels, the sewage system cannot handle toilet paper. This is especially true in old hotels where the antiquated plumbing system was designed in the pre-toilet paper era. Also, in rural areas there is no sewage treatment plant – the waste empties into an underground septic tank and toilet paper will really create a mess in there. For the sake of international relations, be considerate and throw the paper in the wastebasket.

And while we're on the subject of toilets,

in most Asian countries, including ultra-modern Japan, you will encounter squat toilets. For the uninitiated who don't know what I'm talking about, a squat toilet has no seat for you to sit on while reading the morning newspaper...in other words, it is a hole in the floor, but it does flush. These take some getting used to, though you may be pleased to know that the squatting position is better for your digestive system.

While most people in Taiwan now have Western-style toilets in their homes, many public restrooms still have the squat variety. While you are balancing yourself over one of these marvellous devices, take care that your comb, wallet, keys and the other valuables in your pockets don't fall into the abyss.

## MEDIA
### Newspapers

Taiwan produces two English-language newspapers, the *China Post* and the *China News*. They're available from many hotels, bookstores or by subscription from the post office. In Taipei, you can also subscribe by telephone to the *China Post* (tel (02) 5969971) and the *China News* (tel (02) 3210882). At NT$12 for 12 pages, they rate as two of the most expensive newspapers in the world, and it doesn't take very long to read the 12 pages since about half the space is advertising. However, they are good for learning about the local news.

The *Taiwan Grapevine* (tel (02) 5960838), PO Box 28-186, Taipei, is a monthly paper more of interest to resident expatriates than to tourists. It's a free publication, though finding it takes some doing. Subscriptions cost NT$250 a year. In Taipei, you can get free copies at AIT and the following pubs: Ploughman, Mariners, Sam's, Farmhouse, City Light, Hope & Anchor; or the following hotels: Lai Lai, Howard Plaza, Ritz, Imperial and President. In Taichung, you can get copies from Sam's. In Kaohsiung, from Sam's, Brass Rail, Snow's, Stormy Weather, Pizza Pub and the Kingdom Hotel. The addresses of all these pubs and hotels are listed in the appropriate sections of this book.

The *International Herald-Tribune* is produced jointly by the *New York Times* and the *Washington Post* for distribution outside the USA. It's rather expensive but it's comprehensive. It can be purchased in Taiwan at major hotels, bookstores or by subscription from the Taiwan English Press.

### Radio

Taiwan has one English-language radio station, ICRT, which stands for International Community Radio Taipei. ICRT broadcasts 24 hours a day on the following wavelengths: Taipei – AM-1548 kHz, FM-100.1 mHz; Taichung – AM-1570 kHz, FM-100.9 mHz.

### TV

There are three TV stations in Taiwan but they broadcast almost entirely in Chinese. English-language programmes are broadcast late at night, usually starting from 10 pm. Unfortunately, all three stations tend to broadcast their English programmes at the same time. Check the local English-language newspapers such as the *China Post* and the *China News* for the schedule. A few hotels and pubs catering to foreigners have satellite dish antennas enabling them to receive programmes from Europe and the USA.

If you have access to a video cassette player there are plenty of English-language movies available for rent cheaply on video cassette from numerous shops in any major city in Taiwan.

Unfortunately, the world has many incompatible video standards. A 'video standard' refers to the many little dots that appear on the screen that make up the picture. If the TV station is broadcasting a different number of dots from what your TV can display, you'll get nothing but garbage on your screen.

Taiwanese TV uses the NTSC standard, as does the USA, Japan and several other countries. It is totally incompatible with the PAL standard used in Europe, or the many other standards found throughout the world. If you bring a video tape player from Europe, don't expect it to work with a Taiwanese TV or vice versa. The same applies to those little mini-TVs like the Sony Watchman – they will not work in Taiwan unless they're built

to NTSC standards. There is no TV that can convert PAL transmissions to NTSC or vice versa, nor can it be adjusted by a technician.

Even an American (NTSC) TV or video player will not work properly in Taiwan because the broadcast frequencies are different, but this is a relatively minor problem. The frequency can be adjusted by a technician. A shop charged me NT$500 to adjust an American video player to work with a Taiwan TV, but you may be able to bargain it cheaper. There is no problem playing an American or Japanese video tape on a Taiwan TV or vice versa, but European tapes won't work.

If you wonder why Chinese characters are displayed on the TV screen during a Chinese dialogue, it is because many older Chinese from the mainland can read and write characters but cannot speak Mandarin. Also, having the characters displayed helps children learn how to read.

### Magazines

No discussion of the local media would be complete without mentioning *Bang*, Taipei's avant-garde magazine which is published monthly. It's a little expensive at NT$85 a copy, but many foreigners seem to find it worth the price. It's available from Lucky Bookstore, or you can subscribe by contacting the Bang office (tel (02) 7189195), 4th floor, Room 2, 207 Fuhsing N Rd.

If you are interested in the news, politics and economy of Taiwan and all of Asia, the best magazine by far is the *Far Eastern Economic Review*, produced weekly in Hong Kong but available throughout the region.

Those planning a long stay in Taiwan can subscribe to foreign publications. You can pay for the subscription locally in NT$ by contacting Formosa Magazine Press (tel (02) 3612151), 6th floor, 189 Yenping S Rd, Taipei; the postal address is PO Box 65, Taipei 100. Another competing magazine distributor is Taiwan English Press (tel (02) 3114727, 3713291), PO Box 225, Taipei. They import such publications as *US News & World Report, National Geographic*, the *Economist, Time* and *Newsweek*.

## STUDYING IN TAIWAN

Students who have a reasonably good level of proficiency in Chinese can be admitted to a university in Taiwan and receive a degree after completing a course of study. University entrance is highly competitive in Taiwan, but foreigners, mostly overseas Chinese, are given special consideration.

I have one American friend who doesn't speak Chinese but who gained entrance into a medical school in Taiwan, so I guess anything is possible. For further information, write directly to the university you wish to attend or contact the Bureau of International Cultural & Educational Relations, Ministry of Education (tel (02) 3513111), 5 Chungshan S Rd, Taipei.

### Universities in Taiwan

Central University (*zhōngyāng dàxùe*)
    Chungli, Taoyuan County (tel (034) 427151)
Chengchi University (*zhèngzhì dàxùe*)
    Mucha, Taipei (tel (02) 9398335)
Chengkung University (*chénggōng dàxùe*)
    Tahsueh Rd, Tainan (tel (06) 2361111)
Chiaotung University (*jiāotōng dàxùe* or *jiāodà*)
    100 Tahsueh Rd, Hsinchu (tel (035) 712121)
Chinese Cultural University (*zhōnggúo wénhùa dàxùe*)
    Huakang, Yangmingshan, Taipei (tel (02) 8610511)
Chunghsing University (*zhōngxīng dàxùe*)
    250 Kuokuang Rd, Taichung (tel (04) 2873181)
Chungyuan University (*zhōngyúan dàxùe*)
    Chungli, Taoyuan County (tel (034) 563171)
Fengchia University (*féngjiǎ dàxùe*)
    100 Wenhua Rd, Port District, Taichung (tel (04) 2522250)
Fujen Catholic University (*fǔrén dàxùe*)
    Hsinchuang, Taipei County (tel (02) 9031110)
National Taiwan University (*táiwān dàxùe* or *táidà*)
    Roosevelt Rd, Section 4, Taipei (tel (02) 3510231)
Soochow University (*dōngwú dàxùe*)
    Waishuanghsi, Shihlin, Taipei (tel (02) 8819471)
Sun Yatsen University (*zhōngshān dàxùe*)
    Hsitszwan, Kaohsiung (tel (07) 5316171)
Taiwan Normal University (*shīfàn dàxùe* or *shīdà*)
    Hoping E Rd, Section 1, Taipei (tel (02) 3415101)
Tamkang University (*dànjiāng dàxùe*)
    151 Yingchuang Rd, Tanshui, Taipei County
Tsing Hua University (*qīnghúa dàxùe*)
    855 Kuangfu Rd, Hsinchu (tel (035) 715131)

Tunghai University (*dōnghǎi dàxùe*)
    Taichung Kang Rd, Taichung (tel (04) 2521121)

### Schools for Expatriates

Many expatriate business people come to Taiwan with children. Although some parents want their children to attend a Chinese school, others prefer that their kids have a Western-style education in the English language.

There are two major schools that cater to foreigners and offer education up to the 12th grade. The Morrison Christian Academy has branch schools in Taipei, Taichung and Kaohsiung. The Taipei American School is more expensive but has a very good reputation. For more information, contact these schools directly: Taipei American School (tel (02) 8739900), 800 Chungshan N Rd, Section 6, Taipei; Morrison Christian Academy (tel (04) 2921171), 136-1 Shuinan Rd, Taichung (PO Box 27-24, Taichung).

### Student Cards

Full-time students coming from the USA, Australia and Europe can often get some good discounts on tickets with the help of an International Student Identity Card (ISIC). This card entitles the holder to a number of discounts on airfares, trains, museums, etc. To get this card, inquire at your campus.

Unfortunately, these cards are only good outside Taiwan. Within Taiwan you will need some sort of Chinese student ID to get discounts. You may be able to get such an ID card if you study Chinese at a Taiwan university, but don't count on it. They aren't happy about giving these cards to part-time students. I have seen some fake student IDs, but quality varies. Moreover, in Taiwan it's a serious offence to possess a fake ID – the official designation is 'document forgery' and it carries a penalty of several years in prison.

## HEALTH

Visitors to Taiwan will be happy to know that in general the health conditions are good. Nevertheless, there are a few special health conditions and precautions that are worth noting. Remember also that it's a good idea to see your doctor before travelling overseas for up-to-date medical advice.

For a discussion of medical problems that might arise if you go hiking (eg, snake bite), refer to the Hiking section further on in this chapter.

## Pre-Departure Preparations

**Vaccinations** No special vaccinations are required for Taiwan. However, that doesn't mean you shouldn't get any. For Taiwan, the most useful vaccinations are for hepatitis B, tetanus and influenza. While none of these are essential, a little bit of precaution never hurt.

**Health Insurance** Although not absolutely necessary, it is a good idea to take out travellers' health insurance. The policies are usually available from travel agents, including student travel services. Some policies specifically exclude 'dangerous activities', which may include motorcycling, scuba diving and even hiking. Obviously, you'll want a policy that covers you in all the circumstances you're likely to find yourself in.

Hopefully you won't need medical care, but do keep in mind that any health insurance policy you have at home is probably not valid outside your country. The usual procedure with travellers' health insurance is that you pay in cash first for services rendered and then later present the receipts to the insurance company for reimbursement after you return home. Other policies stipulate that you call collect to a centre in your home country, where an immediate assessment of your problem is made.

If you are unfortunate enough to get very ill while travelling in Taiwan, at least you can be grateful for one thing – medical care is much cheaper in Taiwan than in most Western countries.

**Medical Kit** You can buy almost any medication across the counter in Taiwan, even antibiotics. Pharmacies (*yàojú*) are everywhere in the cities, but hard to find in rural areas. If you're going to be hiking in the

mountains, a basic medical kit would be handy. It should include panadol for pain and fever, a pin and tweezers for removing splinters, plaster for blisters, band-aids, an antiseptic, insect repellent, sunscreen, suntan lotion, chap stick and water purification tablets.

**General Thoughts** If you need vitamins it's best to bring them from home or from Hong Kong, as good ones are very expensive in Taiwan.

If you wear glasses, bring an extra pair of spectacles and/or a copy of your lens prescription with you. Spectacles are reasonably cheap in Taiwan, though Hong Kong is cheaper. Dental work is fairly cheap in Taiwan.

Sunglasses come in useful, and sunblock and a hat will protect you from getting burned.

Don't walk around in bare feet. In hotel showers, thongs are useful protectors against athlete's foot and other fungal infections.

## Common Ailments

Some simple precautions can save you a lot of misery. Some of the more common ailments are as follows:

**Skin Diseases** The most common summertime afflictions that visitors to Taiwan suffer from are skin diseases. This is because of the hot, humid climate. The most common varieties are 'jock itch' (a fungal infection around the groin), athlete's foot (known to the Chinese as 'Hong Kong feet'), contact dermatitis (caused by a necklace or watchband rubbing the skin) and prickly heat (caused by excessive sweating). Prevention and treatment of these skin ailments is often a matter of good hygiene.

For fungal infections, bathe twice daily and thoroughly dry yourself before getting dressed. Standing in front of an electric fan is a good way to get thoroughly dry. Dust the affected area with an antifungal powder such as Desenex, Tinactin or Mycota. An inexpensive antifungal ointment, Fundex, is available in Taiwan and is more effective than powders. It's also available as a liquid, but the ointment is more effective. Wear light cotton underwear or very thin nylon that is 'breathable' – maybe even no underwear at all if the condition gets serious. Wear the lightest outer clothing possible when the weather is really hot and humid. For athlete's foot, wearing open-toed sandals will often solve the problem without further treatment. It also helps to clean between the toes with a warm soapy water and an old toothbrush.

Treat contact dermatitis by removing the offending necklace, bracelet or wristwatch. Avoid anything that chafes the skin, such as tight clothing, especially elastic. If your skin develops little painful red 'pin pricks', you probably have prickly heat. This is the result of excessive sweating which blocks the sweat ducts, causing inflammation. The treatment is the same as for fungal infections: drying and cooling the skin. Bathe often, soak in hot soapy water to get the skin pores open and dust yourself with talcum powder after drying off. Sleeping in a room that has air-con will help. If all else fails, a trip to Taiwan's high, cool mountains will do wonders for your itching skin.

**Diarrhoea** Tap water is not too bad in Taiwan, but the government does recommend that it be boiled before drinking. Most Chinese do boil their water anyway out of habit, even when it is not necessary. I have drunk unboiled water in Taiwan often without any ill effect, but I have seen others rapidly develop that well-known ailment, 'travellers' diarrhoea'. Should it happen to you, first try a simple cure by switching to a light, roughage-free diet for a few days. White rice, bananas, pudding and boiled eggs will usually see you through. Further relief can be obtained by chewing tablets of activated charcoal. These are expensive in Taiwan so bring some with you.

More serious cases can be treated with prescription drugs such as Lomotil and Imodium. These drugs only treat the symptoms, not the underlying disease. Use such drugs with caution because they can cause serious side effects. Only take the minimum

dose needed to control the diarrhoea. Don't take so much that you become plugged up, as the diarrhoea serves a function – your body is trying to expel the unwanted bacteria. If you continue to suffer, you may have a serious infection that requires antibiotics. Although prescription drugs are available across the counter in Taiwan, you would be wise to see a competent medical authority if you get to this stage.

I highly recommend that you visit a hospital with a medical laboratory rather than a private doctor. In Taiwan, private doctors will almost always just hand you a bottle of pills without doing a stool examination under a microscope, but without a stool examination the doctor is only guessing what your condition is.

**Hepatitis** Infectious hepatitis also continues to pose a minor health hazard to those visiting Taiwan. Hepatitis is a viral disease which affects the liver. There are two kinds of hepatitis: infectious (A) and serum (B).

Hepatitis A is spread if food, water or cooking and eating utensils have been contaminated. Hepatitis is often spread in Taiwan due to the Chinese custom of everybody eating from a single dish rather than using separate plates and a serving spoon. It is a wise decision to use the disposable chopsticks now freely available in most restaurants in Taiwan, or alternatively to spare a thought for the world's forest resources and travel with your own chopsticks.

No true vaccine exists for hepatitis A. However, there is gamma-globulin – an antibody made from human blood which is effective for just a few months. Most people don't consider it worthwhile in Taiwan, where hepatitis A isn't all that widespread, but if you're heading for Africa or India you might consider it. The best preventive measures are to eat food that is clean and well cooked, and to use disposable chopsticks.

Hepatitis B is usually transmitted in the same three ways the AIDS virus spreads: by sexual intercourse; contaminated needles; or through being inherited as an infant from an infected mother. For reasons unknown, infection rates are very high in Taiwan, but it is probably a case of being passed down from mother to child and then spread sexually. In recent years, it has also been spreading rapidly in developed countries due to casual sex and drug use. The innocent use of needles – ear piercing, tattooing and acupuncture – can spread the disease. Fortunately, a vaccine exists against it, but the vaccine must be given before you've had any exposure whatsoever. Once you've got the virus, you've got it for life. Therefore, you need a blood test before the vaccine can be given to determine if you've been exposed. The vaccine requires three injections each given a month apart. Unfortunately, the vaccine is expensive. It's available in Taiwan from large hospitals.

For both kinds of hepatitis, the usual symptoms are fever, loss of appetite, nausea, depression, total lack of energy and pain near the bottom of the rib cage where the liver is. The skin and whites of the eyes become yellow and urine turns a deep orange colour. There is no curative drug, but rest and good food are vital. Also stay clear of alcohol and tobacco for a full 6 months – the liver needs a long time to recover. Hepatitis A makes you very sick but complete recovery is the norm. You can also recover from hepatitis B but the disease can lead to liver cancer many years later – the vaccination is indeed worthwhile.

**Dengue Fever** This is a problem during the summer months in Taiwan, especially in the cities. Biting mosquitoes transmit this disease between humans. Also known as breakbone fever, the disease causes a sensation of extreme aching in the legs and joints at the onset of the illness. This gives way to high fever, sweating, headaches and a rash which spreads over the body. Although the patient feels very ill, the symptoms rapidly subside after about 3 or 4 days, then suddenly return. It may take up to 3 weeks to recover fully. There is no effective medication, but aspirin, panadol or codeine (15 to 60 mg every 4 hours) can help reduce the headache. Bed rest is important.

Although the disease is not dangerous in adults, it often has fatal complications in children under 10, especially infants. There is no vaccine, so the best prevention is to avoid mosquito bites. If you are taking care of a dengue fever patient, keep him or her under a mosquito net and use insect repellent or mosquito incense to prevent a mosquito transmitting the disease to you too. Having the disease produces immunity that lasts for about a year.

**Tetanus** There do seem to be quite a few motor accidents in Taiwan and although there is no vaccination that can protect you from getting run over by a bus, it would be prudent to get a tetanus shot before your arrival in Taiwan if you haven't had one for a few years.

**Bronchitis** Not so much a disease as a side-effect of influenza, bronchitis can nevertheless be very distressing. Basically, it's an infection of the bronchial tubes which lead into the lungs. The disease is found worldwide. Just why it's so common in Taiwan is not certain, but the pollution in Taiwan's urban areas is probably a major reason. Taipei and Kaohsiung residents are the worst affected. The unheated buildings in winter may also be a factor, and crowded living conditions make it easier to get the flu. Foreigners in mainland China are even more familiar with bronchitis, where it's been affectionately dubbed 'the China Syndrome'.

The main symptom is a cough that produces a lot of phlegm, usually growing worse at night and making sleep impossible. It can persist for a month or longer. The disease will normally go away by itself, but is so miserable that patients will do almost anything to get well. In a few patients, bronchitis occasionally leads to pneumonia.

There are a few things you can do. An influenza vaccination might prevent you from catching the flu in the first place, but that's not certain. If you get bronchitis, don't even go near people who smoke! One whiff of cigarette smoke will send you into a coughing fit. Steam inhalation helps. A trip to a sauna or hot springs could be the best medicine, especially if you get away from the city and its dirty air. All the usual things people do for colds – drinking hot tea, eating soup, maintaining proper nutrition, resting and keeping warm – can be useful. If you're coughing up thick green phlegm for several days, you should probably visit an ear, nose and throat (ENT) specialist, of which there are many in Taiwan. You may need to get the phlegm tested by a lab to prescribe the correct antibiotic.

## Sexually Transmitted Diseases

Sexual contact with an infected sexual partner spreads these diseases. While abstinence is the only 100% preventative, using condoms is also effective. Gonorrhoea and syphilis are the most common of these diseases; sores, blisters or rashes around the genitals, discharges or pain when urinating are common symptoms. Symptoms may be less marked or not observed at all in women. Syphilis symptoms eventually disappear completely but the disease continues and can cause severe problems in later years. The treatment of gonorrhoea and syphilis is by antibiotics.

There are numerous other sexually transmitted diseases, for most of which effective treatment is available. However, there is no cure for herpes and there is also currently no cure for AIDS. Using condoms is the most effective preventative.

AIDS can be spread through infected blood transfusions; most developing countries cannot afford to screen blood for transfusions. It can also be spread by dirty needles – vaccinations, acupuncture and tattooing can potentially be as dangerous as intravenous drug use if the equipment is not clean. If you do need an injection it may be a good idea to buy a new syringe from a pharmacy and ask the doctor to use it.

## Women's Health

**Gynaecological Problems** Poor diet, lowered resistance due to the use of antibiotics for stomach upsets, and even contraceptive pills can lead to vaginal infections when travelling in hot climates. Keeping the genital area clean, and wearing skirts or loose-fitting trousers and cotton underwear will help to prevent infections.

Yeast infections, characterised by a rash, itch and discharge, can be treated with a vinegar or even lemon-juice douche or with yoghurt. Nystatin suppositories are the usual medical prescription. Trichomonas is a more serious infection; symptoms are a discharge and a burning sensation when urinating. Male sexual partners must also be treated, and if a vinegar-water douche is not effective medical attention should be sought. Flagyl is the prescribed drug.

**Pregnancy** Most miscarriages occur during the first 3 months of pregnancy, so this is the most risky time to travel. The last 3 months should also be spent within reasonable distance of good medical care, as quite serious problems can develop at this time. Pregnant women should avoid all unnecessary medication, but vaccinations and malarial prophylactics should still be taken where possible. Additional care should be taken to prevent illness and particular attention should be paid to diet and nutrition.

## Herbal Medicine

*(zhōngyào)* 中藥
In virtually every town and nearly every street of the main cities of Taiwan, one can find traditional herbal medicine shops. Although there are now plenty of doctors and an abundance of modern clinics, many people like to back up Western medicine with a few herbs 'just in case'.

Some herbs are taken to cure disease while others are taken as preventive measures to ward off colds and flu. Some herbs serve as aphrodisiacs while others are longevity treatments. Many herbs are specific to a particular organ – one herb for good eyesight and another for a healthy liver, etc. No matter what your ailment or other motive, a Chinese herbal medicine dealer is certain to have some remedy for your condition.

Many Westerners will be surprised when

they learn the ingredients of some herbal medicines. Many are spices like ginger, cinnamon, anise, nutmeg and the dried skins of particular fruits. Other ingredients are more exotic: powdered deer antlers, rhinoceros horn, cockroach droppings, dead bees and snake bile. Some Chinese herbs, such as ginseng and rosehips, are well known in the West.

Adherents of herbal medicine claim that you don't use a single herb but rather a combination of herbs to produce the desired result. The herbs, when properly mixed, are believed to have a synergistic effect. That is, the whole is greater than the sum of its parts.

Another important property of herbal medicine is that the effects are supposed to be gradual, not sudden or dramatic. That is, you start taking herbs at the first sign of illness, such as a scratchy throat, or even before you get sick as a preventive measure. So in the cold and flu season you might start taking herbs before you even have your first cough or sniffle, so that you can build up resistance.

When reading about the theory behind Chinese medicine, the word 'holistic' appears often. Basically, this means that Chinese medicine seeks to treat the whole body rather than focusing on a particular organ or disease. Using appendicitis as an example, a Chinese doctor may try to fight the infection using the body's whole defences, whereas a Western doctor would simply cut out the appendix. While the holistic method sounds great in theory, in practice the Western technique of attacking the problem directly often works better. In the case of appendicitis, surgery is very effective. On the other hand, in the case of migraine headaches, asthma or chronic stomachache, herbs may well be more effective in the long run.

Understanding Chinese medicine involves a knowledge of the Yin and Yang theory. It's too complex to go into any detail here so I'll just briefly introduce it. All things in the universe have two aspects, a Yin aspect and a Yang aspect. Examples would include female and male, cold and hot, night and day,

down and up, passive and active, and so on. In terms of illness, Chinese often speak of 'too much fire' which is very Yang, or of being cold which is Yin. Weakness is Yin, hypertension is Yang. The trick is to keep these two forces in balance.

Many Chinese practise *jìnbǔ*, the consumption of tonic food as well as herbs, in order to build strength, and in some cases to increase their sexual potency. It is a widely held belief in Taiwan that sex wears down the body and that frequent sex will result in a short life. To counter the wear and tear of sexual activity you should eat snake, since snakes are long and strong. Poisonous snakes are considered the most effective. An elixir made from deer antlers (also long and strong) is a good medicine for men whose virility is on the wane. However, bamboo shoots and sugar cane apparently are not effective. Another treatment requires drowning bees in a strong alcoholic drink. Drinking the resulting potion will bring out the machismo in any man. The flesh of a tiger will also really give your hormones a recharge, but it's very expensive, especially the sex organs.

To fight off those coughs and colds in winter, goat and dog meat are just what you need. Black goats and black dogs are the best. Eat liver to fight off hepatitis, and eat brains to increase your knowledge. The more expensive the herb, the greater its reputation. Apples, once very expensive in Taiwan, were widely sought after as a medical treatment. Now that the price of apples has fallen drastically due to cheap imports, few people still believe in their medicinal value.

Does herbal medicine really work? In my opinion, the answer is both yes and no. I say yes because it is true that herbalists have made some important medical discoveries. And I say no because many people, even in the West, expect too much from herbs. If herbs could effect miracle cures for cancer, heart disease and pneumonia, then all Chinese should have a life expectancy of at least 100 years or more. Herbs are useful, as long as one doesn't catch the California Syndrome of trying to cure cancer and heart disease holistically with herbs, wheat germ,

White Flower Oil

vitamin C and yogurt made from unpasteurised goats milk.

Herbs are not candy, and reckless consumption of these and any other medicines can be harmful. One friend of mine experienced serious allergic reactions and broke out in boils after taking a herbal medicine. He went on taking the medicine for several months and his condition only got worse. It cleared up miraculously when he stopped taking the herb. Many Chinese take herbs for years hoping to build up their bodies, and wind up destroying their liver because many herbs are partially toxic. Liver disease is a major cause of death in Taiwan.

All that having been said, there are some successful herbal treatments. One example of a dramatic herbal cure is the bark of the cinchona tree, which is used to make the antimalarial drug quinine. This particular herb was not discovered by the Chinese, but herbal medicine has a long history in many countries. Deficiency diseases were successfully treated with herbs. For example, scurvy, caused by vitamin C deficiency, can be cured with rose hips, while other vitamin-rich herbs can cure beriberi, night blindness, pel-

lagra and rickets. A more recent discovery by Japanese researchers is that glycyrrhizin, a licorice ingredient used in herbal medicine, can stop the growth of the AIDS virus.

My own experience with herbs is that they can be useful for relieving some symptoms and discomforts, but should not be considered a cure-all or replacement for surgery and antibiotics. For example, ginger root, placed in soup, seems to be helpful as a mild decongestant for colds. Other herbs such as mint and menthol soothe a sore throat, while liniment relieves sore muscles. Some herbs work well for an upset stomach. The oil of cloves is used worldwide to numb an aching tooth.

I'll recommend a couple of herbs, not unique to China, that I sometimes use. The most common is angelica (dānggūi), which is placed in Chinese winter stew (huǒgūo). It's supposed to offer protection from colds and other illnesses. Visit any hospital ward in Taiwan during lunchtime and you will easily catch the scent of angelica in the air – the patients' relatives bring it in, sometimes over the protests of doctors.

I have achieved very good results with a

herbal medicine called *língzhī*. Made from a rare mushroom, it's very expensive and therefore not something you take regularly. It might also be toxic in the long run. I used it when I was suffering from a serious intestinal disorder, and it was the *only* thing that helped when Western medicine had failed. It's widely available in Taiwan but care must be taken against fake or bad quality *língzhī*.

The Chinese make regular use of various liniments which are rubbed into the body where pain is felt. These liniments are claimed to cure just about anything, including headaches, stomachaches, backaches and nappy rash. I have tried many of these liniments and I can report that some of them really seem to work, at least for temporary relief of symptoms. Again, don't use liniments as if they were perfume – they may be harmful if overused and definitely should not be swallowed or put in the nose. Typical ingredients include eucalyptus oil and turpentine, both of which are toxic. They are available everywhere in Taiwan, as well as in Hong Kong and Singapore. My favourite one is called White Flower Oil (*bái huā yóu*).

Before shopping for herbs, keep in mind that in Western medicine doctors talk about broad-spectrum antibiotics such as penicillin, which are good for treating a wide range of infections. But for many illnesses, a specific antibiotic might be better for a specific type of infection. The same is true in Chinese medicine. A broad-spectrum remedy such as snake gall bladder may be good for treating colds, but there are many different types of colds. The best way to treat a cold with herbal medicine is to see a Chinese doctor and get a specific prescription. Otherwise, the herbs you take may not be the most appropriate for your condition.

If you visit a Chinese doctor, you might be surprised by what he or she discovers about your body. For example, the doctor will almost certainly take your pulse and then may tell you that you have a slippery pulse or perhaps a thready pulse. Chinese doctors have identified more than 30 different kinds of pulses. A pulse could be empty, prison, leisurely, bowstring, irregular or even regularly irregular. The doctor may then examine your tongue to see if it is slippery, dry, pale, greasy, has a thick coating or maybe no coating at all. The doctor, having discovered that you have wet heat, as evidenced by a slippery pulse and a red greasy tongue, will prescribe the proper herbs for your condition.

Those interested in studying herbal medicine more thoroughly can find a number of reference books on the subject. For a good introduction to Chinese medicine, about the most clearly written introductory text is *The Web That Has No Weaver: Understanding Chinese Medicine* by Ted J Kaptchuk (Congdon & Weed, New York). A more advanced text, sprinkled with Latin terms and much more difficult to comprehend, is *The Theoretical Foundations of Chinese Medicine* by Manfred Porkert (MIT Press, Cambridge). Finally, there is *Treasures of Chinese Medicine* (*běn cǎo gāng mù*), a classic published in the 16th century by Chinese doctor Li Shinchen. Although it has been over 400 years since it was written, it still remains the best reference in Chinese herbal medicine. An even older reference is the *Yellow Emperor's Classic of Internal Medicine* (*huángdì nèijīng sūwén*) – written, it's claimed, by the mythical Huang Ti around 2600 BC.

## Acupuncture
*(zhēnjiǔ)* 針灸

Chinese acupuncture and massage have received enthusiastic reviews from many satisfied patients who have tried it. Of course, one should be wary of overblown claims. Acupuncture and massage are not likely to cure terminal illness, in spite of any testimonials you might read in Western countries about curing cancer holistically. Nevertheless, acupuncture and massage are of genuine therapeutic value in the treatment of chronic back pain, migraine headaches and arthritis. Indeed, it has been demonstrated that major surgery can be performed using acupuncture alone as the anaesthetic.

For those not already familiar with the term, acupuncture is a technique employing needles which are inserted into various points of the body. In former times, needles were probably made from bamboo, gold, silver, copper or tin. These days, only stainless steel needles of hairlike thinness are used, causing very little pain when inserted. Dirty acupuncture needles can spread disease rather than cure it, so good acupuncturists sterilise their needles or use disposable ones. As many as 2000 points for needle insertion have been identified, but only about 150 are commonly used.

The exact mechanism by which acupuncture works is not fully understood by modern medical science. The Chinese have their own theories, but it is by no means certain they really know either. Needles are inserted into various points which are believed by the acupuncturist to correspond to a particular organ, joint, gland or other part of the body. These points are believed to be connected to the particular area being treated by an energy channel, also translated as a meridian, but more likely associated with the nervous system. By means not fully understood, it would appear the needle can block pain transmission along the meridian. However it works, many report satisfactory results.

Should you wish to try this technique while visiting Taiwan, try to get a Chinese person to recommend a good acupuncturist. A bad one is worse than none and there are quacks in this business, so a recommendation would certainly be helpful. If you don't know someone who can recommend an acupuncturist, call the China Acupuncture Association (tel (02) 3312468, 3810111/3), 4th floor, 66-1 Chungching S Rd, Section 1, Taipei, for a recommendation.

### Massage
*(ànmó)* 按摩
Massage is an effective technique for treating a variety of painful ailments such as chronic back pain, rheumatism and sore muscles. Of course, I'm talking about legitimate massage. To be most effective, a massage should be administered by someone who has really studied the techniques. An acupuncturist who also practises massage would be ideal.

Traditional Chinese massage is somewhat different from the increasingly popular do-it-yourself techniques practised by people in the West. One traditional Chinese technique employs suction cups made of bamboo placed on the patient's skin. A burning piece of alcohol-soaked cotton is briefly put inside the cup to drive out the air before it is applied. As the cup cools, a partial vacuum is produced, leaving a nasty-looking but harmless red circular mark on the skin. The mark goes away in a few days. Other methods include bloodletting and scraping the skin with coins or porcelain soup spoons.

A related technique is called moxibustion. Various types of herbs, rolled into what looks like a ball of fluffy cotton, are held just near the skin and ignited. A slight variation of this method is to place the herb on a slice of ginger and then ignite it. The idea is to apply the maximum amount of heat possible without burning the patient. This heat treatment is supposed to be good for such diseases as arthritis.

However, there is no real need to subject yourself to such extensive treatment if you would just like a straight massage to relieve normal aches and pains. I speak from experience when I say that a good massage can unknot those aching muscles and is an excellent way to relax. There's no harm in trying it while you're in Taiwan if you don't mind spending the cash. If you really get into it, you could consider studying Chinese massage techniques during your stay in Taiwan.

### WOMEN TRAVELLERS
There are all-too-frequent reports of young, unescorted females who have been raped and/or robbed by a taxi driver, usually at night. Most of the victims are Chinese, but there have been a few attacks on foreign women as well. Most taxi drivers are OK, but there are enough bad apples to spoil the bunch. Unfortunately, a large number of ex-convicts drive taxis in Taiwan because it's the only job they can get.

There is no way to be 100% safe, but a few precautions can help. Most importantly, a woman shouldn't take a taxi alone at night. Of course, it's easy to say that, but in practice some women must travel alone at night and sometimes a taxi is the only mode of transportation available.

A few tips for playing it safe: note that there are two designs for taxis, sedans and hatchbacks, and that hatchbacks pose an extra danger – in one common type of assault, an accomplice hides in the rear storage area and enters the passenger compartment by pushing forward the rear seat. Thus, the woman is faced with two attackers at once. This cannot happen with a sedan since the boot (trunk) is separated from the rear seat by a metal wall. To be safe, learn to recognise sedans and use only this form of taxi.

Before getting into the vehicle, make sure the rear window can be rolled down. Rapists have been known to remove the inside door and window handles so the victim cannot escape or yell for help.

Write down the taxi's licence plate number before entering the vehicle. If an attempt is made and you escape, you can at least send the police after the attacker. The licence plate number is also displayed on the rear window and should be highly visible. Never get into a taxi if the licence plate number appears to have been obscured, since potential rapists often deliberately try to hide the number.

Finally, don't be overly paranoid. These attacks do happen, but not so frequently that you need to bottle yourself up indoors. Nevertheless, a little bit of caution never hurt.

## DANGERS & ANNOYANCES

The biggest danger and annoyance in Taiwan is the traffic, but that is discussed thoroughly in the chapter on Getting Around.

Taiwan is one of the safer places in Asia in terms of street crime, but it is always wise to be careful with money. Pickpockets do exist, so keep your cash in a money belt or a small pouch under your clothes. Be sure to have a receipt and/or written record of the numbers of your travellers' cheques. This makes it much easier to replace them if they are lost

or stolen. Many of the better hotels have a safe where you can deposit your valuables rather than carrying them around with you. If you're staying for a long time, you can rent a safe-deposit box.

Although street muggings are exceedingly rare, there is a serious problem with residential burglaries in the cities. Youth hostels are not immune, especially since they tend to leave the door unlocked. Also, it's sad but true that some of your fellow travellers may take a liking to your camera or Walkman, so never leave valuables lying around the dormitory.

## FILM & PHOTOGRAPHY

Major brands of colour print film such as Kodak, Fuji and Sakura are available at reasonable prices in Taiwan. Colour photofinishing stores are abundant and many offer 1 hour service. The quality varies between different establishments but is about the same standard as in Western countries. I personally like Konica, which operates a chain of fast photofinishing stores throughout the island.

Slide film is available, mostly Ektachrome and Fujichrome. Slide photofinishing service is available from most stores that sell slide film. Agfachrome is hard to come by, and Kodachrome is not available at all and cannot be processed in Taiwan. If you want prints made from your slides, have it done when you get home or in Hong Kong or Japan. They can do it in Taiwan, but most stores still use the old-fashioned internegative process rather than the much more attractive direct positive method.

B&W film is available in Taiwan at very reasonable prices. Popular brands are Agfa and Fuji. If you need B&W film processed, I recommend you wait until you get home or do it in Hong Kong or Japan. B&W film can indeed be processed in Taiwan, but only at a few places and the quality varies tremendously as it is usually done by hand, not by machine. If you have the necessary skills, you'd be better off developing your own B&W negatives and sending them out to get the prints made. At least this way there is no risk of the store ruining your film.

For some reason, in the USA most stores will only process Kodak B&W film. So unless you do your own processing, you'd best use Kodak film if you want it developed in America.

At the airport all hand luggage and checked baggage are x-rayed, so keep your film in an x-ray proof bag or carry it in your hands when boarding the plane. Sometimes the machines say 'film safe', but the major manufacturers of film say repeated exposures to 'film safe' machines will fog the film, especially high-speed films faster than ASA 400. The magnetic metal detectors you must walk through in the airport will not affect film.

These days most cameras are made in Japan, but Taiwan is starting to challenge the Japanese by making similar cameras which are relatively inexpensive. However, most of these cameras are of the pocket, automatic type, not the sophisticated reflex cameras with changeable lenses. If you'd like a small, easy-to-use 'point and shoot' camera, you can pick one up cheaply in Taiwan.

Any Japanese cameras or lenses bought in Taiwan are expensive because of the import tax. Overall, I'd say that if you come to the Orient looking for photographic equipment, Hong Kong is really the place to get it because everything there is duty-free. However, in Taiwan there are good deals on locally made camera accessories, like an electronic flash or tripod.

It is illegal to take photos around the airports, harbours and many coastal areas in Taiwan. It is also prohibited to take photos out of the window of a plane, though I've seen this rule violated numerous times. You can photograph quite freely in Taiwan's temples as long as you don't disturb the worshippers.

Chinese people feel much the same about being photographed as Westerners do — they'll pose for photos if they know you but they don't like being photographed by strangers. If you want candid photos of people doing their everyday tasks, it would be best to take them from afar, using a long telephoto lens, so as not to upset anyone.

Chinese (and Japanese) people have a near obsession with collecting photos of themselves posing in front of something. Thus, virtually everyone in Taiwan has hundreds or thousands of photos of themselves usually posed in the same rigid position. They can't understand why Westerners take pictures of scenery with no people posing. Pictures without people are considered 'boring'.

## ACCOMMODATION

Taiwan is well endowed with hotels and there is a wide selection to fit any budget. Nevertheless, demand sometimes exceeds supply so it is wise to make a reservation if you are going to stay in one of the more expensive international hotels.

One way to save money on accommodation is to travel with a companion. Most hotels in Taiwan charge nothing extra for two people as long as you're willing to share a double bed. Hotels usually charge by the number of beds in the room, not by the number of people sleeping there. Most 'single rooms' in Taiwan are in fact doubles. Twin rooms have two separate beds and cost considerably more.

Westerners are often steered into the more expensive rooms. This is not because the owners are trying to cheat you. They assume that you, a Westerner, will want good accommodation, so often the first room they show you is the best. If you want a cheap room, just say so. If you think the price they have quoted is high, tell them it is 'too expensive' (tài gùi le). You can try to bargain a little, but remember that Taiwan is not a Third World country.

In Taiwan, hotel proprietors may knock off 10% or they may give you a cheaper room, but in general prices are fixed and not subject to haggling. If you bargain for more than a minute then you're really just arguing, which is a waste of time. Would you argue like that in your own country?

At the bottom end of the scale, reservations are usually not accepted and those planning to stay in youth hostels can usually

Top: View from Suao-Hualien Cliff Highway (Storey)
Left: Yushan (Strauss)
Right: Taiwanese lady (Storey)

Top: Lanyu, North shore (Strauss)
Bottom: Aboriginal village, Lanyu (Strauss)

find a bed. To save yourself some running around you can telephone ahead from the airport. The people at the information desk in the airport will do this for you for free. It's certainly better to call ahead than to scramble from place to place in search of a room.

## Hotels

Top end hotels can easily cost more than NT$3000 per night for a basic single; mid-range hotels cost from around NT$600 to NT$1500 for a single; budget hotels can be as little as NT$200 in rural areas up to NT$600 in cities.

Many hotels have some very cheap Japanese-style *tatami* rooms, a legacy of the 50 years of Japanese occupation in Taiwan. A tatami room consists of straw mats or quilts laid out on the floor. Be sure to take your shoes off before entering these places! Even if you don't speak a word of Chinese, just say the word tatami (*tātāmǐ*). They may say they have 'no tatami', in which case you could see if they have a dormitory (*tuántǐfáng*). If they don't, then ask for a room with shared bath (*pǔtōngfáng*). Rooms with private bath (*tàofáng*) are more expensive. All resort areas have discounts from Monday to Friday, excluding holidays. The usual discount is 20% but sometimes it's as much as 50%.

A dormitory (*tuántǐfáng*) is usually meant for large groups. In resort areas, the week-days are slow and they will usually let you sleep in the dormitory but on the weekends or holidays they will move other people into your room. If the hotel you are staying at is booked out by a tour group, you might be asked to move into another room which may be more expensive. If they have no room left, you might have to leave. The management isn't trying to be nasty or anti foreigner, but if a large tour group arrives and you happen to be occupying a needed dormitory room, somebody has got to move. Most of these resort hotels only survive off the weekend traffic. On two occasions on a Saturday night, the hotel management asked me to leave. I hasten to add that on both occasions they were extremely apologetic and even found another room for me in a different hotel.

One traveller who stayed at the Tienhsiang Youth Activity Center in east Taiwan wrote to Lonely Planet and said:

...the 2nd day we were asked to check out at 1.30 pm because Chinese people had arrived and wanted a room. This is normal procedure – Westerners must move out of rooms if Chinese people want to move in.

To which I must reply – not so! All hotels in Tienhsiang are heavily booked by tour groups – especially the Youth Activity Center because it's cheap. So if you are asked to move, try and understand that demand exceeds supply and a busload of tourists with a prepaid deposit gets preference over a single budget traveller without a reservation.

It is very difficult to contact your Western friends in other hotels or even in the same hotel by giving their name. Best results are obtained by asking face to face rather than on the telephone. Having a room number greatly increases the chance of success. Knowing when your friend checked in is also helpful. The problem here is communication – most Chinese desk clerks have no idea how to deal with Western names. Rather than lose face by admitting this, the usual response to an inquiry will be: 'he checked out', even if 'he' is a 'she'.

One thing to keep in mind is that Chinese people bathe in the evening rather than in the morning. In less expensive hotels the hot water will not be turned on until the evening. Of course, you can bathe any time if you don't mind cold water. Although they expect madness from foreigners anyway, the management will probably be quite perplexed if you complain that there is no hot water for your morning shower.

Expensive hotels will often have a sign in English, but cheaper places usually will not. Probably the two most important Chinese characters that you can learn represent the word for 'cheap hotel' (*lüshè*). You will save yourself a good deal of time and money by learning to recognise this. The best way to learn is by writing it many times. The characters are:

Cheap hotel (*lǔshè*)

**Hot Springs Hotels** 溫泉 There are many hot springs in Taiwan and they tend to be commercialised. That is, the hot water is pumped into a pool or tub, rather than left in its natural condition. Hotels are built right next to the hot springs and water is pumped into private tubs in individual rooms. However, some of the better resorts have outdoor pools in beautiful natural settings.

You do not usually have to stay in a hotel to use the hot spring facilities. If you want a private pool, most hotels will permit you to bathe in one for about half the price of a room. Outdoor public pools are much cheaper. They almost always rent out swimsuits for outdoor pools. To recognise a hotel that has hot spring facilities, look for this symbol:

Hot springs symbol

**Youth Hostels**

Most of Taiwan's youth hostels are run by a government organisation called the China Youth Corps (CYC). This organisation is not connected with the International Youth Hostel Association (IYHA) and therefore you do not need an IYHA card. You also do not need a sleeping sheet and the hostels are open all day, unlike IYHA hostels which often kick you out during the daytime. Some of the urban hostels may lock their doors at

midnight, but other than that there are no restrictions on your movements. Unlike IYHA places, these hostels do not provide kitchen facilities for your use, although they do have cheap cafeteria meals if you reserve them in advance.

In addition to CYC hostels, there are urban hostels in Kaohsiung and Tainan called Laborers' Recreation Centers. Note that the so-called Mountain Hostels in Juili and Taiho are really hotels rather than hostels.

Dormitory-style accommodation in the hostels costs between NT$100 and NT$150, except at the Kenting Hostel where prices start at NT$250. Most of these places have private rooms available at higher prices and they are quite reasonably priced for the good quality of accommodation provided. Reservations are advisable at these hostels, especially during holidays. The hostels in Taipei are normally full and difficult to get into.

A list of all the CYC hostels and Laborers' Recreation Centers with telephone numbers is provided. The English addresses aren't very useful for those hostels in rural areas, so outside the big cities use the Chinese address. The Taipei International will book a bed for you in the other hostels around the island. If booking by telephone, the hostels ask for a postal money order. These are very reliable, but you'll probably need a Chinese person to help you fill in the form.

1   *Chinshan Youth Activity Center* (tel (032) 981191/3) (*jīnshān húodòng zhōngxīn*), Chinshan, Taipei County
2   *Chientan Youth Activity Center* (tel (02) 5962151) (*jiàntán húodòng zhōngxīn*), 16 Chungshan N Rd, Section 4, Taipei
    *Taipei International* (tel (02) 7091770) (TIYAC)(*gúojì húodòng zhōngxīn*), 30 Hsinhai Rd, Section 3, Taipei
    *International House* (tel (02) 7073151) (*gúojì xúeshè*), 18 Hsinyi Rd, Section 3, Taipei
3   *Fuhsing Mountain Hostel* (tel (03) 3822276) (*fùxīng shān zhuāng*), North Cross-Island Highway, Taoyuan County
4   Paling Mountain Hostel (tel (03)

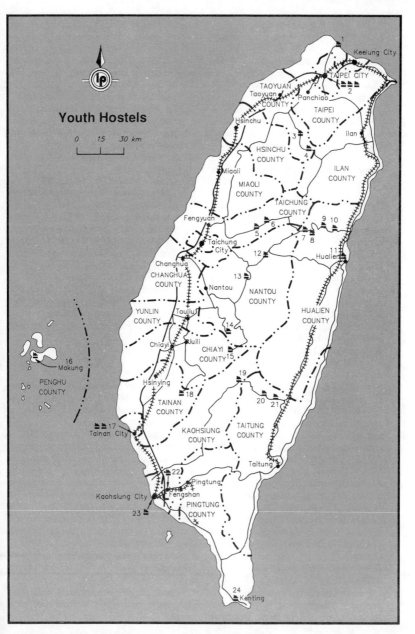

3332153/4) (*bālíng shān zhuāng*),
North Cross-Island Highway, Taoyuan
County

5  *Chingshan Mountain Hostel* (tel (045)
244103) (*qīngshān shān zhuāng*),
Central Cross-Island Highway,
Taichung County

6  *Techi Mountain Hostel* (tel (045) 981
592) (*déjī shān zhuāng*), Central
ross-Island Highway, Taichung County

7  *Tayuling Mountain Hostel* (tel (038)
691111/3) (*dàyúlíng shān zhuāng*),
Central Cross-Island Highway, Hualien
County (inquire at Tienhsiang Hostel)

8  *Tzuen Mountain Hostel* (tel (038)
691111/3) (*cīēn shān zhuāng*), Central
Cross-Island Highway, Hualien County
(inquire Tienhsiang Hostel)

9  *Loshao Mountain Hostel* (tel (038)
691111/3) (*luòsháo shān zhuāng*),
Central Cross-Island Highway, Hualien
County (inquire at Tienhsiang Hostel)

10  *Tienhsiang Youth Activity Center* (tel
(038) 691111/3) (*tiānxiáng húodòng
zhōngxīn*), Hualien County

11  *Hualien Student Hostel* (tel (038)
324124) (*hūalián xúeyùan*), 40-11
Kungyuan Rd, Hualien

12  *Wushe Mountain Hostel* (tel (049)
223441) (*wùshè shān zhuāng*), Wushe,
Nantou County

13  *Sun Moon Lake Youth Activity Center*
(tel (049) 850070) (*rì yùe tán húodòng
zhōngxīn*), Sun Moon Lake, Nantou
County

14  *Hsitou Youth Activity Center* (tel (049)
612161) (*xītóu húodòng zhōngxīn*),
Nantou County

15  *Alishan Mountain Hostel* (tel (05)
2770482/3) (*ālǐshān shān zhuāng*),
Alishan, Chiayi County

16  *Penghu Youth Activity Center* (tel (06)
9271124) (*pénghú húodòng zhōngxīn*),
11 Chiehshou Rd, Makung, Penghu
County

17  *Tainan Student Hostel* (tel (06)
2670526/8, 2689018) (*táinán
xúeyùan*), Lane 300, Funung St,
Section 1, Tainan
*Tainan Laborers' Recreation Center* (tel

(06) 2630174) (*láogōng xiūjià
zhōngxīn*), 261 Nanmen Rd, Tainan

18  *Tsengwen Youth Activity Center* (tel (06)
5752575, 5753164) (*zēngwén húodòng
zhōngxīn*), Tainan County

19  *Meishan Mountain Hostel* (tel (07)
7470134/5) (*méishān shān zhuāng*),
Southern Cross-Island Highway,
Kaohsiung County

20  *Yakou Mountain Hostel* (tel (089)
329891) (*yǎkǒu shān zhuāng*),
Southern Cross-Island Highway,
Taitung County

21  *Litao Mountain Hostel* (tel (089)
329891) (*lìdào shān zhuāng*), Southern
Cross-Island Highway, Taitung County

22  *Chengching Lake Youth Activity Center*
(tel (07) 3717181) (*chéng qīng hú
húodòng zhōngxīn*), Kaohsiung County

23  *Kaohsiung Laborers' Recreation Center*
(tel (07) 3328110) (*láogōng yùlè
zhōngxīn*), 132 Chungshan 3rd Rd,
Kaohsiung

24  *Kenting Youth Activity Center* (tel (08)
8861221/4) (*kěnding húodòng
zhōngxīn*), Kenting Village, Hengchun,
Pingtung County

## Camping

Taiwan does not have any organised system
of campgrounds or caravan parks. Most
established campgrounds are attached to
youth hostels and the tents are usually
already set up. A fee of about NT$30 is
charged per person and campers are permitted to use the hostel's showers and other
amenities at no extra charge. Some of the
hostels in mountain areas will allow you to
set up your own tent next to the hostel for
free, but always ask first. Some remote
mountain hostels (Yakou, for example) will
permit you to 'camp out' on the dining room
floor if all the beds are occupied. Usually you
have to pay a small 'camping fee'. Not every
hostel allows you to do this, so don't count
on it.

In back country areas, there is usually no
objection to setting up a tent just about anywhere.

# FOOD

If Chinese food continues to receive rave reviews, it's for a good reason. Through the generations, the Chinese have perfected their own unique style of cooking, which they regard as a fine art. As anyone who has been to China will tell you, the Chinese love to eat.

There are many different styles of Chinese cooking, originating from the different regions of China. Fortunately these regional variations are well represented in Taiwan as a result of immigration from the mainland. Westerners are generally most familiar with Cantonese cooking, but visitors should also try the food of Peking, Szechuan, Hunan and, of course, the native Taiwanese cuisine.

The different styles of Chinese cooking tend to reflect the ingredients most readily available in that region of China. For example, northern Chinese food is based on wheat flour whereas southern Chinese food has rice as its base. Szechuan food, from south-west China, uses lots of meat, tofu and hot spices. Taiwan, being a subtropical island, has a rich supply of rice, sugar and seafood, which are all basic staples

Most Westerners have eaten Chinese food but on arrival in Taiwan they may be in for some surprises. For example, there are numerous bakeries in Taiwan producing all sorts of delicacies which look very tempting. They smell and look wonderful, but the Chinese have their own tastes when it comes to baked goods. You may purchase what appears to be a sweet, cream-filled pastry, only to find it filled with dried, salted pork and red beans. Probably not exactly what you had in mind! You may also encounter the opposite problem: things which you don't expect to be sweet in fact contain a lot of sugar. For example, the corn and ham bread would probably be much better if it wasn't sweetened. Chinese peanut butter is so sweet it turns your teeth inside out.

Looks and odours can deceive. What looks good might taste strange and vice versa. A notorious example is the '1000 year egg' (*pídàn*) – it looks good but tastes like ammonia. Originally, these eggs were produced by soaking them in horse's urine, but now they are manufactured by a chemical process. On the other hand, smelly tofu (*chòu dòufù*) doesn't look or smell good, but it is absolutely delicious. Many foreigners eventually come to love it after getting past the odour. Try to think of it as Chinese blue cheese. Most Chinese, incidentally, can't tolerate the smell of Western cheese and don't know how we could eat such a thing.

Try to keep an open mind and don't be afraid to taste something new. In time, you may acquire a taste for the salted plums and seaweed dishes. Don't head straight for McDonald's at the first sign of trouble or you'll be missing one of the prime attractions of a trip to Taiwan.

You may be surprised to see a restaurant displaying a big swastika. In fact, the swastika is an old Buddhist religious symbol seen on many temples. On restaurants, it indicates that the food is vegetarian, in accordance with Buddhist beliefs.

Another surprise for Westerners is the interesting English translations on packaged food. Some examples: 'chocolate sand' turns out to be a chocolate sandwich cookie and 'hot spicy jerk' is spicy beef jerky. A popular soft drink imported from Japan is 'Pocari Sweat'. One restaurant in Taipei innocently advertised its hamburgers as 'the best piece of meat between two buns'.

Don't laugh too hard at other people's English mistakes. Imagine how silly you sound when trying to order food in broken Chinese. Once, when trying to explain to the waitress what vegetables I wanted, I asked for venereal disease (*cài hūa*) instead of cauliflower (*hūa cài*).

Certain foods are sold at particular times of the day or year. Bread, fruit and smelly tofu are sold mostly at night. Soybean milk, steamed buns and clay-oven rolls (*shāobǐng*) are sold only in the morning. Spring rolls are sold mostly during April; moon cakes during the Mid-Autumn (or Moon) Festival; rice dumplings (*zòngzǐ*) are at their best during the Dragon Boat Festival. 'Red turtle cakes' are for birthdays and temple worship. Snake meat and snake blood are mostly served in the night markets. 'Bear palm', an exotic food that you might hear about in Taiwan, is a gourmet delicacy that costs hundreds of US$ a plate.

It's true that some Chinese eat dog and it's for the same reason that they eat snake, tiger and other exotic animals – because it is believed to have medicinal value. As a medicine, it is expensive and therefore no one is going to sneak it into your soup, noodles or fried rice as a replacement for beef. If you want to eat dog, you have to seek out a restaurant that specialises in it. Such restaurants are not common because not many Chinese eat dog. Dog meat is most readily available in winter, since the Chinese believe it can prevent colds.

Cafeterias (zìzù cān) offer cheap, good meals for lunch and dinner, but get there either just before noon or around 5.30 pm for the best selection. As soon as the crowd arrives, the good stuff disappears quickly. Another thing you should definitely try are the dim-sum (yǐn chá) restaurants, in which various Cantonese delicacies are wheeled around the restaurant on pushcarts and you select what you want as they pass your table. Again, arrive before the lunch and dinner crowd or all the best goodies will have already been consumed.

A tip for those concerned about their health: Chinese cooks make liberal use of monosodium glutamate, or MSG. I personally have had no difficulty with this. However, I have heard other Westerners complain that they are allergic to it. Heart patients in particular must avoid salt because of its sodium content, and MSG is loaded with sodium. If you are really worried about MSG, just tell the cook you don't want it by saying (búyào wèijīng) 不要味精. Most cooks will readily comply.

### Etiquette

You'd better learn how to use chopsticks if you haven't already mastered this skill. People rarely use forks, and spoons are usually for soup. Eating with a knife is almost unheard of except in Western-style restaurants serving steak.

## Using Chopsticks

Place first chopstick between base of thumb and top of ring finger. (Bend fingers slightly.)

Hold second chopstick between top of thumb and tops of middle and index fingers.

Keeping the first chopstick and thumb still, move the other one up and down using index fingers.

Proper etiquette demands that you hold your rice bowl close to your face rather than leaving it on the table – exactly the opposite of what would be considered proper behaviour in Western countries. This only applies to rice bowls, not to soup bowls or plates.

It is also OK to spit out fish bones and pile them on the table next to your plate. When not eating, never leave your chopsticks sticking pointed-end down into the bowl. Always place them across the top of the bowl or on the table. To the Chinese, leaving chopsticks sticking vertically into the bowl looks like sticks of incense in a bowl of ashes, a clear death sign. This is a common cultural blunder committed by Westerners.

Rather than greeting someone by saying 'How are you?', many Chinese open a conversation by asking, 'Have you eaten yet?'. That might seem like a strange question to ask someone at 10 am, but Chinese regard eating as vitally important.

Proper hosts *must* feed their guests. If the guests aren't hungry, that is too bad – they must be force-fed. A proper guest, to avoid appearing greedy, *must* refuse. One of the most amusing scenes you'll encounter in Taiwan goes something like this:

*Host* – Here, have something to eat.
*Guest* – Oh, no thank you, I just ate.
*Host* – Oh, but you must, I insist. Have some cake, some fruit.
*Guest* – No, no, I'm on a diet.
*Host* – But you must. Don't be shy. Have something.
*Guest* – Really, it's not necessary...(ad infinitum).

The best solution to this dilemma is to visit people when you are hungry. Such formidable hospitality not only means that you must eat with the appetite of a normal person but your host will see to it that you eat, eat and eat until you reach bursting point and then insist that you have some more.

If you are invited to a feast – for instance, to a Chinese New Year celebration, a temple worship or a wedding – the meal will include at least 10 courses, so eat slowly and sparingly or you'll soon be filled to capacity with seven courses left to go. If you are a man, people will try to toast you. One of the best ways to avoid this is to choose a table with only women sitting around it. Alternatively, seat yourself between two women. Women rarely smoke or drink in Taiwan, at least not publicly. Bowls of delicious food will be put on the table and most of the guests will put their chopsticks right into them and help themselves. The idea of a serving spoon is only starting to catch on, mostly in high-class restaurants.

Fruit, rather than cake, ice cream or other sweets, is usually served at the end of the meal. The Chinese almost never eat the skin on apples, pears and grapes. If you do, expect to draw a few amused stares and comments. They feel the same way about eating uncooked vegetables, like carrots. They figure only rabbits do that.

Comments like 'This food is delicious!' will be much appreciated. However, don't be surprised if your hosts apologise that the food was 'so poor', even though it was excellent. In accordance with the custom of Chinese humility, your hosts will often indicate that the service is inadequate and that the food is not enough. What they really mean is that nothing is too good for you, the honoured guest.

When it comes time to pay the bill be prepared for a rather amusing scene. If you are with a group of five people, don't be surprised if all five rush up to the cash register, each one insisting on paying for the entire group. It can turn into quite a battle as everybody pulls out their money and simultaneously tries to stuff it into the hands of the bewildered cashier. As a foreign guest, everyone will certainly insist that they pay for you. Keep smiling and insist at least a few times that you should pay. It's unlikely they will let you, but part of the ritual is that you pretend you really want to.

### Prices

Pay careful attention to prices, especially with seafood. The Chinese try to impress each other by ordering exotic, high-priced fish which costs the earth. Don't just point to a fish that somebody else is eating and say you want that one, ask the price first. It could be NT$100 – or NT$3000, even if you buy it from what looks like a cheap foodstall in the night market.

Breakfast is the cheapest meal, especially if you buy soybean milk and steamed buns. Western breakfasts are considerably more expensive. In resort areas food can be expensive, so your best bet is probably instant noodles which are widely available from grocery stores. Stores like 7 Eleven have instant meals which can be heated in their microwave oven.

### Fast Food

Western-style fast food is readily available in the cities though still hard to come by in rural areas. It tends to be a lot more expensive than Chinese food and has considerable snob appeal to the 'face'-conscious Taiwanese.

**McDonald's as a Tourist Attraction** When McDonald's first announced that they would open a branch in Taipei, both Chinese and foreign residents laughed. 'The Chinese will never go for it,' everyone agreed. Every foreigner who had lived in Taiwan for any length of time knew very well that the Chinese don't eat hamburgers, fries and milk shakes. And the

Chinese unanimously agree that cheese is positively revolting. 'McDonald's will go bankrupt in a month,' everyone chuckled.

From the day it opened, Taipei's first McDonald's has broken all records for sales volume. The company quickly opened up other branches in Taipei's fashionable neighbourhoods, and the customers just kept coming. Significantly it's not the foreign tourists who have been flocking to McDonald's – the customers are overwhelmingly Chinese. Still, you can see foreigners hanging around. As one traveller, Jan Hader, wrote: 'Thank goodness for all those McDonald's. We never actually *ate* there – preferred local noodle and dumpling places – but they are an excellent source for toilet facilities.'

Ironically, while McDonald's is one of the cheapest places to eat in Western countries, in Taiwan it's expensive and prestigious. Notice all the Mercedes-Benzes and BMWs parked outside, and the fashionably dressed Chinese clientele hanging out sipping their Cokes and chatting over an Egg McMuffin.

Superficially, it would seem that McDonald's foray into the Taiwan market has been a complete success. However, there is a touch of indigestion in the air. As one McDonald's employee told me: 'This place has become a tourist attraction. It's always packed, but we don't sell much food. Many people hang out here for hours, smoke cigarettes, read magazines, and maybe just buy a Coke. Some customers even have the nerve to bring their lunch boxes in here and eat noodles. They get all dressed up and take pictures of each other standing in front of Ronald McDonald. On Sunday, our playground attracts more kids than the city park.'

Nevertheless, McDonald's must be doing something right. No company stays in business for long unless it's making a profit, and McDonald's shows no sign of abandoning the Taiwan market. Perhaps the greatest tribute to McDonald's success is the traditional Taiwanese reaction to a profitable business – copying. A number of Taiwanese companies have opened up Chinese fast-food chains in America.

## Food List

A list of some of the more common food items is included in the following pages. The reason for such a long list is that many of the food items in this book are not found in the dictionary or are frequently mistranslated. For example, the Chinese usually translate plain white bread as 'toast' and carrots as 'radishes'. There are many food items which have no translation at all. All food given in the list includes the Pinyin transcript as well as the Chinese characters. For a list of drinks, see the Drinks section further on in this chapter.

## Breakfast

fried bread stick
  *yóutiáo* 油條
clay oven rolls
  *shāobǐng* 燒餅
sliced bread
  *tǔsī* 土司
bread, pastry, rolls
  *miànbāo* 麵包
egg & flour omelette
  *dànbǐng* 蛋餅
egg boiled in tea
  *cháyè dàn* 茶葉蛋
egg boiled in gravy
  *lǔ dàn* 滷蛋
salty hard-boiled egg
  *xián dàn* 鹹蛋
rice & vegetable roll
  *fàntuán* 飯團
watery rice porridge
  *xīfàn* 稀飯
shredded dried pork
  *ròusōng* 肉鬆
soybean milk
  *dòujiāng* 豆漿
steamed bun
  *mántóu* 饅頭
steamed meat bun
  *bāozi* 包子
steamed rice dumpling
  *zòngzi* 粽子
sushi
  *shòusī* 壽司

## Dumplings

boiled dumplings
  *shuǐjiǎo* 水餃
fried meat dumplings
  *guōtiē* 鍋貼
steamed dumplings
  *zhēngjiǎo* 蒸餃
sweet & sour dumpling
  *tián búlà* 甜不辣
rice-meat dumplings
  *ròu yuán* 肉圓
fried vegetable roll
  *shuǐjiān bāo* 水煎包

## Noodles

noodle soup
  *tāng miàn* 湯麵
plain noodles
  *gān miàn* 乾麵
noodles & sesame sauce
  *májiàng miàn* 蔴醬麵
rice noodles
  *mǐfěn* 米粉
beef noodles
  *niú ròu miàn* 牛肉麵
sliced noodles
  *dāoshāo miàn* 刀削麵
pork noodles
  *ròusī miàn* 肉絲麵
instant noodles
  *pào miàn* 泡麵
wanton & noodle soup
  *húndùn miàn* 餛飩麵

## Rice

plain cooked rice
  *fàn* 飯
fried rice
  *chǎofàn* 炒飯
fried rice with egg
  *dàn chǎofàn* 蛋炒飯
fried rice with pork
  *ròusī chǎofàn* 肉絲炒飯
rice & vegetable lunchbox
  *biàndāng* 便當
salty rice pudding
  *wǎgùi* 碗粿

## Soup

clear soup
  *qīng tāng* 清湯
seaweed soup
  *zǐcài tāng* 紫菜湯
snake soup
  *shé tāng* 蛇湯
sweet & sour soup
  *sūan là tāng* 酸辣湯
tofu soup
  *dòufǔ tāng* 豆腐湯
wanton soup
  *húndùn tāng* 餛飩湯

## Meat

beef 牛肉
  *niú ròu*
chicken
  *jī ròu* 雞肉
chicken feet
  *jī jiǎo* 雞腳
chicken leg
  *jī tǔi* 雞腿
chicken nuggets
  *yán sū jī* 鹽酥雞
Chinese stew
  *hǔoguō* 火鍋
dog meat
  *xiāng ròu* 香肉
duck
  *yā ròu* 鴨肉
goat or mutton
  *yáng ròu* 羊肉
intestines
  *cháng* 腸
Peking duck
  *běipíng kǎoyā* 北平烤鴨
pork
  *zhū ròu* 豬肉
snails
  *gūo niú* 蝸牛

## Seafood

clam
  *gělì* 蛤蜊
crab
  *pángxiè* 螃蟹
fish
  *yú* 魚
lobster
  *lóngxiā* 龍蝦
octopus
  *zhāng yú* 章魚
oyster
  *mǔlì* 牡蠣
shrimp
  *xiāzi* 蝦子
squid
  *yóu yú* 魷魚

## Vegetables

bamboo shoots
  *zhúsǔn* 竹筍

broccoli
  *měiguó hūa cài* 美國花菜
cabbage
  *gāolì cài* 高麗菜
pickled cabbage
  *pào cài* 泡菜
carrot
  *hóng lóbō* 紅蘿蔔
cauliflower
  *hūa cài* 花菜
celery
  *qíng cài* 芹菜
corn
  *yùmǐ* 玉米
kelp
  *hǎidài* 海帶
mushrooms
  *xiāng gū* 香菇
peas
  *wǎn dòu* 豌豆
green pepper
  *qīng jiāo* 青椒
sweet potato
  *dìgūa* 地瓜
seaweed
  *hǎitái* 海苔
soybean
  *huáng dòu* 黃豆
bitter squash
  *kǔgūa* 苦瓜
tomato
  *fānqié* 蕃茄
white radish
  *lóbo* 蘿蔔

## Fruit
apple
  *pínggǔo* 蘋果
banana
  *xiāngjiāo* 香蕉
'crab apple'
  *zǎozi* 棗子
'dragon eyes'
  *lóngyǎn* 龍眼
grape
  *pútáo* 葡萄
guava
  *bālè* 芭樂
lychee
  *lìzhī* 荔枝

mango
  *mánggǔo* 芒果
orange
  *liǔdīng* 柳丁
pear
  *lí* 梨
pineapple
  *fènglí* 鳳梨
starfruit
  *yángtáo* 楊桃
sugar cane
  *gānzhè* 甘蔗
tangerine
  *júzi* 橘子
watermelon
  *xīgūa* 西瓜

## Condiments
garlic
  *dàsùan* 大蒜
ginger
  *jiāng* 薑
black pepper
  *hújiāo* 胡椒
hot pepper
  *làjiāo* 辣椒
hot sauce
  *làjiāo jiàng* 辣椒醬
ketchup
  *fānqié jiàng* 蕃茄醬
mayonnaise
  *měinǎizhī* 美乃滋
MSG
  *wèijīng* 味精
salt
  *yán* 鹽
sugar
  *táng* 糖
sesame seed oil
  *xiāng yóu* 香油
soy sauce
  *jiàng yóu* 醬油
vinegar
  *cù* 醋

## Miscellaneous
almond
  *xìngrén* 杏仁
betelnut
  *bīnláng* 檳榔

cabbage roll
　*gāolì cài juǎn* 高麗菜捲
cake
　*dàngāo* 蛋糕
candy
　*tángguǒ* 糖果
peanut candy
　*huāshēng táng* 花生糖
sesame seed candy
　*zhīmá táng* 芝蔴糖
cookies
　*bǐnggān* 餅乾
crackers
　*sūdǎ bǐng* 蘇打餅
dried duck's blood
　*yāmǐxǐe* 鴨米血
ice cream
　*bīngqílín* 冰淇淋
crushed ice & fruit
　*bābǎo bīng* 八寶冰
ice, milk & red beans
　*hóngdòu niúnǎi bīng* 紅豆牛奶冰
*'1000-year' egg
　*pídàn* 皮蛋
peanuts
　*huāshēng* 花生
popsicle
　*bīng bàng* 冰棒
potato chips
　*mǎlíng shǔ* 馬鈴薯
pudding
　*bùdīng* 布丁
rice crackers
　*mǐ guǒ* 米菓
puffed rice (popcorn)
　*bàomǐhūa* 爆米花
sandwich
　*sānmíngzhì* 三明治
sherbet
　*miánmián bīng* 綿綿冰
peanut sherbet
　*huāshēng bīng* 花生綿綿冰
pineapple sherbet
　*fènglǐ bīng* 鳳梨綿綿冰
strawberry sherbet
　*cǎoméi bīng* 酸梅綿綿冰
egg roll
　*chūn juǎn* 春捲
tofu
　*dòufu* 豆腐

dried tofu
　*dòufu gān* 豆腐乾
smelly tofu
　*chòu dòufu* 臭豆腐
tofu pudding
　*dòuhūa* 豆花
vegetarian gelatin
　*aìyù* 愛玉

## DRINKS
### Tea

Tea is to China what coffee is to Brazil. Chinese tea is justifiably famous and Taiwan produces many top-grade varieties. Taiwanese tea has a delightful fragrant aroma that is unmatched by any other tea I've tried. Tea seems to grow best in tropical to subtropical climates at high elevation with lots of moisture. Such conditions exist in many mountain areas in Taiwan.

What is there to know about tea? More than you think. There are many varieties and the price varies tremendously depending on what type you wish to buy.

Black tea, called 'red tea' by the Chinese, is the type most Westerners are familiar with. Black tea is fully fermented, making it dark and strong, and it's relatively inexpensive.

Green tea is not fermented at all. In order to kill the microbes the tea leaves are steamed immediately after the tea is picked, and then the tea is dried.

Oolong tea is a partially fermented tea and is considered prime quality. Some oolong teas fetch incredibly high prices, nearly worth their weight in gold. As oolong tea is so highly prized, there is a tendency among tea vendors to label teas 'oolong' which are in fact green tea.

Apart from these basic types of tea, there are other kinds produced by blending ingredients. For example, jasmine tea is a mixture of tea and flowers. The possible combination of blends is endless.

Having good tea is only half the battle. To enjoy tea, one has to know how to prepare it. Most Chinese are dumbfounded by the Western custom of putting milk and sugar in tea. They drink it straight, and the more bitter the taste, the better.

There are two basic methods of preparing tea. The most popular way for a group to drink tea is 'old man style'. A tiny teapot is stuffed full of tea leaves and scalding hot water is poured inside. With very little time to steep, the tea is quickly poured into a small flask to cool, then served in very tiny cups which allows the tea to cool faster. More boiling water is poured into the teapot and a second brew is prepared. As the tea gets weaker, the time needed for steeping is progressively longer. Eventually, the leaves are discarded and the pot can be stuffed with fresh leaves again. In Taiwan, you can buy beautiful tea sets cheaply to make 'old man tea'.

The easiest way to prepare tea is to put the leaves directly into the cup or large teapot, pour boiling water into it, and then let it steep for no less than 6 minutes. The longer it steeps the more bitter it will become. Tea bags are not very popular in Taiwan, but they are available.

Taiwanese tea is high in caffeine. However, there are a few herbal teas available in Taiwan, though not nearly as many as most Westerners expect. Herbal teas are usually not sold in tea shops, but you can buy hibiscus tea (*lùoshén*) in grocery stores. Also available from grocery stores is wheat tea (*mài chá*), which tastes a lot like coffee. There is also chrysanthemum tea (*júhūa chá*), which is sold in many street markets.

## Coffee

Taiwan does not produce any coffee. The coffee you buy in Taiwan is imported and usually grossly overpriced. Nevertheless, hanging out in a coffee shop with friends is a pleasant and popular pastime. The coffee itself comes in a tiny cup which costs as much as a whole dinner, about NT$100, so if you're hungry order the dinner instead. Ironically, the dinner often includes a free cup of coffee, but it's usually iced coffee and already flavoured with (too much) sugar and milk. If you ask for hot coffee instead, you'll be charged an extra NT$100.

Coffee shops usually have excellent ice cream sundaes which are much better value

than the coffee. The atmosphere is comfortable and sometimes a band is provided especially on Saturday night. Some places show video movies and serve 'old man tea as well.

## Alcohol

Taiwanese beer is cheap and excellent and it's easy to remember the brand name, which is simply Taiwan Beer. Apart from beer Chinese liquor doesn't attract much of a following amongst Westerners. Most liquors are rather harsh, although Taiwan produces a good sweet red grape wine and plum wine There is also a white grape wine which some Westerners like.

Some of the liquors make a fairly good mixed drink, but the Chinese do not like to drink liquor mixed. They prefer it straight from the bottle. The strongest stuff, called Kaoliang, is made out of sorghum. It's 65% alcohol and makes a reasonably good substitute for gasoline. The most popular liquor is Shaoshing, distilled from rice with an alcohol content of 15%. Taiwanese rum mixes well with Coca-Cola.

If you attend a feast or dinner party, be careful of getting drawn into the 'finger game' (*húa jiǔ qúan*). It's rather hard to describe, but it's a drinking game and the loser is obliged to empty his glass. If you lose too many times, you're going to get smashed.

As a Westerner, you may find yourself being toasted. This only applies to men, as women aren't expected to drink. Someone will lift his glass and say *gān bēi*, which literally means 'dry glass'. If you accept the challenge, see the local herbal medicine shop for some hangover remedies. If you'd prefer not get wasted, just answer *súi yì*, or 'as you like'. You can then just take a sip.

All liquor and tobacco products are controlled by the government. The price is regulated uniformly throughout the island, no matter if you buy these products from a street stall, grocery store or department store. Restaurants, however, charge tax in addition to the list price. There is no minimum age for purchasing liquor or for drinking it.

Most stores keep only a small stock of

liquor. To see all the liquor products on display in one place, visit the Taiwan Tobacco & Wine Monopoly Bureau, 83 Chungshan N Rd, Section 3, Taipei. They have branch offices in all the major cities around the island. You can purchase liquor and tobacco directly from them, and they carry some imported brands too. Any imported liquor and tobacco products carry an import tax, so bring the maximum if you need this stuff. You are permitted 1 litre of liquor and 200 cigarettes duty-free.

These days more and more young women are smoking and drinking, but overall these vices are still regarded as being suitable for men only. A women who smokes and drinks in public is regarded as a 'bad girl' (sexually loose). This is especially true in the conservative hinterland outside of Taipei.

### Drink List

drinking water
  *kāishuǐ* 開水
beer
  *píjiǔ* 啤酒
carrot juice
  *hóng lóbo zhī* 紅蘿蔔汁
orange juice
  *liǔchéng zhī* 柳橙汁
passionfruit juice
  *bǎixiānggǔo zhī* 百香果汁
starfruit juice
  *yángtáo zhī* 楊桃汁
sugar cane juice
  *gānzhè zhī* 甘蔗汁
papaya milkshake
  *mùgūa niúnǎi* 木瓜牛奶
pineapple milkshake
  *fènglí niúnǎi* 鳳梨牛奶
watermelon milkshake
  *xīgūa niúnǎi* 西瓜牛奶
black tea
  *hóng chá* 紅茶
chrysanthemum tea
  *júhūa chá* 菊花茶
green tea
  *lü chá* 綠茶
hibiscus (herb) tea
  *lùoshén chá* 洛神茶

jasmine tea
  *mòlìhūa chá* 茉莉花茶
oolong tea
  *wūlóng chá* 烏龍茶
wheat tea
  *mài chá* 麥茶

## BOOKS

Books dealing exclusively with Taiwan are scarce. Most people with an interest in this part of the world want to read about China. Taiwan, being only one small province of China, hardly merits a footnote as far as most authors are concerned.

A good coffee-table book is *Images of Taiwan* by Daniel Reid & Dan Rocovits (Hong Kong Publishing Co Ltd), available in Taiwan for NT$400. Also check out *Arts & Culture in Taiwan* by B Kaulbach & B Proksch (Southern Materials Center; NT$378).

One of the most beautiful coffee-table books is *Taiwan with a View* by the Independence Evening Post, Taipei, which sells for NT$500. *Taipei*, a Times edition, has good photos, an interesting text and historical information.

Those whose interests are more on the monetary side might want to read *Doing Business in Taiwan* by James Cheng. Reading through this book sometimes gives you the impression that it's one big advertisement for Cheng & Cheng Law Offices in Taipei, but it does contain some very useful information for business people.

Hikers might want to look at *Walking in Taiwan* by R Warburton & F Haas. It's an excellent book but it hasn't been updated for many years. The *Insight Guide to Taiwan* (APA Productions, Singapore) has lots of information (besides travel information) and contains excellent illustrations and photographs.

## MAPS

Every bookstore in Taiwan sells maps and atlases. However, the maps are almost exclusively in Chinese characters. Also, they tend to be outdated and somewhat inaccurate. Your best source of English or Romanised maps is the Tourism Bureau. Their map collection is far from complete, but has the great advantage of being free.

## HIKING

A Chinese farmer once confronted me with this question: 'Why do you climb the mountains?'. He was sincere and wanted an answer. 'Because,' I said, 'it feels so good when you stop.'

The fact is that mountain climbing is a hobby of those who live on the flat lands. Mountain folk just don't see the sense in it. They observe us hikers going up and down the mountain, up and down, up and down, like a toilet seat. As that farmer said to me, 'I guess you city folks just have nothing else to do'.

### Mountain Permits

If you hike or travel in certain remote mountain areas, a permit might be required. At times, this can be a real nuisance. Fortunately, they are not required in all mountain areas. On the other hand, they are required for some of Taiwan's most spectacular peaks such as Yushan and Tapachienshan.

There are two basic types of mountain permit, one which is easy to obtain and another which is difficult. The difficult one is called a class A pass (*jiǎzhǒng rùshānzhèng*) and the easy one is a class B pass (*yǐzhǒng rùshānzhèng*).

Class B permits can usually be obtained right at the roadside entrance or trail head in a few minutes, after you've filled out a simple form. It's no hassle to get a class B pass except that the local official in charge probably won't speak English and the forms are in Chinese. You can also get class B passes easily in Taipei. In fact, it's usually better to get the pass in Taipei because the officials there speak English and they can explain all the rules about where you can and cannot go. Be sure to ask for more time than you think you need, since a 2 day trip could wind up taking 3 days.

To apply for a class B mountain permit, you need your passport. Foreign residents of

Taiwan also need their alien resident certificates. The processing fee is NT$5. The pass will be issued on the spot after only a few minutes wait if all the paperwork is in order.

The place to apply for a mountain permit is at the Foreign Affairs Office, Taiwan Provincial Police Administration, 7 Chunghsiao E Rd, Section 1, Taipei – directly across the street from the Lai Lai Sheraton Hotel.

The other type of mountain permit, which I call a class A pass, must be applied for in advance and is not easy to get. For most travellers, there are only two ways to obtain such a pass: join a mountain club and go on one of their regularly scheduled trips, or hire a government-licensed mountain guide.

If you go with a mountain club, they will need photocopies of your passport and alien resident certificate (if you have one) at least a week in advance. The club will apply for the permit and make all the arrangements. The best club for arranging this is the Alpine Association ROC (tel (02) 5911498), 10th floor, 185 Chungshan N Rd, Section 2, Taipei.

If you choose to hire a licensed mountain guide, the Alpine Association can also arrange this. You need at least four people in your climbing party, and you must submit the following documents to the Association: itinerary (one copy); member list (five copies); photocopies of members' passports (one copy). The climbing party is expected to pay the guide's expenses including food, accommodation and transportation. You must obtain suitable climbing gear, which you can buy, rent, borrow or whatever. In other words, don't expect to climb Yushan in thongs and a T-shirt.

If you want to climb solo, there are only two ways in which to obtain a class A pass. You must be a genuine missionary (with credentials to prove it) or a scientific researcher. Supporting documentation is definitely required – for example, a letter from a university saying you are studying botany, meteorology or archaeology. In addition, a letter from a consulate or the American Institute in Taiwan (AIT) endorsing your travel plans would be useful. Even with all this, it is by no means certain that the permit will be granted.

If you are not in Taipei, you can still apply for a class A pass at any office of the Foreign Affairs Police or at the main police station in any major city or county seat. However, they must send all the paperwork to Taipei, which delays the process by several days.

Remember, only some areas of Taiwan require these permits. If you don't want to bother with these passes, hike in the places where they are not necessary.

## Problems & Dangers

Overall, hiking is a safe, healthy and exciting pastime. However, there are a few things to be careful of if you wish to have a safe and pleasant journey.

**Unstable Weather** The most immediate threat to hikers in Taiwan is the unstable mountain weather. It rains frequently, especially in the spring and summer months. It can be beautiful one minute, then the clouds and fog come out of nowhere and it starts pouring. This is not only unpleasant but dangerous. If you get soaking wet, you may die of exposure (hypothermia is the technical term) even in summer. Therefore, adequate waterproof clothing is a must. Cheap plastic rain boots, widely available in Taiwan, are great for keeping the feet dry too.

The rain and steep mountains produce another hazard – landslides. In most cases, you won't have to worry about them if you stick to the trails, but be warned that trails and even roads get wiped out regularly in Taiwan by landslides, especially during the rainy season.

**Hypothermia** Hypothermia occurs when the body loses heat faster than it can produce it and the core temperature of the body falls. It is surprisingly easy to progress from very cold to dangerously cold due to a combination of wind, wet clothing, fatigue and hunger, even if the air temperature is above freezing. It is best to dress in layers; silk, wool and some of the new artificial fibres are all good insulating materials. A hat is import-

ant, as a lot of heat is lost through the head. A strong, waterproof outer layer is essential, as keeping dry is vital. Carry basic supplies, including food containing simple sugars to generate heat quickly and lots of fluid to drink.

Symptoms of hypothermia are exhaustion, numb skin (particularly toes and fingers), shivering, slurred speech, irrational or violent behaviour, lethargy, stumbling, dizzy spells, muscle cramps and violent bursts of energy. Irrationality may take the form of sufferers claiming they are warm and trying to take off their clothes.

To treat hypothermia, first get the patient out of the wind and/or rain, remove their clothing if it's wet and replace it with dry, warm clothing. Give them hot liquids - not alcohol - and some high-kilojoule, easily digestible food. This should be enough for the early stages of hypothermia, but if it has gone further it may be necessary to place victims in warm sleeping bags and get in with them. Do not rub patients, place them near a fire or remove their wet clothes in the wind. If possible, place a sufferer in a warm (not hot) bath.

**Snakes** Another physical danger is that Taiwan has a thorough assortment of the world's most poisonous snakes. The ones I've seen have mostly been the small but venomous bamboo snake. They are green and camouflage themselves in the bushes and trees. They are not limited to bamboo trees. Another interesting snake is the '100 pacer', so called because if it bites, you can expect to walk about 100 paces before dropping dead. There are also cobras, though I've yet to see one in Taiwan, except on a dinner plate in Taipei's exotic night market.

Now that I've got you thoroughly paranoid, let me add the following: I have seen many snakes and almost all species are timid and will flee from humans. Even those which are not timid are unlikely to attack a big creature like a human unless you inadvertently step on one of them. Remember, snakes eat insects, birds and rodents, not people. They only bite humans when they feel threatened. Wearing boots rather than running shoes will help protect you from a bite on the leg should you step on a snake. There is such a thing as snakeproof trousers, though I haven't seen them for sale in Taiwan.

Don't be a fool and attack a snake with a stick – that's the most likely way to get bitten. Whenever I see a snake by the trail, I try to make some noise to scare it off before it can be attacked by a vicious hiker. Some Chinese hikers attach a small bell to their pack to scare off snakes – not a bad idea if you can tolerate all that damn noise.

If by some chance you do get bitten, the important thing to remember is to remain calm and not run around. Authorities differ widely on how to treat a snake bite in emergencies without a specific antivenin, but the conventional wisdom is to rest and allow the poison to be absorbed slowly. The use of tourniquets is discouraged by the medical profession, as a tourniquet could possibly cut off circulation and cause gangrene. The old 'boy scout' method of treating snake bite – cutting the skin and sucking out the poison – has also been widely discredited. The main result of such treatment will likely be a deep cut, loss of blood and an infection. Even if done by an expert, only about 20% of the poison can be removed this way. Immersion in cold water is also considered useless.

Treatment in a hospital with an antivenin would be ideal. However, getting the victim to a hospital is only half the battle – you will also need to identify the snake. In this particular case, it might be worthwhile to kill the snake and take its body along, but don't attempt that if it means getting bitten again. Try to transport the victim on a makeshift stretcher which you can fashion from two bamboo poles and an overcoat.

Although I hate to say it, there isn't a whole lot you can do for a snake bite victim if you are far from civilisation. Fortunately, the vast majority of snake bite victims survive even without medical treatment. However, prevention is still the best medicine.

**Insects & Stings** Wasps, which are common in the tropics, are a more serious hazard than snakes because they are more aggressive and will chase humans when stirred up. If you see a wasp nest, the best advice is to move away quietly. They won't attack unless they feel threatened, so don't do anything foolish like seeing how close you can get to their nest.

Every year, several people in Taiwan are killed or injured by swarms of angry wasps; the victims are most often children who throw rocks at their nests. Should you be so unfortunate as to be attacked by wasps, the only sensible thing to do is run like hell.

Mosquitoes are a nuisance and they can be numerous in Taiwan's mountains, especially after a rainstorm. There are two things you should have in your arsenal to keep them at bay. One is mosquito coils; these are made of slow-burning incense which contains a poison that stops them cold. Of course, they're no use while actually hiking, but they're great when you stop to rest or eat lunch or camp. In Taiwan, the backpacking shops sell neat little holders for the incense that makes it easy to carry without it breaking into 100 pieces.

Your second defence against mosquitoes should be insect repellent, especially those containing the magic ingredient diethyl toluamide, commonly known as 'deet'. Nothing is more effective. In Taiwan it's hard to find and expensive, though it can be readily bought in any pharmacy or supermarket in Western countries. Cutters is a popular brand in the USA, and in Europe or Hong Kong you should look for Autan.

Spiders are not something you need to worry much about, but if you do much hiking, you will probably encounter a large spider which looks very much like a tarantula. They reside in trees and I've occasionally bumped right into them. Fortunately, they are neither poisonous nor aggressive and will flee from humans.

A more serious problem is posed by a type of scorpion which is fortunately not common – in fact, the only place I've seen such scorpions is in the Tsaoling-Fengshan area, at about 800 metres elevation. They look nasty. They are found on the ground, usually on

'Bite People Cat' nettle

roads, where they frequently get squashed by passing vehicles. Boots should give you ample protection. When confronted by a human, they will not attack but will assume an aggressive posture with claws and stinger bristling. The best thing to do is walk away from them. If you have an irresistible urge to kill one, use a rock or a stick, never your foot. I'll bet they can move that stinger awfully fast when under attack.

**Poisonous Plants** A minor but painful hazard is caused by a particular type of stinging nettle, a plant called *yǎorénmāo* (literally 'bite people cat') in Chinese. I have touched this plant once in Taiwan and can report it's much worse than a cat's bite. It took 3 days for the swelling to go away. It's a rather ugly plant with splotches on the leaves and is common at around 1500 metres elevation. Should you accidentally touch it, you'll never forget what it looks like.

**Miscellaneous** Many people will tell you not to drink unboiled water in Taiwan, but I feel the danger is exaggerated, especially in the mountains where the water is generally unpolluted. If your choice is between dying of thirst or drinking unboiled water, I suggest you choose the latter. The worst that is likely to happen to you is a mild case of diarrhoea, which is best treated by bringing extra toilet paper. Dysentery is very unusual in Taiwan and you needn't worry about it.

Sunburn is a hazard while hiking and some cases can be serious, especially at high elevations. A wide-brimmed sun hat is your best protection. Sunscreen (UV) lotion works fine but it's not widely available in Taiwan, so bring your own from elsewhere. It can be bought cheaply in Hong Kong.

Getting lost is another hazard, especially for travellers who can't speak Chinese. Many trails are well marked in Taiwan – in Chinese characters of course. Local people will gladly give you directions, if you can understand them. If you are concerned about getting lost and don't have a Chinese person to accompany you, consider the advantages of going out with a Chinese hiking club.

## Hiking Clubs

There are many clubs in Taipei and in the other big cities. Many of these clubs are commercial outfits, taking a whole busload of hikers out for about NT$250 a head for day hikes, and considerably more for overnight trips. Most things are included: transport, meals, lodging and required mountain permits. The only bad thing I can say about these clubs is that at times their trips can be rather crowded. The Chinese like to do things in groups, so you may get 50 or 100 people or more hiking together. Fortunately, overnight trips are usually smaller, involving about 20 or so people.

To find these clubs, inquire at any shop which sells backpacking equipment. There are several in Taipei and elsewhere around the island. Many of these shops run their own trips. Additionally, all universities in Taiwan have hiking clubs, but usually these clubs only welcome students and faculty. Do bear in mind that most of these clubs are thoroughly Chinese and that few people will speak English. These trips are a great way to practise your Chinese. Some hiking clubs are:

ROC Alpine Association (*zhōnghúa shānyùe xiéhùi*), 10th floor, 185 Chungshan N Rd, Section 2, Taipei (tel (02) 5911498). Annual membership

NT$300, nonmembers welcome. Members receive the club's newsletter every 2 months. This is Taiwan's largest mountain club.

Rain Road Mountain & Rafting Club, 2nd floor, 12 Chungshan N Rd, Section 1, Taipei (tel (02) 3811530, 3319093)

Shan Yuan Mountain Climbing Education Training Center, 4th floor, Room 400, 2 Chungshan N Rd, Section 1, Taipei (tel (02) 3147271)

Chungho City Mountain Climbing Club (*zhōnghé shì dēngshān huì*), 4th floor, 4 Lane 26, Chunghsiao St, Yungho City, Taipei County (tel (02) 9291576)

## THINGS TO BUY

Shopping is something of a national sport amongst the Chinese. When they travel abroad, the Chinese spend more time in the department stores than sightseeing. Prices in Taiwan may or may not be a big bargain depending on what you buy. The golden rule for shoppers is to buy Taiwan-made products rather than imported goods. Import taxes are high in Taiwan, especially on luxury items like chocolate, cosmetics, liquor and medicines.

Taiwan is no longer the bargain it used to be. There are still a few bargains to be had on toys, clothing, shoes, sporting goods, camping equipment, luggage, jade and coral jewellery and certain electrical appliances. But overall, Hong Kong is much better for shopping.

Some good-natured bargaining is permissible in small shops and street markets, but usually not in large department stores. I say usually because in fact I have occasionally been given a discount simply by asking for it. In Taiwan, most department stores lease space to smaller vendors rather than trying to run the whole store under one management. If you speak to the manager of the particular department you may get a discount, but usually only if you are making an expensive purchase like a suit or some furniture.

Some good deals in Taiwan include hiking and camping equipment, rain gear, Oriental paintings and pottery, padlocks and special locks for motorcycles and cars.

You may see carved ivory products and leopard skin rugs in Taiwan. However, such products are made from rare animals and many countries now ban the import of goods made from endangered species. An international ivory ban went into effect in 1990, and if effective it will probably put the ivory carvers out of business – good news for the elephants.

Clothing sizes are different in Taiwan. Most things, such as shoes, gloves, garments, even bicycles, are smaller than in the West. 'Extra large' in Taiwan is about equal to medium in the West. Don't believe the sales assistants when they say, 'It will stretch'. It won't.

Shopkeepers may follow you all around the store, standing right on your heels. This is considered polite not pushy. However, many Chinese customers don't like it any more than Westerners do.

Chinese shopkeepers are shrewd and will try to soften up a customer with little gifts like soft drinks, cigarettes and chewing gum. That's all very nice, but don't feel obliged to buy unless you really want the goods. Better yet, refuse such gifts unless you really intend to buy something.

Beware of counterfeit merchandise. Taiwan used to be notorious for fake labels, but is now much less so since the government has cracked down. It probably doesn't matter so much when it comes to designer jeans, but it can be crucial when buying electronics. Many of those fake 'Rolex' watches don't work at all.

### Computers

Taiwan is one of the world's leading centres for manufacturing IBM-compatible personal computers. There are many retail stores all over the island selling computers. For export, Taiwan's best known name brand is Acer (*hóngjī*). It is a good quality brand, and you should be able to find an Acer dealer in your home country to supply you with parts and service. Unfortunately, Acer is not highly compatible with other computers. That is, the parts are not interchangeable with the other widely available computers on the market. So if your Acer needs repairs, you will be forced to go to an Acer dealer and pay a premium for parts once your warranty

Author's name chop

expires. Of course, before you buy a computer in Taiwan you should check prices in your home country. You may find that Taiwan is not that much cheaper, and if you buy the computer in your home country you'll have the benefit of a local dealer who will honour the warranty.

Within Taiwan, the most popular computer brand names are DTK (*xùqīng*) and Asia (*yǎzhōu*). They are both good quality and highly compatible with generic brands so parts are never a problem. They are also cheaper than Acer and DTK is marketed in many other countries as well.

You can also buy generic computers in Taiwan. These are priced about the same as DTK and Asia, but quality varies. In general, I advise against buying a generic computer unless you know that the local dealer will service it. Beware of tiny fly-by-night shops selling no-name computers.

The Apple Macintosh is also available in Taiwan, but it's imported and prices are higher than in most Western countries. However, some Macintosh accessories are made in Taiwan – modems are a particularly good buy. Good Chinese-language word-processing software is also available, one of the strongest selling points of the Macintosh.

Anyone interested in computers should visit the electronics show (October) and the computer show (June) at the Taipei World Trade Center. It's often possible to pick up electronic equipment for half-price at these shows as 'samples'.

## Name Chops

The traditional Chinese name chop or seal has been used for thousands of years. It is quite likely that people began using name chops because Chinese characters are so complex and few people in ancient times were able to read and write. In addition, chops date back to a time when there was no other form of identification such as fingerprinting, picture ID cards and computer files.

A chop served both as a form of identification and as a valid signature. All official documents in China needed a chop to be valid. Naturally, this made a chop quite valuable, for with another person's chop it was possible to sign contracts and other legal documents in their name.

Today, most Chinese are literate, but the tradition is still kept alive in Taiwan. In fact, without a chop it is difficult or impossible to enter into legally binding contracts in Taiwan. A chop is used for bank accounts, entrance to safe-deposit boxes and land sales. If you extend your visa in Taiwan, the official who grants the extension must use their chop to stamp your passport. Only red ink is used for a name chop.

If you spend any length of time in Taiwan, you will almost certainly need to have a chop made. If you're staying a short time, a chop makes a great souvenir. A chop can be made quickly, but first you will need to have your name translated into Chinese characters.

There are many different sizes and styles of chops. Inexpensive small chops can be carved from wood for about NT$50 or so. Chops costing several thousand NT$ can be carved from ivory, jade, marble or steel. Most Chinese people have many chops to confuse a possible thief, though they run the risk of confusing themselves as well. One chop might be used for their bank account, another for contracts and another for a safe-deposit box. Obviously, a chop is important and losing one can be a big hassle.

Most foreigners in Taiwan do not like to have access to their bank accounts or safe-deposit box with a chop. Fortunately, international banks recognise this fact and permit foreigners to use just a signature.

## Rip-Offs

Getting ripped off is seldom a problem in Taiwan. Foreigners occasionally get overcharged, but as a general rule if the store says it's a diamond, it will be a diamond, not glass. If they say it's a genuine Rolex watch, then it should be real, not a fake. In all the years I've lived in Taiwan, I can't say that I've ever been really cheated.

Nevertheless, not everyone is honest. If you think you've been ripped off, there are a few places you can take your complaint. First, try to obtain a refund or exchange from the store itself. In many cases that will work if you do it immediately. If you can't get any satisfaction that way, call the ROC Consumers' Foundation (tel (02) 7001234) (*xiāofèizhě jījīn hùi*). The Consumers' Foundation can't enforce the law, but they have publicised many cases of dishonesty and the manufacture of defective merchandise. Finally, in cases of outright fraud, file a complaint with the Foreign Affairs Police at the main police station in any large city.

## WHAT TO BRING

As little as possible. Many travellers try to bring everything and the kitchen sink. Keep in mind that you can and will buy things as you travel, so don't burden yourself down with a lot of unnecessary junk.

That advice having been given, there are some things you will want to bring from home. But the first thing to consider is what kind of bag you will use to carry all your goods. There is nothing more convenient than the old trusty backpack.

There is a bewildering variety of backpacks to choose from. A frameless backpack has the advantage of being very easy to load on and off luggage racks. A framed model is easier on your back if you are walking long distances. They are available in many different sizes, from huge expedition packs to cheapie models made in Taiwan and South Korea. Travel packs with shoulder straps that zip away into a hidden compartment and internal frames are a modern innovation; they're halfway between the regular backpack and a shoulder bag.

I prefer an inexpensive, medium-size, short-frame backpack. Why spend a fortune on a backpack when it might get lost, stolen or damaged? If that does happen to you, a cheap replacement can be bought in Taiwan.

If you're a business traveller, I would recommend bringing your luggage in a shoulder bag of some sort. It is a lot more convenient than a suitcase and if you find that you run out of room, you can easily buy another bag before you leave.

The following items are either expensive or not readily available in Taiwan: shaving cream, deodorant, multivitamins, special medications, chocolate, cosmetics, good quality running shoes, dental floss, UV lotion (sunscreen), mosquito repellent, a good camera and Kodachrome film.

The following is a checklist of everyday travel items. Most are readily available in Taiwan. You don't necessarily need to bring all these but the list is here for you to consider while you are packing your bag: shorts, T-shirt, trousers/skirts and shirts, sweater, rain gear, underwear, socks, sunhat, toilet paper, razor, nail clipper, comb, towel, water bottle, small knife, sewing kit, daypack, wristwatch, swimsuit, name cards, small flashlight (torch), some paperback books, passport, air ticket, money and moneybelt.

## What to Wear

From May to October the lightest summer clothes will do, except in the mountains, where it can get quite cold at night any time of the year. A good quality rainsuit or poncho will come in handy.

Western-style clothing is certainly acceptable. Indeed, with Taiwan's export-oriented garment industry, you are likely to see people dressed in the same brand-name clothes you find at home.

'Face' is important. The Chinese tend to judge people by their clothing far more than Westerners do. If you saunter around the cities in a dirty T-shirt, shorts and floppy sandals, you may attract some rude stares. The rule to follow is to look neat and clean, even if dressed in shorts and sandals. This is especially important when visiting people, eating in restaurants, or going to discos and nightclubs.

A sandal with a strap across the back of the ankle is considered much better than thongs. Thongs are for indoor wear. True, you will see people wearing thongs outdoors, but some restaurants, theatres and other establishments may refuse you admission. Other people won't say anything but will stare at your feet. It's like walking around outside with torn trousers while you're wearing bright red underwear.

The Taiwanese are certainly more conservative regarding beachwear than their counterparts in Hong Kong and Singapore. Foreign women who wear bikinis will be vigorously stared at. Many Chinese women who swim do so with all their clothes on. Nudity in public places is a definite no-no.

Sunbathing is a peculiar Western custom that the Chinese don't understand at all. Proper Chinese ladies always carry a sun umbrella. The Chinese feel that white skin is much more beautiful than suntanned skin. A suntan is associated with labourers and farm workers, which are low-class positions according to the Chinese. On a hot, sunny day in Taiwan, when the Western expatriates head to the beach or swimming pool to bask in the sun, the Chinese stay indoors. They're likely to go to the swimming pool at night, when there is no risk of getting a tan.

Although tourists may get away with wearing jeans and a T-shirt, those coming to Taiwan on business will be expected to dress very formally. Taiwan is more formal than most Western countries, though not so formal as Japan.

# Getting There

### AIR

Except during the busy times, like the summer vacation and Chinese New Year, there is no shortage of air services to Taiwan. Taipei lies right on the major air routes between Japan and Hong Kong, so there are numerous daily flights on many of the major airlines.

Buying a plane ticket to Taiwan is simple if money is no object. It gets more difficult when you want to buy a ticket for a rock-bottom price and still have the flexibility to stop off in numerous countries en route for indefinite periods of time. Indeed, many travellers to Asia plan to visit Japan, Korea, Hong Kong, Thailand or the Philippines in addition to Taiwan. The trick then is to find an inexpensive ticket that will allow you the maximum number of stopoffs but will not lock you into a rigid, unchangeable schedule of departure dates.

If you are coming directly to Taiwan for a definite period of time, then the best deal is an advance purchase ticket. Such tickets often but not always lock you into a fixed date of departure and return. If you want to change the itinerary you usually have to pay a substantial penalty, often 50% of the purchase price. For that reason I don't recommend buying such tickets for round trips, because travellers often end up changing the return date.

That having been said, it's not unreasonable to buy an advance purchase ticket for a one-way trip. You can purchase your return ticket in Taiwan, Hong Kong, or several other places in Asia. This allows you maximum flexibility. In addition, there are good bargains to be found if you buy plane tickets in Asia – travel agents in Hong Kong are known for giving particularly good discounts. However, Taiwan is not especially cheap for air tickets and Japan is ridiculously overpriced.

How to find the cheapest ticket to Taiwan? That depends partly on where you are coming from and where you will be going to after you leave Taiwan. A ticket bought in Hong Kong will often include a stopoff in Taiwan for free or very little extra if you are continuing on to the USA west coast or Japan.

Buying plane tickets from a travel agent is almost always cheaper than buying directly from the airline because airlines don't give discounts. It's a good idea to call the airline first and see what their cheapest ticket costs. Use that as your starting point when talking to travel agents.

The only word of caution is to watch out for fly-by-night travel agents who insist on receiving the full fare in advance and who ask you to come back in a few days to pick up the ticket. If you use a fairly large travel agency with a good reputation there should be no problems.

Use common sense before handing over the cash and always get a receipt. Whenever possible, try to avoid handing over the cash until they hand over the ticket, or else pay only a deposit until you receive the ticket. I want to add that I've never been ripped off by a travel agent in any country, but I have heard occasional horror stories from fellow travellers, especially in Thailand, Indonesia and the Philippines.

I have bought tickets in a number of countries and I can report that good discount prices are available from the Council on International Educational Exchange (CIEE). This organisation, usually just known as Council Travel, supposedly exists for the benefit of students, but in fact they will sell discount plane tickets to anybody. Another one to try is Student Travel Australia (STA), who also have offices in many countries.

### From the USA

Cut-throat competition between airlines has greatly reduced the cost of flights from the USA west coast to Japan, Korea, Taiwan and Hong Kong. You can often pick up a ticket which includes several free stopoffs along the way in places such as Alaska and Hawaii. The cheapest airlines seem to be China Airlines and Korean Air.

I usually buy my tickets from Council Travel. They are listed in the phone directory and have offices in the following cities: California – Berkeley, Long Beach, Los Angeles, San Diego, San Francisco; Georgia – Atlanta; Illinois – Chicago; Massachusetts – Amherst, Boston, Cambridge; Texas – Austin, Dallas; Minnesota – Minneapolis; New York City; Oregon – Portland; Rhode Island – Providence; Washington – Seattle.

### From the UK

There are practically no direct flights from the UK to Taiwan. Getting a cheap ticket to Taiwan from the UK usually means first going to Hong Kong. In Hong Kong, you can easily change planes and be in Taiwan an hour later.

If you will be travelling to several countries in Asia, it's usually cheaper to fly to Hong Kong first, and then buy a ticket to Taiwan and other destinations. Keep in mind that if you arrive during the Chinese New Year (late January to mid-February) you may get stuck in Hong Kong, as all flights are heavily booked at this time.

It is possible to get quite good discounted plane tickets in London from the travel agents known as 'bucket shops'. To find out what is going on look through the travel ads in *Time Out* and the *News & Travel Magazine*.

Two reliable London travel agents are Trailfinders at 46 Earls Court Rd, London W8, and STA at 74 Old Brompton Rd, London SW7 or 117 Euston Rd, London NW1.

Taiwan's flag carrier, China Airlines, has flights from Amsterdam to Taipei several times a week, but this may not necessarily be the cheapest way to go. First see what fare you can get to Hong Kong and then compare it with China Airlines' economy fare.

### From Australia

There are no direct flights from Australia to Taiwan. The cheapest routes are via Singapore or Bangkok and you have to stop off in either city.

From the east coast the cheapest fare is A$1540 with Singapore Airlines. From Perth it's A$1326, also with Singapore Airlines. You can also stop off in Hong Kong if you want to.

If you intend to visit other countries in the region, Thai International flies to Melbourne, Singapore, Bangkok, Hong Kong, Taipei, Tokyo and Osaka.

From Perth, Thai International flies to Bangkok, Hong Kong, Taipei, Tokyo and Osaka.

### From Japan

Japan is not a good place to buy cheap air tickets. In fact, I can't think of anything you can buy cheaply in Japan. The cheapest way to get out of Japan is by ferry boat. However, if you need a plane ticket, Council Travel (tel (03) 5817581) does have an office in Tokyo at the Sanno Grand Building, Room 102 14-2 Nagata-Cho, 2-Chome, Chiyoda-ku, Tokyo 100.

### From Korea

The USO in Seoul offers some of the best deals on air tickets to Taiwan.

### From Hong Kong

Reasonable prices and a zero chance of getting ripped off are good reasons to recommend the Hong Kong Student Travel Bureau. Of course, there are plenty of other travel agents offering discount tickets in Hong Kong. Some places to check out include:

Hong Kong Student Travel Bureau
   10th floor, Room 1020, Star House, Kowloon (tel 3-694847)
Hong Kong Student Travel Bureau
   130-132 des Voeux Rd, Central (tel 5-414841)
Traveller Services
   7th floor, 57 Peking Rd, Kowloon (tel 3-674127)
Time Travel
   16th floor, Chungking Mansions, Kowloon (tel 3-687710)

## Arrival in Taiwan

The vast majority of travellers will arrive in Taiwan at Chiang Kaishek (CKS) International Airport, in the city of Taoyuan 40 km south-west of Taipei. In the main lobby there is an information desk and it's well worth your while to go over and see them. Firstly, they can give you a free map of Taiwan and Taipei, plus a copy of the free magazine *This Month in Taiwan*.

The next thing they will do for you is make a call to Taipei and book a hotel room for you. This service is free and they will do this whether you are staying in the most luxurious VIP suite or the scruffiest youth hostel. If you have no idea where you want to stay, they can recommend all sorts of places in any price range you'd care for. Of course, these places are all listed in this guidebook too. The service is excellent and of great value to first-time tourists to Taiwan who don't speak Chinese. I can't praise it enough.

Your next priority is to change money. The airport bank gives as good a rate as anywhere else in Taiwan, so don't hesitate to change as much as you think you'll need. Save the receipt because you will need it to re-exchange NT$ back into another currency when you leave Taiwan.

## OVERLAND

You can't reach Taiwan overland, but you can reach Hong Kong from Europe without setting foot on a ship or plane. It's slow going and not necessarily cheaper than flying, but it can be interesting. Several routes are possible, the fastest being the trans-Siberian. Other routes are by way of the Middle East and India.

## SEA

Travelling to and from Taiwan by ship is possible and economically feasible from either Macau or Japan. From anywhere else forget it, unless you have friends in the sea-freight business.

## From Macau

A twice weekly passenger ferry runs between Macau and the port of Kaohsiung in southern Taiwan. The name of the ship is the *Macmosa*, a combination of Macau and Formosa. At present, this is the cheapest way to enter and exit Taiwan.

From Taiwan, one-way 1st-class tickets cost NT$3000; 2nd class is NT$2500; 3rd class is NT$2000. Round-trip fares are exactly double. From Macau, a one-way 1st-class fare is M$850; 2nd class is M$700; and 3rd class is M$550. A 1st-class cabin sleeps two people, 2nd class has four beds and 3rd class is a dormitory for eight. The ship leaves Kaohsiung at 4 pm on Monday and Thursday. From Macau, departures are at 9 am on Sunday and Wednesday. The trip is supposed to take 22 hours, but from my experience it can take from 2 to 8 hours longer depending on how rough the water is. The sea is invariably rougher in winter. Be sure to check on the scheduled departure times because they may change.

In Macau tickets are most easily purchased at the ferry pier. In Hong Kong, you can buy tickets at Shun Tak Shipping (tel 5-8593333), 1st floor, Shun Tak Centre, Hong Kong Island. This is the same building where you get the jetfoils to Macau. In Kaohsiung, you can buy tickets at the pier, from some travel agents, or from their ticket offices in Taipei and Kaohsiung. The Taipei office (tel (02) 7155028) is on the 14th floor, 205 Tunhua N Rd. The Kaohsiung ticket office (tel (07) 2821166) is in Room 2, 6th floor, 79 Chunghua 3rd Rd. In Kaohsiung, the boat departs from Pier 1 on Penglai Rd – take bus No 1 to get there. Taiwan charges a departure tax of NT$200. Macau has no departure tax.

The ticket price entitles you to three free meals of rather poor quality. There is a better restaurant on board where you have to pay for your meals. There is also a small shop on the ship selling a few snacks, but nothing outstanding. If there is something you particularly crave (chocolate, fruit, biscuits, etc) bring your own. It's wise to bring books or magazines to help pass the time. The only entertainment on board is the kung fu videos shown in the cocktail lounge and the slot machines in the mini-casino.

The *Macmosa* doesn't stop in Hong Kong, but this is no problem. Fast and cheap jetfoils, hydrofoils and hovercraft run between Hong Kong and Macau approximately every 30 minutes and the trip only takes about an hour.

## From Japan

There is a weekly passenger ferry that operates between Taiwan and the Japanese island of Okinawa. From Okinawa, there are many passenger ferries to Japan's major port cities, Tokyo, Osaka, Fukuoka and Kagoshima.

If you travel economy class on the ferry it is cheaper than going by plane, and student discounts are available. From Okinawa, the ship departs every Friday and arrives in Taiwan the next day, after making brief stops at the islands of Miyako and Ishigaki. The ship alternates between the Taiwanese ports of Keelung and Kaohsiung. The fare to Keelung is Y15,600; to Kaohsiung it's Y18,000.

You can buy tickets from travel agents in the port cities from where the ferries depart. Many of the youth hostels in Japan will help you out by referring you to a local travel agent who can speak English.

## LEAVING TAIWAN

Plane tickets are not nearly as cheap in Taiwan as they are in Hong Kong, but they can still be bought at reasonable discounts below the airlines' list price. I've never heard of anybody getting ripped off by a travel agent in Taiwan, but should it happen to you, report it to the police. Travel agents are licensed by the government, and the licence can easily be revoked if the agent indulges in unscrupulous practices. If a foreigner is

involved, the authorities will usually come down like a tonne of bricks on the offending company. On the other hand, don't make a complaint unless you really have something to complain about.

### Air

**From Taipei** The following are some of Taipei's discount travel agencies. Many other travel agencies advertise in the local English-language newspaper, the *China Post*. Jenny Su Travel Service has received good endorsements from travellers.

Eagle International Travel
    20 Changchun Rd (tel (02) 5510336, 5713986)
Jenny Su Travel Service
    10th floor, 27 Chungshan N Rd, Section 3 (tel (02) 5951646)
Rex International Travel Service
    8th floor, 185 Sungchiang Rd (tel (02) 5054455)
Wing On Travel Service
    73-79 Jenai Rd, Section 4 (tel (02) 7722998)

**From Kaohsiung** Almost everyone arrives at and departs from Taiwan at the airport near Taipei, but there is a second, much smaller international airport at the southern end of the island near the city of Kaohsiung. Although there are far fewer flights available than from Taipei, some travellers, especially business people, might find it more convenient to fly from Kaohsiung. Flights go to Hong Kong, Japan, Korea and a few other destinations.

In Kaohsiung, the following travel agencies give a good price on tickets: Southeast Travel Service (tel (07) 2312181), 106 Chungcheng 4th Rd; and Wing On Travel Service (tel (07) 2826760), 125-1 Chunghua 3rd Rd.

**Airline Offices** The following airlines maintain offices in Taipei and at CKS Airport. Some airlines also have branch offices in Kaohsiung.

Air France (*fǎguó*)
    12th floor, 100 Nanking E Rd, Section 2, Taipei (tel (02) 5427345)

Air India (*yìndù*)
Room 1, 9th floor, 341 Chunghsiao E Rd, Section 4, Taipei (tel (02) 7410163)

Air Lanka (*sīlǐlánkǎ*)
65 Minchuan E Rd, Taipei (tel (02) 5943911)

Air New Zealand (*niǔ xīlán*)
6th floor, 98 Nanking E Rd, Section 2, Taipei (tel (02) 5083111)

Alitalia (*yìdàlì*)
4th floor, 169 Chunghsiao E Rd, Section 4, Taipei (tel (02) 7415161)

British Airways (*yīngguó*)
6th floor, 98 Nanking E Rd, Section 2, Taipei (tel (02) 5418080)

British Caledonian (*yīngguó jīnshì*)
10th floor, 52 Nanking E Rd, Section 1, Taipei (tel (02) 5210322)

Canadian International (*jiānádà guójì*)
4th floor, 90 Chienkuo N Rd, Section 2, Taipei (tel (02) 5034111)

Cathay Pacific (*gúotài*)
137 Nanking E Rd, Section 2, Taipei (tel (02) 7152333)
CKS Airport (tel (03) 3832502)
Kaohsiung (tel (07) 2013166)

China Airlines (*zhōnghúa*)
131 Nanking E Rd, Section 3, Taipei (tel (02) 7151212)
CKS Airport (tel (03) 3834106)
Kaohsiung (tel (07) 2826141)

Continental (*dàlù*)
2nd floor, 150 Fuhsing N Rd, Taipei (tel (02) 7120133)

Delta Airlines (*dàměi*)
3rd floor, 50 Nanking E Rd, Section 2, Taipei (tel (02) 5076900)
CKS Airport (tel (03) 3834500)

Garuda Indonesia (*yìnní gúojiā*)
6th floor, 82 Sungchiang Rd, Taipei (tel (02) 5612311)
CKS Airport (tel (03) 3834106)

Japan Asia (*rìběn yǎxìyǎ*)
2 Tunhua S Rd, Taipei (tel (02) 7765151)
CKS Airport (tel (03) 7765151)

Iberia (*xībānyá*)
1st floor, 78 Fuhsing S Rd, Section 1, Taipei (tel (02) 7733266)

Korean Air (*dàhán*)
53 Nanking E Rd, Section 2, Taipei (tel (02) 5214242)
CKS Airport (tel (03) 3833787)
Kaohsiung (tel (07) 2715351)

KLM Royal Dutch (*hélán*)
1 Nanking E Rd, Section 4, Taipei (tel (02) 7171000)
CKS Airport (tel (03) 3833034)
Kaohsiung (tel (07) 2811131)

Lufthansa (*déháng*)

3rd floor, 90 Chienkuo N Rd, Section 2, Taipei (tel (02) 5034114)

Malaysian Airlines (*mǎláixīyǎ*)
2nd floor, 102 Tunhua N Rd, Taipei (tel (02) 7168384)
CKS Airport (tel (03) 3834855)

Northwest (*xīběi*)
181 Fuhsing N Rd, Taipei (tel (02) 7161555)
CKS Airport (tel (03) 3832471)

Pan American (*fànměi*)
2nd floor, 28 Nanking E Rd, Section 3, Taipei (tel (02) 5076900)

Philippine Airlines (*fēilǜbīn*)
2nd floor, 90 Chienkuo N Rd, Section 3, Taipei (tel (02) 5053030)
CKS Airport (tel (03) 3832419)
Kaohsiung (tel (07) 2017181)

Qantas (*àozhōu*)
11th floor, 9 Nanking E Rd, Section 3, Taipei (tel (02) 5083111)

Royal Brunei (*húangjiā wènlái*)
11th floor, 9 Nanking E Rd, Section 3, Taipei (tel (02) 5212311)
CKS Airport (tel (03) 3833746)

Scandinavian Airlines (*běi'ōu*)
2nd floor, 150 Fuhsing N Rd, Taipei (tel (02) 7120138)

Singapore Airlines (*xīnjiāpō*)
148 Sungchiang Rd, Taipei (tel (02) 5516655)
CKS Airport (tel (03) 3832247)
Kaohsiung (tel (07) 2013303)

South African Airways (*nánfēi*)
12th floor, 205 Tunhua N Rd, Taipei (tel (02) 7136363)
CKS Airport (tel (03) 3834106)

Thai Airways (*tàigúo*)
1st floor, 152 Fuhsing N Rd, Taipei (tel (02) 7154622)
CKS Airport (tel (03) 3834134)

United Airlines (*liánhé*)
12th floor, 2 Jenai Rd, Section 4, Taipei (tel (02) 7358868)
CKS Airport (tel (03) 3832781)

## Sea

A ferry usually leaves every Monday at 8 am for the Japanese island of Okinawa . Departures alternate between Keelung and Kaohsiung. For further information, including the exact schedule, contact Yeong An Maritime Company (tel (02) 7715911), 11 Jenai Rd, Section 3, Taipei. Some travel agents can also sell tickets for this ferry, so ask around. The cheapest one-way fare in tatami dormitories is NT$2815, while 1st-class tickets are NT$3949. Discounts are available for students.

## Departure Tax

If you are leaving Taiwan by air, there's a departure tax of NT$300. It should be paid in local currency. If you are leaving Taiwan by ferry or ship, departure tax is NT$200.

## Duty-Free

When you leave Taiwan, the duty-free shops at the airport offer reasonably good buys on cigarettes, liquor, perfume and gold coins.

# Getting Around

Inter-city buses, trains and planes are frequent, fast and dependable. There is almost no place on the island that is not served by some means of public transport. You should have no trouble getting to wherever you wish to go except on a Sunday or public holiday, when all means of transport can be very crowded.

If you must travel by train or bus on a Sunday, you will probably have to stand during the trip unless you've bought a reserved-seat ticket in advance. If there is a shortage of seats, expect any queue to quickly deteriorate into a push-and-shove match when the bus arrives. However, the advantage of travelling on local buses and trains – as opposed to taxis or private cars – is that you will have plenty of opportunities to meet the local people. Some of them will be happy to practise their English with you, even though you may not necessarily welcome the practice. You can always use the opportunity to practise your Chinese.

## AIR

Due to Taiwan's small size there is little need to fly in most cases unless you are in a big hurry or plan to visit some of the smaller islands around Taiwan, like Penghu or Lanyu. If you do fly, carry your passport with you and arrive at the airport about an hour before departure time. This is especially true during the holidays, when they could quite likely give away your seat if they need the space.

Most domestic flights are with China Airlines (CAL) or Far Eastern Air Transport (FAT), both of which use comfortable jet aircraft. Formosa Airlines, Taiwan Aviation Corporation (TAC), Foshing and Great China Airlines operate small propeller-driven aircraft on less heavily used routes such as Green Island and Lanyu. For these smaller airlines, check-in should be at least 30 minutes before departure time.

Buy domestic air tickets directly from the airlines. Travel agents give discounts only on international tickets. If you buy directly from the airline, it will be much easier to obtain a refund if your plans change or if the flight is cancelled due to bad weather or mechanical problems. This happened to me once – I obtained my refund right in the airport, but others who had purchased tickets from agents were told they had to go back to the agent and apply for a refund.

## BUS

With the completion of the North-South Freeway, highway buses are able to compete with trains for comfort and speed. A trip from Taipei to Kaohsiung typically takes 4½ hours now by bus, which is faster than the train unless there is a big accident on the freeway (a common occurrence). The buses make a 10 minute stop en route at a freeway rest area, where OK food and drinks are available.

There are two basic classes of bus, the Kuokuang (*gúoguāng hào*) and the Chunghsing (*zhōngxīng hào*). The Chunghsing is the cheaper of the two but not by much. The Kuokuang has a restroom on the bus and gives you a smoother ride than the Chunghsing. Both cover the route in the same amount of time. The Kuokuang and Chunghsing are both air-conditioned in summer and winter and in my opinion are often too cold. There is no way to turn off the air-conditioning. Rather than freezing for several hours, I've gone so far as to tape up the vents. Some travellers carry tape especially for this purpose – the bus company is not amused.

In rural areas, the bus service has been gradually deteriorating over the years thanks to Taiwan's 'car revolution'. As more people buy cars, fewer ride the bus, forcing the bus companies to reduce their services. Ironically, in urban areas bus use is increasing because the parking problem is now so severe that many people don't dare to bring their car into the city. Unfortunately, the actual number of cars is increasing since everyone wants to have a car whether they drive it or not, and virtually every road is plugged up with double-parked cars, slowing Taipei's traffic to a crawl. There are no special bus lanes, so bus passengers have to suffer too.

On all buses you must save your ticket stub. You should turn it in to the driver or conductor when you get off the bus or you will have to pay the full fare again.

Here are some sample bus fares from Taipei to different destinations around the island.

| | Kuokuang | Chunghsing |
|---|---|---|
| Touliu | NT$274 | NT$223 |
| Chiayi | NT$294 | |
| Hsinying | NT$320 | NT$259 |
| Tainan | NT$362 | |
| Kaohsiung | NT$414 | NT$334 |
| Pingtung | NT$428 | |
| Kenting | NT$546 | |
| Keelung | | NT$28 |
| Suao | | NT$159 |
| CKS Airport | | NT$72 |
| Hsinchu | | NT$76 |
| Taichung | NT$194 | NT$156 |
| Changhua | NT$208 | NT$168 |
| Sun Moon Lake | | NT$242 |

## Wild Chicken Bus Companies

Taiwan has some supposedly illegal bus companies affectionately known as 'wild chickens' (yějī gōngchē). The wild chickens have been known to use all sorts of methods to attract customers, including the installation of video cassette players on the bus to entertain passengers during a long journey. While these buses may not win points for safety or reliability, they are faster, cheaper and becoming more popular.

The wild chicken buses also let passengers smoke, supposedly against the rules. If you don't smoke you'd better avoid these buses, as the air gets as thick as oyster sauce after a few hours. The government keeps declaring that they will put the wild chicken bus companies out of business – instead, it appears that the wild chickens may soon put the government bus company out of busi-ness. I don't like to give the addresses of wild chicken bus terminals, as there are so many of them and they move frequently, but you can be sure that they are close to the govern-ment bus terminal with a sign prominently displayed in Chinese.

## Travel Sickness

I don't know why, but Chinese people seem to be unusually susceptible to motion sick-ness. It may be something in the diet, or the fact that the Chinese like to eat big meals while travelling, or maybe it's just a psycho-logical fear of travelling which is not surprising considering how people drive. Children are particularly susceptible. If the person sitting next to you looks very pale, change your seat or give them a plastic bag if you have one handy. Most highway buses in Taiwan are prepared for this and place a barf-bag by each seat, as in planes.

## TRAIN

The train services are frequent and generally good, though not quite up to the standards of Japan and Europe. There are two major lines, the west coast line, which is electrified, and the east coast line, which still uses diesel trains. There are several spur routes to places like Alishan and Shuili. Taiwanese trains are more expensive than the buses.

Currently, there are five classes of train and it is fair to say that you get what you pay for. In descending order they are:

1. Tzuchiang (zìqiáng hào). An express with air-con, it's very fancy and usually has a dining car.
2. Chukuang (jǔguāng hào). Also has air-con but is slightly slower than Tzuchiang.
3. Fuhsing (fùxīng hào). Has air-con, but is slower and not as luxurious as chukuang.
4. Pingkuai (píngkùai chē). Slow with no reserved seats, it's cheap and stops in many small towns – the best bargain for budget travellers. No air-con, but since the windows can be opened these trains are better for photography. There isn't much to photo-graph on the west coast line, but on the east coast and spur lines there is good scenery.

Another advantage Pingkuai has over the more luxurious trains is that no one likes to take this train. Therefore on a Sunday or holiday it is relatively easy to get a seat, while the express trains are packed.

5. Common Train (pǔtōng chē). The slowest train of all, it stops everywhere and it costs the same as the Pingkuai.

On the better trains (Nos 1, 2 and 3) it is often wise to buy your ticket a day or 2 in advance, especially on weekends and holidays. There is no need to buy advance tickets on the slower trains (Nos 4 and 5) as there are no reserved seats. If no seats are available, you are permitted to board but will have to stand. You can receive a 15% discount on round-trip tickets, but the ticket must be used within 15 days of purchase.

If you buy a round-trip ticket from Taipei to Kaohsiung, for example, you reserve the return seat when you get to Kaohsiung. You cannot do this from Taipei as the booking system is not computerised. On any advance ticket sales you cannot reserve a seat more than 3 days in advance. This includes the return portion of a round-trip ticket. If you don't use the return portion of a round-trip ticket, you can refund it (minus the 15% discount you previously received) within 15 days of purchase.

If you are rushing for the train, you can board without a regular ticket if you have bought a platform ticket for NT$4. You must then find the conductor and upgrade your ticket. The same applies if you buy a cheap ticket and then decide to get on a more expensive train. When you find the conductor, you must say 'upgrade ticket' (bǔ piào) 補票. Of course, if you only have a platform ticket, you also have to tell him where you intend to get off.

Food is available on trains. A few trains have dining cars, but most of the time you will have to settle for biàndāng, precooked rice, meat and vegetables in a cardboard box. There is little variety and the quality is so-so, but it beats starving. Food bought on the train and in or around the train and bus stations tends to be more expensive than elsewhere,

but not outrageously so. However, there is free hot tea on the train and you can help yourself. If you're going to be spending a long time on a train, it's best to buy something before you board.

Car Nos 1 and 10 are *usually* for smokers. To be sure, look for a 'No Smoking' sign in the front of the car – if it's not there, smoking is OK. Unfortunately, the no smoking rules are frequently broken when the conductor isn't around.

Save your ticket when you get off the train. You need to turn it in at the gate when you leave the train station. If you lose it you have to pay a big penalty.

Unlike the automobile traffic, the trains run on the left. This is a legacy of the Japanese occupation. Although that might seem like a useless bit of trivia, in fact it can be quite helpful to know when trying to figure out which platform is for southbound trains and which is for northbound.

Timetables (shí kè biǎo) are available but they are written completely in Chinese. If you can read any Chinese, they are very handy. They cost NT$20 and can be purchased at the service counter in almost any train station – the service counter is also the place where you buy the platform tickets. The timetables cover the entire railway system and are updated every few months.

Toilets on the trains discharge the waste directly onto the tracks, so you are not allowed to use them while the train is in a station or in tunnels. The Railways Administration says that they plan to eventually install chemical toilets, as in the buses.

### West Coast Trains

The following table gives some indication of the train fares from Taipei to cities on the west coast. Prices are only quoted for the first three classes of train.

| Destination | Tzuchiang | Chukuang Fare | Fuhsing |
|---|---|---|---|
| Taichung | NT$259 | NT$224 | NT$188 |
| Tainan | NT$504 | NT$435 | NT$366 |
| Kaohsiung | NT$576 | NT$497 | NT$418 |

## East Coast Trains

This table indicates the prices to some of the cities on the east coast from Taipei.

| Destination | Tzuchiang | Chukuang Fare | Fuhsing |
|---|---|---|---|
| Fulung | | NT$77 | NT$65 |
| Ilan | NT$150 | NT$130 | NT$109 |
| Hualien | NT$300 | NT$259 | NT$218 |

## TAXI

You won't have to look for a taxi in Taipei, they will be looking for you. Just stand on a street corner, raise your arm and three or four of them will stop. However, this does not apply during rush hour. During peak hours the competition for taxis is keen. This is usually only a problem in Taipei, not in other cities.

In Taipei, the taxi service is good but there are two negative points that you must deal with. Firstly, the drivers seldom speak a word of English and secondly, many of them wish to demonstrate their Grand Prix racing skills. The first difficulty can be overcome easily enough if you speak Chinese, have a Chinese person with you or if you have your destination written down in Chinese characters. Be sure to have the name of your hotel written in Chinese for the return trip.

The second problem is a little more difficult to solve. To avoid getting into a demolition derby, I employ several tactics. The first is to look for an old driver, as they are usually wiser (how else did they survive so long?) than a young driver. I also prefer the simpler taxis to the ones with racing stripes, air scoops and Christmas lights. Finally, you can tell the driver to slow down by saying *kāi màn yìdiǎn, hǎo bù hǎo*. If that doesn't work, you can always ask to get out by saying *xià chē*.

The taxis in Taipei, Taichung, Tainan and Kaohsiung are required to have meters. In the big cities the metered fare is set by the government and there is no bargaining; just make sure they use the meter. However, with country taxis you should agree on the fare before you get in. The usual price is around NT$50 to NT$70 for any place within the town or city and the drivers usually won't bargain. However, when going out into the country, bargaining with the driver is essential, especially if you are a foreigner. Don't get into an unmetered taxi until you've settled on the price.

Meters charge for both time and distance. The fare at the time of writing was NT$35 at flagfall, which is good for the first 1½ km. Each additional 400 metres will cost you NT$5. You are also charged an extra NT$5 for every 5 minutes of waiting when the taxi is travelling less than 5 km per hour. From 11 pm to 5 am you are charged 20% extra, but this extra charge is automatically calculated by the meter.

Taxis waiting at train stations and airports have a minimum charge because they must line up and wait for a long time, sometimes several hours. The minimum charge is around NT$200 or more, so don't get a taxi from the train station if you're only making a short trip. For NT$200, you could go about 10 km in a regular taxi. To get a regular taxi, walk a couple of blocks from the station or airport and hail a passing cab.

Tipping is not necessary, although you could leave the change. If you do tip, don't get carried away or you'll make it tough on other foreigners who come after you.

Never ask taxi drivers for directions, and don't believe anything that they tell you. As one traveller wrote:

Without our Chinese speaker, we would have been at the mercy of taxi 'hucksters' telling us that our map (your book) was wrong and that the bus station moved, must take taxi. Kept walking and asking questions – took only 5 minutes walk – found the station (obviously been there for years).

Women travellers should take note of the warning about travelling alone by taxi (see the Facts for the Visitor chapter).

## Wild Chicken Taxis

It's not easy to define a wild chicken taxi. It's not necessarily an illegal taxi, but they do have a poor reputation in Taiwan, which accounts for the name. Generally, they are long-distance taxis and are usually painted dark red or black. They are bigger than city taxis and often have diesel engines. The drivers hang around bus and train stations and practically arm wrestle passengers into their cars.

If you speak Chinese, you may enjoy listening to their sales pitch as they solicit customers. They often approach people standing in line at a ticket window and say something like: 'The bus you want is out of order', or 'It has just left', or 'It drove off a cliff', or whatever. Most people ignore them and wait for the bus to arrive, on time, 5 minutes later.

Foreigners should be careful around resort areas. The drivers may approach you and yell out the name of the destination they think you want to go to and they'll usually quote a ridiculously low price. The price then gets raised once you are out in the middle of nowhere. If you refuse to pay more, you might get kicked out on a country road. Of course, I should point out that the majority of taxi drivers are honest, but you never really know.

If you've definitely been cheated, be sure to get the licence plate or ID number of the taxi so you can report the driver to the police. The Foreign Affairs Police in major cities and county seats speak English. They are generally sensitive about complaints by foreigners and will try to assist you.

## SEA

There are several ferry trips which can be made to the islands around Taiwan, and they are mentioned in the appropriate sections of this book. Some destinations reached by boat include the Penghu Islands, Hsiao Liuchiu, Lanyu and Green Island. You must bring your passport with you on boat trips, even though it may not be checked.

## DRIVING

An International Driving Permit is necessary in Taiwan unless you obtain a Taiwanese driver's licence. If you intend to drive and will be travelling to other countries in the region, an international licence will save you much trouble. They are valid for a year.

If you remain in Taiwan for over 2 months, you are expected to obtain a Taiwanese licence. If you wish to obtain a local driver's licence be sure to bring along your home country's licence – you can use it to get the Taiwanese licence without taking a written exam or driving test. You'll also need two B&W photos of yourself, approximately 3 x 2 cm in size. These can be obtained easily and cheaply in Taiwan from photo shops, and they know exactly what size is needed. Finally, you will need to go to the Foreign Affairs Police and obtain a Report of Alien Residence. The address you put on this report will also be put on your driver's licence, so don't use a hotel address. Take these documents and photos to the Department of Motor Vehicles, and you can receive your licence in about an hour. You'll need to pass an eye exam, so if you normally wear glasses or contacts be sure to bring them. A Taiwanese driver's licence is valid for 6 years. Separate licences are issued for cars and motorcycles. The Department of Motor Vehicles can also issue an International Driving Permit in case you need one for other countries that you'll be visiting.

### Rules of the Road

For many years foreign residents have complained steadily about Taiwan's chaotic traffic situation. Now the former complainers are beginning to think they've created a monster – the police are cracking down (in some cities) but the cure seems worse than the disease. The problem is that the police appear to be more interested in filling quotas than solving the traffic problem. Citations seem to be handed out at random for the most minor infractions, while the most serious traffic violations continue to go unpunished.

Furthermore, every city seems to have its own rules, and the rules don't seem to make much sense. For example, in Taipei, you can't ride a motorcycle in the car lane, though it seems to be OK for cars to block the motorcycle lane. Motorcycles are *required* to park on the pedestrian sidewalks, which means pedestrians must walk in the motorcycle lane (I'm not making this up). Driving

Top: Sunset in Tainan (Storey)
Left: Boat in museum, Lanyu (Storey)
Right: Locally made baskets (Strauss)

Top: Ceremony during Chinese New Year, Luerhmen (Storey)
Left: Pagoda at Carp Mountain, Taitung (Storey)
Right: Mural in Kaiyuan Temple, Tainan (Storey)

at night with no lights seems to be legal, and is very popular because Chinese drivers believe (erroneously) that the headlights consume more petrol. Driving on the sidewalks also seems to be OK, but it appears that motorcycles aren't permitted to make left turns in Taipei, though it's allowed in other cities. Things are a lot simpler in Tainan – there are no rules and you can do whatever you like.

The most obnoxious policy is the use of hidden cameras to catch traffic violators. The citation will be charged against the owner of the vehicle, even if they weren't driving at the time. It takes the slumbering bureaucracy many months to finally send the citation by mail, but if not paid promptly the fine will be automatically tripled! By this time, the driver of the vehicle may have long left Taiwan, leaving the unfortunate vehicle owner holding the bag – a big headache for the car rental agencies. Because of the time lag, if the vehicle is sold the new owner may inherit the tickets!

## Car Rental

If you've got the cash and feel the need to hire a car, you'll find plenty of rental agencies ready, willing and able to put you in the driver's seat. When you rent a car, be sure that it's fully insured against accidents and theft, and that the rental company will cover repairs and towing costs. If you're renting for a long time, discounts should be available. Many companies now demand some sort of deposit to protect themselves against traffic citations that they may receive months after your departure thanks to the hidden cameras. Rather than cash, they may ask you to leave a blank, signed cheque or to run off an extra signed receipt from your credit card. How should you deal with this request? Don't ask me, I've yet to figure it out myself. The agencies given in the following list all have English-speaking staff. Good luck.

Avis Rent-A-Car
    Chienkuo N Rd, Section 2, Taipei (tel (02) 5006633)

Central Auto Service
    1098 Chengte Rd, Taipei (tel (02) 8819545, 8821000)
Hertz Rent-A-Car
    642 Minchuan E Rd, Taipei (tel (02) 7173673)
VIP Rent-A-Car
    606 Minchuan E Rd, Taipei (tel (02) 7131111)

Hertz also has branches in Taoyuan, Hsinchu, Taichung, Changhua, Tainan and Kaohsiung.

## MOTORCYCLE

A motorcycle can be a mixed blessing in Taiwan. Public transportation isn't too bad, and motorcycles aren't all that comfortable in the often rainy weather. Nevertheless, a bike can give you a lot of freedom. In the cities, a motorcycle is usually the fastest way to get around since the buses get bogged down in traffic, and parking is usually not such a serious problem for motorcycles as it is for cars.

Touring the island by bike is most enjoyable during the summer season when the warm breeze feels good. Taiwan may be subtropical, but it can get damn cold in the mountains even in summer, especially when it's raining. Since rainy weather is almost guaranteed, equip yourself with a rainsuit and plastic boots – cheap and available at almost any good grocery or hardware store in Taiwan. A helmet with faceshield will not only help keep your head in one piece, but will also keep the rain off your face. Don't forget your hands either – a pair of cheap rubber gloves (the kind used for washing dishes) will make an enormous difference in cold, wet weather. After all, you can't put your hands in your pockets while driving.

Proper clothing is one thing, but what about the motorcycle itself? Buying a motorcycle is easy enough – any motorcycle shop can sell you one, either new or used – but renting can be difficult. Some motorcycle shops are willing to work out a deal whereby you buy a bike and sell it back to them a few months later – it winds up costing you perhaps NT$4000 for 2 months, which is not too bad if you get a lot of use out of it. In Taipei, motorcycle shops are very reluctant to rent vehicles thanks to the hidden cameras mentioned previously. It's much easier to rent in rural areas, especially tourist resorts like Hualien. Rentals cost about NT$400 per day. At that price, it would be better to buy a bike if you plan to use it for a month or more. To rent a motorcycle you must have a licence valid for motorcycles. A car licence is not acceptable, though most motorcycle shops are not capable of reading an International Driving Permit written in English. They much prefer you to have a Taiwanese licence.

About the best all-round touring bike you can (legally) buy in Taiwan is the Sanyang (Honda) 125cc. Be sure it has a four stroke engine because the two stroke model sounds like an overstressed lawn mower and generates as much pollution as a small petrochemical plant. A larger bike would be more comfortable, but they aren't available except on the black market at premium prices. The government doesn't want large motorcycles, only large cars. The Sanyang uses very little petrol, is reliable, and repairs of any kind are very cheap in Taiwan anyway. Motor scooters are no good for long distances – the small wheels are dangerous on rough roads and will quickly vibrate your posterior into marshmallows. Motorcycles are not permitted on the freeway, no matter how large the engine.

### Road Safety

In Taiwan you're officially supposed to drive or ride on the right, though many drivers don't seem to be aware of this. There are many motorcycles in Taiwan. Indeed, Taiwan boasts the world's highest per capita motorcycle ownership and quite possibly the world's highest accident rate. Should you contemplate riding on two wheels, be sure to wear a sturdy helmet and have your will updated. Few drivers in Taiwan carry liabil-

Rush hour in Kaohsiung

ity insurance, so you'd be wise to have medical insurance, not to mention life insurance. Riding with your headlights on makes you more visible, but every time you stop at a traffic light people will remind you to turn off your lights.

Is there anything positive that I can say about riding in Taiwan? Yes, there is – the death rate from traffic accidents seems to be declining in Taipei. This is not because there are fewer accidents, but because the traffic now moves so slowly that injuries are seldom serious.

One foreign visitor actually seemed to enjoy riding his bike in Taiwan. As he wrote:

The free-form traffic pattern is unnerving, what with disregard of traffic signals; disregard of life and limb; disregard of common sense; disregard of accepted (Western) vehicle maintenance practices, etc. But myself? Being a desert car and motorcycle racer who kind of thrives on running on the ragged edge, it's OK. Always a challenge. But for others it may not be their cup of oolong.

Anthony H Tellier

## BICYCLE

Taiwanese-made 10 speed bicycles are cheap, though the quality is not as good as European and Japanese bikes. However, the bikes they keep in stock are usually the smaller frame sizes. If you need a larger frame they may have to order it for you; you'll probably get it within 1 or 2 days. You can ship bicycles cheaply on the train in case you get tired of riding. If you decide to take the bike to another country, it can be taken on a plane for free as a piece of checked baggage if it's properly boxed.

## HITCHING

It is certainly possible to hitchhike in Taiwan, but a few warnings are in order. Most important is that it can be very difficult to hitch in urban areas, so you should really confine your hitching to rural regions. In cities, most people assume that you want to get to the bus station, and that's where they will take you. You'll need a good command of the Chinese language to explain otherwise. Furthermore, bus services are so good and cheap in urban

areas that it really doesn't make sense to hitch unless you're dirt poor. And most Chinese will be shocked if they learn that you're only hitching to save money.

In rural areas it's a different situation. Although public transportation is good along main highways, some remote mountain areas are served by only one bus a day or none at all. In such places, hitching may be the only alternative to walking. Country people are friendly and will usually pick you up, though on a few occasions I've been asked for money. Communicating can be a problem since almost no one speaks English. If you can't speak Chinese, you and the driver will probably spend the whole journey grinning at each other.

Attacks on hitchhikers are almost unheard of, though this is probably because the Chinese never hitchhike. A lone female would be wise to travel with a male companion rather than hitching solo.

The biggest danger to hitchhikers is getting picked up by drunks. It's happened to me a few times, and the last time was pretty exciting. A motorcycle pulled over. The driver was friendly enough – he even pulled a bottle of Kaoliang out of his coat pocket and offered it to me. The problem was that he kept zigzagging all over the twisting, precipitous mountain road we were travelling on. Worse still, he was speeding, turning his head to talk to me, driving with one hand and holding the bottle of Kaoliang with the other. The brakes weren't working very well and music blasted us from a stereo he had built into his motorcycle. After 5 minutes of this, I was suffering from a severe case of sensory overload and finally had to get off.

## LOCAL TRANSPORT
### Airport Transport
**To/From Taipei** A bus is the cheapest way to get to Taipei. There are two classes: a 1st-class express line (Chunghsing Line) for NT$72, which has large luggage racks; and the Express Bus Line for NT$34, which is just as fast but is more crowded and has scant luggage space.

Buses run every 15 to 20 minutes, beginning at 6.30 am and ending at 10.30 pm. There are two routes. The more popular one with travellers goes to the Taipei train station right in the city centre. The other bus goes to Sungshan Domestic Airport in the north-east part of the city. Should you accidentally get on the wrong one, don't panic – city buses connect Sungshan Airport to the train station area.

The bus drivers rarely speak a word of English. You might find it helpful if the staff at the airport information desk write down your destination in Chinese characters.

Taiwan seems to have as many taxis as people and you'll have no trouble finding them. In fact, one of the biggest problems with taxis is that there are too many of them. Competition between drivers is keen and you may well find several hundred taxis lined up at the airport when you arrive.

Due to an oversupply of taxis, the drivers generally have to wait an hour before they get a customer. Therefore the taxi drivers have a standard policy of charging 50% more than what the meter reads, making the fare from the airport to central Taipei about NT$1000. However, going the other way, from Taipei to the airport, the drivers are only supposed to charge you the meter fare.

If you are staying at one of the better hotels in Taipei, they may have a limousine service from the airport directly to your hotel. However, if you want them to meet you at the airport you'd better fax, write or telephone ahead. Otherwise, you'll have to call them from CKS Airport and wait nearly an hour or more for them to arrive. If they know when you are coming, they will stand at the arrival gate just after you clear customs and hold up a sign with your name on it. Personally, I don't think it's worth it. Limousine service is seldom free unless you're a VIP. They charge about NT$1000, the same as for a taxi.

**Southbound Passengers** About 99% of arriving tourists head directly to Taipei, which is north-east of the airport. However, if for some reason you are heading to south or to central Taiwan, there is no need to go to Taipei, which is in the opposite direction. If you are one of those rare few who want to head directly south, first take the local bus into nearby Taoyuan to catch the southbound train. Another option is to take a bus from the airport directly to the city of Taichung. These buses don't run at night. If you arrive late you can take a taxi to Taoyuan, but the cost is around NT$300 – so it may be cheaper to go to Taipei unless you're sharing the cab with someone.

**To/From Kaohsiung** Only a handful of foreigners arrive by air in Kaohsiung, mostly coming from Hong Kong. Airport transport is not terribly fast, but there is a bus about once every 30 minutes to central Kaohsiung. It doesn't go all the way to the train station – it stops at Chungcheng Rd, a 10 minute walk south of the train station. The cost is only NT$10. The airport taxis have a set fee, usually NT$200 minimum, but ask first. You can save some money by walking outside the airport and hailing a passing cab. They will use the meter and the cost to the train station is about NT$130.

**TOURS**
Most Chinese and Japanese tourists prefer organised tours to individual travel. The tour guide wears a smart uniform, carries a brightly coloured flag and speaks through a megaphone. Those who attend the tours get to wear bright yellow caps with visors and sing songs together. It's customary to dress formally (black suits and ties for the men) – you'd think they were attending a funeral rather than going on holiday. The tours are usually spending sprees with frequent 'rest stops' at shopping plazas. Many people claim that the tour companies get a commission from the vendors for bringing in customers. A huge lunch at a fancy restaurant is a major feature of Chinese tours and is always included in the tour price. The actual sightseeing part of the tour tends to be rushed – most of the time is wasted shopping, eating and posing for group photos.

I won't say much about package tours, but if a tour appeals to you it can easily be booked in Taipei. Some reputable tour agencies in the capital include:

Travel Service
    58 Chungshan N Rd, Section 2 (tel (02) 5713001)
Huei-Fong Travel Service
    4th floor, 50 Nanking E Rd, Section 2 (tel (02) 5515805, fax 5611434)
Edison Travel Service
    4th floor, 190 Sungchiang Rd (tel (02) 5635313, fax 5634803)

**Budget Tours** Group tours can be arranged for rates as low as US$20 per day, including food, accommodation and transport around Taiwan. This is possible thanks to the government youth hostels. The accommodation is either dormitory-style rooms or tatami mats. These tours are very popular with groups of visiting overseas Chinese. If you belong to a group that might be interested contact the following address: China Youth Corps (tel (02) 5435858) (*jiùgúotúan*), 219 Sungchiang Rd, Taipei, Taiwan, ROC.

The centres and hostels are heavily booked during the summer vacations and the Chinese New Year. All arrangements should be made well in advance.

# Taipei 台北

Not long ago, the valley of the Tanshui River was home mainly to rice and vegetable farmers but today it's the site of Taipei, the bustling centre of commerce, government and culture in Taiwan. Almost without exception, Taipei is the first stop for Western visitors arriving in Taiwan; also it is home for most of the Western expatriates. As far as most people are concerned, this is the heart of Taiwan's activity and the place where things happen.

With a population of 3 million, Taipei is easily the largest city on the island and the number of residents is growing rapidly. The population increase is due primarily to an influx of people from other parts of the island who are attracted to the city by the economic and educational opportunities. In an attempt to prevent the population of Taipei from overflowing, the government has made a sincere and largely successful effort to locate industry and educational institutions in other parts of the island. The cities of Kaohsiung, Tainan and Taichung have benefited most from this policy. Nevertheless, most people in Taiwan still see Taipei as the golden land of opportunity and continue to flock there. As far as they are concerned, if you want to make it big, you must live in Taipei.

As a boom town, Taipei has its share of problems. Social problems such as crime and drug addiction have increased sharply. More noticeable to the visitor are environmental problems such as overcrowding, pollution, noise and incredible traffic jams. Too much money and too little space has led to sky-rocketing real estate prices which have made home ownership an impossible dream for the lower classes. In an attempt to deal with the onslaught of people, industry and automobiles, there is a tremendous amount of construction going on. Commercial and residential buildings spring up overnight. A gigantic new subway system is being built, though work seems to be proceeding at a snail's pace. The city is undergoing a badly

needed facelift. To see the hoped-for results, you should go out to the Dinghao area in east Taipei, along Chunghsiao E Rd east of Fuhsing Rd. This is the new Taipei and when it is compared to old Taipei in the centre of the city the difference is striking.

Whether or not you like Taipei depends on how you feel about big, booming cities. Physically, Taipei is not very attractive, yet some travellers come here and like it so much that they stay for months and never seem to get out of the city at all. Others just can't wait to leave. Even if you like Taipei, one thing is for sure – it's an expensive place to hang out unless you're working there.

Although Taiwan's magnificent scenery lies beyond the city's glittering glass and concrete, Taipei should not be missed. It's the economic, cultural and trendsetting heart of the island, and if you haven't seen Taipei then you haven't seen Taiwan.

## Orientation

Taiwan's cities – and Taipei in particular – might at first seem like a confusing sprawl to the uninitiated. However, there is a system to finding your way around. Naturally, this task is made easier if you can speak, read and write Chinese, but that isn't absolutely necessary. It's certainly helpful to have your destination written down in Chinese characters and of course you should always have the name card of your hotel so you can find your way back.

The city of Taipei is divided into sections. Chunghsiao Rd bisects the city into its north and south sections. All major roads that cross Chunghsiao Rd are labelled accordingly. Thus, we have Linsen North Rd and Linsen South Rd, Yenping North Rd and Yenping South Rd, etc.

Chungshan Rd bisects the city into east and west sections. Roads to the east of Chungshan Rd are labelled east and those to the west are labelled west. Thus, we have Nanking East Rd and Nanking West Rd.

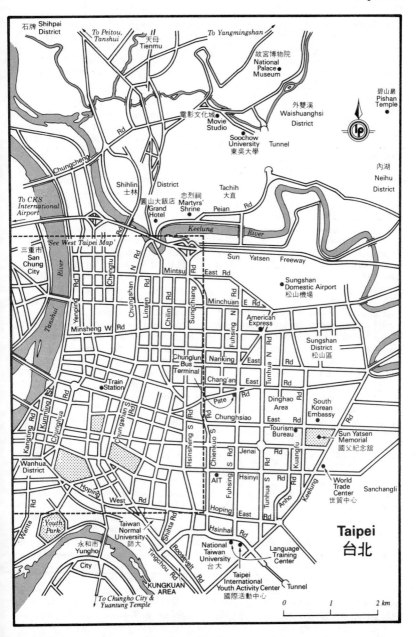

石牌 Shihpai District
To Peitou, Tanshui
天母 Tienmu
To Yangmingshan
故宮博物院 National Palace Museum
碧山巖 Pishan Temple
電影文化城 Movie Studio
外雙溪 Waishuanghsi District
Soochow University 東吳大學
Tunnel
內湖 Neihu District
Chungcheng Rd
Shihlin 士林 District
忠烈祠 Martyrs' Shrine
大直 Tachih
To CKS International Airport
圓山大飯店 Grand Hotel
Peian Rd
Keelung River
三重市 San Chung City
'See West Taipei Map'
Sun Yatsen Freeway
Tanshui River
Chengtu Rd
Mintsu
East Rd
Sungshan Domestic Airport 松山機場
Chungshan N Rd
Linsen Rd
Chilin Rd
Sungchiang Rd
Minchuan Rd
Fuhsing N Rd
E Rd
American Express
Yenping Rd
Minsheng W Rd
Sungshan District 松山區
Tunhua N Rd
Chunglun Bus Terminal
Nanking East Rd
Kunming Rd
Chunghua Rd
Train Station
Chungshan S Rd
Hsinsheng S Rd
Chang'an East Rd
Pate Rd
Chunghsiao
Dinghao Area East Rd
South Korean Embassy
Kangting Rd
Chienkuo S Rd
Chunghsiao East Rd
Tourism Bureau
Kuangfu Rd
Sun Yatsen Memorial 國父紀念館
Wanhua District
Jenai Rd
Tunhua S Rd
Keelung Rd
Hoping Rd
AIT
Fuhsing Rd
Hsinyi Rd
Anho Rd
World Trade Center 世貿中心
Sanchangli
Wanta Rd
West Rd
Hoping East Rd
永和市 Yungho
Youth Park
Taiwan Normal University 師大
Shihta Rd
Hsinhai Rd
Taipei 台北
City
Tingchou Rd
Roosevelt Rd
National Taiwan University 台大
Language Training Center
To Chungho City & Yuantung Temple
KUNGKUAN AREA
Taipei International Youth Activity Center 國際活動中心
Tunnel

0    1    2 km

So far that sounds easy enough, but things are a little more complex than that. Major roads, such as Chungshan N Rd, are divided into sections. Thus, in Taipei we have Chungshan N Rd, Section 1, Section 2, Section 3 and so on right up to Section 7. Sometimes, instead of writing 'Wufu Rd, Section 3', they might write 'Wufu 3rd Rd', but the meaning is the same. A section is normally about three blocks long. When finding an address you really have to pay attention to which section you are in.

Taipei also has lanes. A lane, as the name implies, is a small side street and they never have names, just numbers. A typical address might read like this: 16 Lane 20, Chungshan N Rd, Section 2. The 16 simply refers to the house number and Lane 20 is the name of the lane which intersects with Section 2 of Chungshan N Rd. Now that doesn't sound too difficult, but is there an easy way to locate Lane 20?

Fortunately, the answer is yes. As you walk along Chungshan N Rd, Section 2, keep your eye on the house numbers. Lane 20 should intersect with Chungshan N Rd just near a building bearing the street address number 20. Once you understand this system, it becomes very easy to find the lane you are looking for.

Occasionally, you'll have to find an alley. An alley is a lane which runs off a lane. Again, the same system is used. Alley 25 will intersect with a lane, and the house at the corner of this intersection should be number 25. A typical address could be 132 Alley 25, Lane 20, Chungshan N Rd, Section 2, Taipei. It may sound complicated, but it's very systematic.

Budget travellers in particular should learn this method of finding places, as many of the inexpensive youth hostels in Taipei are in these small lanes.

It's worthwhile spending your 1st day in Taipei exploring the city on foot – it's a bustling place with plenty to see. Chungshan N Rd is a good place to start, as it is full of shops, restaurants and tempting bakeries. If you are looking for a cheap meal, get off the main street and into the narrow lanes and alleys where you will find all sorts of tiny restaurants selling various inexpensive Chinese delicacies. The Dinghao area in east Taipei and Kungguan near National Taiwan University are other good walking areas.

## Information

**Visas** The place to go in Taipei for visa renewals is the Foreign Affairs Police (tel (02) 3817475) (*wàishì jǐngchá*), 96 Yenping S Rd, close to Chunghua Rd.

**Tourist Information** The Taiwan Tourism Bureau (tel (02) 7218541), 9th floor, 280 Chunghsiao E Rd, Section 4, is not far from the Sun Yatsen Memorial and the South Korean Embassy. While you are there, be sure to pick up a copy of *This Month in Taiwan* and some maps.

There is a Tourist Information Hot Line (tel (02) 7173737), which accepts calls from 8 am to 8 pm, every day of the year. The operators speak English and can provide useful information such as the schedule of cultural events, exhibitions, even current bus and train schedules. They also provide an emergency translation service if you need to summon the police or an ambulance. They will also forward your complaints to the relevant authorities. I have called them a few times for information and I can report that the service is excellent.

The most useful information for many tourists is a street map. The ones available from the Tourism Bureau (for free) are pretty good, but it's worth investing NT$50 in a more detailed map if you intend to spend any length of time in Taipei. The maps available from the street stalls by the bus stops are usually just in Chinese characters; from bookstores and hotel gift shops you can pick up English-language maps, though they aren't nearly as detailed as the Chinese ones. I also find it useful to carry a small pocket compass to get the map oriented correctly, though it isn't absolutely necessary.

Apart from the notice boards at the youth hostels, there is a good notice board for travellers at Taiwan Normal University,

Mandarin Training Center, 6th & 7th floors, 129-1 Hoping E Rd, Section 1, Taipei.

**Post** The GPO in Taipei is on Chunghsiao W Rd, close to the train station, and is called the North Gate Post Office. The North Gate is that old monument just across the street from the post office.

**Telecommunications** The government-owned company ITA is responsible for calls within the island and overseas. You can also send fax messages, telegrams and telexes from the offices listed. The main office (tel (02) 3443781) is at 28 Hangchou S Rd, Section 1; it is open 24 hours a day. Other ITA branch offices are at:

CKS International Airport (tel (03) 3832790), 7 am to 9 pm
23 Chungshan N Rd, Section 2 (tel (02) 54174340), 8 am to 10 pm
118 Chunghsiao W Rd, Section 1 (tel (02) 3443785), 8 am to 10 pm
Sungshan Domestic Airport (tel (02) 7126112), 8 am to 9 pm

**Money – local banks** The International Bank of China (ICBC) is the best place to change money, as they have numerous branches strategically located throughout the city and they handle almost any brand of travellers' cheques.

Branch near Train Station
6 Chunghsiao W Rd, Section 1 (tel (02) 3118298)
Chungshan Branch
15 Chungshan N Rd, Section 2 (tel (02) 5119231)
Nanking Branch
198 Nanking E Rd, Section 3 (tel (02) 7516041)
Dinghao District
233 Chunghsiao E Rd, Section 4 (tel (02) 7711877)
Shihlin District
126 Chungshan N Rd, Section 6 (tel (02) 8345225)

The other most likely place to change money is at the Bank of Taiwan. Expect more forms to fill out here than at other banks. Major branches in Taipei include:

Main Branch
120 Chungching S Rd, Section 1 (tel (02) 3147377)
Chungshan Branch
150 Chungshan N Rd, Section 1 (tel (02) 5423434)
Dinghao District
560 Chunghsiao E Rd, Section 4 (tel (02) 7073111)
Shihlin District
248 Chungshan N Rd, Section 6 (tel (02) 8367080)

You can also change money at the main branches of the Changhua Commercial, First Commercial and Hua Nan Commercial banks.

**Money – foreign-owned banks** American Express only cashes American Express travellers' cheques. Similarly Bank of America, Citibank, etc will only change travellers' cheques issued by their own banks.

American Express
214 Tunhua N Rd (tel (02) 7151581)
Bank of America
Bank Tower, 205 Tunhua N Rd (tel (02) 7154111)
Chase Manhattan Bank
72 Nanking E Rd, Section 2 (tel (02) 5378100)
Citibank
742 Minsheng E Rd (tel (02) 7155931)
Dai-Ichi Kangyo Bank
137 Nanking E Rd, Section 2 (tel (02) 5614371)
Grindlays Bank
2nd floor, 123 Nanking E Rd, Section 2 (tel (02) 5427456)
Hollandsche Bank-Unie
61-1 Sungchiang Rd (tel (02) 5818131)
Metropolitan Bank & Trust
107 Chunghsiao E Rd, Section 4 (tel (02) 7766355)
Morgan Bank
Bank Tower, 205 Tunhua N Rd (tel (02) 7122333)
Security Pacific National Bank
2nd floor, 62 Tunhua N Rd (tel (02) 7775533)
Société Générale
683 Minsheng E Rd (tel (02) 7155050)
Standard Chartered Bank
337 Fuhsing N Rd (tel (02) 7166261)
Toronto Dominion Bank
2nd floor, 337 Fuhsing N Rd (tel (02) 7162160)

**Bookstores** The most popular place at which to buy English-language books in

Taipei is Caves Books (tel (02) 5371666) (*dūnhúang shūjú*), 103 Chungshan N Rd, Section 2. They also have a shop at 107 Chungshan N Rd, Section 2, which sells Chinese books. Besides books they sell major foreign newspapers, magazines, music cassettes and tickets for concerts and other cultural events.

Lucky Bookstore (tel (02) 3927111), 129-1 Hoping E Rd, Section 1, is similar to Caves and is well known in Taipei as the place to buy books and cassette tapes for studying Chinese. The store is in the same building as the Mandarin Training Center, Taiwan Normal University.

Lai Lai Book Company (tel (02) 3414265), 8 Lane 94, Hsinsheng S Rd, is close to National Taiwan University and has a good selection of books even though it's a small store. They import a lot of books directly from abroad and distribute to other stores.

Bookman Books Ltd (tel (02) 3924715, 3928617) (*shūlín shūdiàn*), 5 Lane 62, Roosevelt Rd, Section 4 (near National Taiwan University), is a very small store but has a reasonably good collection of English literature.

For expensive coffee table books, the best place in Taipei is Eslite (tel (02) 7755977) 477 Tunhua South Rd, at the corner with Jenai Rd. Another English-language bookshop in Taipei is Imperial Book, Sound & Gift (tel (02) 5917633), 615 Linsen N Rd.

**Libraries** The American Institute in Taiwan (AIT) maintains a library at 54 Nanhai Rd (tel (02) 3075639), across from the Botanical Gardens. The sign on the library says 'American Cultural Center'. Hours are noon to 6 pm Monday to Saturday.

Those whose interests are business-oriented will find the library at the American Trade Center (tel (02) 7132579), 600 Minchuan E Rd, more useful. Perhaps an even better business library is maintained by the China External Trade Development Council (CETRA) (tel (02) 7251111), 5 Hsinyi Rd, Section 5.

National Taiwan University (*táiwān dàxúe* or *táidà*) on Roosevelt Rd, Section 4, has a good library with mostly Chinese but also English books. Other large universities in Taiwan have English-language sections in their libraries. For Chinese books, there is the National Central Library (*zhōngyāng túshūgŭan*) on Chungshan S Rd near the Chiang Kaishek Memorial.

**Laundry** The logical places to look for inexpensive laundry services are in the alleys around National Taiwan University (*táidà*) and Taiwan Normal University (*shīdà*). One of the many places is *shīdà zìzhù xǐyī* (tel (02) 3621047), 72 Lungchuan St. Lungchuan St is one block east of Shihta Rd and runs parallel to it.

**Hospitals** The Adventist Hospital has English-speaking doctors and caters to foreigners. It also charges very high prices for medical care, but if you have health insurance you might be covered. The other hospitals are government-run and very cheap for the high standard of service provided, but public hospitals in Taipei can be unbelievably crowded.

Adventist Hospital (*tái ān yīyùan*) 台安醫院
  424 Pate Rd, Section 2 (tel (02) 7718151)
Chang Gung Memorial Hospital (*cháng gēng yīyùan*) 長庚醫院
  199 Tunhua N Rd (tel (02) 7135211)
Mackay Memorial Hospital (*mǎjiē yīyùan*) 馬偕醫院
  Chungshan N Rd, Section 2 (tel (02) 5433535)
National Taiwan University Hospital (*táidà yīyùan*) 台大醫院
  1 Changte St (tel (02) 3123456)
Tri-Service General Hospital (*sānjūn zhōng yīyùan*) 三軍總醫院
  226 Tingchow St (tel (02) 3117001)
Veterans General Hospital (*róngmín zhōng yīyùan*) 榮民總醫院
  201 Shihpai Rd, Section 2 (tel (02) 8712121, English extension 3530)

**Mountain Permits** To get a mountain permit, visit the Foreign Affairs Office, Taiwan Provincial Police Administration, 7 Chunghsiao E Rd, Section 1, directly across the street from the Lai Lai Sheraton Hotel.

**Baggage Storage** If you want to leave some of your luggage in Taipei, the best place to store your things is in the baggage checkroom at the Taipei train station. Actually, the checkroom is in a separate building about 100 metres to the east of the train station. The charge is NT$12 per day per bag and you can get your luggage whenever you want it. The checkroom is open daily from 7 am to 10 pm. A passport or some other identification is needed.

In most other large cities in Taiwan you can also find baggage checkrooms at train stations, but the hours will be shorter, around 8 am to 8 pm, and they will probably close for lunch.

## National Palace Museum
*(gùgōng bówù yùan)* 故宮博物院

It's no exaggeration to say that Taipei's National Palace Museum, in the northern suburb of Waishuanghsi, ranks as one of the four best in the world, in a class with the Louvre, British Museum and Metropolitan Museum of Art. Of course, museums are not for everybody, but for those who love art and archaeology the National Palace Museum is a must. The museum holds the world's largest collection of Chinese artefacts, over 600,000 items in all. There are so many that they cannot possibly be displayed all at once. Therefore, the display is rotated, with the majority of the treasures kept well protected in air-conditioned vaults buried deep in the mountainside.

Most of this priceless art was moved from the Forbidden City in Peking at the end of WW II because it was feared the communists would destroy the artefacts. These fears may well have been justified, given the massive destruction to temples and historical sites in China caused by rampaging Red Guards during the Cultural Revolution of the 1960s.

You can see artefacts made from jade, bronze, porcelain, lacquerware and enamel. There is also tapestry and embroidery, and many priceless documents and books containing excellent examples of ancient Chinese calligraphy.

There are good English tours of the museum twice daily at 10 am and 3 pm. The tours will run even if only one person shows up. In October, there are special showings of rare and fragile artefacts and this is the best time to visit. You can buy excellent reproductions of rare paintings for the low price of NT$50 each – probably the best buy in Taiwan. Photography is prohibited inside the museum and you are requested to check cameras at the entrance.

Just to the east of the museum steps is the Chihshan Garden, which has fine landscaping but costs NT$10 for admission. The museum has its own restaurant, which is not too expensive and much better than the not-too-good restaurants across the street.

The museum is open from 9 am to 5 pm every day of the year; admission is NT$30. It's too far to walk there from the centre of the city. Buses which go to the museum are Nos 210, 213, 255 and 304. You must pay double fare (NT$20) as it is a long way out.

## Chinese Culture & Movie Studio
*(zhōngguó diànyǐng wénhùa chéng)*
中國電影文化城

The movie studio is within walking distance of the National Palace Museum so a lot of foreigners come here to take a look. Basically, it's a movie set where the buildings are all designed in the traditional style of ancient China. If you watch TV in Taiwan, you are sure to see some Chinese kung fu dramas – this is where they are filmed. The buildings are a good introduction to Chinese architecture and you may also have the chance to see some filming.

The movie set is open to the public daily from 8.30 am to 5 pm, but is closed during lunch hour (noon to 1 pm). There is an entrance fee of NT$80. There is also a wax museum – entrance fee NT$30 – which contains some realistic figures from Chinese history.

Overall, my impression is that the movie studio is a bore. Only the wax museum is interesting. If you're fortunate enough to catch them filming a movie, that might be worth seeing. Most travellers give this place the thumbs down. However, it has been heavily promoted in the tourist literature and that's why I mention it here.

The Chinese Culture & Movie Studio (tel (02) 8812681), 34 Chihshan Rd, Section 2, Shihlin, is a 10 minute walk from the National Palace Museum. It's on the left side of the road as you walk away from the museum and has a big sign in Chinese but not in English. Right next to the movie studio is Soochow University (*dōngwú dàxúe*), but there isn't anything much to see there either.

### Martyrs' Shrine
*(zhōng liè cí)* 忠烈祠

The shrine is a rather peaceful place with beautiful buildings set against a backdrop of hills overlooking the city. It was built to honour those who died fighting for their country. There are two rifle-toting military police who stand guard at the gate in formal dress – absolutely rigid, not moving a muscle or blinking an eye – while tourists harass them. It's a wonder these guys don't run amok and bayonet a few of their camera-clicking tormentors.

The Martyrs' Shrine is less than a 10 minute walk along Peian Rd, due east of the Grand Hotel. You can go there on bus Nos 21, 42, 208, 213, 247 or 267.

### Fine Arts Museum
*(měi shù gǔan)* 美術館

This museum (tel (02) 5957656), 181 Chungshan N Rd, Section 3, is just south of the Grand Hotel. As art museums go it's OK, but it pales into insignificance when compared to the National Palace Museum. It's open from 9 am to 5 pm daily, except Monday, and from 1 pm to 9 pm on Wednesday. Bus Nos 21, 40, 42, 203, 208, 210, 213, 216, 217, 218, 220, 224, 240, 260, 266, 301, 304, 308 and 310 pass by.

### Botanical Gardens
*(zhíwù yúan)* 植物園

The Botanical Gardens, on Nanhai Rd, south of the central area and near the American library, are a pleasant retreat from the noisy city. There is a beautiful lotus pond in the gardens; it's one of the ponds adjacent to the

National Museum of History, National Science Hall and National Arts Hall – all worth looking into.

The National Museum of History seems to be most popular with travellers. It's sort of a scaled-down version of the National Palace Museum. It has a good pottery collection and is open from 9 am to 5 pm, 7 days a week, NT$10 admission. You can get there on bus Nos 1, 24, 204, 242 or 259.

### New Park
*(xīn gōngyúan)* 新公園

Taipei New Park is another good place to take refuge from the urban chaos. The pleasant tree-shaded grounds contain a lake, pagoda and pavilions. Just adjacent to the park is the Taiwan Provincial Museum. You can get to New Park on bus Nos 0-North, 20, 48, 65, 69, 222, 224, 237, 241, 243, 245, 251 or 259.

### Taiwan Provincial Museum
*(shěnglì bówùgǔan)* 省立博物館

This museum (tel (02) 3814700) is at 2 Hsiangyang Rd, adjacent to New Park. There are interesting displays of artefacts made by Taiwan's aborigines. Of special interest to some is an excellent, well-organised display of herbs on the main floor. It's open daily from 9 am to 5 pm. The museum can be reached on bus Nos 5, 20, 27, 48, 65, 222, 224, 236, 245, 249, 252, 259 or 263.

### Presidential Building
*(zhǒngtǒng fǔ)* 總統府

Very close to New Park is the Presidential Office Building in Presidential Square. Normally, there is not much to see here, but on Double 10th Day (10 October or National Day) there are enormous rallies and military parades at this site. Should you be in Taipei at this time you may want to see these impressive parades. For several weeks after Double 10th, the area is lit up like a Christmas tree and presents an excellent opportunity for night photography. One of the world's most dazzling displays of fireworks is held on the night of Double 10th over an island in the middle of the Tanshui

River. You can watch the fireworks from Huanho S Rd near the Chunghsing Bridge. The fireworks start around 7.30 pm, but be there earlier to secure a good viewing place. The fireworks run for 1 hour.

## Chiang Kaishek Memorial
*(zhōngzhèng jì niàn táng)* 中正紀念堂

This memorial hall is a fantastic piece of architecture and is surrounded by a magnificent garden, making it a popular place in the morning for joggers and practitioners of taichichuan (Chinese shadow boxing). These days it is more common to see people practising jazz dancing to the thump of disco music in the morning. There is a museum downstairs inside the memorial.

Within the grounds of the Chiang Kaishek Memorial is the National Chiang Kaishek Cultural Center (tel (02) 3925060). The Cultural Center consists of two buildings, the National Opera House and National Concert Hall. A schedule of events is published monthly and is available from the Tourism Bureau.

The Chiang Kaishek Memorial is on Hsinyi Rd, Section 1. Buses which pass nearby are Nos 18, 22, 20, 25, 38, 48, 60, 67, 70, 204, 209, 236, 237, 249, 253, 263, 270, 274 and 275.

## Postal Museum
*(yóuzhèng bówù gǔan)* 郵政博物館

If you have a particular interest in stamps, this is the place to go. Actually, historians might enjoy it too because there are many exhibits explaining the history of China's postal service all the way back to the Yuan Dynasty. The Postal Museum (tel (02) 3945185) is at 45 Chungching S Rd, Section 2. It's open from 9 am to 4.30 pm daily except Monday; admission is NT$5.

## National Taiwan University
*(táidà)* 台大

National Taiwan University is Taiwan's largest and reputedly best institution of higher learning. You can stroll around the large campus, visit the bookstore and use the library. If you want to meet Chinese students, you will find that most of them are quite friendly and are anxious to practise their English.

The university does have a good programme for foreign students who wish to learn Chinese, though many Westerners prefer the programme at nearby National Taiwan Normal University *(shīdà)* on Hoping E Rd, Section 1. Both these universities have excellent Chinese departments. National Taiwan University is on Roosevelt Rd, Section 4, in the city's Kungkuan district. Buses that stop near the campus include Nos 0-South, 10, 30, 52, 60, 236, 251, 252, 253, 311 and 501.

## Youth Park
*(qīngnián gōngyúan)* 青年公園

Youth Park is the largest park in the city. It's not special, but its facilities include swimming pools, tennis courts and a roller skating rink. This park is in the south-west part of the city along the Tanshui River. Buses that go there include Nos 0-West, 30 and 79.

## Chinese Opera
*(píngjù)* 平劇

There are not very many places in Taipei where you can see regularly scheduled operas. Operas are frequently performed at the Armed Forces Cultural Activity Center (tel (02) 3716832) *(gúo jūn wényì zhōngxīn)*, 69 Chunghua Rd, Section 1. The National Chiang Kaishek Cultural Center (adjacent to the Chiang Kaishek Memorial Hall) publishes a monthly schedule of events which often includes Chinese opera performances. The schedule is available from the Tourism Bureau. Unfortunately, performances at the Cultural Center tend to be expensive.

## Sun Yatsen Memorial
*(gúofù jì niàn gǔan)* 國父紀念館

This is an interesting place for history buffs, as it is stocked with many photographs of mainland China taken during the early part of the 20th century. Dr Sun Yatsen is an important figure in China's history. He is highly regarded, as a national hero and the father of his country, for the key role he played in the 1911 revolution, which overthrew the last dynasty and created the Republic of China. He is revered by both the Kuomintang and the Communist Party for his role in overthrowing China's last dynasty.

The Sun Yatsen Memorial contains an auditorium which is used for staging cultural events. Unfortunately, it isn't getting much use these days because the building has been closed for some time now. The reason is that Taipei has experienced several earthquakes recently and cracks have appeared in the building's structure. An attempt is being made to repair this, but when it will open again is anybody's guess. Still, you may want to have a look at the building from the outside. The Sun Yatsen Memorial is on Jenai Rd, Section 4, near the Tourism Bureau and the South Korean Embassy.

Buses which come close to the Sun Yatsen Memorial are Nos 19, 27, 31, 33, 43, 55, 207, 212, 240, 259, 263, 266, 270 and 504.

### World Trade Center
*(shì mào zhōngxīn)* 世貿中心

This huge exhibition complex is home to the product display shows of the China Export Trade Development Council (CETRA). The Center hosts several large trade shows every year and some are definitely worth seeing. The shows are not just for looking – you can often buy 'samples' directly from the manufacturer for bargain prices. Even if you don't buy, the shows can be a lot of fun. Most popular with foreigners are the Sporting Goods Show (April), the Cycle Show (bikes and accessories – April), the Footwear & Leather Goods Show (May), Computex (computer show – June), the Jewellery & Timepiece Show (September), the Toy Show (September) and the Electronics Show (October). You can get a complete schedule of the shows from the Tourism Bureau or from CETRA (in the World Trade Center).

The World Trade Center (tel (02) 7251111), 5 Hsinyi Rd, Section 5, is in east Taipei near the Sun Yatsen Memorial Hall. It's open Monday to Friday from 8 am to 5.30 pm and from 8.30 am to noon on Saturday. Children under 15 are not admitted.

### Lin Gardens
*(línjiā huāyúan)* 林家花園

The Lin Gardens (tel (02) 9653061) are in the suburb of Panchiao *(bǎnqiáo)*, southwest of Taipei proper. These classical gardens were constructed in 1894 as part of the Lin family's home. In the succeeding years the gardens were allowed to deteriorate – until 1976, when they were donated to the government. After a financial outlay of NT$157 million, the gardens were finally restored in 1987 and opened to the public.

Covering an area of only 1.2 hectares, the gardens are scenic and of historical interest. The area has been declared a historic site. The grounds have numerous pavilions, arches and ponds.

Admission is NT$60 and the gardens are at 9 Hsimen St, a 10 minute walk from the Panchiao train station. You could take a train to Panchiao, and then take a taxi or walk to the gardens. Also, bus Nos 264, 307 and 310 from Taipei pass nearby. The gardens are open from 9 am to 5 pm every day, except Monday and the day after public holidays.

### Lungshan Temple
*(lóngshān sì)* 龍山寺

This is an example of a mixed Buddhist-Taoist temple. It's extremely colourful and is packed with worshippers most of the time; the air is heavy with smoke from burning incense and 'ghost money'. Adjacent to the temple is an active market and two blocks away is the famous Snake Alley. You can get there on bus Nos 0-West, 9, 25, 38, 49, 62, 65, 201, 210, 215, 221, 231, 233, 242, 264, 265 or 601.

### Snake Alley
*(húaxī jiē)* 華西街

The night market held in Snake Alley is much more lively than the day market. At night you can see skilled snake handlers play with real live cobras as though they were wind-up toys. For a small fee, you can sample snake soup or drink a cup of snake bile – not for children. This is also the place to stock up on snake-penis pills and powdered gall bladder.

One of the reasons why the Chinese

Temple art

consume such exotica is that Chinese herbalists have claimed for a long time that the sexual organs of wild and venomous animals act as aphrodisiacs when eaten by people. If you care to experiment with these mysterious revitalising potions from the Orient, Snake Alley is the place to do it.

As you might have guessed, the presence of all those aphrodisiacs means there is also a good deal of prostitution in the Snake Alley vicinity. However, foreigners aren't likely to encounter it. Snake Alley is a tourist attraction, and the police have put heavy pressure on brothel operators to leave foreigners alone in this neighbourhood. Thus, Western males can walk through the alley without being solicited.

Buses going to Snake Alley include Nos 9, 25, 38, 49, 62, 65, 201, 210, 215, 221, 231, 233, 242, 264, 265 and 601.

### Paoan Temple
*(bǎo'ān gōng)* 保安宮
This lovely old Taoist temple is a short walk from the Confucius Temple. The address is 16 Hami St, not far from the Grand Hotel. Many travellers consider this to be one of the most interesting temples in Taipei. Take bus Nos 0-North, 2, 24, 26 or 246.

### Confucius Temple
*(kǔngzǐ miào)* 孔子廟
In sharp contrast to the Lungshan Temple, the Confucius Temple is a sedate place. There are no statues or deities and the only

time it comes to life is on 28 September, the birthday of Confucius (Teacher's Day), when there is an interesting festival held at dawn. Check with some of the tourist offices or your hotel to see if you can get a ticket if you are in Taiwan at this time. The temple is on Talung St, near Chiuchuan St and the Paoan Temple.

### Hsingtien Temple
*(xíngtiān gōng)* 行天宮
This is another Taoist temple worth visiting. It's at 261 Minchuan E Rd, at the intersection with Sungchiang Rd (north-east corner).

### Pishan Temple
*(bì shān yán)* 碧山巖
The Chinese name means 'Green Mountain Crag' but it refers to a magnificent temple perched on the side of a mountain with a breathtaking view of Taipei. The Pishan Temple gets surprisingly few visitors, at least on weekdays. The scenery is great and the area is laced with hiking trails. You can stay overnight in the temple for a NT$200 'donation' but food costs extra.

The temple is in the Neihu district, which is the high-class north-east part of Taipei. From the Hilton Hotel area (near the train station) take bus No 247 to the last stop. From there you must walk up the hill, following a paved road. Along the way you will pass the small Golden Dragon Temple *(jīnlóng sì)*; this is also a nice temple, but don't mistake it for your final destination,

which is higher up the mountain. Even if you're not particularly interested in temples, coming up here is a great way to escape the madness of Taipei.

### Places to Stay – bottom end

One of the cleanest and newest hostels in Taipei is the *Formosa-II* (tel (02) 5116744). How long it might stay clean is anybody's guess, but at the time I was there it was absolutely spotless. The hostel is on the 2nd floor, 5 Lane 62, Chungshan N Rd, Section 2. The price is NT$160.

The nearby *Formosa Hostel* (tel (02) 5622035), 3rd floor, 16 Lane 20, Section 2, Chungshan N Rd, is under the same management but does not have such a high standard as the Formosa-II. The location off Chungshan N Rd is convenient. It has a kitchen and washing machine and costs NT$150 in the dormitory.

Another favourite with travellers is the *Amigo Hostel* (tel (02) 5420292), 4th floor, 286 Chilin Rd. It is clean, has a quiet atmosphere and friendly management. The price is NT$160 in the dorm. Unfortunately, it's a fair distance from the centre of things, so you will have to quickly become familiar with Taipei's bus system. From the train station, take bus No 502 and get off at the corner of Minchuan E Rd and Chilin Rd, opposite the Ritz Hotel.

The *Happy Family Hostel* (tel (02) 3753443) is on the 4th floor, 16-1 Peking W Rd, about a stone's throw from the train station. The location couldn't be better! This very popular place is often full. The friendly management makes an effort to keep it clean in spite of the constant flow of travellers. The cost is also NT$160.

Under the same management is the *Happy Family II* (tel (02) 5810716), 2nd floor, 2 Lane 56, Chungshan N Rd, Section 2; it's a short walk away from the train station. It's a small hostel but very clean, and the owner lives on the premises. Call first because it's often full. Dorm beds cost NT$180.

The *Taipei Hostel* (tel (02) 3952950), 6th floor, 11 Lane 5, Linsen N Rd, is also very popular. It's not terribly clean, but has a very central location near the Lai Lai Sheraton Hotel. They charge NT$160 for a dormitory bed and they have a very good notice board for travellers, a laundry service and TV set, but no kitchen.

*Wendy's Hostel* (tel (02) 3718277) is attached to the Wan Bang Language Center, which is only open in the daytime – so that's when you must arrive if you want to get a room here. The dormitory costs NT$160. The hostel is near the train station, 4th floor, 41 Chunghsiao W Rd, Section 1. It's in the same building as the Cosmos Hotel – take the door just to the right of the main hotel entrance.

*Shoe's Trips Youth Hostel* (tel (02) 3819750) is on the 4th floor, 16 Kungyuan Rd, very close to the train station. They have double rooms with shared bath for NT$250 to NT$300. They also run the *Cambridge Cultural Exchange Restaurant* on the 3rd floor of the same building.

If you'd prefer to have your own room instead of a dormitory, Hankou St (*hànkǒu jiē*) 漢口街 near the train station is a good place to look.

If you'd prefer to have your own room instead of staying in a dormitory, about the best deal around is the *Phoenix Palace Hotel* (tel (02) 3713151) (*fènggōng dàfàndiàn*) at 4 Hankou St, Section 1, right near the train station. Prices are NT$500 to NT$600 for a double – not exactly cheap, but this is Taipei. The hotel is clean, friendly and comfortably air-conditioned.

Huaining St (*húainíng jiē*) 懷寧街 is just opposite the train station and is a happy hunting ground for relatively cheap hotels in the NT$500 to NT$600 range. Among the choices are the *Paradise Hotel* (tel (02) 3313311) (*nánguó dàfàndiàn*), 7 Huaining St, where doubles cost NT$550 to NT$700. Nearby is the *Yon Hong Hotel* (tel (02) 3611906) (*yǒngfēng bīnguǎn*), 10 Huaining St, where doubles are NT$500. Also nearby is the plush-looking *Chuan Chia Huam Hotel* (tel (02) 3814755) (*quánjiā huan bīnguǎn*), 4th floor, 6 Huaining St. Doubles cost NT$700.

**Government Hostels** The government operates a number of youth hostels which are very popular and rarely have room for a traveller. Most of the people staying in these hostels are students, both Chinese and foreigners, but others are visiting tour groups of overseas Chinese. Students are permitted to reside on a long-term basis. If you enrol in classes at either National Taiwan University or Taiwan Normal University, you might consider staying at one of these government hostels. Otherwise, you probably won't be able to get in.

*International House* (tel (02) 7073151) (*gúojì xúeshè*), 18 Hsinyi Rd, Section 3, dormitory costs NT$100
*Taipei International Youth Activity Center* (TIYAC) (tel (02) 7091770) (*gúojì húodòng zhōngxīn*), 30 Hsinhai Rd, Section 3, dormitory/double costs NT$100/300. Bus Nos 3, 209, 237 and 501 go there.
*Chientan Youth Activity Center* (tel (02) 5962151) (*jiàntán húodòng zhōngxīn*), 16 Chungshan N Rd, Section 4, dormitory/double costs NT$120/500

## Places to Stay – middle
There are literally hundreds of hotels in Taipei that fall into this price category. Some of the better known ones are listed here.

*China Hotel Taipei* (tel (02) 3319521, fax 3812349) (*zhōngguó dàfàndiàn*), 14 Kuanchien Rd, doubles and twins NT$2000 to NT$2200
*Cosmos Hotel* (tel (02) 3617856, fax 3118921) (*tiānchéng dàfàndiàn*), 43 Chunghsiao W Rd, Section 3, doubles NT$1600, twins NT$1800 to NT$2000
*First Hotel* (tel (02) 5418234) (*dìyī dàfàndiàn*), 63 Nanking E Rd, Section 2, doubles are NT$1700
*Flowers Hotel* (tel (02) 3123811, fax 3123800) (*húahúa dàfàndiàn*), 19 Hankou St, Section 1, doubles NT$1100 to NT$1500, twins NT$1250 to NT$2000
*Gala Hotel* (tel (02) 5415511, fax 5313831) (*qìngtài dàfàndiàn*), 186 Sungchiang Rd, doubles NT$2730, twins NT$2940
*Golden Star Hotel* (tel (02) 5519266, fax 5431322) (*jīnxīng dàfàndiàn*), 9 Lane 72, Chungshan N Rd, Section 2, doubles NT$900 to NT$1100, twins NT$1100 to NT$1200
*Keymans Hotel* (tel (02) 3114811, fax 3115212) (*húainíng lüdiàn*), 1 Huaining St, singles NT$1280, doubles NT$1360
*Kilin Hotel* (tel (02) 3149222) (*qílín dàfàndiàn*), 103 Kangting Rd, doubles NT$1680, twins NT$1890
*Leofoo* (tel (02) 5813111, fax 5082070) (*liùfú kèzhàn*), 168 Changchun Rd, doubles NT$2010, twins NT$2200
*Merlin Court Hotel* (tel (02) 5210222) (*húamào dàfàndiàn*), 15 Lane 83, Section 1, Chungshan N Rd, doubles/twins NT$1600/1800
*Mingfu Hotel* (tel (02) 5316068, fax 5628000) (*míngfù dàfàndiàn*), 1 Chungching N Rd, Section 1, doubles NT$1100 to NT$1300, twins NT$1400
*New Asia Hotel* (tel (02) 5117181, fax 5224204) (*xīnyà dàfàndiàn*), 139 Chungshan N Rd, Section 2, doubles/twins are NT$1600/1800
*Olympic Hotel* (tel (02) 5115253) (*aòlínbìkè dàfàndiàn*), 145 Chungshan N Rd, doubles NT$1200 to NT$1500, twins NT$1300 to NT$1700
*Orient Hotel* (tel (02) 3317211, fax 3813068) (*dōngfāng dàfàndiàn*), 85 Hankou St, Section 1, doubles NT$1200 to NT$1300, twins NT$1500
*Paradise Hotel* (tel (02) 3142122, fax 3147873) (*yílèyúan dàfàndiàn*), 24 Hsining S Rd, doubles NT$1400, twins NT$1700 to NT$1900
*Plaza Hotel* (tel (02) 5515251) (*húachéng dàfàndiàn*), 68 Sungchiang Rd, doubles NT$1100 to NT$1400, twins NT$1750
*Rainbow Guest House* (tel (02) 5965515) (*căihóng bīngŭan*), 91 Chungshan N Rd, Section 3, NT$1210 for a double
*Star Hotel* (tel (02) 3943121) (*fùmíngxīng dàfàndiàn*), 11 Hoping W Rd, Section 1, doubles/twins are NT$1300/1800
*YMCA* (tel (02) 3113201, fax 3113209) (*jīdūjiào qīngnián huì*), 19 Hsuchang St, doubles NT$940 to NT$1050, twins NT$1140 to NT$1250

## Places to Stay – top end
If a scenic view takes precedence over a convenient location, then the *Grand Hotel* wins first prize in Taipei for its beauty and magnificent setting. The hotel itself is an architectural masterpiece and the view overlooking the city can't be beaten. Visiting dignitaries usually stay there. However, the Grand Hotel is too far from just about everywhere to get around on foot, though it's a short taxi ride to the central area.

The *Hilton Hotel* and the *Lai Lai Sheraton* are close to the train station. All the hotels along Chungshan N Rd should also be considered. In fact, Chungshan N Rd is a much more pleasant part of town than the train station area. However, the upper-crust district of Taipei is in the eastern part of town, near the intersection of Chunghsiao E Rd and Tunhua Rd. The *Asiaworld Plaza* is another excellent hotel in this area. Many of these

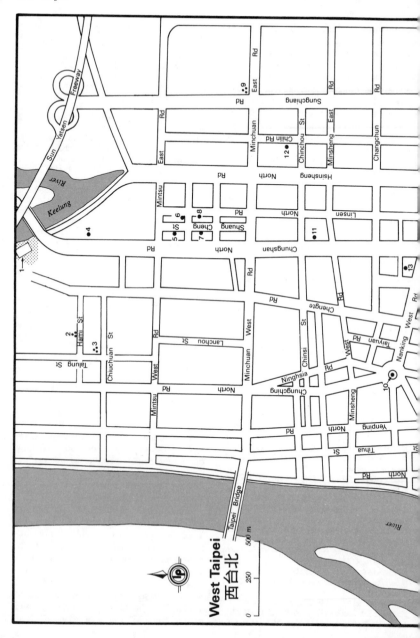

**West Taipei** 西台北

| | | | | | |
|---|---|---|---|---|---|
| 1 | Swimming Pool 游泳池 | 16 | East Coast Buses (Suao-Hualien) 台汽北站 | 29 | Far Eastern Department Store 遠東百貨 |
| 2 | Paoan Temple 保安寺 | 17 | Lai Lai Shopping Mall 來來百貨 | 30 | Presidential Building 總統府 |
| 3 | Confucius Temple 孔子廟 | 18 | GPO 郵政總局 | 31 | Foreign Affairs Ministry (Visa Changes) 外交部 |
| 4 | Fine Arts Museum 美術館 | 19 | Hilton Hotel 希爾頓大飯店 | | |
| 5 | Pubs | 20 | YMCA 基督教青年會 | 32 | Lungshan Temple 龍山寺 |
| 6 | President Hotel 統一大飯店 | 21 | Phoenix Palace Hotel 鳳宮大飯店 | 33 | National Central Library 中央圖書館 |
| 7 | Pubs | 22 | Provincial Police Administration (Mountain Permits) | 34 | Telephone Company Main Office 電信總局 |
| 8 | Imperial Hotel 華國大飯店 | | | | |
| 9 | Hsingtien Temple 行天宮 | 23 | Taipei Hostel | 35 | National Museum of History 歷史博物館 |
| 10 | Food Circle 圓環 | 24 | Lai Lai Sheraton Hotel 來來大飯店 | | |
| 11 | Caves Books 敦煌書局 | 25 | Chinese Handicraft Mart | 36 | Mandarin Daily News 國語日報 |
| 12 | Amigo Hostel | 26 | Wulai Bus Stop | 37 | International House 國際學舍 |
| 13 | Formosa Hostel | 27 | Bank of Taiwan 台灣銀行 | | |
| 14 | Happy Family Hostel | 28 | Police (Visa Extensions) 外事警察 | 38 | Lucky Bookstore 師大書苑 |
| 15 | West Coast Buses (Airport & Kaohsiun) 台汽西站 | | | | |

hotels have a 10% service charge and a 5% value-added tax (VAT).

*Ambassador Hotel* (tel (02) 5551111, fax 5617883) (*gúobīn dàfàndiàn*), 63 Chungshan N Rd, Section 2, doubles NT$3700 to NT$4600, twins NT$4300 to NT$5500

*Asiaworld Plaza* (tel (02) 7150077, fax 7134148) (*húanyà dàfàndiàn*), 100 Tunhua N Rd, doubles and twins are NT$4900

*Brother Hotel* (tel (02) 7123456, fax 7173334) (*xiōngdì dàfàndiàn*), 255 Nanking E Rd, Section 3, doubles NT$2800 to NT$3500, twins NT$3500

*Emperor Hotel* (tel (02) 5811111) (*gúowáng dàfàndiàn*), 118 Nanking E Rd, Section 1, doubles/twins are NT$1750/2000

*Empress Hotel* (tel (02) 5913261, fax 5922922) (*dìhòu dàfàndiàn*), 14 Tehuei St, doubles/twins cost NT$1900/2200

*Ferrary Hotel* (tel (02) 3818111, fax 3147055) (*húalì dàfàndiàn*), 41 Kangting Rd, doubles/twins NT$1600/2450

*Fortuna Hotel* (tel (02) 5631111, fax 5619777) (*fùdū dàfàndiàn*), 122 Chungshan N Rd, Section 2, doubles NT$3300 to NT$4200, twins NT$4200 to NT$4850

*Fortune Dragon Hotel* (tel (02) 7722121, fax 7210302) (*lóngpǔ dàfàndiàn*), 172 Chunghsiao E Rd, Section 4, doubles and twins NT$2940 to NT$4620

*Gloria Hotel* (tel (02) 5818111, fax 5815811) (*húatài dàfàndiàn*), 369 Linsen N Rd, doubles and twins NT$3500 to NT$4500

*Golden China Hotel* (tel (02) 5215151, fax 5312914) (*kānghúa dàfàndiàn*), 306 Sungchiang Rd, doubles and twins NT$2500 to NT$3500

*Grand Hotel* (tel (02) 5965565, fax 2948243) (*yúanshān dàfàndiàn*), 1 Chungshan N Rd, Section 4, doubles NT$3360 to NT$3900, twins NT$3780 to NT$4410

*Hilton International Taipei* (tel (02) 3115151, fax 3319944) (*xī ěrdùn dàfàndiàn*), 38 Chunghsiao W Rd, Section 1, doubles NT$3800 to NT$4600, twins NT$4250 to NT$5100

*Howard Plaza Hotel* (tel (02) 7002323, fax 7000729) (*fúhúa dàfàndiàn*), 160 Jenai Rd, Section 3, doubles NT$4400 to NT$5700, twins NT$4700 to NT$6600

*Imperial Hotel* (tel (02) 5965111, fax 5927506) (*húagúo dàfàndiàn*), 600 Linsen N Rd, doubles and twins NT$3100 to NT$4000

*Lai Lai Sheraton* (tel (02) 3215511, fax 3944240) (*láilái dàfàndiàn*), 12 Chunghsiao E Rd, Section 1, doubles and twins NT$4750 to NT$5800

*Majestic Hotel* (tel (02) 5817111, fax 5623248) (*měiqí dàfàndiàn*), 2 Minchuan E Rd, doubles/twins are NT$2600/3000

*Mandarin Hotel* (tel (02) 7121201, fax 7122122) (*zhōngtài bīnguǎn*), 166 Tunhua N Rd, doubles NT$3300 to NT$4500, twins NT$3900 to NT$4500

*Miramar Hotel* (tel (02) 5313456, fax 5029173) (*měilìhúa dàfàndiàn*), 420 Minchuan E Rd, doubles/twins are NT$3400/3600

*President Hotel* (tel (02) 5951251, fax 5913677) (*tǒngyī dàfàndiàn*), 9 Tehuei St, doubles NT$3600 to NT$4000, twins NT$4410 to NT$4810

*Rebar Crown Hotel* (tel (02) 7635656, fax 7679347) (*lìbā dàfàndiàn*), 32 Nanking Rd, Section 5, doubles NT$4200, twins NT$4200 to NT$4500

*Ritz Hotel* (tel (02) 5971234, fax 5969222) (*yǎdū dàfàndiàn*), 155 Minchuan E Rd, doubles and twins cost NT$4950

*Riverview Hotel* (tel (02) 3113131, fax 3613737) (*háojǐn dàjiǔdiàn*), 77 Huanho S Rd, Section 1, doubles/twins are NT$3500/4400

*Royal Hotel* (tel (02) 5423266, fax 5434897) (*lǎoyé dajiudian*), 37-1 Chungshan N Rd, Section 2, doubles/twins NT$4000/5000

*Royal Palace Hotel* (tel (02) 7766599, fax 7527388) (*háolì dàfàndiàn*), 81 Taan Rd, doubles/twins NT$2050/2550

*San Polo Hotel* (tel (02) 7722121) (*sānpú dàfàndiàn*), 172 Chunghsiao E Rd, Section 4, doubles are NT$3570

*Santos Hotel* (tel (02) 296311, fax 5963120) (*sāndé dàfàndiàn*), 439 Chengte Rd, doubles and twins cost NT$3100

*United Hotel* (tel (02) 7731515, fax 7412789) (*gúoliàn dàfàndiàn*), 200 Kuangfu S Rd, doubles NT$3250 to NT$3350, twins NT$3600 to NT$4000

## Places to Eat

Many cheap foodstalls and restaurants can be found in the small lanes and alleys off the main streets. It is possible to enjoy a filling noodle dish for around NT$20. Keep your eyes open for cafeterias where you can just point to what you want. Restaurants on the main boulevards are of course more expensive.

**Budget Eats** Besides back alley foodstalls, there is a large collection of cheap restaurants in a place called the *Food Circle* (*yúanhúan*), at the intersection of Chungching N Rd and Nanking W Rd. In addition to the Food Circle itself, street vendors appear at night in all the side streets adjoining the circle. It's one of Taipei's busiest night markets.

Where you find students, you find cheap restaurants. Just south of the train station is Wuchang St, the home of numerous 'cram schools' that train students to pass Taiwan's rigid university entrance exams. The high concentration of schools and students guarantees an infinite choice of cheap eating places in this area.

Cheap restaurants also surround Taiwan University and Taiwan Normal University. Don't forget to look in the small alleys.

A great place to sample Taiwan's famous dumplings (*shǔijiǎo*) is at the row of restaurants on the north-west corner of Linsen N Rd and Nanking E Rd. These places charge NT$2 for each dumpling.

The 2nd floor of the Taipei train station has a collection of reasonably priced restaurants.

A place you must visit – if only to look at it – is *FM Station* (tel (02) 3615788), 36 Chunghsiao W Rd, Section 1, next to the Hilton Hotel. The basement is chock-a-block with food stalls and is a popular hangout for Taipei's trendy set. Prices are moderate. Upstairs you can buy everything from Elvis Presley posters to bright orange underwear.

**Fast Food** American-style fast-food chains seem to be everywhere in Taipei. The Dinghao area of east Taipei is a haven for gourmets in search of fast-food cuisine. Among the choices are *McDonald's* at 183 Chunghsiao E Rd, Section 4; *Wendy's* at 209 Chunghsiao E Rd, Section 4; *Kentucky Fried Chicken* at 71 Chunghsiao E Rd, Section 4; and *Pizza Hut* at 130 Chunghsiao E Rd, Section 4.

In north-east Taipei there is a *Swensen's* at 218 Tunhua N Rd; *Wendy's* at 116 Tunhua N Rd; and *Dunkin' Donuts* at 1032-2 Minsheng E Rd. There are plenty of fast-food restaurants along Chungshan N Rd, such as...well, why go on? Just follow the familiar odours wafting down the street and you are sure to find what you're looking for.

**Coffee Shops** Not cheap places to hang out, but coffee shops are so pervasive that you can't help but fall over them. I happen to like

*I Love My Home Coffee Shop* (tel (02) 5616458), 56 Minsheng E Rd.

**Taiwanese Food** Traditional Taiwanese food largely consists of endless courses of exotic seafood, which is very expensive. One of Taipei's most notable Taiwanese restaurants is *Hai Pa Wang* (tel (02) 5626345) (*hǎi bà wáng*) 7 Hsining N Rd. They have several branch stores, including 59 Chungshan N Rd, Section 3 (tel (02) 5963141), and 169 Nanking W Rd, near the Food Circle (tel (02) 5377323).

**Mongolian Barbecues** A Mongolian barbecue is a fantastic feast. Make sure you don't eat breakfast, because you'll want plenty of extra room in your stomach so you can gorge yourself. One very popular Mongolian barbecue can be found in the basement of the *Ploughman Inn* (tel (02) 7733268), 8 Lane 460 Tunhua S Rd in the Dinghao area. Prices per person are typically in the NT$300 to NT$350 range.

Another Mongolian barbecue place is the *Fauchon Barbecue* (tel (02) 8712000), 105 Tienmu W Rd. They charge NT$280 for adults. Also try the *Log Cabin* (tel (02) 5367144), 1 Lane 39, Chungshan N Rd, Section 2 (by the Hotel Royal) and the *Genghis Khan Restaurant* (tel (02) 7113655), 176 Nanking E Rd, Section 3.

**Other Speciality Restaurants** Korean food can be had for moderate prices at the *Seoul Korean Barbecue* (tel (02) 5112326) (*hànchéng cāntīng*), 4 Lane 33, Chungshan N Rd, Section 1. You can try Thai food at *Ban-Thai Restaurant* (tel (02) 5233362), 8 Lane 78, Sungchiang Rd. *Hai Pa Wang* (tel (02) 5312205) operates a Szechuan-style restaurant at 287 Chang'an W Rd.

The place to go for German food is *Zum Fass* (tel (02) 5313815), 55 Lane 119, Linsen N Rd. Fine French food is available at *Cannes Restaurant* (tel (02) 7006488), 26-3 Jenai Rd, Section 3. The best Italian food in town is at *La Bettola* (tel (02) 8828290), 57 Wenlin Rd, Shihlin. You can guess what kind of food is served at *Chalet Swiss* (tel (02)

7152051), 47 Nanking E Rd, Section 4. Taiwan's first Mexican restaurant is *La Casita* (tel (02) 3415680), 2nd floor, 782 Tingchou Rd, near National Taiwan University. They also serve vegetarian dishes.

If you want Japanese food, you have to pay Japanese prices. You can thin out your wallet at *Tsu Ten Kaku* (tel (02) 5117372), 8 Lane 53, Chungshan N Rd, Section 1. Japanese *teppanyaki* (steak with mushrooms and bean sprouts) can be had at *Flamingo Teppanyaki* (tel (02) 5217722), 23 Chang'an Rd, Section 1.

There is a budget vegetarian restaurant near Taiwan Normal University called *Yeang Sheng Jai* (tel (02) 3212830) at 4 Lane 59, Shihta Rd. Actually, the whole area abounds in vegetarian restaurants.

The *Wooden Nickel Saloon* (tel (02) 7211312), 124 Chunghsiao E Rd, has the usual darts and pub decor, but also serves such delicacies as Texas chilli and tacos.

*Jake's Country Kitchen* (tel (02) 8715289) serves such exotica as blueberry pancakes, tacos, pizza and cheesecake. The address is 705 Chungshan N Rd, Section 6, Shihlin. There is a 5 to 7 pm happy hour. *Sam's Place* (tel (02) 5942402), 2-2 Lane 32, Shuang Cheng St, specialises in chilli, hamburgers, pizza and sandwiches.

**Entertainment**
Taipei is a good city for nightlife. It may be more conservative than Bangkok or Manila, but if you've got even a little money to burn, you can have a great time in Taipei. Most businesses close around 11 pm to midnight, but clubs and dance halls may stay open until dawn.

In addition to the information in this book, read the advertisements in *This Month in Taiwan* and the *China Post*.

**Night Markets** A trip to Taipei wouldn't be complete without a trip to one or more of the city's colourful night markets. They are most active on weekends. The most exotic night market is in the Wanhua area between Chunghua Rd and the river (near the Lungshan Temple, in the oldest and most traditional part of Taipei). The centre of activities is Snake Alley.

There is also a night market around the Food Circle (*yúanhúan*) at the intersection of Nanking W Rd and Chungching N Rd. The biggest night market of all exists in the suburb of Shihlin, between Wenlin Rd and Dadung St, north-west of the Grand Hotel.

These markets are a gourmet's delight. Try the delicious oyster omelettes, steamed meat buns, tofu pudding, fruit milkshakes and whatever else looks good.

The Kungguan Night Market (*gōnggǔan yèshì*) is on Roosevelt Rd, Section 4, near Hsinsheng S Rd and National Taiwan University. It's very interesting and often so crowded with students that there is hardly enough room to walk.

The area around the Lai Lai Department Store is really busy at night. Ditto for Linsen N Rd near the Imperial Hotel.

**Cinemas** The largest collection of movie theatres is on Wuchang St, Section 2, near the Lai Lai Department Store. See the English-language newspapers – *China News* and *China Post* – for the current movie selection. The *China News* gives a much more thorough listing than the *China Post*. For some reason the newspapers don't have the addresses of the theatres, so they are given in the following list. The *yìshù diànyǐng yùan* is not listed in the newspapers but specialises in artistic, mostly European movies.

*Ambassador* (*gúobīn*)
    88 Chengtu Rd (tel (02) 3611222)
*Chang Chun* (*cháng chūn*)
    172 Changchun Rd (tel (02) 5074141)
*Golden Lion* (*jīn shī*)
    36 Hsining S Rd (tel (02) 3122993)
*Governor* (*zhǒng dū*)
    219 Chang'an E Rd, Section 2 (tel (02) 3633909)
*Great Century* (*dà shìjì*)
    136 Roosevelt Rd, Section 4
*Great World* (*dà shìjiè*)
    81 Chengtu Rd (tel (02) 3313017)
*Hoover* (*háo húa*)
    91 Wuchang St, Section 2 (tel (02) 3719380)
*King* (*gúowáng*)
    10th floor, 72 Wuchang St, Section 2 (tel (02) 3713594)

*Majestic*
    7th floor, 13 Chengtu Rd (tel (02) 3312270)
*New World* (*xīn shìjiè*)
    1 Chengtu Rd (tel (02) 3312752)
*Oscar* (*jīn xiàng jiǎng*)
    215 Chang'an E Rd, Section 2 (tel (02) 7118298)
*Shin Shin* (*xīn xīn*)
    4th floor, 247 Linsen N Rd (tel (02) 5212211)
*Sun*
    89 Wuchang St, Section 2 (tel (02) 3315256)
*Tashin* (*dà xīn*)
    87 Wuchang St, Section 2 (tel (02) 3315256)
*Tung Nan Ya* (*dōngnán yǎ*)
    3 Lane 136, Roosevelt Rd, Section 4 (tel (02) 3416839)
*yìshù diànyǐn yùan*
    7th floor, 116 Hanchung St

**MTV** Music & TV (MTV) clubs offer the chance to see movies on video tapes in either a large group room or in the privacy of your own little cubicle. These clubs are extremely popular in Taipei and offer a good opportunity to meet people, at least in the larger group rooms.

The competition between MTV clubs is keen and many of these places fold quickly. Among the best clubs that were still open at the time of writing was *Wall Street* (tel (02) 3811477) (*húa ěr jiē*), 5th floor, 83 Chunghsiao W Rd, Section 1.

*Attraction* is a good MTV club with several branches. The Fuhsing branch (tel (02) 7715937) is on the 2nd floor, 158 Fuhsing S Rd, Section 1. The Hankou branch (tel (02) 3822903) is on the 2nd floor, 3 Hankou St, Section 1.

*Kiss MTV* (tel (02) 5624052), 3rd floor, 289 Linsen N Rd, is open 24 hours. *Solar Systems*, 2nd floor, 8 Tunhua N Rd (just above the pub called Passion), is famous for its huge screens.

**Kala OK** If you like amateur singing contests, visit a *kala OK* (from the Japanese word *karaoke*). The Chinese love singing and if you visit a kala OK you will certainly be asked to sing. No matter how badly you sing, you will undoubtedly receive polite applause. The Chinese love to hear foreigners sing even if they can't understand a word you say. However, if your singing is truly

Kala OK advertisment

awful don't subject the audience to more than one song, for the sake of international relations.

You can easily find a kala OK even if you don't read Chinese. Just look for the neon sign that says 'OK'.

**KTV** This is kala OK and MTV combined. Want to sing along with your own movie? It seems to be popular with the Chinese, but not many foreigners get into it.

**Pubs** Taipei has an assortment of English-style pubs offering darts, beer and good Western food. Some places have live music, especially on Saturday night. If this interests you, the magic word to remember is Shuang Cheng St (*shuāng chéng jiē*). Shuang Cheng St is sandwiched between Linsen N Rd and Chungshan N Rd and runs in a north-south direction. It is lined with pubs and Western restaurants, but some of the best are in the little alleys running off this street.

The one place in this neighbourhood that continues to get rave reviews from travellers is *The Farmhouse* (tel (02) 5951764), 5 Lane 32, Shuang Cheng St. They have live music every night from 9.30 pm to 12.30 am. Some other places to check out in this area are the *Hope & Anchor Pub* (tel (02) 5962949), 16-3 Shuang Cheng St; *Mariner's Pub* (tel (02)

5963341), 6 Lane 25, Shuang Cheng St; *Pub Kristina* (tel (02) 5926573), 4-2 Lane 32, Shuang Cheng St; *City Music Pub* (tel (02) 5947788), 5 Lane 25, Shuang Cheng St; *Waltzing Matilda Inn* (tel (02) 5943510, 5961474), 3 Lane 25, Shuang Cheng St; and *Ploughman Pub* (tel (02) 5949648), 9 Lane 25, Shuang Cheng St.

One interesting pub not on Shuang Cheng St is the *Martini Pub* (tel (02) 5966360), 6 Chungshan N Rd, Section 3, on the south side of the Tatung Building.

The *Top Pub* (tel (02) 3923958), 1 Fuchou St, is close to the Mandarin Daily News.

Yet another popular gathering place for foreign devils is *The Doors* (tel (02) 7386658), 383 Fuhsing S Rd, Section 2. It's a nice pub, with good sandwiches, cheap beer and live music on Sunday.

*Passion* (tel (02) 7765692) is a large, classy pub in the fashionable Dinghao area. There's good food and music and a lot of foreigners go there, but it's still expensive even though there's no cover charge. There's dancing on Friday and Saturday nights.

One of the most interesting places to visit in Taipei is *Indian* (tel (02) 7410550), 196 Pate Rd, Section 2. It's hard to define what this place is – it's a pub, it's a restaurant, but with a difference. There is a skeleton of a dinosaur on the roof and the sides of the building. The interior decorating follows the same design scheme – dinosaur bones stick out of the walls, ceiling and floor. The waiters and waitresses wear dinosaur bone shirts. Beer is served in large wooden kegs. The place definitely has character and it's usually packed with customers, both foreign and Chinese.

**Discos & Hard Rock Cafes** The place that draws Westerners like a magnet is *Roxy II*, 2nd floor, 27 Pate Rd, Section 1. It has good beer and music. *Roxy III*, a small, jazz-oriented place with excellent music, is on the 2nd floor, 300 Roosevelt Rd, Section 3. It's more stylish than Roxy II and more expensive.

Linsen N Rd is a busy street at night and has numerous discos. One place that has become a landmark with foreigners is *Buffalo Town* (tel (02) 5641172), 12th floor, 289 Linsen N Rd. Foreigners are admitted free but the Chinese pay. Apparently the presence of so many foreign devils attracts a lot of Chinese groupies.

*Birdland* (tel (02) 3940077), 5th floor, 7 Chunghsiao E Rd, Section 1, is a small, cosy place with good music. It's closed on Mondays.

A good hangout close to Taiwan Normal University is *The Bushiban*, 2nd floor, 152 Roosevelt Rd, Section 3. Cover charge is NT$70.

In the fashionable Dinghao area you can brush elbows with Taipei's trendsetters at a place called *U2 Plaza* in the basement at 6 Lane 147, Chunghsiao E Rd, Section 4, where Chunghsiao E Rd intersects with Tunhua S Rd. Within U2 Plaza are several discos, such as *Rock City* tel (02) 7511804) and the *Day & Night Pub* (tel (02) 7771696), which is open 24 hours.

*Touch Disco* (tel (02) 3316957), 13th floor, 41 Chunghua Rd, Section 1, costs NT$200. There is a live band every Saturday at midnight.

Taipei's largest and slickest disco is *Kiss* (tel (02) 7121201), in the Mandarin Hotel, 166 Tunhua N Rd. Admission is NT$350. It's extremely popular with the locals, less so with foreigners.

**Beer Halls** Anho Rd is Taipei's beer house alley. The most famous beer house in the city is *Five Star Beer King* (*wǔ kē xīng*) (tel (02) 7017642), 95 Anho Rd. It's extremely popular and has good food.

Nearby is *Fandango Beer House* (tel (02) 7017540), 136 Anho Rd; it's popular and has a good, cosy atmosphere. A very inexpensive beer house in the same neighbourhood is *yìn jiǎ qiú zhǎng* (tel (02) 7075653), 133 Anho Rd.

**Restaurant Floor Shows** A few classy restaurants feature floor shows with some of Taiwan's most popular singers. Westerners rarely go to these shows because the songs are all in Chinese and the music suits local tastes. So before you shell out the money, you may want to watch some of the variety shows on Taiwanese TV to see if this type of music appeals to you.

One of the most elegant floor-show restaurants is the *Hoover Theatre Restaurant* (tel (02) 5967171) (*háohúa jiǔdiàn*), at 21 Fushun St. They serve Cantonese-style cuisine while you watch the floor show. A good meal will cost upwards of NT$500.

**Activities**
**Barbershops** A trip to a barbershop can be a delightful experience. From amongst the services offered you can have a haircut, shampoo, blow-dry, manicure, and massage of the head, neck and shoulders. Men can have a shave, and for an extra fee they will even clean the wax out of your ears. Prices can be as low as NT$100, though you could spend as much as NT$1000 in a luxurious place for the same thing. It's a real treat and still a bargain if you choose the right place.

Barbershops (*lǐfǎ tīng*) are generally for men. For women, there are beauty parlours (*měiróng yuàn*). But many places are unisex.

Alas, things are not always what they seem. There are barbershops, and then there are 'barbershops'. In some 'barbershops' not a hair gets cut nor a beard gets shaved – they are nothing but brothels!

How to distinguish a real barbershop from a house of ill repute? Usually, you can judge from the outside appearance. Real barbershops have windows that you can look through so you know what's going on inside. The brothels have mirrored glass or no windows at all. The pimp standing outside is also a sure giveaway. Brothels have gaudy bright lights and sometimes a neon butterfly. To the Chinese, a butterfly symbolises a man who cheats on his wife, 'fluttering' from flower to flower.

I'm not going to recommend that you do business at the mirrored-glass barbershops. But if you do, you might be interested in an advertisement from *This Month in Taiwan* (Vol 13, No 11) for the Central VD Clinic which said: 'Having VD problems? Don't hesitate to call us. Your problem is our problem.'

**Mahjong & Chess** Chinese friends may want to teach you how to play mahjong. Remember that gambling is illegal in Taiwan, so it is better to play just for fun. Besides, the Chinese have a well-deserved reputation for being good gamblers, especially when it comes to mahjong. If you are a beginner, the other players may well take you to the cleaners. Your Chinese friends may also teach you how to play Chinese chess (*xiàngqí*), a rather complex but very popular game in Taiwan.

**Exercise** If late-night carousing is making you feel run down, you can get in shape at Clark Hatch Physical Fitness Center (tel (02) 7416670), 86 Tunhua S Rd. Clark's competition is Body-Talk (tel (02) 7713212), 11th floor, 235 Chunghsiao E Rd, Section 4 (side entrance). Alternatively you can go jogging for free at the Taipei Municipal Sports Stadium, at the south-east corner of Nanking E Rd and Tunhua N Rd.

Another alternative is the Taipei Gym, Basement, 58 Hsinsheng S Rd, Section 3. There is a yellow sign with black Chinese letters – you have to walk around the corner and go down a flight of steps to get there. They offer aerobic classes and weightlifting. A 2 month membership for students costs NT$2000. Of course, you can just go running for free on the track at nearby National Taiwan University.

**Sauna** (*sān wēn lǔan*) Having a sauna and jacuzzi seems to appeal mostly to the Japanese tourists, but many Westerners appreciate it during Taipei's chilly, dreary winter. The Hilton Hotel has a good one for NT$500. It's open 24 hours.

**Swimming** There is a public outdoor swimming pool called *zàichūn yóuyǒng chí* on the west side of Chungshan N Rd, Section 3, just south of the Grand Hotel on the south side of the Keelung River. There is also a swimming pool in Youth Park (*qīngnián gōngyúan*) in

south-west Taipei. All outdoor pools are only open during the summer.

**Bowling** Good bowling facilities are available at *rén'ài bǎolíng qiúgǔan* (tel (02) 7719167), 466 Tunhua S Rd; *jiājiā bǎolíng qiúgǔan* (tel (02) 5037216), 223 Sungchiang Rd; *liùfú bǎolíng qiúgǔan* (tel (02) 3815854), 54 Hankou St, Section 2; *shīnjiāpō bǎolíng qiúgǔan* (tel (02) 5115431), 287 Chang'an W Rd; and *yúanshān bǎolíng qiúgǔan* tel (02) 8812277), 3rd floor, 6 Chungshan N Rd, Section 5, Shihlin.

**Things to Buy**
**Clothing** Be sure to check out the Dinghao Market (*dǐnghǎo shìchǎng*) for clothing and shoes. The market is in the alleys just north of Chunghsiao E Rd and east of Tunhua S Rd. A store to try in this area is Longtai (tel (02) 7219654), 48 Lane 390, Tunhua S Rd.

One store that I recommend for clothing is called Madame Fashion Company (*zhǔfù shāngchǎng*). Most of their clothing is made for export, but they have branch outlets throughout Taiwan. In Taipei, you can find their branch stores in FM Station (tel (02) 3615788), 36 Chunghsiao W Rd, Section 1, next to the Hilton Hotel; south of the train station (tel (02) 3315593), at 77 Wuchang St, Section 1; in Shihlin district (tel (02) 8825733), 120 Wenlin Rd, Shihlin; Dinghao Market (tel (02) 7528213), 51 Alley 9, Lane 390, Tunhua N Rd; and near National Taiwan University (tel (02) 3930724), 162 Roosevelt Rd, Section 4.

**Backpacking Gear** The place to go for backpacking gear is *táiběi shānshǔi*, 12 Chungshan N Rd, Section 1, just to the north of the intersection with Chunghsiao Rd. Just a few doors up the street is another good shop, *dēng shān yǒu* (tel (02) 3116027), 18 Chungshan N Rd, Section 1. Both shops have a wide selection of gear for hiking, climbing and camping, but even if you don't indulge in such activities, they're good places to replace a worn-out backpack so you can continue travelling.

**Flower Market** (*jiàrì huāshì*) 假日花市 This incredible outdoor market is only held on Sundays and holidays and is popular with foreigners. Even if you don't like flowers, it's nice to come here and look. The market is under an overpass on Chienkuo N Rd, between Jenai Rd and Hsinyi Rd, not far from AIT and the Howard Plaza Hotel.

**Jade Market** (*jiàrì yùshì*) 假日玉市 This is another outdoor market which is held only on Sundays and holidays. The market is underneath the overpass at the intersection of Pate Rd and Hsinsheng S Rd.

**Handicrafts** The Chinese Handicraft Mart (tel (02) 3217233), 1 Hsuchou Rd (near the intersection with Chungshan S Rd), is a non-profit government-sponsored organisation selling jewellery, furniture, arts and crafts. It's open every day from 9 am to 5.30 pm. They accept credit cards and travellers' cheques, do packing and arrange shipping.

**Cakes** A very good gift for your friends and relatives is some of Taiwan's delicious cakes and biscuits. When I say 'cakes and biscuits', I don't mean the usual kind you find in every bakery. These are special cakes, beautiful in appearance and delicious; they're made just for gift-giving and are unlike anything you've ever tried before. One of the best places for buying these is a shop called Kuo Yuan Ye (tel (02) 3821759, 3314729) (*guō yúan yì*), 12 Huaining St, just a few blocks south of the train station. There is another Kuo Yuan Ye (tel (02) 5946756, 5965719) in the north-west part of the city, near the Confucius Temple at 32-2 Yenping N Rd, Section 3.

**Cameras** Taipei's 'photography street' is Poai Rd, around the intersection with Kaifeng St. There are more than a dozen camera shops here and prices are about as low as you can find in Taiwan. Of course, Hong Kong is cheaper for imported Japanese cameras, but Taiwan-made accessories are very reasonably priced.

**Computers** Reasonably inexpensive Asia-brand computers can be bought from the following dealers: *láixīn* (tel (02) 3965781), 51 Pate Rd, Section 1; *lúolín* (tel (02) 3944812), 10 Roosevelt Rd, Section 2; and *qúanmín* (tel (02) 5962935), 181 Minchuan E Rd.

Macintosh fans should visit McEwan International (tel (02) 5024505), Suite 801, 344 Fuhsing N Rd. Another store specialising in Macs is Light River Information (tel (02) 7554570), 10th floor, 166 Fuhsing S Rd, Section 2.

Underneath the overpass on Hsinsheng S Rd, just north of Pate Rd, is the Kuanghua Bazaar (*guānghúa shāngchǎng*), which houses about a dozen small computer shops and stores selling electronic components. Most of the machines are generic. The quality of the computers is questionable, but it's an interesting place to browse.

**Department Stores** Amongst the large department stores in Taipei are:

Evergreen Department Store
   6 Nanking E Rd, Section 2
   466 Tunhua S Rd
Far Eastern Department Store
   2 Paoching Rd (near Chunghua Rd)
Lai Lai Shopping Mall
   77 Wuchang St, Section 2
Ming Yao Department Store
   200 Chunghsiao E Rd, Section 4
Shin Kong Shopping Center
   12 Nanking W Rd (near Chungshan N Rd)
Shin Shin Company
   247 Linsen N Rd
SOGO Department Store
   45 Chunghsiao E Rd, Section 4
Sunrise Department Store
   15 Fuhsing N Rd
Tonlin Department Store
   201 Chunghsiao E Rd, Section 4

Most of these department stores have supermarkets in the basement.

### Getting There & Away
The train station is easy enough to find, but there are three important bus terminals near the train station and another one 2 km to the east.

Probably most important is the West Bus

Station, where you get highway buses to major cities, including Taichung, Chiayi, Tainan and Kaohsiung. The West Bus Station is on Chunghsiao West Rd, a 3 minute walk west of the train station.

The East Bus Station is almost right in front of the train station. From here you get buses to CKS Airport and to Keelung.

The North Bus Station is on the north side of the train station. Here you can get buses to Hsinchu and Chungli, as well as to Hualien (transfer in Suao).

The Chunglun Bus Station is on the southwest corner of Pate Rd and Fuhsing Rd, over 2 km east of the train station. You can get there by taking city buses Nos 57, 69, 205 or 311. Important departures from Chunglun Station include buses to Chinshan Beach and Fengyuan.

For details of day trips from central Taipei to places of interest in the surrounding area, see the North Taiwan chapter.

### Getting Around

**Bus** Buses are certainly the cheapest way to get around Taipei other than on foot or by bicycle. Buses are frequent and the service is good. There are a few problems for English-speaking foreigners, however, in that the bus drivers don't speak English and the destination is written on the bus in Chinese characters. Armed with a street map, your destination written in Chinese characters and maybe a compass, you should be able to manage.

If you've been studying Chinese characters for a while, you'll be pleased to know that there is an excellent bus route guidebook in Chinese. It can be purchased from kiosks near the bus stops. The name of the guidebook is (*liányíng gōngchē zhǐnán*) 聯營公車指南. But if you can't read Chinese, it's of little use. There is also a reasonably good English bus guide available from Caves Books and Lucky Bookstore for NT$100, but the map (same price) is useless.

If you do get lost, you can always bail out and take a taxi, but again, most of the drivers don't speak English. I certainly recommend having your hotel name and address written

down in Chinese characters so that you can get back. Another tactic is to have the words for train station written down, as it makes a good reference point when using a map. The words for train station are *huǒchē zhàn* 火車站.

Buses cost a mere NT$8 a ride, but longer trips can be double or even triple this amount, as the fare is determined by the number of zones you travel through – also the exact change is required. Rather than fumbling for change and getting the bus driver all upset, it is much more convenient to buy a bus card (*gōngchē piào kǎ*) for NT$80, which is good for 10 rides.

Even though there are several local bus companies operating in Taipei, they will all accept this card. You can easily buy these bus cards from the street vendors near the bus stops in the little booths.

The bus driver will punch the card when you board, though sometimes he does it when you get off. Sometimes he punches it both when you get on and when you get off, but only if you have crossed two zones. Sometimes the driver hands you a ticket with a number on it. Save it, you must return it when you get off. The ticket tells him which zone you were in when you got on the bus. The various systems seem unnecessarily confusing, but this reflects the fact that there are numerous companies operating these buses and each company has its own way of doing things.

Somewhere near the driver should be a sign in Chinese or a red light telling you to pay when you get on (*shàng*) 上 or when you get off (*shà*) 下. Figuring out when you are supposed to pay can be confusing even for the Chinese.

There are air-conditioned buses that cost NT$10 per zone. On the air-conditioned buses you pay by handing over either the exact change or a special token which can be bought at the same roadside booths where bus tickets are purchased. You cannot use a bus ticket on these buses. If you travel across two zones, you need to have two tokens or else pay NT$20. All buses numbered in the 500 and 600 series are air-conditioned, but other buses may not be. You may want to keep two or three tokens handy for these air-conditioned buses, or else carry plenty of NT$10 coins.

The so-called 'cultural buses' are supposed to stop off at all the points of scenic and cultural interest in Taipei. This might sound like a big convenience for tourists, but in practice it's not so convenient because of the limited schedule. Cultural buses only run from 8 am to 5 pm on Sundays and holidays and there is one bus every 30 minutes. The fare is NT$10 and they run in a circular route, both clockwise and anticlockwise.

All other buses begin at 6 am and end around 11.30 pm. Some buses return on the same route, others make a circular route. To help you make some sense out of the bus system, the following section has all the important bus routes. Keep in mind that the routes change periodically so this information can get out of date. Good luck.

## South Area Cultural Bus (clockwise circular route)

Taipei train station, Lai Lai Sheraton Hotel, Dinghao Market, San Polo Hotel, Sun Yatsen Hall, World Trade Center, Howard Plaza Hotel, Holiday Flower Market, Postal Museum, National Museum of History, Youth Park, Lungshan Temple, Armed Forces Museum, North Gate and return to Taipei train station.

## North Area Cultural Bus (clockwise circular route)

Taipei train station, Ambassador Hotel, Fortuna Hotel, Taipei Fine Arts Museum, Shuanghsi Park, Chinese Culture & Movie Center, National Palace Museum, Martyrs' Shrine, Taiwan Visitors' Association, Hsingtien Temple, Mandarin Hotel, Sunday Flower Market, Chiang Kaishek Memorial, Taiwan University Hospital and return to the Taipei train station.

## 0-South (south Taipei circular route)

Kungkuan, pass the National Taiwan University (táidà), Roosevelt Rd, Little South Gate, Chunghua Rd, Taipei railway station, Jenai Rd, Hsinsheng S Rd, National Taiwan University, Roosevelt Rd and Kungkuan.

## 0-North (north-west Taipei circular route)

Kulun St to Chiuchuan St, Confucius Temple, Tihua St, south along Yenping N Rd (Hsimending area) to Chungching S Rd, Provincial Museum, Chingtao E

Rd, YWCA, Shin Shin Department Store, to Linsen N Rd, turn right on Minsheng E Rd to Sungchiang Rd, President Hotel, west to Chengteh Rd, back to Kulun St.

## 0-East (east Taipei circular route)

Minsheng area, turns onto Tunhua N Rd, Mandarin Hotel, Nanking E Rd, American Express, Chungshan N Rd, south to Taipei railway station, Chungching S Rd, Hoping W Rd, Taiwan Normal University, International House, Jenai Rd, Tunhua S Rd, Chang Gung Hospital and return to Minsheng area.

## 3 – GPO to Taipei Train Station

GPO, Taipei International Youth Activities Center, Da An Medical Service, Taipei Normal College, An Dong Market, Taiwan Normal University (shīdà), Electric & Power Company, Judicial Court, Poai Rd and Taipei train station. Return route goes to Henyang Rd (shoe area), Chungching S Rd, Judicial Court, Nanmen Market, Electric Company, Taiwan Normal University and GPO.

## 5 – Yungho to Taipei Train Station

Yungho, National Taiwan University Hospital, Botanical Gardens, Legislative Center and Taipei train station. A slow route due to severe traffic jams.

## 7 – East Garden Area to Train Station (circular route)

East Garden area, wholesale fruit & vegetable market (gǔo cài gōngsī), Fuhsing Theater, Lungshan Temple, Chunghua Rd, train station, National Taiwan University Hospital, Youth Garden, wholesale fruit & vegetable market and East Garden area.

## 9 – Three Happy Village to Snake Alley

Three Happy Village, Yenping Bridge, Tihua St, Da Tung Group Center, Nanking W Rd, North Gate, Chunghua Rd North station, Lungshan Temple and Snake Alley. Return route goes to West Gate Market, Poai Rd and Three Happy Village.

## 12 – Youth Garden to Minsheng E Rd Area

Youth Garden, Chunghua Rd, North Gate, behind the railway station, Food Circle (yuánhúan), Nanking W Rd, Boy Scout Activity Center, Chang Gung Hospital and Minsheng E Rd area. Return route goes by the Mandarin Hotel, Boy Scout Activity Center, Food Circle, behind the train station, Chunghua Rd North station and Youth Garden.

## 17 – Tachih (dàzhí) to Chunghua Rd North Station

Tachih (military language centre), Martyrs' Shrine, American Club, passes Grand Hotel, Tatung Company, Chia Hsin Cement Company, Ambassador

Hotel, Chungshan Market, Taipei railway station, Chungching S Rd, Henyang Rd (shoe area) and Chunghua Rd North station. Return route goes by Hagglers' Alley, Taipei train station and Tachih.

## 20 – Sanchangli to Chunghua Rd South Station

Sanchangli, Hsinyi Rd, GPO, American Institute in Taiwan (AIT), International House, East Gate Market, Kuomintang Headquarters, National Taiwan University Hospital, Henyang Rd and Chunghua Rd South station. Return route goes to Far East Department Store (Paoching Rd), National Taiwan University Hospital, Kuomintang Headquarters, International House, Chienkuo S Rd, AIT, GPO and Sanchangli.

## 22 – Wuhsing St to Chunghua N Rd

Wuhsing St (near Sungshan Temple), Theology College, post office, west on Hsinyi Rd, passing AIT, International House, East Gate Market, turns right past the telephone & telegraph office (get off for Chiang Kaishek Memorial), Chunghsiao E Rd, Lai Lai Sheraton Hotel, Hilton Hotel, Taipei train station, Chungching S Rd, Henyang Rd and Chunghua Rd. Return route goes by the Taipei train station, Lai Lai Sheraton Hotel, Jenai Rd, International House, AIT, post office, Theology College and Wuhsing St.

## 37 – Wuhsing St to Taipei Train Station

Wuhsing St (Sungshan Temple), Tunhua Rd, Regency Hotel, Jenai, Hsinsheng, Chunghsiao E Rd, Lai Lai Sheraton Hotel, Hilton Hotel and Taipei train station.

## 42 – Tachih *(dàzhí)* to North Gate

From Tachih (military language centre), Martyrs' Shrine, American Club, to Chungshan N Rd (get off here for Linkou Bookstore), Tatung Company, Mackay Hospital, turn right at corner to Food Circle and North Gate.

## 45 – Yungho to Food Circle *(yúanhúan)*

Yungho, Roosevelt Rd, turns at Hsinyi Rd, Chunghsiao E Rd, Nanking E Rd, Hsinsheng N Rd, Chang'an E Rd, City Hall, behind Taipei train station and Food Circle. Return by Nanking W Rd, Nanking E Rd, Chunghsiao E Rd, Jenai Rd, Roosevelt Rd and Yungho.

## 48 – Minsheng E Rd to Paoching Rd

Minsheng E Rd, Air Force Hospital, sports complex, Adventist Hospital, bus turns onto Futan Bridge, Jenai Rd, Regency Hotel, Jenai Rd, Country Hospital, Air Force Headquarters on Jenai Rd, Linchi St, Linsen S Rd, Kuomintang Headquarters, Chunghua Rd South station and Paoching Rd (near Poai Rd and shoe area). Returns by Provincial Museum, National Taiwan University Hospital.

## 52 – East Garden Area to Kungkuan

East Garden area, wholesale fruit & vegetable market, Fuhsing Theater, Snake Alley area, Chunghua Rd, Roosevelt Rd, Botanical Gardens, West Gate market, China Theater, Nanking W Rd, Yenping N Rd, Food Circle, Chungching N Rd, Minchuan E Rd, Linsen N Rd, First Hotel, Chang'an E Rd, Adventist Hospital, Tunhua Rd, Hsinyi Rd, Normal University Dormitory, Hoping E Rd, Roosevelt Rd, National Taiwan University and Kungkuan.

## 74 – Chingmei to Fuhsing N Community

Chingmei district (Roosevelt Rd, Section 5), north on Roosevelt Rd past Taiwan Normal University (*shīdà*), National Taiwan University (*táidà*), north on Fuhsing Rd past Jenai Hospital and Sesame Department Store to north end, near Sungshan Domestic Airport.

## 203 – Sungshan to Shihlin

From Sungshan Station west on Pate Rd, past Adventist Hospital and Chang'an E Rd, past Sesame Department Store and Oscar Theater, north on Sungchiang Rd to Hsingtien Temple, west on Minchuan Rd to Chungshan N Rd, north past the Grand Hotel, Minchuan College, Foremost, turns left at Ricardo Lynn furniture shop, left at Taipei American School, enters Shihlin district, returns to Chungshan N Rd and repeats the same route.

## 205 – Nankang to Wanhua

From Nankang district (near Academia Sinica) onto Nankang Rd, west on Pate Rd, past Adventist Hospital, Chunghsiao E Rd, Taipei train station, south on Chunghua Rd to Wanhua district (near Lungshan Temple).

## 206 – Tienmu to Chunghua S Rd

Circles Tienmu Chung 12th Rd, by Fulin Bridge, past the park on Chicheng Rd, right on Fulin Rd, Shihlin, Pailin Bridge, Yenping N Rd, Chunghua Rd North station and Chunghua Rd South station. Return route goes to Poai Rd, GPO, Yenping N Rd.

## 208 – Yungho to Tachih *(dàzhí)*

From Yungho (south Taipei) north on Roosevelt Rd, passes near Bethany School and National Taiwan University (*táidà*), Chungshan S Rd, turns right after the Handicraft Center, north on Linsen Rd to Minsheng Rd, west to Chungshan N Rd, past Grand Hotel, turns right on Peian Rd, past American Club, Martyrs' Shrine, National Defense Language School, Overseas Radio & TV, to Tachih. Return route goes past the Grand Hotel, President Hotel, east to Minsheng Rd, Linsen Rd, south to the Handicraft Center, south on Chungshan Rd, National Taiwan University and Yungho.

## 210 – National Palace Museum to South Gate

From National Palace Museum, Central Movie Studio and Soochow University to Chungshan N Rd, turns left past Grand Hotel, turns right to Food Circle and Yenping area, behind Taipei railway station, North Gate, Chunghua Rd, near Hagglers' Alley, ends at South Gate. Return by same route.

## 212 – Taipei Train Station to Nankang

From Taipei train station on Chunghsiao W Rd to Chunghsiao E Rd, Lai Lai Sheraton Hotel, Dinghao Market, Central Clinic, Continental Building, Sun Yatsen Memorial, Keelung Rd, Yungli Rd, Chunghsiao E Rd (Section 6), Shangyang Rd, Nankang Rd, Tsungyuan Rd, Jo Tsuan St and the Nankang train station.

## 213 – Palace Museum, Chunghua Rd, Waihsuanghsi

From National Palace Museum area through Tzuchiang Tunnel by Tachih (military language centre), Martyrs' Shrine, American Club, down Chungshan N Rd by Taiwan Cement, past the Taipei train station to Chungching S Rd, Hengyang Rd and Chunghua Rd. Returns direct to Taipei train station and goes on to Waihsuanghsi. This bus only runs its full route during rush hours; at other times it turns around at Tachih.

## 216 – New Peitou to Taipei Train Station

From New Peitou through Shihpai, down Wenlin Rd past Taipei American School, goes into Shihlin district and on to the Grand Hotel, down Chungshan N Rd, past the Hilton Hotel, circles around the central city area and the Taipei train station.

## 217 – New Peitou to Taipei Train Station

From New Peitou, past Tatung Electric in Peitou, past Shihpai on Wenlin Rd to Taipei American School, goes into Shihlin district, by the Yangming Theater, past Minchuan College, the Grand Hotel area, near Linkou Bookstore, down Chungshan Rd past Tatung Company and Taiwan Cement to Taipei train station.

## 218 – New Peitou to Chunghua Rd South Station & Wanhua

New Peitou, Shihpai, Shihlin district, south on Chungshan N Rd, Tatung, Taipei train station, Chunghua Rd North station and Chunghua Rd South station. Some of the No 218 buses go a few blocks more to Wanhua and some terminate at the Chunghua Rd South station.

## 220 – Tienmu to Chunghua Rd North Station

From traffic circle in Tienmu, down Chungshan N Rd, Section 7 (or Tienmu Rd 1), past Foremost and Shihlin Electric Company, Mingchuan College, across the bridge, south on Chungshan N Rd, Florida Bakery and Caves Books to Taipei train station, turn south on Chungching S Rd to Hengyang Rd (Far Eastern Department Store), end of line on Chunghua Rd behind the police station.

## 223 – New Peitou to Food Circle (yúanhúan)

From New Peitou, Tienmu W Rd to Shihpai and Shihlin area, to Chungching N Rd and to Circle Restaurant. Makes a loop around the Yenping Market area and back to the Food Circle.

## 224 – Tienmu, Shihpai to Taipei Train Station

From traffic circle in Tienmu (Chungshan N Rd Section 7, also called Tienmu Rd 1), Tienmu W Rd (Rd 3), down Shihpai Rd past the Veterans' General Hospital, Taipei American School through Shihlin district, down Chungshan N Rd, on to Chingtao W Rd, past the YWCA and to the Taipei train station.

## 230 – Yangmingshan to New Peitou Station

From Yangmingshan bus terminal (near the park) behind Yangmingshan, down Cherry Hill and terminates in New Peitou.

## 237 – Mucha to Taipei Train Station

Starts at Chengda University and goes via Hsinhai Tunnel, Taipei Water Works, International Youth Activity Center, Taiwan Normal University (shīdà), Hsinyi Rd, corner of Jenai Rd and Taipei train station.

## 243 – Chungho to Taipei Train Station

From Chungho goes north on Chungching S Rd to Chunghsiao W Rd past the Taipei train station. Returns to Chungho by Chungshan S Rd, Roosevelt Rd and Hoping E Rd.

## 245 – New Park to Panchiao

From the east side of New Park, south on Kungyuan Rd, passes Soldiers' History Museum, Kueilin Rd, Lungshan Temple and crosses Huachiang Bridge to Panchiao.

## 247 – Neihu to Chunghua Rd North Station

From Neihu, Tachih (military language centre), Martyrs' Shrine, American Club, past Mintsu Rd, Linkou Bookstore, down Chungshan N Rd, past Tatung, Taipei train station, Chungching S Rd, New Park, Hangyeng Rd and to Chunghua Rd North station.

## 250 – Yungho to Shihlin

Yungho, Chunghua Rd, behind Taipei train station, Chengchou Rd, Chungching N Rd and Shihlin.

### 251 – Mucha to Taipei Train Station

From Chunghsiao W Rd, south on Chungching S Rd past Presidential Building to Aikuo Rd, east to the circle beside Chiang Kaishek Memorial, south on Roosevelt Rd to Chingmei, east to Mucha. Returns by the same route. To go to the Chihnan Temple, change to the temple bus, which runs every 30 minutes.

### 255 – Waihsuanghsi to Chungching N Rd

From Waihsuanghsi, National Palace Museum, past the Movie Studio, Soochow University, past Foremost corner through Shihlin to Shedz, south on Yenping Rd to Chang'an St, Yenping Market area and the Circle Restaurant. Return route goes to Chungching N Rd and Mintsu W Rd to Shedz, Shihlin and Chungcheng Rd past Foremost and back to Palace Museum.

### 259 – Sungshan to Yungho

Sungshan Rd, Chunghsiao E Rd, Chunghsiao W Rd, Taipei railway station, Chunghua Rd, little South Gate, Botanical Gardens, crosses Chungshan Bridge and Yungho.

### 260 – Chinese Cultural University to Vegetable Market

Chinese Cultural University in Yangmingshan, down Yangte Rd to Shihlin, Foremost, turns south on Chungshan N Rd, Grand Hotel, Taipei train station, Chunghua Rd, Wanta Rd and the wholesale fruit & vegetable market.

### 266 – New Peitou to Sun Yatsen Memorial

From Fushen High School in New Peitou, to Peitou Highway, past Shihpai, Wenlin Rd past Taipei American School, by the Grand Hotel and on to Nanking E Rd, past the China Airlines office and the Municipal Stadium to the Sun Yatsen Memorial.

### 267 – Tienmu to Neihu

Traffic circle on Chungshan N Rd Section 7 (Tienmu), turns right on Tienmu W Rd to Veterans' Hospital in Shihpai, past the Rehabilitation Center, winding through the Shihpai area to Wenlin Rd, past Taipei American School, through Shihlin district, around the base of the Grand Hotel to Peian Rd, past the American Club, Martyrs' Shrine, Dominican School and on to Neihu.

### 268 – Tienmu to Taipei Train Station

Traffic circle on Chungshan N Rd Section 7 (Tienmu), via Tienmu 3rd Rd, Veterans' Hospital, Shihpai, Shihlin district, south on Chungshan N Rd and Taipei train station. Return route goes on Chungshan N Rd only.

### 271 – Yangmingshan, China Hotel, Shihlin

Yangmingshan, post office, Fushou Bridge, China Hotel, Kochih High School, Hsin An, Mingte New Village, Yangming Elementary School, Yungfu, Yungling, Lingtou, Mingshan district, Taipei High School, Fulin district, Chungcheng Rd, Taipower Company, Minchuan Commercial College, Shihlin.

### 277 – Veterans' Hospital to Rehabilitation Hospital

From the Veterans' Hospital in Shihpai to Wenlin Rd, past Taipei American School, through Shihlin district to Chungshan N Rd, Sungchiang Rd, Minsheng E Rd, Tunhua N Rd (near Bank of America), Nanking E Rd, Keelung Rd and Taipei City Rehabilitation Hospital.

### 278 – Chingmei District to Neihu

From Chingmei district to National Taiwan University, Normal University, Chunghsiao Rd and Sun Yatsen Memorial.

### 301 – Yangmingshan to Taipei Train Station

From Yangmingshan Park and bus terminal down Yangteh Rd to Calvary Baptist Church, Foremost, south on Chungshan N Rd, Chungshan S Rd, east on Chingtao W Rd, YWCA and Taipei railway station.

### 302 – Kuantu to Wanhua

From Peitou Park to Wenlin Rd, past Taipei American School in Shihlin district, south on Chungcheng Rd, Chungching N Rd, Food Circle, North Gate, Kunming St to Wanhua district. Goes south to circle at Kueilin Rd, Hsining Rd and Chunghua Rd, right on Kueilin Rd, turns right on Kangting Rd, Kueiyang St to make a circle around the Lungshan Temple district and returns to Hsining Rd. Returns by same route.

### 303 – Yangmingshan, Pingtung to Shihlin

From Shihlin district, Yangteh Da Rd up Yangmingshan, right at San Shih Ho Market onto Chingshan Rd, out into the countryside to Pingtung Village. This bus runs only every 30 minutes to 1 hour.

### 304 – Yungho to Palace Museum

Yungho to South Gate Market (Presidential Hall), Police Headquarters, Chunghua Rd (Hagglers' Alley), Circle Restaurant, north to Minchuan W Rd, Minchuan Girls' College, turns right by Foremost, goes by Shuanghsi Park, Soochow University, Movie Studio and National Palace Museum. Return route is nearly the same, except it goes through Shihlin district.

### 308 – Tanshui to Taipei Train Station

From Mackay Hospital to Chuwei, Christian College, Kuantu, Motion Picture Company, Peitou Military School Army Academy, past Shihpai Rd to central Shihlin district, Yangming Theater, near Grand Hotel, south on Chungshan N Rd and Taipei train station.

Top: Shoreline of Hsiaomen Island, Penghu (Storey)
Bottom: Stone walls to protect crops from the fierce winds, Penghu (Storey)

Top: The sea after a typhoon, Lanyu (Strauss)
Bottom: Temple roof, Lukang (Strauss)

## 310 – Shihlin, Taipei Train Station to Panchiao

From Shihlin station (across street from Catholic Church), south on Chungshan N Rd near Grand Hotel, to Chunghsiao W Rd, Taipei train station, south on Chunghua Rd, Lungshan Temple, Hoping W Rd, Huachiang Bridge, Wenhua Rd and the Panchiao train station. Buses with characters in red on white background go through to Panchiao, buses with characters written in green on white background terminate at Taipei train station.

## 502 – Minsheng E Rd to Food Circle *(yúanhúan)*

From Minsheng E Rd past Chang Gung Hospital, Sungshan Airport, Rong Shin Park, south on Chilin Rd, Chungshan N Rd, Taipei train station and Food Circle.

## 503 – Sanchangli to Chunghua Rd

From Sanchangli (east Taipei), west on Hsinyi Rd to Fuhsing Rd, south to Hoping E Rd, east on Hoping Rd past Taiwan Normal University (*shīdà*), north on Nanchang Rd and west on Aikuo Rd to Chunghua Rd (Hagglers' Alley).

## 504 – Chungching S Rd to Sungshan Movie Studio

Chungching S Rd to Far Eastern Department Store, Taipei railway station, Dinghao Market, Sun Yatsen Memorial, Huling St, Chunghsiao E Rd (Section 5), Sungshan district and Sungshan Movie Studio.

## 508 – Shihlin Bus Station to Cherry Hill

From Shihlin Bus station, Wenlin Rd, by Taipei American School, past Veterans' Hospital, turns left up Cherry Hill, ends at the Chinese high school. Returns by the same route.

## 601 – Tienmu to Wanhua (circular route)

From Tienmu traffic circle (Chungshan N Rd, Section 7), turns right on Tienmu W Rd, Shihpai Rd, past Veterans' Hospital, past Taipei American School on Wenlin Rd, through Shihlin district, turns right at church, down Chungcheng Rd over the bridge, down Chungching N Rd, past Food Circle, Snake Alley, past Lion Plaza, past Yenping Market, back to Chungching N Rd, Shihlin district, Shihpai, upper Tienmu and back to Tienmu traffic circle.

## 602 – Neihu to Paoching Rd in Hsimending

From Neihu, past Fuhsing Opera School, south on Sungchiang Rd, past Hsingtien Temple, Chunghsiao E Rd, to Linsen Rd, Chingtao Rd, past the YWCA, Paoching Rd and ends near the Far Eastern Department Store.

## 603 – Tienmu to Hoping W Rd

From upper Tienmu traffic circle (Chungshan N Rd Section 7), south on Chungshan N Rd to Chunghsiao Rd, Kungyuan Rd (by New Park), south to Hoping W Rd and turns back north on Chungching Rd to Aikuo W Rd (South Gate area).

## 604 – Neihu to Little South Gate

Sungshan area (east Taipei), west on Nanking E Rd, past China Airlines, Boy Scout Activity Center, Linsen N Rd, Taipei railway station, Chunghua Rd and Little South Gate. Return route skips Chunghua Rd and goes by Poai Rd, Hankou St, Provincial Museum, Chungshan Market and Nanking E Rd.

## 606 – Kungkuan Area to Yangming Medical College

Kungkuan, Tri-Services Hospital, East Gate Market, Jenai Rd, Hsinsheng N Rd, Hsingshing Middle School, Chungshan N Rd (Section 5), north to Tienmu W Rd, Veterans' General Hospital and Yangming Medical College.

# North Taiwan 台灣北部

Within a short distance from Taipei, you can forget all about the problems of urban life and find peace and relaxation visiting some of Taiwan's mountains, beaches and hot spring resorts. You can experience some of the pleasures of rural living, enjoy clean air, visit waterfalls and temples, and enjoy some of Taiwan's best seafood.

Many travellers have neither the time nor the inclination to leave Taipei, which is a pity. If you have very limited time, you can spend 1 day visiting the northern region and getting a feel of rural life – it is bound to provide you with a new and different insight into Taiwan.

## YANGMINGSHAN
*(yángmíngshān)* 陽明山

A pleasant mountain park north of Taipei, Yangmingshan is noted for its beautiful flowers – especially in the spring (February to April) when the cherry blossoms are in bloom. The cherry trees are in Chungshan Park, which is part of the Yangmingshan Park area. There are also plenty of birds, squirrels, trees and fresh air. Many wealthy Taiwanese and Westerners live on the lower slopes of Yangmingshan, preferring life in the cooler mountains above the smog to living down in the city. Real estate developers have recently moved into the lower slopes and have erected some ultra-expensive American-style housing projects with names like 'Taipei California'. Fortunately, most of the mountain is protected by a national park.

The park itself offers many opportunities for hiking and provides a most welcome relief from Taipei's bustle. The only bad thing one can say about this place is that on Sundays it tends to be packed out with hordes of people trying to get away from it all, especially during the blossom season. Also, on rare occasions the higher slopes of Yangmingshan get dusted by snow. If this occurs on a weekend, you'll be able to witness the greatest pilgrimage of Chinese people since the Long March.

Yangmingshan has hot spring resorts similar to Peitou. There is a restaurant in the park and also a large, impressive Chinese-style building called the Chungshan Building *(zhōngshān lóu)*, the site of high-level government meetings. You can admire the building from the outside, but getting inside requires connections.

If you would like a moderately difficult hike, climb Seven Star Mountain *(qīxīngshān)*. At an elevation of 1120 metres, it is the highest peak in the area. From the summit, you can look down one side of the mountain and see Taipei. In the opposite direction the ocean is visible.

### Places to Stay

Staying in Yangmingshan may not be as convenient as central Taipei, but it certainly offers more pleasant surroundings. Accommodation there is not very expensive compared with Taipei, but there are no dormitories for budget travellers.

*Yangmingshan Hostel* (tel (02) 8616601) *(liánqíng yángmíngshān zhāodàisuǒ)*, 12 Yangming Rd, Section 1, Grass Mountain, charges NT$600 to NT$700 for a double but gives a sizeable discount if you rent the room by the month.

The *Hotel China, Yangmingshan* (tel (02) 8616661, fax 8613885) *(yángmíngshān zhōngguó dàfàndiàn)* at 237 Kochih Rd, Yangmingshan, has doubles for NT$2400; facilities include a swimming pool.

### Getting There & Away

From Taipei you can get to Yangmingshan on bus No 301, which runs along Chungshan N Rd. The trip only takes about 45 minutes.

From Peitou you can catch bus No 230. Stay on the bus to the very last stop at the top of the mountain. It's about a 10 minute walk to the park entrance – follow the footpath behind the bus terminal.

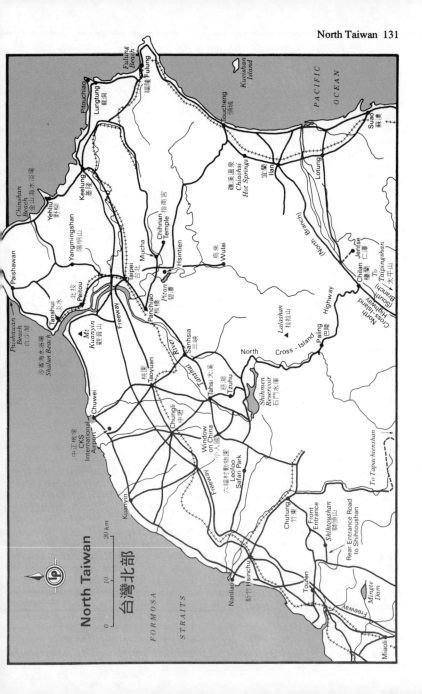

# North Taiwan

台灣北部

Hot springs at Peitou

## PEITOU
*(běitóu)* 北投

A hot spring resort area 13 km north-west of Taipei, Peitou was at one time known as a blatant red-light district. Nowadays, Peitou has been 'cleaned up' – the prostitutes are still there but maintain a very low profile. Mostly they serve upper-class clientele such as visiting Japanese businessmen. Peitou still has many nice inns and spas; they're a legacy of the Japanese occupation when Peitou was one of Taiwan's three big luxury hot spring resorts. The other two were Kuantzuling and Szechunghsi, both of which have deteriorated markedly in recent years.

Peitou may have lost some of its former glory, but it still retains a certain charm. Within the city limits is the community of Wellington Heights, which has a large number of foreign residents from the USA and Europe. The two main sightseeing attractions are Hell Valley and the Lovers' Temple.

### Hell Valley
*(dìyù gǔ)* 地獄谷

An enormous hot spring with scalding hot water, Hell Valley is no place to go bathing but it certainly is interesting. The locals seem to get a kick out of boiling eggs here. It's to the north-east of Peitou Park, off Chungshan Rd.

### Lovers' Temple
*(qíngrén miào)* 情人廟

Also known as *cháo míng gōng*, this exotic temple is one of Peitou's main attractions. Lovers flock to the temple on the 7th day of the 7th lunar month to swear their undying love to each other. You can reach the Lovers' Temple on bus Nos 223, 224, 277 or 601.

### Places to Stay

Peitou is not a place for budget travellers to find a cheap dorm. The accommodation here is all hotels – some with mirrors on the ceiling and heart-shaped waterbeds – where rooms are rented by the hour. But there are straight hotels too for guests who just want to use the hot springs. Among the better known hotels in Peitou is the *Communications Palace* (tel (02) 8913031) *(jiāotōng dàfàndiàn)*, at 30 Yuya Rd, where doubles

cost NT$960. Also well appointed is the
*I-Tsun Hotel* (tel (02) 8912121) (*yìquán
wēnquán lüshè*), 140 Wenchuan Rd, where
doubles are NT$1600.

### Getting There & Away

From Taipei, you can reach Peitou on bus
Nos 216, 217, 218, 219, 223, 302 or 308.
Whenever they finish the new subway line
you will be able to use it to get to Peitou, but
don't hold your breath for it.

From Yangmingshan, you can reach
Peitou by bus No 230, which leaves from the
bus terminal near the park.

## TIENMU
*(tiānmǔ)* 天母

Tienmu (usually misspelled 'Tienmou'), is
not exactly a renowned tourist attraction.
Rather, you might think of it as the
foreigners' ghetto in suburban Taipei. Actually, Chinese make up the overwhelming
majority of the inhabitants, but there are also
many expatriates from the USA, New
Zealand, Australia, Europe and wherever
else expatriates come from.

It used to be much more of a foreigners'
ghetto, but now many have moved into
luxury apartments in east Taipei. Most of the
expats are representatives of foreign companies but some are missionaries, technicians
and teachers at the American School near
Tienmu.

There are numerous stores in Tienmu carrying lots of foreign goods, especially things
from the USA like instant mashed potatoes,
artificial whipped cream, frozen TV dinners,
cheese in a spray can, microwave popcorn
and other plastic foods. If you need a dose of
these things while you are in Taiwan, this is
the place to go looking for them. When
buying such imported foods it might be
prudent to check the expiry dates on the
package, though most of these products have
a shelf life of 25 years or so.

### Hike to Yangmingshan

As far as I'm concerned, the most pleasant
activity in Tienmu is to hike up to the Chinese
Cultural University in Yangmingshan. To do

this hike, take a bus to the last stop on the big
traffic circle, the highest point you can go by
bus in Tienmu. Two streets go uphill from the
traffic circle. If you take the one to the right,
you'll walk steeply uphill but will soon come
to the end of the street where you'll find stone
steps leading up into the forest. It's
signposted as being a 1.8 km hike. Head up
the steps. After a while you'll come to a fork.
The left fork heads back down to Tienmu, the
right fork continues uphill to Shantzehou and
the Chinese Cultural University in Yangmingshan.

### Places to Stay

If you take a liking to Tienmu and plan to
take up long-term residence, the *Lanya Guest
House* (tel (02) 8315722) (*nányǎ bīngǔan*),
280 Chungshan N Rd, Section 6, rents rooms
by the month. A double is NT$15,000 for a
month.

### Places to Eat

The large number of foreigners has made
Tienmu a popular spot for eating non-
Chinese food. Being a somewhat upper-class
neighbourhood, prices are moderate to
expensive. *Súiyúanjū* (tel (02) 8214730),
126 Tienmu W Rd, serves vegetarian food.
They also serve tea, but it's ridiculously
expensive. The meals are a much better deal.
Other fine restaurants with self-explanatory
names include *Da Antonio Pizza & Pasta
Restaurant* (tel (02) 8731027), 2nd floor, 26
Chungshan N Rd, Section 7; *Hugo's French
Restaurant* (tel (02) 8719974, 8314363), 31
Chungshan N Rd, Section 7; *Fauchon Steak
Restaurant* (tel (02) 8717000, 8722576), 6
Tienmu N Rd; *Charlie's Curry Restaurant &
Bar* (tel (02) 8727877), 45 Tienmu N Rd; and
*Dazzle Indian Curry Restaurant* (tel (02)
8733249), 3 Alley 4, Lane 43, Tienmu E Rd.

### Getting There & Away

Buses going to Tienmu include Nos 220,
224, 267, 268, 601 and 603. All these buses
lead to the big traffic circle at the top of
Chungshan N Rd.

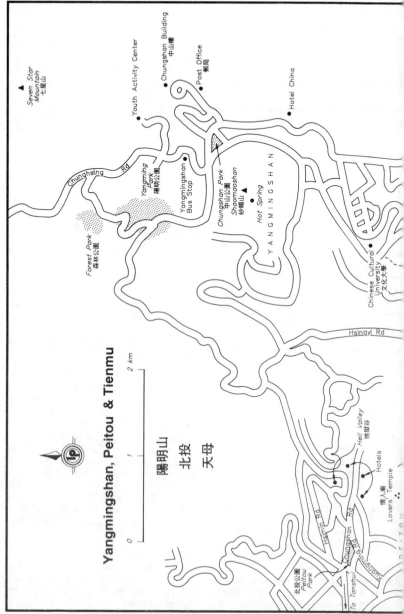

Yangmingshan, Peitou & Tienmu

陽明山
北投
天母

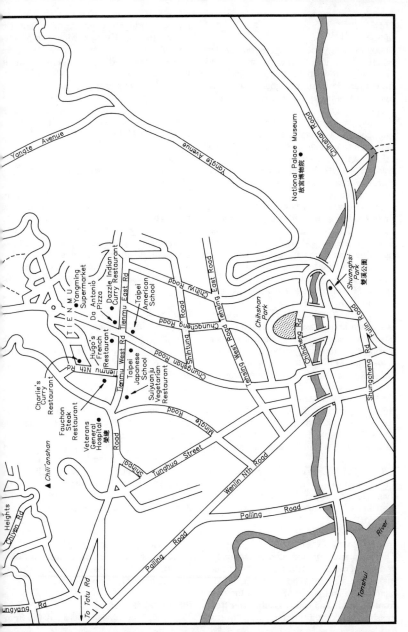

## TANSHUI
*(dànshǔi)* 淡水

Though it was once the largest port on the island, Tanshui (frequently misspelled 'Tamsui') is now a fishing village. Residents from Taipei know it as a good place to eat seafood. The name Tanshui means 'Freshwater'.

Today the town boasts a fine university, a golf course, a good beach and Fort San Domingo *(hóng máo chéng)*, a legacy of the brief Spanish occupation of north Taiwan from 1624 to 1642. The fort also housed the British Consulate until 1972 when the consulate closed.

Tanshui is 20 km north-west of Taipei. From the bus station, it's only a 15 minute walk or 2 minute taxi ride to Fort San Domingo. People will gladly point you in the right direction if you ask the way. Cut over one block to your left as you're walking and you can stroll along the river and get good views of Kuanyin Mountain, a popular place with hikers from Taipei.

Where the Tanshui River meets the ocean is a beach known as Shalun Beach *(shālún hǎishǔi yùchǎng)*. This is one beach where surfing and windsurfing is possible. You can also go horse riding at the nearby Yuanye Chi Horse Riding Club *(yúanyě qímǎ jùlèbù)*.

### Getting There & Away

Buses operated by the Chihnan Bus Company *(zhǐnán kèyùn)* go to Tanshui from Taipei. They depart from the North Gate area west of the train station. Take bus Nos 2 or 5.

From Tanshui, you can continue on to see Chinshan Beach, Yehliu and Keelung, and then return to Taipei. This loop trip can be done in a day and in either direction.

### KUANYIN MOUNTAIN
*(gūanyīnshān)* 觀音山

This mountain, named after Kuanyin the goddess of mercy, is a pleasant half-day hike in the Taipei area. The mountain is 612 metres high and is directly across the river from Tanshui. You can cross the river from Tanshui by taking a tiny ferry or a bus that crosses a bridge several km away, but it i quicker to reach Kuanyin Mountain directl from Taipei. In summer, try to head up in th morning to avoid the frequent afternoo thundershowers.

The Sanchung Bus Company *(sánchón kèyùn)* offers a direct bus service from Taipei. The bus terminal is on Tacheng S *(tǎchéng jiē)*, which is just north of the Nort Gate, by the GPO.

### PAISHAWAN BEACH
*(báishāwān hǎishǔi yùchǎng)*
白沙灣海水浴場

A nice beach to the north of Tanshui Paishawan has surfing, windsurfing an hang-gliding. Of course, it's only reall enjoyable to go there during summer. Ther is a small entry fee but you get snack bars lifeguards, changing facilities and someon to clean up the litter. From Tanshui, there ar plenty of local buses making the north coas run.

### CHINSHAN BEACH
*(jīnshān hǎishǔi yùchǎng)*
金山海水浴場

Chinshan Beach is one of the best beache close to Taipei. Of course, it does ge crowded during summer weekends, but th rest of the time it's very nice.

If this is your first time at a beach ir Taiwan, you'll notice that few people dare t go into the deep water. There is nothing especially dangerous about Taiwan's beaches – the simple fact is most city-bound Taiwanese really don't know how to swim An amazing number of people drown ir Taiwan in perfectly calm water. Public swimming pools are usually no more than wais deep. If you get into neck-deep water you'l leave the crowd behind, but the lifeguards will frantically blow their whistles at you and perhaps launch a rescue effort.

Admission to the beach costs NT$40. Admission to the swimming pool is NT$100. They also have hot spring baths.

### Places to Stay

Most people do Chinshan as a day trip from

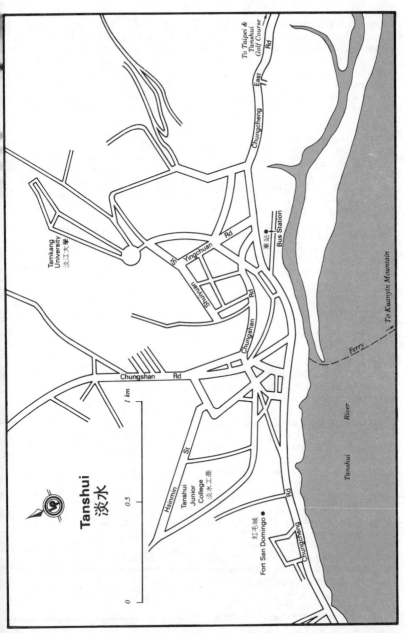

**Tanshui**
淡水

Tamkang University 淡江大學

Shuiyuan St

Yingchuan Rd

Chungshan Rd

車站 Bus Station

Chungcheng East Rd

To Taipei & Tanshui Golf Course

To Kuanyin Mountain

Ferry

Tanshui River

Hsinmin St

Tanshui Junior College 淡水工商

Fort San Domingo 紅毛城

Chungshan Rd

Chungcheng Rd

0    0.5    1 km

Taipei, but if you want to stay, there is the *Chinshan Youth Activity Center* (tel (032) 981190) (*jīnshān húodòng zhōngxīn*). It costs NT$100 to stay in the dormitory, NT$400 for a double and NT$1200 for a bungalow. The youth hostel is by the beach and popular in summer, so try to make a reservation first.

### Getting There & Away

You can reach Chinshan very easily by first taking the bus or train to either Keelung or Tanshui (Keelung is closer), then transferring to a local bus. Chinshan is on the loop road that takes you through Tanshui, Chinshan, Yehliu, Keelung and then back to Taipei, making a fine trip for a day or 2.

A more direct approach from Taipei is the bus that goes over the mountains in Yangmingshan Park. You catch this bus from the Chunglun Station (*zhōnglún zhàn*). Fare is NT$41. It's more appealing to take the coast road going there and the mountain road when returning.

### YEHLIU
*(yěliǔ)* 野柳

This is a popular park known for its bizarre, jagged rock formations which have been moulded by the elements. The rocky coastline is indeed beautiful, but don't go too near the edge. A statue has been built in honour of a man who drowned while trying to save another drowning man at this spot. Unless you want to get your statue built here too, keep away from the cliffs.

After you've seen the main area of rock formations – frequently crawling with camera-clicking tourists – continue along a footpath that climbs steeply up and towards the end of the promontory. When you reach the top you'll see a lighthouse overlooking the coastline; the view is magnificent. Continue out to the end of the promontory and you'll discover nearly deserted little alcoves. The area is rarely crowded, since most of the tourists can't handle walking up the hill and prefer to hang out close to the parking lot.

Admission is NT$25, but on weekdays you may well get in for free, especially if you show up during lunch break.

Yehliu restaurants have earned a bad reputation for overcharging foreign tourists. If you eat there, agree on the price in advance or bring along a suitcase full of money. Better yet, bring your own lunch and thumb your nose at the restaurant owners.

### KEELUNG
*(jīlóng)* 基隆

Keelung – which really should be spelled 'Chilung' – is better known as a container port than as a tourist attraction. It is the second largest port in Taiwan, the largest one being Kaohsiung. Taiwan's booming trade has turned Keelung into a very prosperous city. Being an international seaport, the city has many foreigners passing through it.

Keelung has a pleasant atmosphere and is not that large – the population is around 350,000. It is notorious for its wet winters when it can rain almost continuously. Bring an umbrella or expect to buy one if you go at that time. The weather is more pleasant in summer.

| 1 | Bus Station |
|---|---|
| | 車站 |
| 2 | Police Station (Visa Extensions) |
| | 外事警察 |
| 3 | Long Fa Hotel |
| | 隆發旅社 |
| 4 | Tong Shing Hotel |
| | 東興大飯店 |
| 5 | Anching Temple |
| | 安慶宮 |
| 6 | Okinawa Ferry |
| 7 | Hotel Kodak |
| | 柯達大飯店 |
| 8 | Bank of Taiwan |
| | 台灣銀行 |
| 9 | GPO |
| | 郵政總局 |
| 10 | Telephone Company |
| | 電信局 |
| 11 | McDonald's |
| | 麥當勞 |

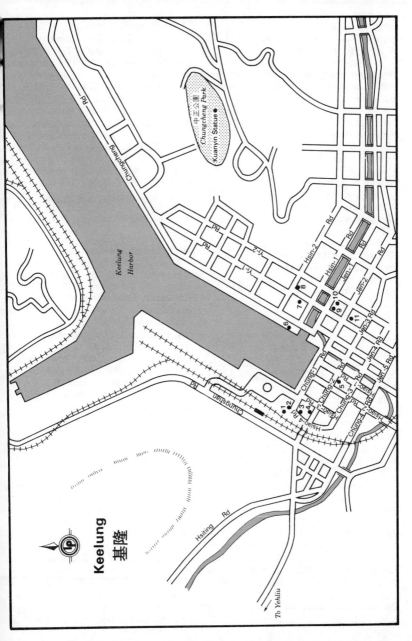

Keelung
基隆

Chungcheng Park
中正公園
Kuanyin Statue •

Keelung Harbor

To Yehliu

## Information
**Money** The Bank of Taiwan (tel (032) 283171) is at 16 Yi-1 Rd.

**Bookstores** Near the harbour there are a few English-language bookstores. The Keelung Bookstore (tel (032) 220325, 255553), 2-1 Chung-1 Rd, has a good selection. Just down the street is the corner of Chung-1 Rd and Hsiao-1 Rd is Frank's Books (tel (032) 223750), 66 Hsiao-1 Rd. Both new and used books are available.

## Chungcheng Park
*(zhōngzhèng gōngyúan)* 中正公園
A fine view of Keelung can be had from Chungcheng Park. The park is not difficult to find: it is dominated by Keelung's main tourist attraction, the huge, white statue of Kuanyin, the goddess of mercy. The statue is visible from many parts of the town. You can climb the stairs inside the statue for a splendid view, particularly at night. There is also a large temple on the hill, not far from the Kuanyin statue.

## Statue of Liberty
*(zìyóu nüshén)* 自由女神像
On the hill just behind McDonald's is a replica of New York's most famous statue. Actually, there are quite a few such replicas in Taiwan – the Statue of Liberty and Mickey Mouse seem to be the two symbols of the USA that have gained most popularity with the Taiwanese. While this may not be one of Keelung's most famous tourist attractions, it makes a great photograph – McDonald's, the Statue of Liberty and some Chinese billboards all together. You have to get far away with a powerful telephoto lens for the best results.

## Places to Stay
You may find it convenient to spend a night in Keelung if you are entering or leaving Taiwan by ship, or if you are touring from there down the east coast. There are no youth hostels, but budget travellers can find reasonable rates at the *Long Fa Hotel* (tel (032) 224059) *(lóngfā lǚshè)*, 23 Hsiao-4 Rd,

which charges NT$450 a double. Somewha nicer is the *Tong Shing Hotel* (tel (032 228206) *(dōngxīng dàlüshè)*, 58 Chung-? Rd, which charges NT$500 for a double.

Moving upmarket, there's the *huashua dàfàndiàn* (tel (032) 223131), 108 Hsiao-? Rd, where doubles are NT$650. Just oppo site the Bank of Taiwan is the *Aloha Hote* (tel (032) 227322) *(ālèhā dàfàndiàn)*, 292-11 Hsin-2 Rd, where doubles cost NT$70C to NT$820. I found the *húaxīng dàfàndiàn* (tel (032) 223166), 54 Hsiao-1 Rd, to be very pleasant and clean; it costs NT$750 to NT$900 for a double. The nicest hote in town is the *Hotel Kodak* (tel (032) 230111) *(kēdá dàfàndiàn)*, 7 Yi-1 Rd, where doubles/twins are NT$970/1300.

## Getting There & Away
Keelung is easily reached from Taipei by train or bus. Buses depart frequently from Taipei's East Bus Station. The fare is NT$28. The Suao to Taipei buses only stop near the ferry departure point rather than at the bus terminal near the train station as well; make sure you get off at the ferry stop, else you could end up in Taipei!

Keelung is the arrival and departure point for the ferry to Okinawa (Japan). The ferry leaves from pier No 2. From Okinawa, you can change boats and reach the main islands of Japan. This is perhaps the most economical way to enter or exit Taiwan. Departure tax is NT$200.

## PITAN
*(bìtán)* 碧潭
South of Taipei is Pitan (Green Lake), which is basically just a nice park on the edge of the city. The lake features rowboats and there is a nearby amusement park. The lake is adjacent to the town of Hsintien *(xīndiàn)*, which can be reached easily from Taipei.

Buses operated by the Hsintien Bus Company *(xīndiàn kèyùn)* depart every 10 minutes or so from the New Park side of Kungyuan Rd near the hospital. I don't recommend going out of your way just to visit this place, but if you are on your way to Wulai

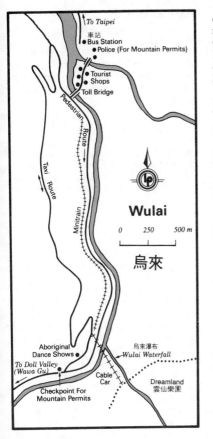

To Taipei
車站
● Bus Station
● Police (For Mountain Permits)
● Tourist
● Shops
Toll Bridge
Pedestrian Route
Taxi Route
Minitrain

**Wulai**

0    250    500 m

烏來

Aboriginal
Dance Shows
To Doll Valley
(Wawa Gu)
Checkpoint For
Mountain Permits

烏來瀑布
Wulai Waterfall

Cable
Car

Dreamland
雲仙樂園

describe this phenomenon as a 'people mountain, people sea' (*rén shān rén hǎi*). Come on weekdays for a more pleasant visit. From Hsintien (*xīndiàn*), buses to Wulai depart every 10 minutes or so from the New Park side of Kungyuan Rd near the hospital.

### Wulai Falls  烏來瀑布

The bus lets you off at a small terminal in the town of Wulai. You walk across a short bridge and enter a small street which is a solid mass of souvenir shops selling everything a tourist desires. So if you'd like to pick up an alligator with a lightbulb in its mouth, or a Buddha with a clock in his stomach, this is the place to do it. When you come to the end of the street, there is another bridge going over the river. You have to pay an admission charge of NT$15 to cross.

After crossing the bridge, you will encounter a congregation of persistent taxi drivers. Ignore them and walk up the steps. You'll soon come to the electric minitrain. It's not expensive, so take the train and you'll be whisked away to the base of Wulai Falls. At the base of the falls, you will almost certainly see a couple of pretty aboriginal girls in red miniskirts who happen to be standing there. They welcome you to take their picture posing by the waterfall, but you are expected to pay a small fee.

From here you can take a cable car up to the top of the falls. The cost of a round-trip ticket is NT$130 for adults. When you get to the top you will find the local equivalent of Disneyland, which is called Dreamland (*yúnxiān lèyúan*). In spite of the amusement park atmosphere, it's fun to go there – as long as you go on a weekday, when it's not crowded.

### Doll Valley
*(wáwa gǔ)* 娃娃谷

If you want to get away from the tourists and see an aboriginal village that hasn't been commercialised, you can do a 4 km (each way) walk from Wulai to Doll Valley (*wáwa gǔ*). However, this does require a mountain permit. You can get the permit fairly easily in Taipei or from the main police station,

you can take in Pitan along the way. The bus that goes to Pitan also continues up to Wulai.

## WULAI
*(wūlái)* 烏來

Wulai has beautiful, though nowadays commercialised, mountain scenery 29 km (a 1 hour bus ride) south of Taipei. It has the advantage of being a lot higher and therefore cooler than Taipei. Among the attractions there is a magnificent gorge and one of Taiwan's highest waterfalls.

Wulai can be wall-to-wall people on weekends and holidays. The Chinese which is near the bus terminal in Wulai. There's not much in Doll Valley itself, but the walk up there – through a gorge with a rushing river below – offers brilliant scenery. Avoid it on Sundays, when the place gets overrun by local hiking clubs. You can also take a taxi or hitch to Doll Valley, but only residents can bring their own vehicles past the police checkpoint.

### Places to Stay
Even though most people prefer to do Wulai as a day trip, you can spend the night at the *Dreamland Hotel* (tel (02) 6616510) (*yúnxiān dàfàndiàn*). The price for a single/double is NT$990/1650 and you can also have a soak in the hot springs. To make a reservation from Taipei, phone (02) 3610068. The hotel is in the Dreamland Amusement Park, which can only be reached by cable car.

### Getting There & Away
For details of getting to Wulai, see the Pitan Getting There & Away section.

### CHIHNAN TEMPLE
(*zhǐnán gōng*) 指南宮
One of the largest temples in north Taiwan, the Chihnan Temple is 19 km south-east of Taipei in the suburb of Mucha (*mùzhà*). The temple is over 100 years old. As it's perched on a mountainside, there are outstanding views of Taipei when the weather is clear. When the weather is not clear, that's OK too – who wants to see Taipei anyway?

You can get there from Taipei by taking a bus operated by the Chihnan Bus Company (*zhǐnán kèyùn*) which departs from Tacheng St, just north of the North Gate or the GPO. Take bus Nos 1 or 2. Bus No 1 starts out from the Food Circle. From where the bus drops you off, you cannot see the temple. Follow the steep steps up and up until you reach a small Taoist temple. The main temple is to your right; to the left are some picnic grounds – a good place to relax, except on weekends when it's crowded.

### TAIPEI-MUCHA ZOO
(*táiběi mùzhà dòngwù yúan*) 台北木柵動物園
The zoo (tel (02) 9382300) is in the suburb of Mucha (*mùzhà*) south-east of Taipei. Bus Nos 236, 258, 282 and 291 go there. Open 8.30 am to 4.30 pm daily. Admission costs NT$40.

### YUANTUNG TEMPLE
(*yúantōng sì*) 圓通寺
This large Buddhist temple is in the foothills of Chungho (*zhōnghé*), a suburb to the south-west of Taipei. It's reminiscent of the previously mentioned Chihnan Temple. You can get there on bus Nos 201, 241, 242 or 244.

### TSU SHIH TEMPLE
(*zǔshī miào*) 祖師廟
Certainly one of the most magnificent temples in Taiwan, the Tsu Shih Temple is still undergoing restoration that began in 1947. It is not expected to be completed until sometime in the 1990s – that is, after some 45 years of painstaking effort. However, don't let the restoration work prevent you from going to see the temple. Indeed, one of the interesting things about the place is to see how the artisans carefully and lovingly recreate the stone carvings and deities, a monumental task. Since much of the work has already been completed, the temple is in good shape and is a paradise for photographers or anybody interested in temple art.

### Getting There & Away
The Tsu Shih Temple is a little inconvenient to get to. It's in the town of Sanhsia (*sānxiá*) about 30 km south-west of Taipei. That isn't really very far, but there aren't any other tourist attractions along the route. Therefore, it's pretty much an out-and-back trip unless you have your own vehicle and want to visit nearby Tzuhu. Sanhsia itself is an historical town with many ancient houses, some dating back to the Ming Dynasty. The departure point for buses to Sanhsia is behind the Presidential Building in Taipei.

## TZUHU
*(cíhú)* 慈湖

Tzuhu, which translates into English as 'Lake Kindness', is where the body of Chiang Kaishek has been entombed. The site is regarded as temporary; it is intended that the body will be returned to the mainland after China is reunited. Most of the Chinese in Taiwan and many foreigners have visited this site.

Go into the main building and you'll find the security desk right near the snack bar. Let them see your passport and they'll fill out a form which you give to the guard at the entrance. You have to walk for about 10 minutes to reach the actual mausoleum. Along the way you'll pass the lake.

You can take photographs outside the mausoleum but I wouldn't do so inside, as it is considered disrespectful. You're allowed about a minute inside to view the granite case in which the body has been placed. It is customary to give a respectful bow.

It's OK to visit Tzuhu on Sundays, as it doesn't get overly crowded.

### Getting There & Away

To reach Tzuhu from Taipei, first take a train to Taoyuan *(táoyúan)* or Chungli *(zhōnglì)*. From there you can get a bus directly to Tzuhu or else to the nearby town of Tahsi *(dàxī)*, from where you'll have to get another bus to Tzuhu. Buses from Tahsi to Tzuhu are not very frequent so you might have to go by taxi. Fortunately, it's not very far so it's not too expensive.

It is possible to combine a visit to Tzuhu with a trip to the Tsu Shih Temple and Shihmen Reservoir. However, there are no direct buses between these places even though they are very close to each other. You must first go back to Tahsi, which is out of the way, and either change buses or take a taxi. The most convenient way to get between these places is to drive yourself.

## SHIHMEN RESERVOIR
*(shímén shǔikù)* 石門水庫

Shihmen Reservoir forms the largest lake in northern Taiwan. The Shihmen Dam is nestled in the foothills south-west of Taipei. Construction on the dam began in 1955 and it was completed in 1964. It's an attractive area, and the best way to really enjoy it is to rent a motorcycle or car so that you can explore the lake at your own pace.

Shihmen Reservoir

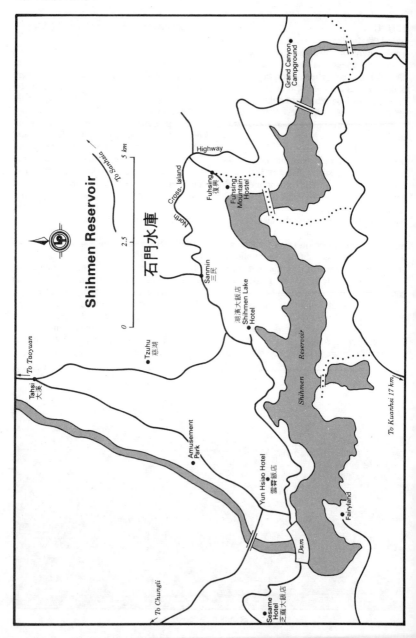

Shihmen Reservoir

石門水庫

If you don't have your own transport, it's usually best to visit the reservoir on Sundays or holidays when there are frequent boat tours cruising the lake. Shihmen Reservoir is off the beaten track for most foreigners, though many Taipei residents go there.

If you arrive by bus, the driver will drop you off right by the dam. From there you can join a boat tour or walk around. The road on the north shore of the lake is an attractive but very long hike. You may want to hire a taxi or try hitchhiking. A bus service exists but it is infrequent. It's a great ride on a motorcycle or 10 speed bicycle, but I couldn't find any bicycle rentals there. Swimming is not permitted in the lake but fishing is allowed.

If you go far enough upstream on the north shore road, you'll reach Fuhsing Village (*fùxīng xiāng*), an attractive place which has a youth hostel – the only cheap place to stay in the Shihmen area.

There is a beautiful trip starting from Shihmen Reservoir and continuing over the mountains, via the North Cross-Island Highway (Highway 7) to Chilan (*qílán*). Details about making this trip are given in the North Cross-Island section further on in this chapter.

### Places to Stay

At Fuhsing Village there's the *Fuhsing Mountain Hostel* (tel (03) 3822276) (*fùxīng shān zhuāng*), where dormitory/doubles are NT$120/360. It is out of the way but it's the cheapest place, and hiking is a definite possibility if you stay here.

The *Sesame Hotel* (tel (034) 712120) (*zhīmá dàfàndiàn*) sets a high standard but does not command a view of the lake, though it overlooks the river below. Doubles cost NT$1000. The *Yun Hsiao Hotel* (tel (034) 712111/2) (*yúnxiāo dàfàndiàn*) is on a hill right next to the dam. Singles cost from NT$550 to NT$850 and twins are NT$1000. The *Shihmen Lake Hotel* (tel (034) 883883) (*húbīng dàfàndiàn*) is in a lovely but secluded spot along the north shore of the lake. Doubles are NT$1000.

**Camping** The *Grand Canyon Campground* is a group camping area and is not really suitable for individual travellers.

### Getting There & Away

To get to Shihmen Reservoir, first take a bus or train to Chungli (*zhōnglì*), which is 36 km south-west of Taipei. Then transfer to a local bus which will take you to Shihmen Reservoir. Buses to the reservoir are not very frequent. If you don't catch one right away, take a bus to Tahsi (*dàxī*) and then get a bus or taxi or hitchhike up to the reservoir.

This trip can be combined with the trip to Tzuhu or with visiting the Leofoo Safari Park and Window on China.

### LEOFOO SAFARI PARK
(*liùfú cūn yě shēng dòngwù yúan*)
六福村野生動物園
Leofoo Safari Park (tel (035) 872626) is an outdoor zoo where the animals wander around loose while you drive through in a car or tour bus. It's very touristy and most suited to families with children.

The park features a wide range of animals including deer, lions, tigers, baboons, giraffes and zebras. As in other tourist areas, it's best to visit it on weekdays, although this safari park doesn't get especially crowded. Admission is NT$185, and it's open from 9 am to 4.30 pm daily.

### Getting There & Away

Certainly the most convenient way to get to the park is to take the bus operated by the Leofoo Hotel (tel (02) 5073211) (*liùfú kèzhàn*) at 168 Changchun Rd, Taipei. Buses depart daily at 9 am. The price of the ticket includes the round-trip fare, admission and a tour around the park.

Should you decide to do the Leofoo Safari Park on your own, you can reach it by taking a train to Chungli (*zhōnglì*) and then catching a bus from the terminal across the street from the train station.

### WINDOW ON CHINA
(*xiǎo rén gúo*) 小人國
Many years ago I read a novel entitled *Slapstick* by Kurt Vonnegut. According to the

story, the Chinese found that the only way they could feed their massive population was to make people smaller. Chinese scientists discovered a way to shrink people. So China closed its borders to the world and began the downsizing process. Several years later, the world was gripped by a massive killer plague. People were dying like flies. An American doctor discovered the reason why – the disease was caused by inhaling microscopic Chinese.

'Nonsense' you say? Then welcome to the Window on China. It's an outdoor park that contains exact models of many of China's famous architectural wonders such as the Great Wall and the Forbidden City. And yes, miniature people too. Some of Taiwan's notable building projects are also included, such as the Chiang Kaishek Memorial, the Sun Yatsen Freeway (with miniature cars) and CKS Airport (with miniature planes). Everything is reduced to ½5 of normal size. The Tourism Bureau calls it a 'world class tourist attraction'. Who says the Taiwanese don't have a sense of humour? Admission is NT$160. The Window on China is open daily from 8.30 am to 5.30 pm.

### Getting There & Away

To reach this place from Taipei, take a train to Chungli (*zhōnglì*) and then a bus from the Hsinchu Bus Company (*xīnchú kèyùn*) terminal, which is near the railway station.

The Window on China is close to Leofoo Safari Park and it is possible to visit both places on the same day. You may also want to visit Tzuhu and Shihmen Reservoir in the same trip, especially if you have your own car or motorcycle.

### NORTH CROSS-ISLAND HIGHWAY

Highway 7, also called the North Cross-Island Highway, is a beautiful but little-travelled mountain road that starts from Taoyuan and then heads up into the hills above Shihmen Reservoir. Buses operated by the Taoyuan Bus Company (*táoyúan kèyùn*) go there. Cars are infrequent, so hitching is not easy except on

weekends. It's a good place to take your own vehicle if you have one.

The highway branches at Chilan (*qīlán*): the north branch heads down to the east coast at Ilan (*yílán*) and the south branch heads still higher up into the mountains until it intersects with the Central Cross-Island Highway at Lishan. If you stay at the Paling Mountain Hostel, there is an interesting day hike that you can do. Just to the north of Paling is the Lalashan Forest Reserve (*lālāshān shéngmù qún*), which can be reached by walking 13 km along the gravel road. You gain about 1000 metres in elevation, so you might consider hitching uphill and walking back, assuming that you see any cars. A mountain permit is needed, but it can easily be obtained along the way. The area is known for its giant cypress trees, some of which are more than 2500 years old.

### Places to Stay

The choices are limited. The *Fuhsing Mountain Hostel* (tel (03) 3822276) (*fùxīng shān zhūang*) is at the entrance to the highway, just above Shihmen Reservoir (see the Shihmen Reservoir map). They have doubles for NT$360 and dormitory beds for NT$120. The *Paling Mountain Hostel* (tel (03) 3332153) (*bālíng shān zhūang*) is further up the mountains and costs NT$100 in the dormitory. For the addresses of the youth hostels, refer to the Youth Hostels map in the Facts for the Visitor chapter.

Camping is another possibility.

### LUNGTUNG
*(lóng dòng)* 龍洞

Taiwan's most beautiful stretch of rocky coastline is between Lungtung (Dragon Hole), to the north-east of Taipei, and Pitouchiao (*bítóujiǎo*). It's not a place for swimming, but the sheer cliffs have made this area Taiwan's prime spot for technical rock climbing. Westerners have started to come here also to test their skills on the cliffs. Even if rock climbing isn't your forte, the scenery is excellent.

To get there, first get yourself to Keelung.

From Keelung, take a bus to Lungtung, about a 40 minute ride. The bus passes Pitouchiao and then enters a tunnel. After it leaves the tunnel it stops in the town of Lungtung, which consists of a few houses and small stores. From where the bus lets you off, walk back towards the tunnel. Just before you reach the tunnel, you will see a path dropping down to your right. Follow the path all the way down to the sea, about a 25 minute walk. When you hit the coast, turn left and continue walking until you see the rock climbing area. As long as you go when the weather is nice, you should see climbers. During the wet winter months you probably won't see anybody.

## FULUNG BEACH
*(fúlóng hǎishǔi yùchǎng)* 福隆海水浴場
Fulung Beach is one of the best beaches in northern Taiwan. The east coast of Taiwan is mostly mountains and jagged rocks, but Fulung is one of the few places on the east coast with a broad, white-sand beach. It's also one of the few places in Taiwan where the waves are good enough for surfing.

Fulung Beach is close enough to Taipei (57 km) to make a good day or weekend trip. During summer it becomes quite crowded on the weekends, but at other times you may have the beautiful surroundings to yourself.

The town of Fulung is very small, pleasant and quiet except on summer weekends and holidays. There is a NT$40 admission fee to the main beach area. The area south of the broad, sandy beach is free and has good coral formations for snorkelling – plus you get away from the music that the management blasts for the customers' enjoyment. The south beach has no lifeguards, which is perhaps a blessing, as Taiwanese lifeguards tend to blow their whistle at you every time the water gets past your knees.

### Places to Stay
The *Fulung Public Hostel* (tel (032) 991211) *(fúlóng gúomín lüshè)* is right on the beach. Actually, it doesn't seem so much like a hostel as a complex of beach cabins and a campground. Prices are NT$500 for doubles,

NT$700 for six people, NT$40 for camping (tent included) and NT$20 if you supply your own tent.

The only other place to stay is *xīnlì dàfàndiàn* (tel (032) 991539), a small hotel next to the train station. Doubles are NT$300 with shared bath, NT$450 with private bath. Most people stay at the Fulung Public Hostel.

### Getting There & Away
You can reach Fulung in less than an hour by train from Taipei's main station. Failing that, take a bus first to Keelung and then transfer to the local bus to Fulung. The bus trip is slower but offers a chance to admire the lovely coastal scenery. If you plan to tour down the east coast towards Hualien you can stop off at Fulung for a day and then continue your journey southwards.

## CHIAOHSI HOT SPRINGS
*(jiāoxī wēnqúan)* 礁溪温泉
The waterfall in the hills above the town is about the best reason for visiting Chiaohsi. Within walking distance of the waterfall is a luxury hotel complex. In winter, residents of Taipei who are weary of the city and cold come to Chiaohsi to soak in the hot springs. Consider it as an alternative to Peitou.

In my opinion there are more attractive hot spring resorts in Taiwan, such as Chihpen, Wenshan and Lushan. Those with limited time should probably bypass Chiaohsi and head on down the east coast towards Hualien where there is more spectacular scenery.

### Places to Stay
There are about a couple of dozen hotels in the town of Chiaohsi itself, but I feel it's only worth spending the night there if you stay by the waterfall area, which is much more beautiful than the town. Near the waterfall is a complex of several luxury hotels with their own restaurants, swimming pools and other amenities. Sorry to say there is no place for budget travellers. Consider the following: *Wufengchi Hotel* (tel (039) 885211/5) *(wǔfēngqí dàfàndiàn)*, where doubles are NT$660; and the *Happy Hotel* (tel (039) 882108, 881511) *(kùailè shān zhūang*

*dàfàndiàn*), with doubles from NT$990 to NT$1320.

## Getting There & Away

Reaching Chiaohsi Hot Springs from Taipei is easy enough. Local trains heading down the east coast stop there, as do numerous buses plying the route between Taipei and Suao. Get off the bus or train in the town of Chiaohsi. From Chiaohsi to the waterfall it is about a 50 minute walk or a short taxi ride. The name of the waterfall is Wufengchi Falls (*wǔfēngqí pùbù*) 五峰旗瀑布. Ask anybody and they'll point you in the right direction.

## TAIPINGSHAN

*(tàipíngshān)* 太平山

Towering majestically over the scenic east coast is Taipingshan, one of the closest places to Taipei where you can experience Taiwan's rugged mountain wilderness. It's close enough to the city to spare you a long, tedious bus ride into the mountains. Yet Taipingshan is so clean, quiet and beautiful that visitors can easily forget Taipei lies only 50 km away. Perhaps this accounts for it's Chinese name, which means 'Peaceful Mountain'.

Hiking is a favourite pastime at Taipingshan. One place worth visiting is Tsuifeng Lake (*cuìfēng hú*). The lake is very small but beautiful. If you have the time and the energy, you could follow the main road and walk back down the mountain to Jentse (*rénzé*), known for its hot springs. It's an 8 hour hike, but at least it's downhill and you'll be rewarded with a nice soak in the hot springs. From Jentse, you can get a bus out the next day to return to Ilan.

If you're going to hike, pay attention to the weather. The best time of the year to visit is during the summer and autumn months. It's usually fine in the morning, although thunderstorms are a distinct possibility in the afternoon. In winter, the weather is similar to Taipei only colder, and snow is a possibility near the summit. Personally, I wouldn't recommend this trip in winter. All of north-east Taiwan is uniformly soggy from about December through to March. If it's raining in Taipei, head further to the south-west (near Lishan, for example) to find drier but equally cold mountain weather.

## Places to Stay

In Taipingshan itself, there is only one place to stay: the *Taipingshan Citizens' Hostel* (tel (039) 544052) (*tàipíngshān gúomín lüshè*), where the dormitory is NT$300 and doubles cost NT$1300. At 1930 metres above sea level Taipingshan gets cold, so come prepared.

The *Jentse Mountain Hostel* (tel (039) 544052) (*rénzé shān zhūang*), Jentse Hot Springs (*rénzé wēnqúan*), is near the base of the mountain at 650 metres. A dormitory room costs from NT$300 and doubles start at NT$1300. The weather is warmer down there and you can enjoy a nice long soak in the hot springs. In summer, I prefer the top of the mountain.

You may notice that both hotels have the same telephone number. In fact, both places use the phone of the Forest Service headquarters at Taipingshan. If you want to make a reservation you have to call this number during the day, which is the only time they are open.

## Getting There & Away

Taipingshan is a remote area and getting there can be a headache. One major tactical problem is that there is no public transport going all the way up the mountain. There used to be, but we can thank Taiwan's car revolution for the bus company's collapse. Fortunately, there are daily buses as far as Jentse. From there you'll have to walk and hitch. Traffic to Taipingshan is rare on weekdays but usually plentiful on weekends. Since walking downhill is easier, probably your best bet is to hitchhike up on Sunday and walk down on Monday.

Buses depart only once a day for Jentse. Departures are from the town of Ilan at 7.50 am. Buses leave from the terminal of the Taiwan Bus Company (tel (039) 322067) (*táiqì kèyùn*). All this poses another problem because getting to Ilan before the Jentse bus departs is no easy feat. The best thing to do is to stay in Ilan the night before to catch the morning bus. The returning bus from Jentse to Ilan departs at 1.30 pm – but check that, because the schedule can (and does) change.

You need a mountain pass for Taiping-shan. Fortunately, it can easily be obtained along the way when the bus stops in the town of Tuchang (*tǔcháng*). Don't leave your passport in Taipei, as you'll need it to get the permit.

If you plan to travel around Taiwan, I recommend doing it in a clockwise direction, first heading down the east coast and then returning to Taipei by the west coast. The main reason for suggesting this is that the east coast presents such a startling change from Taipei's urban jungle, whereas on the west coast the changes are gradual.

Only 10% of Taiwan's population resides on the east side. The simple reason for this is the terrain. The eastern part of the island presents a dramatic coastline of jagged rocks and towering cliffs, not the friendliest environment for agriculture and industrialisation. Furthermore, the east coast gets severe typhoons, another reason why the population prefers to migrate to the west side.

On the east coast it's easy to forget where you are. The sparsely inhabited rugged landscape could pass for the coast of New Zealand rather than crowded Taiwan. The scenery is stunning.

If you do not have the time to go all the way around Taiwan, a good option is to head down the east coast to Hualien and then cut across the island over the mountains to Taichung. This is a very scenic route, although you will miss some of the major attractions in the south of the island.

The amount of time needed to do any travelling in Taiwan is at least 10 days. As small as Taiwan is there is a lot to see, and 2 to 3 weeks would be a much better length of time to spend travelling. To visit all the places in this book and do the hikes, figure on over a month, maybe 2. If you are in a big hurry but have sufficient funds, you could save time by flying to a few scenic spots.

## SUAO TO HUALIEN HIGHWAY

The east coast of Taiwan is lined with spectacular mountains and cliffs. The area between Suao and Hualien is particularly dramatic, especially a section called the Chingshui Cliff (*qīngshǔi dùanyaí*) where sheer walls drop straight into the sea from towering mountains over 1000 metres high. In the 1920s the Japanese, who then occupied Taiwan, managed to carve a narrow road through this section, but ever since it has been a continuous battle between road crews and landslides, rockfalls, typhoons and occasional earthquakes.

Between Suao and Hualien the road is still so narrow that only one-way traffic is permitted. Buses, trucks and cars must drive along in a single-file convoy. There are two convoys daily in each direction between Hualien and Suao, one early in the morning and one in the afternoon. The road is closed at night.

Given the fact that the transport system was poor on the east coast and had been a major impediment to economic development, the government gave priority to opening up a reliable railway line. Incredible as it might seem, in 1980 the railway was finally completed between Suao and Hualien, ending the isolation of the east coast. It cost over US$200 million to construct, as it passes through 15 tunnels and over 91 bridges. The railway line is one of the world's great engineering feats. Previously, the most reliable way to go between Taipei and Hualien was to take a ferry from Keelung Harbor. Since the railway opened the ferry has gone out of business.

If you take the train you'll find it much faster and safer than the bus, but the bus trip is far more scenic. The train spends much of its time going through tunnels, whereas the bus climbs up and down the mountains, passing numerous valleys, beaches and incredible cliffs. This is one of the world's most scenic highways and if you miss it you've missed a lot. But nowadays, the majority of travellers take the train to Hualien.

## SUAO
*(sūaò)* 蘇澳

Although Suao itself is nothing to write

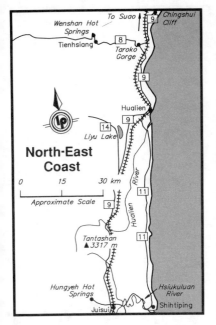

Wenshan Hot Springs
Tienhsiang
To Suao
Chíngshui Cliff
Taroko Gorge
Hualien
Liyu Lake
**North-East Coast**
0     15     30 km
Approximate Scale
Hualien River
Tantashan ▲ 3317 m
Hungyeh Hot Springs
Hsiukuluan River
Juisui
Shihtiping

*dàlüshè*), 49 Chungshan Rd, where singles are NT$150 to NT$300. However, it's very, very basic. A better deal for the money is the *xīnghúa lüshè* (tel (039) 962581), 13 Su'nan Rd, where doubles are NT$200 with shared bath, NT$350 with private bath.

The *hǎitiān dàlüshè* (tel (039) 962576), 96 Chungshan Rd, costs NT$350 for a single, NT$400 for a double. All rooms have a private bath and are clean. The *King Dou Hotel* (*jīndū dàlüshè*) (tel (039) 962586), 6 Taiping Rd, costs NT$400 for a double but doesn't seem worth the money.

If money is no object, the *Suao Hotel* (tel (039) 965181) (*sūaò fàndiàn*), 7 Sutung Chung Rd, offers good, clean doubles for NT$650.

### Getting There & Away

There are three ways to get to Suao from Taipei. The fastest way is to take the train to Suao. The next fastest option is to take a bus over the mountains from Taipei to Suao. The slowest, but by far most scenic route, is to take the coastal bus. Bus departures are from Taipei's North Bus Station. The fare from Taipei to Suao is NT$159.

Suao has two train stations, the old one (next to the bus station in central Suao) and a new one several km out of town called 'Hsin Suao' (*xīn sūaò*). Most express trains from Taipei stop only in Hsin Suao. Therefore, if you arrive from Taipei by express train and want to switch to the Suao to Hualien bus, you have to take a bus from Hsin Suao to the Suao bus station (15 minutes by bus, NT$9). Occasionally, local trains also run between Hsin Suao and Suao.

From Hualien, buses depart for Suao at 6.15 am and 12.10 pm.

### HUALIEN
*(hūalián)* 花蓮

The largest city on the east coast, Hualien is a pleasant place that sees a fair bit of tourist traffic. It's also an area for mining marble and there is a small international port to handle the marble exports.

Actually, Hualien itself is not the main attraction in the area, but rather the nearby

home about, many travellers wind up staying there overnight so they can catch the early morning bus to Hualien. Suao has an attractive harbour, but it's surrounded by fences and a police checkpoint, so you can hardly go wandering around in there. I can't imagine what they're trying to protect – Suao exports only fish and cement. One way to get a look at the harbour is to follow the road that leads out of the south side of town (part of the Suao to Hualien highway), which brings you up a big hill. From there you get a sweeping view of the harbour.

### Information

**Money** The Bank of Taiwan (tel (039) 962566) is at 97 Chungshan Rd.

### Places to Stay

There are a few cheap hotels near the bus station. The cheapest place in town is the *King Ein Hotel* (tel (039) 962372) (*jīnyàn*

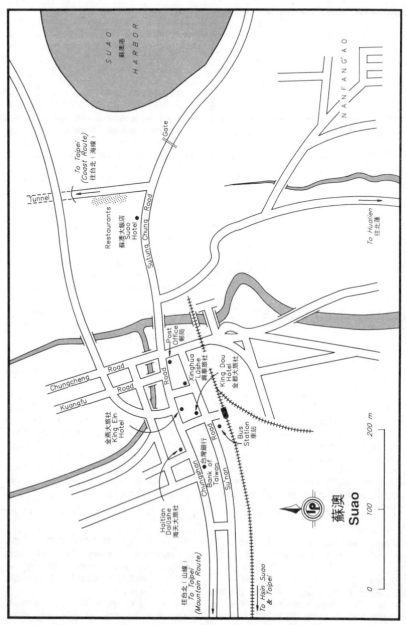

SUAO HARBOR 蘇澳港

NANFANG'AO

To Taipei (Coast Route) 往台北（海線）

Gate

Tunnel

To Hualien 往花蓮

Restaurants

蘇澳大飯店 Suao Hotel

Sytung Chung Road

Post Office 郵局

Chungcheng Road

Road

Kuangfu Road

Xinghua Lüshe 興華旅社

King Dou Hotel 金都大旅社

金燕大旅社 King Ein Hotel

Chungshan Road

Bank of Taiwan 台灣銀行

Bus Station 車站

Haitian Dalüshe 海天大旅社

Su-han Road

往台北（山線） To Taipei (Mountain Route)

To Hsin Suao & Taipei

蘇澳 Suao

0    100    200 m

Taroko Gorge, which is considered one of Taiwan's prime scenic attractions. Don't miss it! Hualien and Taroko Gorge are such a pleasant contrast to the hustle and bustle of Taipei that they are sure to give you a much more satisfying impression of the country.

## Information

**Money** ICBC (tel (038) 350191) is at 26 Kungyuan Rd. The Bank of Taiwan (tel (038) 322151) is nearby at 3 Kungyuan Rd.

## Ami Cultural Village

(*àměi wénhùa cūn*) 阿美文化村

If you arrive in Hualien in the early afternoon and plan to visit Taroko Gorge the next day, you'll have some time to take a look around. If you are into it, there are some Ami aboriginal song and dance shows put on for the tourists at the Ami Cultural Village (tel (038) 525231, 523571) (*àměi wénhùa cūn*). Hotels and travel agents in Hualien can arrange a ticket for you. Admission is NT$100 if you get there by yourself. On a tour, expect to pay NT$160. The dance shows are at 2.20, 3.20, 4.20, 6, 7.20 and 8.20 pm every day, but the schedule can change.

## Liyu Lake

(*lǐyú tán*) 鯉魚潭

If you'd like to get out of town, a nice half-day excursion is to Liyu Lake (*lǐyú tán*), a small but very pretty lake near Hualien. The main activities there are boating, fishing and hiking. If you go there, take the time to walk around the lake. There is a road going all the way. You will also find several well-marked trails leading up from the road behind the lake. These trails lead to the summits of some nearby peaks, a very pleasant walk if you're up to it. There are buses, approximately one every hour, from the local bus station in Hualien. The last bus leaves after 6 pm.

## Hsiukuluan River 秀姑巒溪

Besides the Taroko Gorge excursion, one of the most exciting things to do around Hualien is to take a rafting trip on the Hsiukuluan River. Most travel agents in Hualien can book the trip, which is good value at around NT$800 with transport, equipment and lunch included. Departure time is around 7 am, and you return to town at about 5 pm. These trips are mostly run in the summer. Expect to get soaking wet.

## Beach

If you'd prefer some quiet entertainment, you can stroll down to the beach. It's a pretty beach, but like most of east Taiwan's beaches, it's stony and the surf is too rough for safe swimming.

Ami Cultural Village ticket

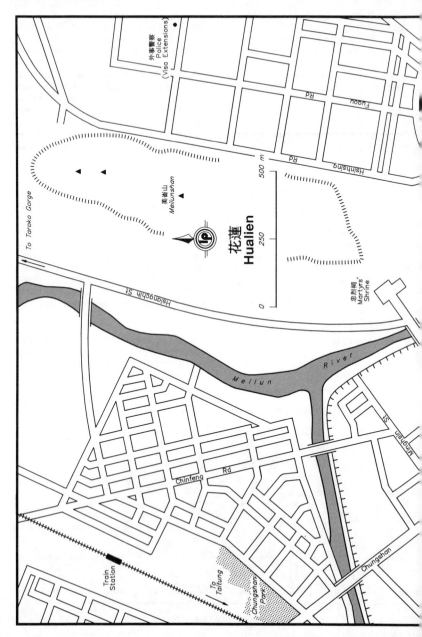

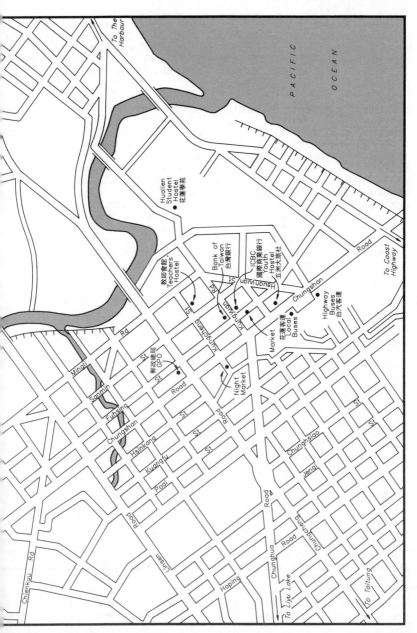

## Places to Stay – bottom end

For budget travellers, the best bargain in town is the *Teachers' Hostel* (tel (038) 325880) (*jiàoshī huìguǎn*), 10 Kungcheng St. They charge NT$130 for dormitory accommodation. In spite of the bargain prices and clean rooms, this place is rarely full. Although supposedly just for teachers, others are welcome to stay.

Another cheap dormitory is the *Hualien Student Hostel* (tel (038) 324124) (*huālián xúeyùan*), 40-11 Kungyuan Rd. Beds are NT$100.

The *Youth Hostel* (tel (038) 324132) (*wǔzhōu dàlüshè*) isn't really a youth hostel but a reasonably cheap hotel. It's at 84 Chungshan Rd, near the bus station. Singles/doubles cost NT$160/250 with shared bath, and NT$350 with private bath.

Most of the hotels are in the central part of town, in the vicinity of Chungshan Rd and the bus station. The *dàxin dàlüshè* (tel (038) 322125), at 101 Chungshan Rd, has doubles with private bath for NT$400. It's nice and clean.

## Places to Stay – top end

*CITC Hualien Hotel* (tel (038) 221171), (*zhōngxìn dàfàndiàn*)中信大飯店, 2 Yunghsing Rd, doubles NT$2310, twins NT$2540 to NT$3230

*Marshal Hotel* (tel (038) 326123, fax 326140) (*tǒngshùai dàfàndiàn*)統帥大飯店, 36 Kungyuan Rd, doubles NT$2000, twins NT$2600

*Toyo Hotel* (tel (038) 326151) (*dōngyáng dàfàndiàn*) 東洋大飯店, 50 Sanmin St, doubles/twins cost NT$840/1280

*Astar Hotel* (tel (038) 326111, telex 22347) (*yǎshìdū dàfàndiàn*) 亞士都大飯店, Seaview Ave, doubles cost NT$1760

## Places to Eat

Hualien has a great market on Fuhsing St just east of Kungyuan Rd. Prices are low and everything is available from complete meals to snacks and milkshakes. Plenty of seafood and traditional Taiwanese cuisine in this area. Also check the night market on Kungcheng St just south of Chungshan Rd.

A popular Western restaurant is *kěn tè lì* (tel (038) 351989), 249 Chungshan Rd. It has good chicken and is moderately priced. A more up-market Western restaurant is *East King* (tel (038) 336166) (*dōngwáng niúpái xīcān*), 255 Chungshan Rd. Good Japanese food is available at *hébā rìběn liàolǐ* (tel (038) 333826), 22 Fuhsing St.

## Things to Buy

Marble is the main export of Hualien. Personally, considering all the environmental destruction being caused by the mining operations, I would prefer to see the marble left in the ground. The Hualien area also produces a lot of cement in case you need to stock up.

For those determined to contribute to the ecological ruin, finished marble items can be bought at the Retired Servicemen's Engineering Agency main factory (*róngmín dàlǐshí gōngchǎng*) at 106 Huahsi Rd near the airport; many of the local shops also sell marble products. Some travel agencies offer a stop at the marble factory along with a trip to Taroko Gorge and the Ami Cultural Village.

## Getting There & Away

**Air** Getting to Hualien by air takes less than an hour from Taipei's Sungshan Domestic Airport (not from CKS International Airport). Both China Airlines and Far Eastern Air Transport fly direct from Taipei to Hualien. The one-way fare is NT$711.

For those with little time but a liberal budget, it is possible to fly to Hualien, take a bus tour of Taroko Gorge and fly back to Taipei the same evening. This can be done on an organised group tour if you don't mind being Tommy Tourist (seven cities in 3 days), but I personally think it is essential to spend at least 1 night in this beautiful part of Taiwan.

**Bus** There is no direct bus between Taipei and Hualien. First you must get to the town of Suao and then take the bus down the spectacular Suao to Hualien Highway. From Suao to Hualien there are only two buses daily, at 6.15 am and noon. The trip takes 3 hours and costs NT$109. If you arrive in Suao too late to catch either of these buses, you can spend the night at one of several hotels near the bus station. They are accustomed to waking people up at 5.30 am to catch the early bus.

When going southwards to Hualien sit on the left (ocean side) for the most spectacular views. The best seat is right up the front. Of course, some will say this seat is the most dangerous, but I always think that if the bus plunges over a cliff, where you sit doesn't make any difference.

Buses to Suao depart Hualien at 6.15 am and 12.10 pm. The fare is NT$109 and the trip takes 3 hours. Buses to Taichung depart Hualien at 7.30, 8 and 11 am. The trip takes 8 eight hours and costs NT$300. Coming the other way, buses depart Taichung at 7.15, 7.50 and 9.30 am.

From Hualien, you can also take a bus westward over the Central Cross-Island Highway (zhōngbù hénggùan gōnglù) 中部横貫公路. This incredible road runs from Taroko Gorge on the east coast to Taichung in the west. The road twists and climbs over Taiwan's awesome central mountain range and offers superb views at every turn.

If your time is limited, you could travel this highway from Hualien to Taichung and just forget about south Taiwan. Of course, you'd be missing a lot. Try to do both. Details of the journey over the Central Cross-Island Highway are provided in the chapter dealing with west-central Taiwan.

**Train** As the trip to Hualien is popular, it's best to book your train ticket a couple of days in advance, especially if you want a reserved seat. The fare of course depends on which class you travel in, but for the first three classes of train, the fares from Taipei range from NT$230 to NT$334.

On this route, avoid the old (cheap) trains which don't have air-conditioning. The trains spend a lot of time going through tunnels, which makes them very noisy and dirty when the windows are open.

**Bicycle** If you are athletically inclined, a bicycle trip down the east coast on a sturdy 10 speed offers an exciting journey. The only problem is that the stretch of highway between Suao and Hualien is so mountainous that you need to be in topnotch physical condition to challenge it. From Hualien to Taitung and to the southern tip of Taiwan is a much easier ride.

If you want to do this beautiful trip as a bicycle tour, consider taking the bicycle from Suao to Hualien on the train. It doesn't cost much to do this. You can ride down the coast to Taitung and then ship the bike back to Taipei, or continue on to Kenting at the southern tip of Taiwan and then up the west coast. The west coast is not as beautiful, so you can ship the bicycle back to Taipei from Fangliao, a small city south of Kaohsiung, if you want to.

Renting a 10 speed bicycle is not easy. Your best bet is to buy a new or secondhand model from a Taipei bicycle shop.

### Getting Around

Hualien is a small city and most points of interest can be reached on foot. The only time you will need to deal with the local transport system is on arrival or departure.

If you arrive by highway bus you can get off in the city centre. If you arrive by train, you will need to take a bus or taxi, as the train station is not in central Hualien. Buses are not that frequent, but bus No 105 goes to the city centre.

Being a resort area, motorcycle rentals are easy to find in Hualien. Most of the rental shops are right by the train station. People who rent bikes may well approach you as you exit the station. Rates are in the range of NT$400 to NT$500 daily depending on bike size.

When you leave the train station, expect to be greeted by a mass of screaming taxi drivers. Hualien taxi drivers do not use meters so you must agree on the fare before you get in. It should be around NT$70. The price is more or less fixed and is not subject to bargaining. The driver will almost certainly try to talk you into a chauffeur-driven tour of Taroko Gorge at NT$1500 or more, so just keep saying 'No'. If you find yourself heading out of town, stop the driver unless you want the tour.

If you stay in a moderate to expensive hotel in Hualien, someone can meet you at the train station if you tell them when you plan to arrive. They will often hold up a sign with your name written on it so you can find them.

## TAROKO GORGE
*(tàilǔgé)* 太魯閣

This fantastic canyon, 19 km long with a rushing white-water river surrounded by sheer cliffs, is considered Taiwan's top scenic attraction.

The highway running through the gorge is an engineering feat rivalling the construction of the nearby Suao to Hualien railway. The road was carved out of the sheer cliffs, at a cost of some 450 lives and US$11 million, and is part of the Central Cross-Island Highway which runs right over the moun-

tains connecting the east and west coasts of Taiwan. The road is an important transportation link for the centre of the island.

During the construction of this highway huge marble deposits were discovered, setting off a mineral boom in the Hualien area. For a while there was considerable pressure by certain interests to mine Taroko Gorge itself. However, after much debate the government came down on the side of the conservationists and the area has now been designated a national park. Whether the legislators were motivated by genuine concern for the environment or tourist revenues is not known – probably both. An equally appalling plan to build a dam in Taroko Gorge was also defeated.

At the entrance of the gorge you can see some mini-skirted aboriginal girls dressed in colourful costumes. Of course, they are there for a purpose – to pose for photos for a fee. They seem to do a thriving business. If you want to take their picture, negotiate the fee in advance.

Taroko Gorge

A short distance above the entrance to the gorge is the Eternal Spring Shrine (*cháng chūn cí*), which features a pavilion with a waterfall passing through it. The shrine is reached by hiking up a short hill from the highway and is well worth the walk. It was built in memory of those who lost their lives while constructing the highway.

## Tienhsiang

*(tiānxiáng)* 天祥

At the top of the gorge, nestled in between the towering cliffs, is the lovely resort village of Tienhsiang. It's a beautiful, relaxing place, certainly more tranquil than Hualien. Of course it offers no nightlife, other than gazing at the moon and stars; the main attraction is the scenery, plus the peace and quiet.

There are a number of short hikes you can do around Tienhsiang. Apart from the gorge itself, there is a pagoda and temple just across the river on a hill; they're easily reached by crossing the suspension bridge.

Up at Tienhsiang, one of the nicer things we did was to just walk upstream along the river. After 100 metres we were completely alone with the beautiful landscape, since nobody else bothered to go this far...On a hot, sunny day, swimming in the cool, crystal-clear water was wonderful – it is not allowed in the centre of Tienhsiang.

Maria Ahlqvist & Staffan Jonsson

**Places to Stay** This resort is popular with honeymooners and other tourists, so hotel space can be a problem at times and a reservation is advisable. On weekends or holidays, forget it.

You are not likely to get lost in Tienhsiang, as it is very small. At the downhill end of the parking area is the *Tienhsiang Lodge* (tel (038) 691155/8) (*tiānxiáng zhāodàisuǒ*). Doubles range from NT$1250 to NT$1350 and twins are NT$1350 to NT$1450. If you want to make a reservation from Taipei phone (02) 5515933.

A much cheaper place to stay and probably the best bargain in town is the *Catholic Hostel* (tel (038) 691122) (*tiānzhǔ táng*), where it is NT$80 in the dormitory and NT$500 for a double. It sits on a hill just

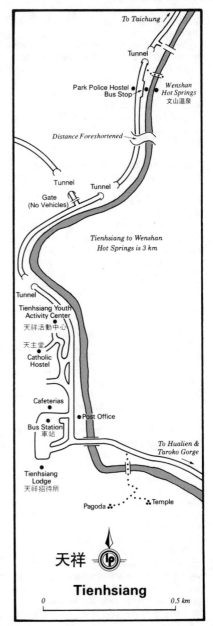

To Taichung

Tunnel

Park Police Hostel
Bus Stop

Wenshan
Hot Springs
文山溫泉

*Distance Foreshortened*

Tunnel   Tunnel

Gate
(No Vehicles)

*Tienhsiang to Wenshan
Hot Springs is 3 km*

Tunnel

Tienhsiang Youth
Activity Center
天祥活動中心

天主堂
Catholic
Hostel

Cafeterias

Post Office

Bus Station
車站

To Hualien &
Taroko Gorge

Tienhsiang
Lodge
天祥招待所

Pagoda        Temple

天祥

**Tienhsiang**

0        0.5 km

above the parking area and resembles a Swiss chalet.

Continuing up the same hill just a little further will bring you to a gleaming white building which is the *Tienhsiang Youth Activity Center* (tel (038) 691111/3) (*tiānxiáng húodòng zhōngxīn*), a government-run place that has dormitory beds. In spite of the fact that it has over 300 beds it's often full, so call ahead. Dormitory/doubles are NT$120/360.

**Places to Eat** You don't have many choices. There are a couple of tiny cafeterias adjacent to the bus terminals. The prices are about double those in Hualien, but that's what the market will bear.

The other alternative is to eat at the *Youth Activity Center*. You don't have to stay there, but if you want to eat with them, buy your tickets at least 30 minutes before meal time. Meals are served from 7 to 7.30 am, noon to 12.30 pm, and 6 to 6.30 pm. Breakfast is NT$30, lunch and dinner both cost NT$70 and the food is good.

**Getting There & Away** For details of getting to Tienhsiang, refer to the Getting There & Away section for Taroko Gorge.

From Tienhsiang, as from Hualien, you can take a bus westward over the Central Cross-Island Highway (*zhōngbù héngguàn gōnglù*) all the way to Taichung on the west coast. Details of the journey over the Central Cross-Island Highway are provided in the chapter dealing with west-central Taiwan.

### Tunnel Hike

If you walk exactly 1 km uphill from Tienhsiang on the main highway, on your left you will find a tunnel with a red gate. The gate is too small to permit motor vehicles to enter but a hiker can easily squeeze through. This is your gateway to a really fun hike, but you'll need a flashlight (torch), mosquito repellent and plastic bag to protect your camera. A raincoat or umbrella wouldn't hurt either because you'll be walking through many tunnels with 'rain' inside. Just follow the road – you can't get lost – and walk for

about 6 km. The destination is a nice waterfall which cascades over the road. I can't tell you where the road will end because it keeps getting longer. They're doing some road construction here, and my big fear is that the final purpose is to open the area up to tour buses, souvenir shops and revolving restaurants. If so, we can only hope for a decisive landslide. Enjoy the great scenery while you can.

### Wenshan Hot Springs
(*wénshān wēnqúan*) 文山溫泉

About 3 km up the main highway is Wenshan Hot Springs, at 575 metres above sea level. You can reach the springs by taking a bus or by hiking. The bus stops in front of a national park police station. Get off there and continue walking up the road for 400 metres. Before you enter the third tunnel up from Tienhsiang, there are some steps leading down to the river. Walk down, then cross the suspension bridge and go down a path on the other side to reach the hot springs.

Many hot springs in Taiwan have been ruined by the fact that the hot water has simply been diverted into the hotels to fill up the bathtubs so that the guests can have a private soak. This has been done because many of the locals are conservative and don't wish to be seen publicly in a swimsuit let alone in the nude. The Wenshan Hot Springs, however, are first rate and totally natural.

### Loop Hike

From Tienhsiang, walk down the gorge road to the park headquarters. Behind the building, which is behind the main 'Taroko Gorge National Park' sign, a trail starts. Stay to the left when you come to an intersection after the first couple of hundred metres, and after an elevation gain of some 200 to 300 metres, walk along the ridge through a lush forest. The trail terminates at Wenshan Hot Springs. Walk across the red suspension bridge and walk the easy 3 km back down the road to Tienhsiang. This hike takes about 4 hours.

### Getting There & Away

There are several tour buses from Hualien going to the gorge, all of which start out in

Top: Fruit market, Lukang (Strauss)
Left: Back street rooftops, Lukang (Strauss)
Right: Temple courtyard, Lukang (Strauss)

Top: Three Sisters Pond, Alishan (Storey)
Left: View just after dawn, Alishan (Storey)
Right: Post Office, Alishan (Storey)

the morning. They stop often so you can admire the scenery while the Chinese tourists take pictures of each other standing in front of the bus. There is a lunch stop before the tour concludes and then they bring you back to Hualien. The total cost is NT$450, lunch included.

If you decide to go by taxi, it's essential that you agree on a price beforehand and don't pay until the tour is over. If you pay in advance, your driver may suddenly vanish while you are still photographing the scenery.

The cheapest way by far to see the gorge is to take the local bus there and then walk back down. If you use this last option make sure you leave in the morning, as the walk down takes 4 hours. The local bus between Hualien and Tienhsiang costs NT$44 one way; the express bus costs NT$51. Departures are at 8.05, 8.15, 8.55 and 9.40 am, but check since the schedule changes periodically. It's best not to go on Sundays or holidays, since the number of cars on the road will be much greater at those times.

There are two routes between Hualien and Taitung. One route follows the coastline and the other runs through a long, narrow inland valley. Both routes are nice, but the coast road wins the prize for being the more scenic. If you take the inland route, you have the option of going by either bus or train. The train is slightly faster and more comfortable, but costs more than the bus.

The best way to enjoy the east coast of Taiwan would undoubtedly be on a motorcycle or 10 speed bicycle. If you can arrange this, it will be worth the effort. One possibility is to rent a motorcycle in Hualien, drive to Taitung on the coast road and drive back through the inland valley. All along the mountainous east coast there are fine, nearly deserted beaches. Most are rocky, but there are a few broad, sandy beaches. If you have your own transport, you can stop and have a look any time you see something particularly interesting.

If you don't have your own transport, one thing you could consider doing is to take the local rather than express bus. You could get off the bus at several places along the way to have a look around, then catch the next local bus. This requires some patience, since east coast buses are not very frequent, but the scenery compensates for the lack of convenience. It's often hard to decide where to get off the bus as the whole coast is nice. An excellent place to visit is Shihtiping (*shítīpíng*), which has great ocean scenery, a beautiful rocky coast and an interesting cemetery up on a hill. The cemetery probably explains why this area does not attract many Chinese tourists.

On Sundays or holidays, tour buses from Taipei come rumbling down the east coast highway. The tour companies focus on three main attractions: Eight Fairy Cave (*bā xiān dòng*), Stone Umbrella Rock (*shí yǔsǎn*) and Three Fairy Platform (*sān xiān tái*). At the risk of being crude, I need to explain – the Eight Fairy Cave resembles the female sexual organs. Chinese men like to stand in front of it and get their pictures taken. The Stone Umbrella Rock is a gigantic phallic symbol. Chinese women like to stand in front of it and get their pictures taken (I'm not making this up). The Three Fairy Platform is just a fancy bridge connecting some offshore rocks to the mainland – I guess that one is for the children.

On the inland valley route, the scenery is rolling farm country surrounded by mountains. There are two good hot springs along the way, Hungyeh and Antung, but they're only easily accessible if you are driving your own vehicle. The Chihpen Hot Springs, near Taitung, feature outdoor pools and have a bus service, making them much more accessible to travellers than Hungyeh or Antung.

## HUNGYEH HOT SPRINGS
*(hóngyè wēnqúan)* 紅葉温泉

If you're driving your own vehicle along the Hualien to Taitung highway (inland route), then these hot springs are well worth visiting. They are 6 km west of Juisui (*rùisùi*), which is on the main highway. If you're determined to visit these hot springs by public transport, take a train to Juisui and then get a taxi or hitch. Juisui is an out-of-the-way place and only local trains – not express – stop there.

There are no outdoor pools. The hot spring water is piped into bath houses which are part of a hotel complex. There is only one hotel, the *hóngyè wēnqúan lüshè* (tel (038) 872176). If you don't want to spend the night, you can rent a room for a few hours and use the hot springs for NT$250. However, for NT$200 you can get a tatami room and spend the night, using the hot springs for free. There are large tatami rooms for groups at NT$150 per person. A double room costs NT$500. The tatami rooms are really pleasant, and popular with the Japanese tourists who occasionally come through here. The food at the hotel is good.

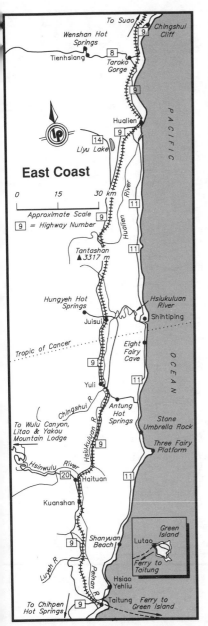

## ANTUNG HOT SPRINGS
*(āntōng wēnquán)* 安通温泉

Another hot spring resort just off the Hualien to Taitung inland highway, Antung is mainly for those who have their own transportation. There is only one hotel, the *āntōng wēnquán dàlüshè* (tel (038) 886108). Beautiful tatami rooms cost NT$300 for a single, NT$400 for a double and NT$450 for three people. If you prefer a bed, double rooms with private bath are NT$600, twins are NT$1000.

The hot springs are piped into private baths, not outdoor pools. Personally, I thought the bath houses at Hungyeh were better.

If you have your own vehicle, the hot springs are reached by first driving 6 km south of Yuli *(yùlí)*, then 5 km to the east on a narrow road. If you want to go to Antung by public transport, first take a train to Yuli (express trains *do* stop there) and then take a taxi (NT$200, 11 km) to Antung. Try to avoid the place on weekends.

## TAITUNG
*(táidōng)* 台東

In the south-east corner of Taiwan, Taitung is a somewhat out-of-the-way place that has escaped the feverish growth and industrialisation that characterises the north and west of the island. Taitung means 'east Taiwan' and the slow pace of the city certainly represents the east coast. This may change in the future as transportation improves, but for the moment Taitung remains a relatively quiet backwater. It is also a departure point for many interesting trips, particularly to Lanyu or Chihpen Hot Springs.

### Information
**Tourist Office** There is a local travel information office in the City Government Building at the corner of Chungshan Rd and Kungsheng Rd.

**Money** The Bank of Taiwan (tel (089) 324201) has a branch at 313 Chungshan Rd.

**Laundry** There are places that do laundry in

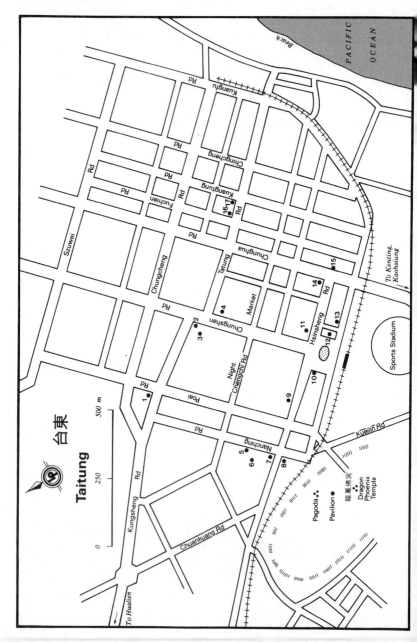

| | |
|---|---|
| 1 | Lanyu Shipping Office<br>台東縣輪船管理處 |
| 2 | Police (Visa Extensions)<br>外事警察 |
| 3 | City Government Building<br>市政府 |
| 4 | Bank of Taiwan<br>台灣銀行 |
| 5 | Swimming Pool<br>游泳池 |
| 6 | Teachers' Hostel<br>教師會館 |
| 7 | Sunshine Man Restaurant<br>香斯曼 |
| 8 | Tungnung Supermarket |
| 9 | Motorcycle Rental<br>榮春機車行 |
| 10 | Hotel Zeus<br>興東園大飯店 |
| 11 | Bus To Chihpen Hot Springs |
| 12 | Bus Station |
| 13 | Lenya Hotel<br>聯亞大飯店 |
| 14 | Dongbin Lüshe<br>東賓旅社 |
| 15 | Laundry<br>志倫洗衣店 |
| 16 | Telephone Company<br>電信局 |
| 17 | Post Office<br>郵局 |

### Dragon Phoenix Temple

*(lóngfèng fóugōng)* 龍鳳佛宮

In Taitung itself, the main attraction is the Dragon Phoenix Temple (*lóngfèng fóugōng*), which is on a hill about 10 minutes by foot from the central bus station. Be sure to go up the stairs in the temple and climb the big pagoda. On a clear day you can easily see Green Island (*lüdǎo*). As you face the main temple, on your left you'll see some stone stairs. Follow those to the top of the big hill for a magnificent view of Taitung and the surrounding coastline.

### Beaches

About 10 minutes walk from the centre is a beach at the end of Tatung Rd. It's pretty, but a little dangerous for swimming. The land seems to drop straight down here, making the water very deep just a few metres offshore. The surf is often rough and there are no lifeguards. Nevertheless, some people do swim here – just be careful.

North of town there is an excellent beach, Shanyuan (*shānyuán hǎishǔi yùchǎng*), which can be reached by bus. Unfortunately, there is an NT$40 admission charge.

Hsiao Yehliu (*xiǎo yěliǔ*) is just north of Fukang Harbor, about 8 km by road north of Taitung. The scenery is great, but it's rocky and the surf is too rough to allow safe swimming. Local residents from Taitung go there to fish off the rocks.

### Places to Stay

All the places listed here are within one block of the bus or train station in central Taitung.

The *rén'ài lüshè* (tel (089) 322423) is just behind the bus station; singles are NT$180. The *dōngbīn lüshè* (tel (089) 322222), at 536 Chunghua Rd, Section 1, has doubles/triples for NT$250/300. The *quánchéng lüshè* (tel (089) 322611), 51 Hsinsheng Rd, is NT$300 for a single.

The *Teachers' Hostel* (tel (089) 310142) (*jiàoshī hùigǔan*), 19 Nanching Rd, is clean, pleasant and popular with foreigners, but not very cheap. Prices for singles/doubles are NT$420/580, NT$630 for twins.

The *Jin An Hotel* (tel (089) 331168,

Taitung, but they're not fast. They need about 2 days. If you're going to Lanyu and Chihpen Hot Springs, you could drop your laundry off as soon as you arrive in Taitung and pick it up when you're ready to leave. Don't forget to ask them when it will be ready. You can speed things up a bit if you make it clear that you don't need it ironed (*búbì tàng yīfú*), just washed. A good place to go is *zhìlún gānxǐ diàn* (tel (089) 310386). It's right at the end of Hsinsheng Rd, where it meets Chunghua Rd.

**Swimming Pool** If you are in the mood to go swimming, the Taitung Municipal Swimming Pool (*yóuyǒng chí*) at 37 Nanching Rd is safer than the beach and not too bad as pools go.

322368) (*jīn'ān lüshè*), 96 Hsinsheng Rd, has singles/doubles for NT$430/500. The *xīngdōng yúan dàfàndiàn* (tel (089) 325101), 402 Chungshan Rd, has nice clean double rooms for NT$500. The *Hsin Hsin Hotel* (tel (089) 324185) (*xīnxīn dàlüshè*) has doubles for NT$550. *Lenya Hotel* (tel (089) 332135) (*liányǎ dàfàndiàn*), 296 Tiehua Rd, has doubles/twins for NT$600/910. *Hotel Zeus* (tel (089) 325101) (*xīngdōng yúan dàfàndiàn*), 402 Chungshan Rd, has doubles for NT$500.

### Places to Eat

Chunghua Rd is lined with numerous restaurants. Between Chunghua Rd and Chungshan Rd are many little alleys which become an active market at night. You can find almost anything imaginable to eat there. Chengchi Rd, between Chunghua Rd and Poai Rd, becomes a fruit market at night. Fruit in this part of Taiwan is particularly good.

A good but inexpensive dumpling restaurant is *tóngxīn jū* (tel (089) 323249) on the south-west corner of Chengchi Rd and Chungshan Rd.

Somewhat expensive, but certainly good, is *Sunshine Man* (tel (089) 323980) (*xiāng shī màn*), 268 Hsinsheng Rd, right next to the Teachers' Hostel. They make good fried chicken. Across the street is Tungnung Supermarket, Taitung's biggest.

### Getting There & Away

From Taitung it is possible to make the spectacular trip over the mountains on the Southern Cross-Island Highway. It is preferable, however, to make this trip from Tainan to Taitung, going west to east, rather than the other way. See the Tainan section in the South-West Taiwan chapter for details.

**Air** Far Eastern Airlines flies from Taipei to Taitung four times daily. The fare is NT$1167 one way.

**Bus** It takes about 4 hours by express bus along the coastal highway to get from Hualien to Taitung. Sit on the ocean side of the bus (left side) for the best views. If you are taking the bus from Taipei you must change buses in Hualien, from where there are frequent buses to Taitung.

There are plenty of buses connecting Taitung with Kaohsiung on the west coast, a 4 hour journey. This same bus also stops at

Poster giving first-aid tips for people who get burnt in the hot springs

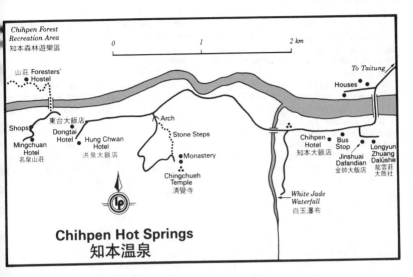

**Chihpen Hot Springs**
知本温泉

Chihpen Forest
Recreation Area
知本森林遊樂區

To Taitung

Houses

山莊 Foresters'
Hostel

東台大飯店
Shops
Dongtai
Hotel
Mingchuan
Hotel
名泉山莊

Hung Chwan
Hotel
洪泉大飯店

Arch
Stone Steps

Monastery

Chingchueh
Temple
清覺寺

Chihpen
Hotel
知本大飯店

Bus
Stop

Jinshuai
Dafandian
金帥大飯店

Longyun
Zhuang
Dalüshe
龍雲莊
大旅社

White Jade
Waterfall
白玉瀑布

0    1    2 km

Fengkang, where you can change buses to go to Kenting. The road is rough and curvy, so try to take the Kuokuang buses rather than the less comfortable Chunghsing buses.

**Train** From Taipei there is a frequent train service direct to Taitung via Hualien. The fastest trains take over 5 hours.

A rail line is under construction connecting Taitung to Kaohsiung. It was not open at the time of writing but perhaps it will be by the time you read this.

### Getting Around
Motorcycles can be rented from *lóngchūn jīchē háng* (tel (089) 328817), 182 Hsinsheng Rd. The cost is NT$300 to NT$500 per day. If you really want a good look at the east coast, you could drive all the way up to Hualien on the coastal route and then back down through the inland valley.

### CHIHPEN HOT SPRINGS
*(zhīběn wēnqúan)* 知本温泉
Chihpen Hot Springs is one of the most pleasant hot spring resorts on the island. It's about 30 minutes south-west of Taitung by either bus or taxi. What makes it such a nice

place is that it has a beautiful natural setting and good outdoor pools. To top it off there are places for hiking nearby, a clean river for swimming, and an interesting Buddhist temple and monastery.

### Hot Springs
The best hot springs are the outdoor pools at the Chihpen Hotel *(zhīběn dàfàndiàn)*. There are three pools, surrounded by swaying palm trees. One pool has cool water, one warm and the other scalding hot. I don't know what they use the super hot pool for, maybe boiling eggs. The medium temperature pool is just right. Admission to the pool is NT$50 and you can hire swimsuits for NT$30 and a towel for NT$5. The swimsuits tend to be small for most Western bodies and the towels are so tiny that you need four of them to dry off. The pool is open until 10 pm and is lit up at night. I certainly suggest that you go on a weekday, when you can have the pool to yourself. On weekends, local kids from Taitung overrun the place.

### White Jade Waterfall
*(báiyù pùbù)* 白玉瀑布
The hot springs are great, but there are other

attractions in the area. After you've soaked in the hot water, head up the road for some sightseeing. Five minutes of walking along the road, following the river upstream, will bring you to a mini-temple on your right side. Just after the temple, on the left side of the road, is a sign in the shape of a white arrow with Chinese characters written on it. It points to a narrow road, on the uphill side to your left. Follow the road uphill for 0.7 km and you'll come to White Jade Waterfall (*báiyù pùbù*). If you go during the dry season (winter) it could be reduced to a trickle. During the wet season, it's magnificent.

### Chingchueh Temple
*(qīngjúe sì)* 清覺寺

Back on the main road, continue walking upstream parallel to the river. Some 10 minutes of walking will bring you to a red steel archway to your left. You can follow the road that goes through the archway to take the stone steps just to the left. A short, steep climb uphill will bring you to a Buddhist monastery, the Chingchueh Temple (*qīngjúe sì*). This temple is most unusual in Taiwan, as it contains a large white-jade Buddha from Burma and a large golden Buddha from Thailand. There are some typically Chinese-looking deities off to either side. Remove your shoes if you go inside the temple.

### Chihpen Forest Recreation Area

Back on the main road, walking uphill again, you will pass the luxurious and expensive Dongtai Hotel. Walk a little further and you will come to a foot suspension bridge across the river. It costs a ridiculous NT$35 to cross the bridge – the admission fee to enter the Chihpen Forest Recreation Area.

Once inside the forest recreation area, there is a hiking trail that follows the north bank of the river, continuing upstream. You can walk in the river if you feel like it. It's likely you won't see anybody as cars and motorcycles cannot get in. The area near the suspension bridge is a great place to go swimming during the summer months. I've spent many an hour here, the rushing white

water gently massaging my body – as good a place as any to reach nirvana.

### Places to Stay

The *Chihpen Hotel* (tel (089) 512220) (*zhīběn dàfàndiàn*) has the nicest hot spring and, since the hot springs are the chief attraction, it's a logical place to stay. If you stay here, you can use the hot springs as many times as you like free of charge. However, the hotel is not cheap. Doubles/twins are NT$1300/1600, but they have some old dumpy rooms for NT$400 for a double. They don't like to tell you about them unless you keep insisting that the hotel is too expensive and start to walk out. Be forewarned that these old rooms have paper-thin walls – they ought to rent out earplugs.

Just to the east of the Chihpen Hotel is the *jīnshùai dàfàndiàn* (tel (089) 512508), where doubles are NT$550. Right next to that is the *lóngyún zhuang dàlüshè* (tel (089) 512627), where doubles cost NT$500.

Up on the western end of the road, just before the foot suspension bridge, is the *Dongtai Hotel* (tel (089) 512290, 512918) (*dōngtái dàfàndiàn*), where doubles/twins go for NT$1600/2000. Fortunately, they offer a 40% discount on weekdays. Nearby is the *Hung Chwan Hotel* (tel (089) 513181) (*hóngqúan dàfàndiàn*), which charges NT$1300 for a double and NT$1800 for a twin.

The *Mingchuan Hotel* (*míngqúan lüyóu shān zhuang*) (tel (089) 513996) is at the western end of the road, past the suspension bridge. It's up on a hill with a nice view, and they have cottages for rent. The cost is NT$800 for a double.

There is a very small hostel, *shān zhuang*, inside the Chihpen Forest Recreation Area that only charges NT$150. Unfortunately, the people who manage the place are elusive and I've never been able to find the man with the keys to open the hostel. However, the workers who sell admission tickets at the suspension bridge insist that it is possible to stay at the hostel. It should be a great place to stay, especially in summer – as you'll be surrounded by forest with a rushing cool river, you could probably get away with swimming nude at night when no one is around. Be sure to bring a torch (flashlight) and some food, as there are no facilities inside the forest recreation area.

## Getting There & Away

From Taitung there is a bus about every 45 minutes between 6.20 am and 10 pm. It departs from a bus stop just next to the Lanyu Travel Agency on Hsinsheng Rd, opposite the main bus terminal. The fare is only NT$18.

Returning to Taitung, the bus departs from the vendor's roadside stand next to the Chihpen Hotel, or further upstream from the Dongtai Hotel.

By taxi, the fare between Taitung and Chihpen is NT$250 or so, subject to bargaining.

## LANYU 蘭嶼

*(lányǔ)*

Some 62 km south-east of Taiwan proper is the tropical island of Lanyu, which has been designated a national park. In English, Lanyu means 'Orchid Island'. The island, which actually has few orchids, is interesting because it is inhabited by some 2000 aborigines from the Yami tribe. The Yami are one of the smaller aboriginal tribes in Taiwan.

The landscape resembles that of a volcanic Pacific island rather than Taiwan, and the island culture is closer to cultures found in the Philippines and the Pacific islands than to Chinese culture. Many of the older islanders still wear loincloths and speak their own dialect, which is definitely not related to Chinese. They live by cultivating taro and sweet potatoes and also by raising pigs and catching fish. The women like to chew betel nut, and unlike Chinese women, they have no fear of getting a suntan. Their traditional homes are built underground to offer refuge from the typhoons, which are severe in this region. There is no industry and most of the island is uninhabited.

If all this sounds like you are about to embark on a journey into the Stone Age, you may be disappointed. Lanyu is very different from Taiwan, but outside influences are definitely creeping in and the native culture is rapidly changing. Christian missionaries have done their job so well that now in each of the six villages on the island there are two churches, one Catholic and the other Presbyterian.

There are a few small Chinese businesses on the island, and taxis, TV, radio, beer and cigarettes are all having an impact on the island culture. There are schools on Lanyu which provide education up to the junior high school level so all the young people can speak Mandarin Chinese. The elders may still wear their loincloths, but young people have discovered blue jeans. Many of the young people now go to work in Taiwan and the majority never return.

The fact that Lanyu is changing is a good reason to see it now, before the native culture disappears forever. Many of the islanders are very poor and will try to peddle their souvenir models of Lanyu canoes which the island is famous for. The people are very friendly, and if you can speak Chinese or Japanese they will gladly chat with you for hours. All that is needed to strike up a conversation is a cigarette. The Yami love them and I advise you to carry a pack or two even if you don't smoke. You can also use cigarettes to barter with.

Lanyu offers excellent coastal scenery. As the island originated from volcanic eruptions, the coastline is of jagged black volcanic rock. It's certainly beautiful but makes swimming difficult. About the only beach where you can swim is south of the airport, near the Lanyu Hotel.

The main activity for tourists is to walk around the island, a distance of 37 km with no big hills. That's a very stiff 1 day or a comfortable 2 day hike.

In winter bring a raincoat, as it rains lightly nearly every day and it is also windy. In summer, carry water as the island is very hot and suffers from drought. As Samuel Coleridge said, 'Water, water, everywhere, but not a drop to drink'. Don't attempt to go anywhere on Lanyu during a typhoon. Although you can buy film on Lanyu, it is

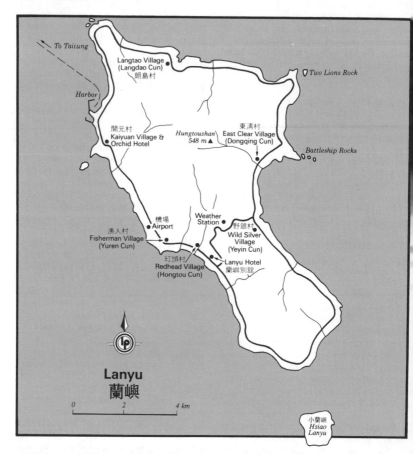

To Taitung

Langtao Village
(Langdao Cun)
朗島村

Two Lions Rock

Harbor

開元村
Kaiyuan Village &
Orchid Hotel

Hungtoushan
548 m ▲

東清村
East Clear Village
(Dongqing Cun)

Battleship Rocks

機場
Airport

Weather
Station

野銀村
Wild Silver
Village
(Yeyin Cun)

漁人村
Fisherman Village
(Yuren Cun)

紅頭村
Redhead Village
(Hongtou Cun)

Lanyu Hotel
蘭嶼別館

**Lanyu**
**蘭嶼**

0        2        4 km

小蘭嶼
Hsiao
Lanyu

much cheaper in Taiwan so bring an adequate supply.

Chinese tourists have not endeared themselves to the local aboriginal population. If you visit on Sundays or holidays, you'll see why. Residents of Taipei catch the morning flight to Taitung, then fly over to Lanyu for a 1 hour tour of the island. Men dressed in suits and ties, and women in high-heels, diamond rings and slit dresses come to Lanyu just to take pictures of each other standing in front of a Lanyu canoe; they point and giggle at the aborigines in their loin-cloths, eat lunch, take in a phony aboriginal song and dance show, and then return to Taitung to catch the afternoon flight back to Taipei.

## Places to Stay

The two hotels in Lanyu know that they have a captive market, and their prices reflect this reality – accommodation costs about twice as much as in Taiwan.

The two airlines which fly to the island also operate the two hotels and both hotels offer a free shuttle service to and from the airport. The *Orchid Hotel* (tel (089) 320033) (*lányǔ dàfàndiàn*), in Kaiyuan village, is operated by Taiwan Airlines. Dormitory accommodation costs NT$250 and doubles range from NT$700 to NT$900. It is also the closer of the two hotels to the harbour, should you arrive by boat. Kaiyuan village has the island's best 'nightlife', which consists of a couple of noodle shops with TV sets.

The *Lanyu Hotel* (tel (089) 326111/3) (*lányǔ biéguǎn*), operated by Formosa Airlines, has dorm accommodation for NT$250, singles for NT$400 to NT$600 and doubles for NT$700 to NT$1500. It's also adjacent to what is probably the best beach on the island.

If you want to save some cash, it is possible to camp out next to a schoolhouse. You should ask permission first, though this will nearly always be granted. Sometimes they'll let you stay inside the schoolhouse, if you can find the person with the key to open it, but nobody speaks English. It is also possible to sleep in a church, but again, ask first. Lanyu is a laid-back place and nobody will hassle you if you set up a tent just about anywhere. You won't need much equipment as it's never cold, but a waterproof tent would be wise. In winter, a blanket would be warm enough, and in summer it's so hot you won't be able to stay in the tent.

### Places to Eat

Food in Lanyu is available at the two hotels – NT$70 for breakfast and NT$140 for lunch or dinner. There are a couple of reasonably priced noodle shops around the island and some closet-size grocery stores selling dried noodles and canned goods. If you're desperate, you could buy some taro roots and sweet potatoes from the locals.

### Getting There & Away

**Air** Two airlines, Formosa Airlines and Taiwan Aviation Company (TAC), fly small propeller-driven aircraft from Taitung to Lanyu. There is no way a jet aircraft can land here as the airport runway is so short. From Taitung, a one-way airfare is NT$907, double that for the round trip. The flight time is about 30 minutes.

Both airlines also operate flights between Kaohsiung and Lanyu once a day. The fare is NT$1406 one way and the flight time is 50 minutes.

It's easy to buy the ticket in Taitung direct from the airline. The airlines both have their offices across the street from the bus station in central Taitung. The Formosa Airlines office is on Hsinsheng Rd. Taiwan Airlines' office is near the Hotel Zeus. The Lanyu Travel Agency is also an agent for Formosa Airlines.

Don't believe the printed timetables published by these airlines. They put on as many flights as they need. Especially on holidays and weekends, the schedule is ignored. When the weather is bad, they won't fly at all.

You can usually get a flight within 24 hours without a reservation. On a weekday, especially in the off season, you can often walk into their office and buy a ticket for a flight leaving within an hour. If you want to make a reservation, call the airlines in Taitung: Formosa Airlines (tel (089) 326677) (*yǒngxīng hángkōng gōngsī*) and Taiwan Airlines (tel (089) 327061) (*táiwān hángkōng gōngsī*).

These airlines both have offices in the major airports throughout Taiwan, including Taipei's domestic airport, Kaohsiung, Hualien and Taichung.

One thing to keep in mind is that both airlines will offer you free transport to and from the airport from their offices in Taitung, a very welcome service. If you are waiting for a flight to Lanyu, you can store your baggage in the airline offices while you mess around in Taitung. If you have extra baggage that you don't want to take to Lanyu, you can leave it with the airlines, even for several days.

**Sea** It is possible to reach Lanyu by ship from Taitung via Green Island, but this is a slow trip and not very comfortable. I certainly wouldn't recommend it if the sea is rough, but in calm water it could be OK. The ship is designed mainly to handle cargo, but they will take passengers. To buy a ticket, you must book it yourself at the Lanyu Shipping Agency (tel (089) 322210, 322290) (*táidōng xiàn lún chúan gǔanlǐ chù*), 306 Poai Rd.

The fare to Lanyu is NT$302 but the boat service is not reliable. If they don't get enough passengers and cargo, they don't sail. The ship is periodically taken out of service for maintenance. Departures are usually twice weekly, on Saturday and Tuesday, from the port of Fukang (*fùgāng*), north of Taitung, at some indefinite time between 5 and 7 am. The ship takes 5 hours to reach Lanyu, 4 hours to return. You must búy the ticket in advance and be at the pier at the crack of dawn before they sail. There are buses to Fukang, but not at this early hour, so you must either get a taxi or stay in a hotel at Fukang.

You must have your passport for this boat trip. You get a free stopoff along the way at Green Island because the boat needs to unload cargo. There will be taxi drivers at the pier to greet you and you can race around the island by taxi if you like, but make sure you

don't miss the boat. The taxi drivers will accommodate you with their Grand Prix driving skills. You will probably enjoy the boat ride to Lanyu, but most people elect to fly back.

### Getting Around

Walking is great for those who have the time and energy, but the island really is large so you'll probably opt for motorised transport. Motorcycles are available for rent from the hotels for NT$500 per day.

A bus goes around the island four times daily, twice in a clockwise direction and twice anticlockwise. The last bus makes a run between 3.30 and 4.30 pm, so don't miss it because there is practically no chance to hitchhike and there are very few telephones around to call a taxi from. These buses are rather expensive for the short distance they travel – it costs about NT$150 to go around the island.

The two hotels occasionally run a touring

Canoe at Lanyu

minibus around the island for NT$280 per person if they can get enough passengers.

## GREEN ISLAND
*(lüdǎo)* 綠島

Relatively few foreign tourists make it to Green Island, even though it is closer to Taitung and cheaper to visit than Lanyu. There are several good reasons for this. Lanyu is larger, more beautiful and has a unique aboriginal culture, whereas Green Island is more typically Taiwanese, more developed and more densely populated. It certainly is not as developed as Taiwan, of course, but it offers few surprises for those already familiar with Taiwan. There is also a lot of military stuff and a prison on the island, neither of which do much to attract tourism.

On the other hand, Green Island does offer some interesting scenery, unspoilt beaches and a chance to get away from it all. Overall, I would say that the trip to Green Island is worth doing if you are in Taitung anyway with an extra day to spare and don't mind paying the additional airfare – just don't expect it to be another Hawaii. The island can be seen in a day if you catch the 7.30 am flight out there and return on the last flight at 4.30 pm. If you take the boat to Lanyu you get a free stopoff in Green Island, but it's uncertain how long the boat will stay there loading and unloading cargo.

### Things to See

I suggest touring the island in a clockwise direction. If you're taking a taxi, make it clear to the driver that you want a chance to stop and see some of the sights along the way and don't simply want to race around at high speed.

You should take the taxi to the hot spring *(xù wēnqúan)* at the south end of the island. First stop off in the village of Kungguan *(gōnggǔan)* and have a look around. It's a very colourfully painted village. Then head up the steep hill and stop at the Kuanyin Cave *(gūanyīn dòng)*, which has a miniature temple inside. One stalagmite is dressed in a cape and represents the deity Kuanyin. There

is always incense burning in the cave. It is placed there in the morning by pilgrims who come from both Green Island and Taiwan to worship.

After the cave, the road continues along the hills of the rugged east coast of the island. The scenery is great. You finally come to the hot spring *(xù wēnqúan)* at the southern tip of the island, right on the beach. It's not a very large spring but it's totally natural and the temperature is comfortable for bathing.

Although it looks like a great place for nude bathing, I don't recommend this in Taiwan. First of all, you could easily offend someone and make it tough on travellers who follow you. Secondly, the Chinese are unabashed starers. When I was there, a couple of foreigners decided to take a swim. No sooner had they taken their clothes off than four taxis pulled up carrying 20 very proper-looking, camera-clicking tourists. When the tourists saw what was going on, they quickly moved in for the best view. Then came the photo session. You know the Chinese – they always like to get a picture of themselves standing in front of something. And what could be a better prop than a few naked foreigners? Although these particular foreigners didn't mind being the centre of attention, all this was a little too much for them.

When you get to the hot spring, pay your driver and head off on foot after you've seen the spring. Soon you will come to a new youth hostel built at the southern tip of the island. Continuing around the island, you will come to a beach called Tapaisha *(dàbáishā)*, which means 'Big White Sands'. You have to wonder why they call it that, because there isn't any sand at all, just coral. Not a place for swimming, but snorkelling should be good here. Continuing along the road, you'll see three beautiful caves in succession. You can go inside two of them, but the third has too much water in it.

If you keep walking, you'll soon reach the boat harbour and then the airport. You can enjoy a good meal at one of the small restaurants in Chungliao while waiting for your flight out.

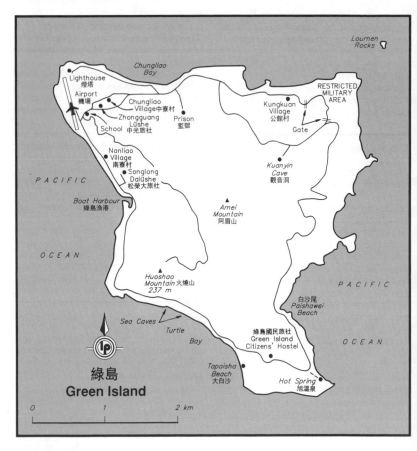

Lournen
Rocks

Chungliao
Bay

Lighthouse
燈塔

Airport
機場

Chungliao
Village中寮村

Zhongguang
Lüshe
中光旅社

School

Prison
監獄

RESTRICTED
MILITARY
AREA

Kungkuan
Village
公館村

Gate

Nanliao
Village
南寮村

Songlong
Dalüshe
松榮大旅社

Kuanyin
Cave
觀音洞

PACIFIC

Boat Harbour
綠島漁港

OCEAN

Amei
Mountain
阿眉山

Huoshao
Mountain 火燒山
237 m

PACIFIC

白沙尾
Paishawei
Beach

Sea Caves

Turtle

Bay

綠島國民旅社
Green Island
Citizens' Hostel

OCEAN

綠島
Green Island

Tapaisha
Beach
大白沙

Hot Spring
旭溫泉

0          1          2 km

## Places to Stay

The only cheap place to stay is *zhōnggŭang lüshè* (tel (089) 672516) in the village of Chungliao (*zhōngliáo*). They asked NT$250 for a double but the price quickly dropped to NT$200 when I started to leave. It's certainly a no-frills hotel, but Green Island doesn't offer many choices.

Near the boat harbour is Nanliao (*nánliáo*), where you can find the comfortable but expensive *sōnglóng dàlüshè* (tel (089) 672515). It's nice, clean and friendly, which it should be at NT$1200 for a double.

At the very southern tip of the island is the *Green Island Citizens' Hostel* (tel (089) 672314, 672244) (*lüdǎo gúomín lüshè*). Doubles are ridiculously priced at NT$1300. It's a long way from the airport and just about everything else, except the hot springs and Tapaisha Beach.

## Getting There & Away

The details of getting to Green Island are exactly the same as for Lanyu. There are direct flights from Taitung on Formosa Airlines and Taiwan Airlines (TAC). Make sure you book your return flight as soon as you arrive in Green Island and make them write it on your ticket, as they have a habit of 'forgetting' and giving your seat to someone else. The one-way airfare between Taitung and Green Island is NT$454, double for a round trip.

There is an occasional direct flight between Green Island and Lanyu but there is no published schedule and it seems to be more or less a charter. Don't count on it.

The twice weekly ship to Lanyu has a 2 hour stop at Green Island. You must show your passport if you travel by this boat.

### Getting Around

There is supposed to be a bus service around the island but it seems to be very irregular. Groups visiting the island often charter the one bus available, thereby taking it out of circulation.

Motorcycle rentals are available right at the airport for a daily rate of NT$300. You won't have to look hard for the bikes – people will approach you and make the offer.

Another way to go is by taxi. Try to find a decent taxi driver to take you halfway around the island. We paid NT$300 for a taxi when I was last there and felt it was worth it. It's 17 km around the island, which isn't terribly far but too far if you must get back to catch your plane the same day. If you are staying overnight, it's no problem to walk the entire route.

### SOUTH OF TAITUNG

After the highway south of Taitung passes Chihpen Hot Springs it clings to the cliffs, offering beautiful scenery all along the way. When it reaches the small aboriginal town of Tawu (*dàwǔ*), the highway turns west and climbs steeply over the mountains to reach the town of Fengkang (*fēnggǎng*) on the west coast. Unfortunately, you'll have to admire the scenery from the window of the bus unless you have your own transport. If you do drive yourself, there are plenty of places where you can stop and walk along the beach.

### KENTING
(*kěndīng*) 墾丁

Situated on a bay just a few km from Taiwan's southernmost tip, Kenting has beautiful white sandy beaches, a national park filled with lush tropical vegetation and, not surprisingly, the warmest weather in Taiwan. Although there is a chilly wind in winter, it is just warm enough for year-round bathing. It's one of the most relaxing places in Taiwan.

Kenting has become a popular recreation area for both Chinese and expatriate workers from Taipei, Taichung and Kaohsiung, so it tends to become a sea of humanity on weekends and holidays. It's best to visit during the weekdays to avoid the crowds.

### Livestock Research Station 墾丁牧場

Adjacent to the beach at Kenting is a Livestock Research Station. It's open to the public and you can have a look around. Be careful of the fences as some of them are electrified. The voltage is low and not dangerous, but it's enough to restrain a cow or to give someone a thrill.

### Lungluan Marsh 龍鑾潭

If you're a bird-watcher, bring your binoculars and head for Lungluan Marsh just north of the power plant. A large number of birds nest there because this is a migratory route between the Asian mainland and the Philippines. The birds were once relentlessly hunted but are now under the protection of the Park Service. Autumn and spring are the best times for viewing migratory species.

### Kenting National Park

After you've enjoyed the sun and surf in Kenting, head towards the national park. The park is famous for its Botanical Gardens. Just inside the park is a tall, steep, pointed peak named Big Sharp Mountain (*dàjiānshān*). You can't miss it, as it dominates the skyline. At first sight it looks as if it would be impossible to climb, but in fact there are two routes going up that are not terribly difficult so long as you are not afraid of heights. One route goes right up the steep front face and the

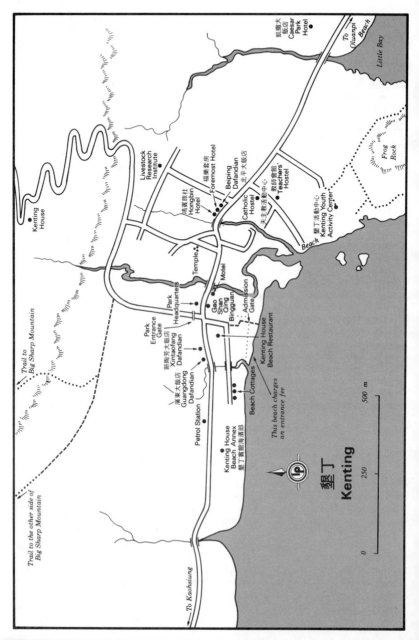

To Oluanpi Beach

Little Bay

凱撒大飯店 Caesar Park Hotel

Frog Rock

Livestock Research Institute

福樂套房 Foremost Hotel

北平大飯店 Beiping Dafandian

教師會館 Teachers' Hostel

鴻賓旅社 Hongbin Hotel

天主教活動中心 Catholic Hostel

墾丁活動中心 Kenting Youth Activity Center

Beach

Kenting House

Temple

Motel

Gao Shan Qing Bingguan

Park Headquarters

Admission Gate

Park Entrance Gate

新陶芳大飯店 Xintaofang Dafandian

廣東大飯店 Guangdong Dafandian

Kenting House Beach Restaurant

Beach Cottages

This beach charges an entrance fee

Petrol Station

Kenting House Beach Annex 墾丁賓館海濱部

Trail to Big Sharp Mountain

Trail to the other side of Big Sharp Mountain

To Kaohsiung

墾丁 Kenting

500 m

250

0

other safer, but longer, route is at the back. If you want to climb it, I suggest ascending on the steep front side and descending on the other side, which is gentler.

To find the way up, first walk through the gate that enters the park. A short walk will bring you to a dirt road on your left. Walk down the road a short distance until the mountain is directly in front of you. There are some cow pastures and a gate which you enter through. Walk uphill through the pastures, following the fence, and eventually the path becomes obvious. The view from the top is fantastic.

Inside the park, high on a hill overlooking the area, is the luxurious Kenting House hotel and restaurant. There is an infrequent bus that goes up into the park for NT$8. One of the highlights of the park is the sea-viewing tower – it is claimed that on a clear day, one can see Lanyu and the Bataan Islands of the Philippines. I've been able to spot Lanyu but not the Philippines. You can often see military patrol boats – not surprising since this is the prime smuggling route for Philippine-produced drugs and firearms.

## Places to Stay

It's easy to find accommodation in Kenting, except on weekends and holidays. If you arrive during the week you can book into a room, but be warned that some places will ask you to leave on Saturday because another group has booked and paid for all the rooms in advance. Weekend prices may be double, if you can get a room at all. On weekends, you might be forced to stay in Hengchun, a not-very-attractive town 9 km to the north.

The *Teachers' Hostel* (tel (08) 8861241) (*jiàoshī hùiguǎn*) offers good rooms at bargain prices. The dormitory costs NT$100 and doubles cost NT$300 but, unfortunately, it is usually full. Anyway, you are supposed to be a teacher to stay there. The nearby *Catholic Hostel* (tel (08) 8861540) (*tiānjǔjiào húodòng zhōngxīn*) is also cheap but not nearly as attractive as the Teachers' Hostel. The dormitory costs NT$100.

I found the *Hongbin Hotel* (tel (08) 8861003) (*hóngbīn lüshè*) in the centre of town to be quite a pleasant place to stay. Singles/doubles cost NT$300/400 during the week, but on weekends prices escalate and rooms are usually not available. Right next door is the *Foremost Hotel* (tel (08) 8861007) (*fùlè tàofáng*), where singles/doubles cost NT$300/400.

One place has a sign outside which just says 'Motel' but it actually has a dorm. The Chinese name is *yǎkè zhījiā* (tel (08) 8861272). The dorm costs NT$150 and double rooms are NT$960.

The *Kenting Youth Activity Center* (tel (08) 8861221) (*kěndīng húodòng zhōngxīn*) is a government-operated place that boasts a unique architecture designed to resemble an ancient Chinese village. On the negative side, it's expensive for a youth hostel with dormitory beds costing NT$250. It is also somewhat isolated from the centre of town, where you will probably want to eat and stroll around at night.

*Kenting House* (tel (08) 8861370) (*kěndīng bīnguǎn*) has been a long-time favourite for those able to afford the beach-front cottages and the fine Western restaurant. A beach cottage for four people costs NT$3200 and twins cost NT$1600. Kenting House has two branches, one right on the beach and one several km away on a mountain inside the park. The mountain branch is slightly cheaper at NT$1200 for a double.

The *Caesar Park Hotel* (tel (08) 8895222, fax 8894729) (*kǎisà dàfàndiàn*) is a five star place designed to attract international tourists. The facilities are magnificent but you pay for them – doubles start at NT$4200. This place seems to be popular with the Japanese. The hotel operates a shuttle bus from Kaohsiung's train station which also stops at Kaohsiung airport – it costs NT$250 one way. Even if you don't stay there, you may want to go to their disco, the only real nightlife in Kenting. They have a money-changing service but only for their own guests.

There are a few other hotels worth considering: at the *xīn tǎofáng dàfàndiàn* (tel (08) 8861021), a double or triple room costs

NT$600. The *běipíng dàfàndiàn* (tel (08) 8861028) has doubles for NT$500. The *gǔangdōng dàfàndiàn* (tel (08) 8861263) also has doubles for NT$700. Right opposite the park gate is the *gāo shān qīng bīngǔan* (tel (08) 8861527), which has doubles for NT$1600.

### Activities
**Water Sports** Kenting is a beach resort so the main activities are swimming, sunbathing, windsurfing, snorkelling and scuba diving. You can swim and lie in the sun for free at all the beaches, except for the beach next to the Kenting House Beach Restaurant, where an admission fee is charged. There is a very nice beach at Little Bay, just opposite the Caesar Park Hotel.

The other sun and water activities require equipment which can easily be hired. Everything from diving masks to sea scooters are available. Most of the sea toys are available at shops in central Kenting and at the beach. You won't have a hard time finding what you want.

**Walks** All around the youth hostel are nice walks that lead down to the beach. Be sure to climb Frog Rock, the big rock adjacent to the hostel. There is a steep path leading to the top, but it's not a difficult climb.

### Getting There & Away
There are no buses which go directly to Kenting. You must first go to Hengchun (*héngchūn*), which is 9 km north of Kenting. Shuttle buses connecting Hengchun with Kenting run about every 40 minutes between 8 am and 6 pm. Wild chicken taxis are numerous, and you can always try hitching.

**To/From Taitung** To reach Hengchun from Taitung, buy a ticket to Fengkang (*fēnggǎng*). All buses going to Kaohsiung stop in Fengkang. From Fengkang there are numerous buses heading south to Hengchun, from where you can get a shuttle bus to Kenting.

If you look at a map, it appears that there is a road running directly between Taitung and Kenting. Unfortunately, that road is closed to the public because of a military base in the area. You must go by way of Fengkang.

**To/From Kaohsiung** There are frequent buses from the Kaohsiung main bus station to Hengchun. The fare is NT$140.

**To/From Taipei** If you have the money but not much time, you may consider flying to Kaohsiung airport and catching a bus south to Hengchun. Buses go right by the airport entrance and can be flagged down, so it's not necessary to go into Kaohsiung city.

The bus fare from Taipei to Kenting is NT$558.

### Getting Around
There is a regular bus service between Hengchun and Oluanpi, stopping at Kenting along the way. Wild chicken taxis also regularly patrol the roads. Hitching is another possibility.

It is a very nice area for walking or cycling. There are plenty of bicycles for hire in Kenting and you'll have no trouble finding a rental shop. A bike costs about NT$100 for 8 hours. However, Taiwanese bicycles do tend to be on the small side, which is a handicap for tall Westerners.

You can hire motorcycles and 4WDs at restaurants all over Kenting. You won't have any trouble finding a rental place – you'll have to climb over the vehicles just to get into some of these restaurants. For a motorcycle, prices are NT$100 per hour or NT$500 for 8 hours. As for hiring a 4WD, I can't see the point. The roads are all surfaced and smooth, so why would anyone need a 4WD vehicle? I suppose that many of the locals have never driven one before, so this is their chance to do it.

## AROUND KENTING
### Maopitou
*(māobítóu)* 貓鼻頭

Maopitou is the peninsula across the bay from Kenting, near the nuclear power plant. It has beautiful coral formations. To get there by bus, first go back to Hengchun, then get a

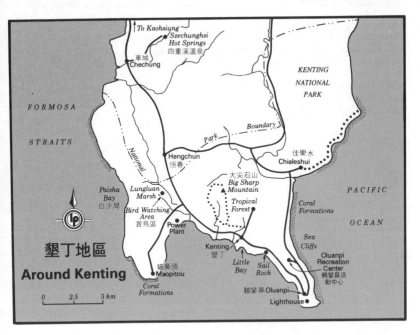

**Around Kenting** 墾丁地區

bus to Maopitou. The town of Maopitou occupies pretty much the whole peninsula, which isn't very large.

### Oluanpi
#### (élúanbí) 鵝鑾鼻
The southernmost tip of Taiwan is 8 km south-east of Kenting. Oluanpi has pretty coral gardens and a lighthouse. There is a small admission charge for the gardens.

Most people prefer to stay in Kenting, but there are a few hotels in Oluanpi, mostly luxurious and expensive. The *Oluanpi Recreation Center* (tel (08) 8851210) (*élúanbí húodòng zhōngxīn*) is in an isolated location about 3 km north of Oluanpi on the Oluanpi to Chialeshui highway. In their annexe they have relatively cheap rooms at NT$550 for a triple. In the main building, twins cost NT$1430. A 20% discount is available on weekdays. The hotel sits up on a hill and has fine views but no beach.

In Oluanpi itself, the *Oluanpi Inn* (tel (08)

8851261) (*élúanbí xiūjià*) costs NT$1300 for a double. A 20% discount is available on weekdays. Nearby is the luxurious *Wen Chyi Hotel* (tel (08) 8851367) *wénqí dàfàndiàn*) where doubles start at NT$1800.

### CHIALESHUI
#### (jiālèshúi) 佳樂水
Located on the east coast north-east of Kenting, Chialeshui has some of the nicest rock formations on the island. Again, it is reached by bus from Hengchun. If you hire a bicycle or motorcycle, you can ride from Kenting to Oluanpi, Oluanpi to Chialeshui, Chialeshui to Hengchun, and then back to Kenting, making a pleasant loop trip. If you've still got excess energy, you can ride up to Szechunghsi Hot Springs.

### SZECHUNGHSI HOT SPRINGS
#### (sìchóngxī wēnquán) 四重溪溫泉
During the Japanese occupation Szechunghsi was one of Taiwan's top three hot springs

resorts, along with Peitou and Kuantzuling. These days, it's sort of a bad joke. Nevertheless, the local tourists keep coming: the springs attract busloads of weekend tourists from Taipei who come here to get their picture taken in front of the Szechunghsi Guest House (proves they've been there), take a quick dip in the hotel hot springs, gorge themselves on 'famous mountain food' and throw it all up on the bus on the way back home.

If you want to see tourists in their native habitat, come on Sundays or holidays. During the week, the place is dead. It's 14 km from Hengchun. The ride up there on a tree-lined road is pretty.

# South-West Taiwan 台灣西南部

This is Taiwan's banana belt. Flat and fertile, this area was until recently the most prosperous part of the island. Now that honour goes to Taipei, but the booming seaport of Kaohsiung is a close second.

The south-west is the cradle of Taiwanese culture. The old city of Tainan was the island's first capital. Temples are pervasive in this region and it's not uncommon to see a huge Buddhist-Taoist festival or parade. Most of the people in this part of the island still speak Taiwanese.

Of course, modern influences have made their mark. New skyscrapers and factories sprout up from former farms. The coastal regions in particular have become heavily industrialised and pollution has fouled Kaohsiung's once beautiful Love River. In spite of this, south-west Taiwan has much to offer the visitor. The rural areas are endless expanses of sugar cane, rice paddies and betel nut trees. And it is in the south-west that you will find Taiwan's largest and most beautiful temples, where much of the traditional Taiwanese way of life has been preserved. Some 50 km to the west are the Penghu Islands – unspoilt, starkly beautiful and home to much of Taiwan's fishing fleet.

## KAOHSIUNG
*(gāoxióng)* 高雄

Kaohsiung is the second largest city in Taiwan and the number one seaport. The city has witnessed rapid growth and industrialisation and now has a population of over 1½ million. The home of the China Steel Corporation, China Shipbuilding and the world's fourth largest container port, Kaohsiung is where one can really see what Taiwan's export-oriented economy is all about.

Those looking for peace, quiet and a view of traditional China may be less impressed. Kaohsiung's booming economy has some unpleasant spin-off effects in the form of crime, traffic, pollution, noise and overcrowding. For many travellers, Kaohsiung will be an overnight stop on the way to some of Taiwan's major scenic attractions, like the Penghu Islands. On the other hand, if you'd like a break from beaches and mountains, Kaohsiung does offer pretty good nightlife. In addition, the city has a few worthwhile places to visit.

## Information

**Tourist Offices** Kaohsiung has two branch offices of the Tourism Bureau. Just what Kaohsiung did to deserve two branches I don't know, but it's not because the city is overflowing with scenic attractions. Anyway, the main branch (tel (07) 2811513) is on the 5th floor, 253 Chungcheng 45th Rd. The Hsinhsing branch (tel (07) 2013001) is on the 3rd floor, 308 Chungshan 1st Rd.

**Money** There is an ICBC (tel (07) 2013001) at 308 Chungshan 1st Rd, very close to the train station. There is another ICBC (tel (07) 2510141) at 253 Chungcheng 4th Rd near the City Government Building. Just across the street is the Bank of Taiwan (tel (07) 2515130), at 264 Chungcheng 4th Rd.

There is an American Express Bank (tel (07) 3123003) at 5 Chungcheng 3rd Rd, and a Citibank (tel (07) 2719101) at 154 Chungcheng 3rd Rd.

**American Institute in Taiwan** Another place to look into is the American Institute in Taiwan (AIT) (tel (07) 2512444) *(měiguó zài tái xiéhùi)*, 3rd floor, 2 Chungcheng 3rd Rd. AIT serves as an unofficial embassy for the USA. For travellers, its chief attraction is that they handle visas for the USA and have a notary service.

**Book & Music Stores** For English-language books, the store with the largest selection is Caves Books (tel (07) 5615716) *(dūnhuáng shūjú)*, 76-78 Wufu 4th Rd, near the Hotel Kingdom. It's open daily from 10 am to 10 pm. Not far away is George's Bookstore (tel

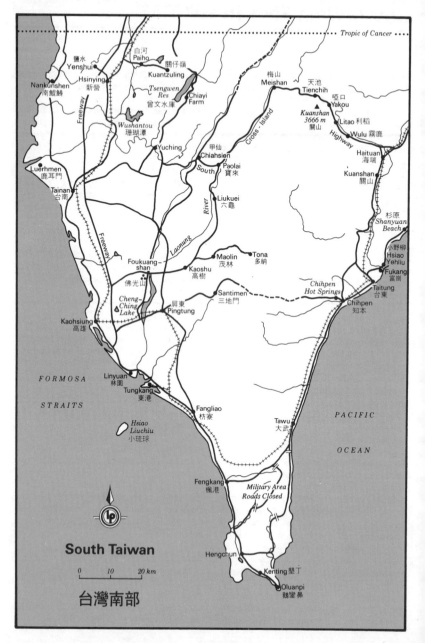

Tropic of Cancer

鹽水
Yenshui

白河
Paiho

關仔嶺
Kuantzuling

Hsinying
新營

Nankunshen
南鯤鯓

Tsengwen
Res
曾文水庫

Chiayi
Farm

梅山
Meishan

天池
Tienchih

啞口
Yakou

Kuanshan
3666 m
關山

Litao 利稻

Wulu 霧鹿

Wushantou
珊瑚潭

Yuching

甲仙
Chiahsien

Paolai
寶來

Haituan
海端

Luerhmen
鹿耳門

Tainan
台南

Kuanshan
關山

杉原
Shanyuan
Beach

Liukuei
六龜

小野柳
Hsiao
Yehliu

Fukang
富岡

Foukuang-
shan

Maolin
茂林

Tona
多納

Chihpen
Hot Springs

Taitung
台東

佛光山

Kaoshu
高樹

Santimen
三地門

Chihpen
知本

Cheng-
Ching
Lake

屏東
Pingtung

Kaohsiung
高雄

FORMOSA

STRAITS

Linyuan
林園

Tungkang
東港

Fangliao
枋寮

Tawu
大武

PACIFIC

OCEAN

Hsiao
Liuchiu
小琉球

Fengkang
楓港

Military Area
Roads Closed

Hengchun

Kenting 墾丁

Oluanpi
鵝鑾鼻

**South Taiwan**

0    10    20 km

台灣南部

(07) 5618596), 84-1 Chihsien 3rd Rd, which has a smaller but good collection. Right next to George's Bookstore is Angela's (tel (07) 5518318), 82-1 Chihsien 3rd Rd, a good place for buying music tapes.

**Hospitals** If you need medical attention, English-speaking Western doctors are available at the Kaohsiung Adventist Clinic, (tel (07) 2010148), suite 503, 5th floor, 101 Wufu 3rd Rd. Prices are definitely at the high end of the scale. More extensive treatment and emergency services are available at Chang Gung Memorial Hospital (tel (07) 7317123) (*cháng gēng yīyùan*) 長庚醫院 near Chengching Lake, 7 km north-east of central Kaohsiung. Medical care is good and very reasonably priced at Chang Gung, but only some of the staff speak English. Bus No 60 goes there; the hospital is the last stop.

**Travel Agents** Two agents that give reasonable prices on international tickets are Southeast Travel Service (tel (07) 2312181), 106 Chungcheng 4th Rd, and Wing On Travel Service (tel (07) 2826760), 125-1 Chunghua 3rd Rd.

### Sun Yatsen University
(*zhōngshān dàxúe*) 中山大學
Sun Yatsen University and the adjacent beach are most easily reached by walking through a tunnel bored straight through Long Life Mountain. The campus is pleasant and seems to serve as an unofficial park for locals. Behind a glass showcase you can see Chiang Kaishek's old limousine. At one time this campus was the Generalissimo's personal retreat. It's also worth having a look at the fishing harbour adjacent to the campus.

### Underground Market
(*dìxià jiē*) 地下街
The entrance to the underground market is just across the street from the City Government Building, by the Love River. This market has three levels below the ground; take any of the steps going down and you'll find it. It is quite an interesting place. The second level down has a large bowling alley, an amusement park for kids, video game arcades and *pachinko* halls (pachinko comes from Japan and is rather like pinball). The third level down has a skating rink with thumping disco music.

### Chungcheng Cultural Center
(*wénhùa zhōngxīn*) 中正文化中心
The Chungcheng Cultural Center is similar to the Sun Yatsen Hall in Taipei. It has art exhibits, operas, exhibitions and classical performances. The programme often changes so you'll have to drop by to get the current schedule of events.

The cultural centre is a very large building in a parklike setting, so you are unlikely to have trouble finding it. It is east of the centre at the intersection of Wufu 1st Rd and Hoping 1st Rd.

### Temples
Kaohsiung has some interesting temples but the place to go if you're really into visiting temples is the nearby city of Tainan.

The largest temple in Kaohsiung is the Yuanheng Temple (*yúanhēng sì*), built on a big hillside just west of Kushan Rd (*gǔshān lù*). Unfortunately, this is also close to a big cement factory which spews out a lot of dust, but it is still a nice temple. On the 1st floor there are three enormous Buddhas, and if you take the elevator to the 5th floor there are three large statues of the goddess Kuanyin. Bus Nos 19, 31, 43 and 45 stop directly across the street from this temple. Just walk up the big hill. The temple is so large that you can't miss it.

In the suburb of Tsoying (*zǔoyíng*) are two magnificent temples within a 10 minute walk of each other. Both are on the shore of a lake. The Spring Autumn Temple (*chūn qiū gé*) has a unique design and includes two pagodas that extend into the lake.

The nearby Confucius Temple (*kǒngzǐ miào*) is a very tranquil place. Just adjacent to the Confucius Temple is another red building which also looks like a temple, but is in fact the temple library. Bus Nos 5 and 19 from Kaohsiung stop near both these temples, and there are trains once an hour.

高雄中部
**Central Kaohsiung**

| | | | |
|---|---|---|---|
| 1 | Cement Factory 水泥廠 | 18 | City Government Building 市政府 |
| 2 | Yuanheng Temple 元亨寺 | 19 | Martyrs' Shrine 忠烈祠 |
| 3 | City Buses | 20 | Sun Yatsen University 中山大學 |
| 4 | Highway Buses (Taipei) | 21 | George's Bookstore 僑助書藝社 |
| 5 | Country Buses (Taitung) | 22 | CITC Kaohsiung Hotel 中信飯店 |
| 6 | International Commercial Bank of China 國際商銀 | 23 | Underground Market 地下街 |
| 7 | Highway Buses (Tainan, Pingtung) | 24 | Hotel Kingdom 華王大飯店 |
| 8 | YMCA 青年會 | 25 | International Commercial Bank of China 國際商銀 |
| 9 | Telephone Company 電信局 | 26 | Ambassador Hotel 國賓飯店 |
| 10 | Zhan'an Boat Company 占岸輪船公司 | 27 | President Department Store 大統百貨 |
| 11 | American Institute of Taiwan 美國在台協會 | 28 | YWCA 女青年會 |
| 12 | Cultural Center 文化中心 | 29 | Talee Department Store 大立百貨 |
| 13 | GPO 郵政總局 | 30 | Movie Theatres 三多大戲院 |
| 14 | Hsinhsing Market 新興市場 | 31 | Far Eastern Department Store 遠東百貨 |
| 15 | Hotel Crane Palace 鶴宮大旅社 | 32 | Laborers' Recreation Center 勞工休假中心 |
| 16 | Police (Visa Extensions) 外事警察 | | |
| 17 | Bank of Taiwan 台灣銀行 | | |

## Chichin Island

*(qíjīn)* 旗津

At one time you could only reach this island by boat. Recently, a cross-harbour tunnel was completed and Chichin is beginning to turn into a container port. In spite of this, there is a pleasant though not spectacular beach, and a string of seafood restaurants in the main villages. Chichin is much quieter and nicer than Kaohsiung and is a welcome break from the city.

You can reach Chichin by taking a short ferry ride from the fishing harbour, which is next to Sun Yatsen University. One of the best seafood restaurants is *jīnshènchūn hǎixiān diàn* (tel (07) 5713603), 68-22 Chungchou Hsiang, about 1½ km north of the tunnel.

## China Steel & Shipbuilding

*(zhōngguó zào chúan chǎng)* 中國造船廠

This is not a place for tourists, but you can go there and take perverse pleasure in seeing ships torn to pieces. Kaohsiung has one of the world's largest shipwrecking facilities and it is possible to buy old relics salvaged from the ships. Inquire at the shipyard if you're interested. These two companies also offer tours of their facilities. Students of economics might find it interesting.

## Kaohsiung Export Processing Zone

*(jiāgōng chūkǒu qū)* 加工出口區

Again, this is not a place for the average traveller. It's a huge complex of factories built on a peninsula in the harbour. The

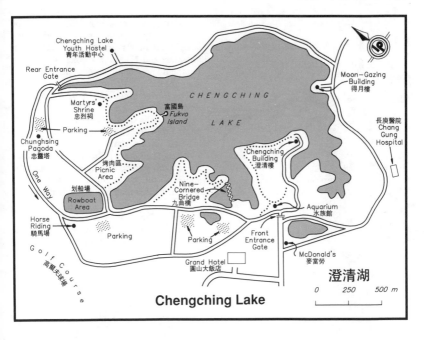

CHENGCHING LAKE

Chengching Lake Youth Hostel 青年活動中心
Rear Entrance Gate
Moon-Gazing Building 得月樓
Martyrs' Shrine 忠烈祠
富國島 Fukvo Island
長庚醫院 Chang Gung Hospital
Chunghsing Pagoda 忠靈塔
Parking
烤肉區 Picnic Area
Chengching Building 澄清樓
One Way
划船場 Rowboat Area
Nine-Cornered Bridge 九曲橋
Aquarium 水族館
Horse Riding 騎馬場
Parking
Parking
Front Entrance Gate
McDonald's 麥當勞
Golf Course 高爾夫球場
Grand Hotel 圓山大飯店
澄清湖

Chengching Lake

0    250    500 m

government's policy is that all raw materials and parts which enter the zone are duty free, but all manufactured items made in the Export Processing Zone (EPZ) are only for export. They cannot be sold in Taiwan unless exported and re-imported, with appropriate duties paid. Unfortunately, the area is not a place you can wander around without permission. As one traveller wrote:

In Kaohsiung I decided to take a look at the harbour. When I entered the area at one of these police posts, they let me in without asking any questions. I wandered around the harbour for 2 hours. But when I wanted to leave again, they gave me trouble. They demanded my passport and wanted to know what I, not being a seaman, did in the area. I answered them according to the truth. So then they searched me for a camera. Luckily, I hadn't brought mine. Finally, they let me go, warning me not to come again. I should add that they didn't speak English, so if I hadn't known Chinese, I might possibly have had to wait there for an interpreter to arrive. Still, the whole affair took about a quarter of an hour. Perhaps it's a good idea to

enter a warning in the guide book not to take too close a look at Taiwan's largest seaport.

Wolfgang Spude

### Chengching Lake
(*chéngqīng hú*) 澄清湖

Seven km from the centre of town, Chengching Lake is a city reservoir surrounded by a well-landscaped park. In fact, it's the only green spot in Kaohsiung besides Sun Yatsen University. The huge Grand Hotel, which resembles a palace, overlooks the lake. This is undoubtedly one of the nicest hotels in Kaohsiung. Around the lake are some pagodas, pavilions, a golf course and a place for rowboats.

Visit Chengching Lake any time, except on Sundays and holidays when it becomes unbelievably crowded. There is an entrance fee of NT$20 for the lake area. Bicycles are not permitted on the road around the lake. As I was told by the guard at the gate, 'The bicycles confuse the cars and motorcycles'.

If it's full, you rent as many blankets as you need and stay in a tent (already set up). They have good meals, which cost NT$30 for breakfast and NT$60 for lunch and dinner. Let them know in advance if you want to eat at the hostel.

The *Chengching Lake Hostel* is on the far side of the lake. Take bus No 60 to the last stop, which is Chang Gung Memorial Hospital. From there, you must walk past the hospital on the same main road for about 1½ km. The lake will be to your left. Take the first paved road to your left; it follows the shore of the lake. About 30 minutes of walking on this road brings you to the hostel.

### Places to Stay – middle

The mid-range hotels can be found in the train station area. Expect to pay at least NT$400 for a double room in these places. Even though the Hung Pin Hotel and the Hotel Jui Chung have the same address, they are actually next door to each other.

*Hung Pin Hotel* (tel (07) 2913173) (*húangbīn lüshè*), 40 Chienkuo 3rd Rd, doubles/twins are NT$350/650
*Hotel Jui Chung* (tel (07) 2725761) (*rùichéng biégŭan*), 40 Chienkuo 3rd Rd, doubles are NT$430
*Hotel Crane Palace* (tel (07) 2213356) (*hègōng dàlüshè*), 41 Chungcheng 4th Rd, doubles/twins are NT$450/750
*Hotel Chien Kuo* (tel (07) 2712149) (*jiàngúo dàfàndiàn*), 44 Chienkuo 3rd Rd, doubles/twins cost NT$550/1350
*Kaohsiung First Hotel* (tel (07) 2218881) (*dìyī dàfàndiàn*), 6 Chungcheng 4th Rd (near GPO), doubles are NT$900
*Hotel Empire* (tel (07) 2216011, telex (85)71535 EMPIRINN) (*dìgúo dàfàndiàn*), 71 Chungshan 1st Rd (near GPO), doubles cost from NT$540 to NT$750
*Hotel Shalom* (tel (07) 3122131) (*tiān'ān dàfàndiàn*), 1 Poai Rd, just behind the train station, doubles/twins are NT$540/840
*Unic Business Hotel* (tel (07) 3215030) (*yōushì dàfàndiàn*), 2 Poai Rd, just behind train station, doubles are NT$640

Sounds to me like that's not the only thing confused. To reach Chengching Lake, take bus No 60 from the city bus terminal.

### Places to Stay – bottom end

Kaohsiung is great for luxury accommodation, but it isn't the best place for budget travellers. The cheapest place in town is the *Laborers' Recreation Center* (tel (07) 3328110) (*láogōng yùlè zhōngxīn*), 132 Chungshan 3rd Rd, near the intersection with Minchuan 2nd Rd. It's a huge place occupying a whole block. Singles/triples are NT$200/400. From the train station, you can get there on bus Nos 7, 12, 25, 26 or 30.

Close to the Grand Hotel is the *Chengching Lake Hostel* (tel (07) 3717181) (*chéngqīng hú húodòng zhōngxīn*). It's a beautiful place to stay, but it's 7 km from the city centre and involves some walking if you don't have your own transport. The dormitory costs NT$100 and there's usually room.

### Places to Stay – top end

For those who can afford luxury accommodation, the Ambassador Hotel combines luxury with a convenient location. However, the most beautiful hotel in town is the Grand Hotel on the shore of Chengching Lake.

*Ambassador Hotel* (tel (07) 2115211, fax 2811113) (*gúobīn dàfàndiàn*), 202 Minsheng 2nd Rd, doubles cost from NT$3000 to NT$3600, twins NT$3400 to NT$5000

*Buckingham Hotel* (tel (07) 2822151, fax 2814540) (*báijīnhàn dàfàndiàn*), 394 Chihsien 2nd Rd, doubles are NT$1700 to NT$2000, twins are NT$1900 to NT$2400

*Grand Hotel* (tel (07) 3835911, fax 3814889) (*yúanshān dàfàndiàn*), 7 km from the centre, doubles from NT$2000 to NT$2200, twins NT$2300 to NT$2500

*Hotel Holiday Garden* (tel (07) 2410121, fax 2512000) (*húayúan dàfàndiàn*), 279 Liuho 2nd Rd, doubles from NT$2650 to NT$3460, twins from NT$2850 to NT$3600

*Hotel Kingdom* (tel (07) 5518211, fax 7522364) (*húawáng dàfàndiàn*), 42 Wufu 4th Rd, doubles cost NT$2500 to NT$3400, twins NT$3000 to NT$3600

*CITC Kaohsiung Hotel* (tel (07) 5217111) (*zhōngxīn gāoxiúng dàfàndiàn*), 43 Dahjen Rd, doubles are NT$2800

*Summit Hotel* (tel (07) 3845526, fax 3844739) (*húangtǒng dàfàndiàn*), 426 Chiuju 1st Rd, doubles/twins NT$2000/2200

## Places to Eat

**Budget Eats** The *Hsinhsing Street Market* (*xīnxīng shìchǎng*) is adjacent to the GPO in a long alley running parallel to Chungshan Rd. Mostly it's a good place to buy ultra-cheap clothing and shoes, but there are also many inexpensive foodstalls, especially at night.

Liuho 2nd Rd (*liùhé èr lù*) has an active night market where the chief form of entertainment is eating. Liuho Rd is a very long street, but the night market is only between Chungshan Rd and Tzuli Rd. Plenty of cheap seafood and fried chicken is available, but the snake soup and anteater are more interesting. During the day, Liuho 2nd Rd is known for its low-priced steak restaurants. Only at night do the street vendors move in.

To escape the heat of summer, excellent ice cream and sherbet sundaes are served at *Taro Ice Town* (*zhǐ zǎi bīng chéng*). They have a few shops: 36 Chungshan 1st Rd (tel (07) 2314168); 209 Chengkung Rd (tel (07) 2240618); 190 Chengchung 2nd Rd (tel (07) 2515689); and 176 Linsen 1st Rd (tel (07) 2515229). Their prices are cheap and at night they're always crowded with students.

The *President Department Store* at the corner of Wufu Rd and Chungshan Rd has something like a traditional Chinese market on the 9th floor. Prices are cheap and there is a wide selection of food.

**Fast Food** If you need a break from Chinese food, there is *Wendy's* (tel (07) 2728561) at 209 Wufu 2nd Rd, just opposite the President Department Store. Similar cuisine can also be found at *McDonald's* on the corner of Chungshan 2nd Rd and Sanduo 3rd Rd, next to the Far Eastern Department Store. On the other side of the Far Eastern Department Store is *Kentucky Fried Chicken*.

For buying various frozen, canned and preserved Western foods, the place to go is *American Eatables* (tel (07) 2311906), 213 Tatung 1st Rd.

**Coffee & Tea Shops** I particularly like *I Love My Home Coffee Shop* (tel (07) 2319657), 258 Chungshan 1st Rd. You can sit and drink coffee, but it's also a restaurant with good food. They show video movies and it's a popular place. There is another branch (tel (07) 2715273) at 104 Liuho 1st Rd.

Designed in Japanese tatami style, tea-houses are popular hang-outs for young people. A good one is *yù shūfáng* (tel (07) 7213556), 149-14 Hoping 1st Rd.

**Speciality Restaurants** Good and inexpensive Szechuan food can be had at *liújiā xiǎogǔan* (tel (07) 2012648), 52 Minsheng 1st Rd.

You can try traditional Taiwanese food at the *Wei Won Manhan Restaurant* (tel (07) 2512814) (*wéiwáng mǎnhàn fàndiàn*), 67 Liuho Rd, or at their Chungcheng branch (tel (07) 2112141), 200 Chungcheng 2nd Rd – it's good but expensive.

Kaohsiung is famous for seafood, but mostly it isn't cheap. One excellent place is the *Crab's House* (tel (07) 2116127) (*xún zhīwū*), 93 Minsheng 1st Rd. Another high-class seafood restaurant (with prices to match) is *Hai Pa Wang* (tel (07) 3335168) (*hǎi bà wáng*), 2 Hsingchung 2nd Rd. There

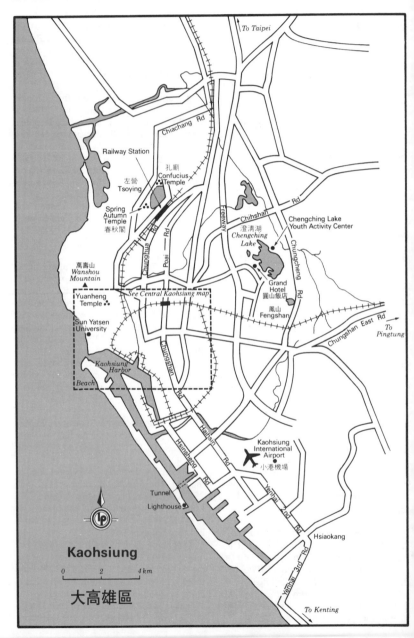

*To Taipei*

Chiachang Rd

Railway Station

孔廟
Confucius
Temple

左營
Tsoying

Spring
Autumn
Temple
春秋閣

Chihshan

Chengching Lake
Youth Activity Center

澄清湖
*Chengching
Lake*

萬壽山
*Wanshou
Mountain*

*See Central Kaohsiung map*

Yuanheng
Temple

Grand
Hotel
圓山飯店

鳳山
Fengshan

Sun Yatsen
University

*Kaohsiung
Harbor*

*Beach*

Chungshan East Rd

*To
Pingtung*

Kaohsiung
International
Airport
小港機場

Tunnel

Lighthouse

Hsiaokang

**Kaohsiung**

0        2        4 km

大高雄區

*To Kenting*

is another branch (tel (07) 2829638) (*dōngqū hǎi bà wáng*) at 160 Kuanghua 1st Rd.

## Entertainment

**Cinemas** There are some movie theatres in town specialising in English-language movies. The best theatres are all clustered into one large complex at the intersection of Sanduo 4th Rd and Chengkung Rd. The complex is known as the *sānduō xìyùan*.

**MTV** One of the biggest MTV places that I've ever seen is *jù jiàng* (tel (07) 2018065), 2nd floor, 40 Minsheng 2nd Rd, on the north-west corner of the intersection with Chungshan Rd. It's open 24 hours.

**Pubs** The Yenchen district of Kaohsiung (near the Hotel Kingdom) is the place to look for pubs and restaurants catering to Westerners. One of the most popular pub/restaurant places is *Stormy Weather* (tel (07) 5514407), 30 Wufu 4th Rd. In addition to being a good place to eat, they organise the Kaohsiung Yacht Club and many social events. At *Sam's Place* (tel (07) 5211564), 27 Wufu 4th Rd, near the Hotel Kingdom, you can play darts, eat great Western food and drink beer. In the same area is *Snow's Pub* (tel (07) 5311886, at 49 Wufu 4th Rd. On the same street is also the *Brass Rail Tavern* (tel (07) 5315643), 21 Wufu 4th Rd; *Key Largo Beer House* (tel (07) 5616901), 88 Wufu 4th Rd; and the *Formosa Pub* (tel (07) 5618045), 19 Wufu 4th Rd.

Behind the Hotel Kingdom is the *Dewdrop Inn* (tel (07) 5612428), 39 Hsin Lo St, which also has darts, drinks and serves a good lunch and dinner. In the same neighbourhood, but closer to George's Bookstore, is *Amy's Beer House* (tel (07) 5318599) at 74 Chihsien 3rd Rd; it's known for good pizza. On the same street is the excellent *Pizza Pan Pub* (tel (07) 5517741) at 90-1 Chihsien 3rd Rd).

**Discos** The most popular disco in town is *Kiss Disco* (tel (07) 3314275), 5th floor, 62 Tzuchiang 3rd Rd, not far from the Sanduo Rd and Chengkung Rd intersection.

## Activities

**Sauna** Kaohsiung has one of Taiwan's largest saunas, *xǐxiāng féng sānwēnnŭan* (tel (07) 3330661, 3330711), at 18 Chunghua 4th Rd. It's very luxurious and the admission is only NT$200. Unfortunately, it's for men only.

## Things to Buy

One of the biggest department stores in Taiwan is the President Department Store (*dàtŏng bǎihùo gōngsī*), on the corner of Chungshan Rd and Wufu Rd. The nearby Talee Department Store (*dàlì bǎihùo gōngsī*) is under the same management but is generally more expensive. Both stores have good restaurants on the top floor and an amusement park on the roof. Kaohsiung's newest store is the Far Eastern Department Store (*yŭandōng bǎihùo gōngsī*), at the corner of Chungshan 2nd Rd and Sanduo 4th Rd, on the traffic circle – there's a great supermarket in the basement.

As in Taipei, good export-quality clothing can be bought in Kaohsiung from Madame Fashion Company (tel (07) 2414153) (*zhŭfù shāng chǎng*), on the traffic circle at 166 Chungshan 4th Rd. If you're in the market for an IBM-compatible computer, quality and good service is provided by the English-speaking management at Longking Computer Store (tel (07) 2714271), 312 Minsheng 1st Rd. There is also an Apple Macintosh dealer (tel (07) 2828181) at 190 Chungcheng 4th Rd.

All types of sporting goods equipment are available from the Good Time Sporting Goods Department Store (tel (07) 5512296), 2 Wufu 4th Rd. As their advertisement says, 'Our store believes in being honesty'.

## Getting There & Away

**Air** Kaohsiung has domestic air services to Taipei, Taitung, the Penghu Islands, Lanyu and Hualien. There are international flights to Hong Kong, Tokyo, Osaka, South Korea and a few other destinations.

**Bus** From Taipei and other major cities there are direct express buses, both legal and wild chicken. The bus fare (legal bus) from Taipei is either NT$415 or NT$334, depending on which class you travel in.

Coming from Taitung on the east coast, there are express buses day and night. From Kenting, take a bus to Hengchun, and then another to Kaohsiung.

**Train** All the major west coast trains pass through Kaohsiung. From Taipei, the fare ranges from NT$418 to NT$576 on the express trains.

**Sea** There are occasional passenger ferries to Okinawa in Japan and a twice weekly ferry to Macau.

### Getting Around

City buses cost NT$6 per ride. It is useful to buy a bus ticket that's valid for 10 rides from the roadside vendors near the major bus stops. Sad to say, if you have any leftover bus tickets from Taipei you can't use them here.

In Kaohsiung, there are three bus terminals adjacent to the train station. If you're facing the front of the station, the terminal to your left is for local city buses. The terminal to your immediate right is for long-distance buses to north Taiwan, and the terminal further to the right is for buses to the surrounding suburban and rural areas, including Taitung. There is another bus station on Linsen Rd, one block south of Chienkuo Rd – this terminal has buses to Tainan and Pingtung.

The wild chicken buses have several small terminals that frequently get moved, but they're always near the big bus station.

### AROUND KAOHSIUNG
### Fokuangshan
*(fóguāngshān)* 佛光山

Fokuangshan is a large Buddhist monastery about a 1 hour ride from Kaohsiung. Besides the temple, pleasant grounds and a Buddhist university, there is a mountain with a huge 32 metre high golden Buddha surrounded by 480 smaller Buddhas, each one almost 2 metres tall – a rather impressive sight.

There is an artificial cave with some rather bizarre mechanical statues that move like the ones at Disneyland. Good inexpensive vegetarian meals can be bought in the monastery and it is possible to stay in the dormitory for the night. A donation of around NT$200, which includes food, is customary. In the big temple with the carpeted floor, make sure you remove your shoes.

**Getting There & Away** To get there take a bus from the eastern bus terminal (to the far right of the train station as you face it). Buses depart about every 20 minutes and the fare is NT$33.

### SANTIMEN
*(sāndìmén)* 三地門

A small town situated where the plains dramatically meet the mountains, Santimen has peaceful surroundings and a white-water rushing river. The population consists mostly of aborigines belonging to the Paiwan tribe.

Santimen actually consists of three areas – Santimen village, Shuimen and the touristy Machia Aboriginal Culture Park. Shuimen is the main market town. Santimen village is on the opposite side of the river from Shuimen, up on a cliff behind trees, and no part of it is visible from Shuimen. Santimen village is great – an authentic and not touristy aboriginal village surrounded by trees and farmland. Many people in Santimen are employed doing embroidery, as aboriginal craft has now become a big business.

The Machia Aboriginal Culture Park (tel (08) 7991219, 7991372) *(mǎjiā shāndì wénhùa zhōngxīn)* is designed for mass tourism. Admission is NT$80 and it's open from 9 am to 5 pm daily. The park has the usual aboriginal song and dance shows at 11 am and 3 pm. The houses are designed to look like the traditional aboriginal homes. It's a somewhat scaled-down version of the Formosan Aboriginal Cultural Village near Sun Moon Lake. It might be interesting to visit Machia first and then Santimen village, as this'll give you a chance to compare fantasy with reality.

As you are entering the Santimen area, the road is lined with farms with tall palm trees.

Top: 'Sea of Clouds' as seen from South Cross-Island Highway (Storey)
Bottom: Bamboo grove in Chiayi County (Storey)

Top: Worship festival in Nankunshen (Storey)
Left: Cable car at Tsaoling (Storey)
Right: View from Chushan (Storey)

These are not coconut palms but betel nut trees, locally referred to as 'Chinese chewing gum'. If you want to try betel nut you can purchase some for NT$10 a piece. It's something you acquire a taste for; it stains the teeth reddish-black and chewers can often be seen spitting red saliva. It's popular in many tropical countries.

### Getting There & Away

From Kaohsiung, you can reach Santimen by first taking a bus to Pingtung (*píngdōng*), from where you can get a bus to Santimen. From where the bus lets you off, you can take another bus to Shuimen, and from there it's a 15 minute walk to the Machia Aboriginal Culture Park. On weekends and holidays, buses go directly to Machia.

From Santimen, a road heads due east into fantastic mountains towards the aboriginal village of Wutai. It would be a lovely place to visit, but a class A mountain permit is needed, and these are very difficult to obtain.

### LIUKUEI
(*liùgūi*) 六龜

Liukuei, or 'Six Turtles', is a lovely spot north-east of Kaohsiung. The town occupies a valley walled in by high mountains with a white-water river rushing by. The scenery is even better than in Santimen, but not many people bother to go there. Camping, hiking and rafting along the Laonung River are popular activities.

### Getting There & Away

Although the bus service from Kaohsiung is not very frequent, you can take a direct bus from Kaohsiung. Failing that, take a bus to Pingtung and then another to Liukuei. If you have your own car or motorcycle it is better, as the trip is very impressive and offers many places to stop and relax by the river.

Just beyond Liukuei, the road continues north until it connects with the South Cross-Island Highway. It's a spectacular hike, which you might want to consider doing. The details for this hike are in the South Cross-Island section further on in this chapter.

If you have your own transport and you visit Liukuei, then try to see Maolin as well.

### MAOLIN
(*mào lín*) 茂林

Maolin is an absolute gem. It's hard to believe a place so unspoilt can be found so close to the sprawling metropolis of Kaohsiung. The area is almost entirely free of commercial development and mass tourism. There are no hotels, but camping is permitted.

The road from Maolin going up into the mountains is only 18 km long and terminates at the village of Tona (*dūo nà*). The scenery is impressive, and there are a number of places to stop and walk down to the river. You can cross one of the several suspension bridges and find waterfalls on the opposite side.

Tona is definitely worth visiting. It's a small aboriginal village where the main industry is stonecraft. Flat, smooth slabs of stone of all sizes stand everywhere against walls. Tables, chair seats and small decorative pieces are available for sale. Some of the houses are built from these stones piled like bricks. Some simple food is available in Tona, but it would be prudent to bring your own. You'll need some biscuits and dried food in case you want to hike in the area.

### Getting There & Away

Transport is a bit of a problem. During the day, there are buses to Maolin about once every hour or 2. There are no buses going the last 18 km up to Tona, so you'll have to walk unless you are driving or hitching. Alternatively, you could go by bus to the nearby town of Kaoshu (*gāoshù*), and from there you could hire a taxi up to Tona. If you don't want the taxi to wait, you could walk back down to Maolin and then catch a bus back. Hitching from Kaoshu is a possibility too.

This is one place where having your own set of wheels is definitely an advantage. A motorcycle is better than a car because the road is narrow, mountainous and winding. It is possible to do it on a 10 speed bicycle, but you'll need to be in good condition because

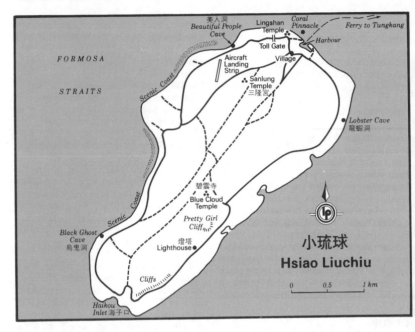

Beautiful People Cave
美人洞
Lingshan Temple
Coral Pinnacle
Ferry to Tungkang
FORMOSA
Toll Gate
Harbour
Aircraft Landing Strip
Village
STRAITS
Scenic Coast
Sanlung Temple
三隆宮
Lobster Cave
龍蝦洞
碧雲寺
Blue Cloud Temple
Pretty Girl Cliff
Black Ghost Cave
烏鬼洞
Scenic Coast
燈塔
Lighthouse
小琉球
Hsiao Liuchiu
Cliffs
0    0.5    1 km
Haikou Inlet 海子口

of the hills. If you decide to go by bicycle, you can first send the bike to Pingtung by train, which will save you a long ride through Kaohsiung's traffic.

You need a mountain pass to enter this area, but fortunately it is very easy to obtain. You get it in Maolin, right at the entrance to the area. Just fill out an application (in Chinese) and the pass will be issued immediately. You should bring your passport, although one time I forget mine and they let me in anyway.

## HSIAO LIUCHIU
### (xiǎo liúqiú) 小琉球

Hsiao Liuchiu is a small island only 50 minutes by boat from the fishing harbour at Tungkang (dōnggǎng). It can be done as a relaxing day trip from Kaohsiung, but it's even better to spend the night in one of the hotels on the island.

Hsiao Liuchiu, which is visible from Kaohsiung on a clear day, is known for its seafood, secluded coves and coral formations. The island is pretty but not stunningly beautiful. Nevertheless, it is a wonderful, tranquil retreat from the madness of Kaohsiung. You can walk all the way around the island in a day. Riding a bicycle is more convenient but they don't seem to be available for hire. You can bring a bicycle on the ferry, but it'll cost you as much as for a passenger. The island also seems like a good place to go snorkelling; again, bring your own equipment.

### Places to Stay

There are two places to stay in the village on the island. The báilónggōng lüshè (tel (08) 8612536) has doubles at NT$200 for a room with shared bath (pǔtōngfáng) and NT$350 for a room with private bath (tàofáng). The xiǎo liúqiú dàfàndiàn (tel (08) 8611133, 8612558) costs NT$550 for a double on weekdays, but the price rises to NT$800 on weekends.

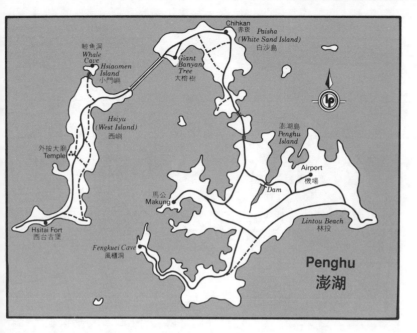

## Getting There & Away

There are two fairly cheap ways to reach Hsiao Liuchiu. The cheapest way is to take a bus to Tungkang fishing harbour. Buses leave from the suburban bus terminal in Kaohsiung. Once you get to the fishing harbour, you can get a boat to to the island. Boats depart at 7.30, 8.30 and 10.30 am, and 1.30 and 4 pm. The last boat returns to Tungkang at about 4 pm. The boats are crowded only on Sundays. The fare is NT$80 one way. You are supposed to show your passport before you get on the boat, but they don't always check.

The other way to get there is to buy a ticket from the Chan'an Boat Company (tel (07) 2112123) (*zhàn'àn lúnchúan gōngsī*), 65 Mintsu 2nd Rd, Kaohsiung. The ticket costs NT$260 and that includes transport to the ferry and the ferry ride both ways. If you make your own way to the ferry, the ticket costs NT$200. They make the trip about eight times daily. Their boat leaves from a small harbour north of Tungkang called Linyuan (*línyúan*).

As nice as Hsiao Liuchiu is, the Penghu Islands are much more scenic.

## PENGHU
*(pénghú)* 澎湖

Consisting of 64 islands about halfway between Taiwan and mainland China, the Penghu Group offers a sharp contrast geographically to Taiwan. Penghu is much drier, and covered with brush and grassland rather than dense forests like Taiwan. While Taiwan has towering mountains, Penghu has none – but makes up for it with lovely, unpolluted beaches, quaint fishing villages, great seafood and a culture similar to that of Taiwan some 50 years ago. From about May to October, the islands are bathed in brilliant sunshine and take on a special stark beauty that's hard to describe.

Historically, Penghu is significant as

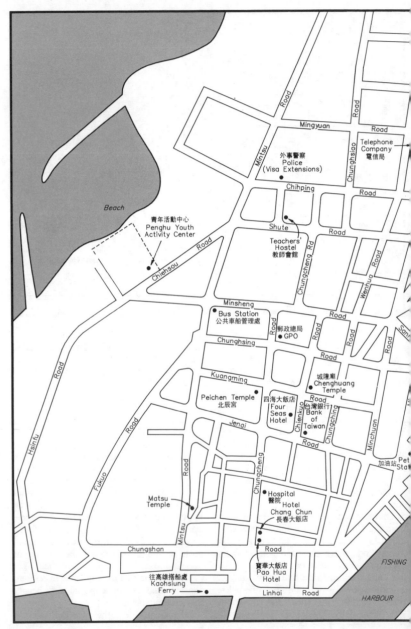

Mingyuan Road

Chunghsiao Road

Telephone Company
電信局

Mintsu

外事警察
Police
(Visa Extensions)

Chihping Road

Shute

Teachers'
Hostel
教師會館

Chungcheng Rd

Wenhua Road

青年活動中心
Penghu Youth
Activity Center

Beach

Chiehsou Road

Minsheng Road

Bus Station
公共車船管理處

郵政總局
GPO

Chunghsing Road

Son

Kuangming Road

城隍廟
Chenghuang
Temple

Peichen Temple
北辰宮

四海大飯店
Four
Seas
Hotel

台灣銀行
Bank
of
Taiwan

Chienkuo

Chungching

Minchuan

Jengi Road

Hsintu Road

Fukuo Road

Chungcheng Road

Road

加油站
Pet
Sta

Matsu
Temple

Hospital
醫院

Hotel
Chang Chun
長春大飯店

Mintsu

FISHING

Chungshan Road

寶華大飯店
Pao Hua
Hotel

往高雄搭船處
Kaohsiung
Ferry

Linhai Road

HARBOUR

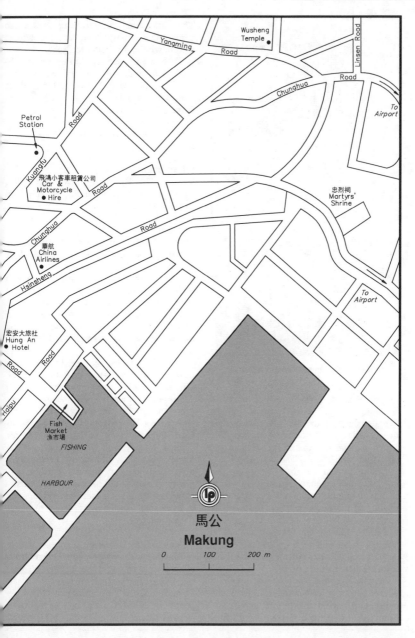

Wusheng Temple

Yangming Road

Linsen Road

Chunghua Road

Road

To Airport

Petrol Station

Kuangfu Road

飛鴻小客車租賃公司
Car & Motorcycle Hire

Road

忠烈祠
Martyrs' Shrine

Chunghua Road

華航
China Airlines

Hsinsheng

To Airport

宏安大旅社
Hung An Hotel

Road

Road

Haipu Road

Fish Market 漁市場

FISHING

HARBOUR

馬公
**Makung**

0    100    200 m

Fishing fleet in the Penghu Islands

the route used by European invaders of Taiwan. A large fort still remains on the Penghu Islands. When the Portuguese visited they called these islands the Pescadores. The Dutch occupied the islands for a time, a role emulated by the French and Japanese.

Unlike Taiwan, Penghu is not overpopulated; the locals tend to migrate to Taiwan in search of greater economic opportunities. Fishing is the main industry, followed by some limited farming, a difficult occupation in Penghu's harsh, windswept climate. The islanders have built coral walls to protect the crops (peanuts, sweet potatoes and sorghum) from the fierce winter winds.

Penghu is a great place to visit, but not in winter. From mid-October to March the chilly north wind makes life unpleasant. From May to the end of September, it's fine.

The winter winds also cause heavy seas, so a boat trip is doubly unpleasant. If you must visit in winter, it is better to fly.

There are 147 temples in Penghu by official count and, not surprisingly, they are mostly dedicated to Matsu, goddess of the sea. Matsu is believed to protect fishermen from harm on their hazardous journeys. Many of Penghu's temples are old, but they have been restored and are well worth visiting.

### Information
**Money** The Bank of Taiwan (tel (06) 9279935) is at 24 Jenai Rd, Makung, on Penghu Island.

### Penghu Island
Makung (*mǎgōng*), the only city in the islands, is on the largest island, which is simply called Penghu. Makung has a population of 60,000. It is a picturesque city with its fishing harbour, outdoor fish markets and temples. Needless to say, good seafood is available. One temple in Makung (*māzǔ gōng*) is over 400 years old, making it the oldest temple in Taiwan. It has been fully restored.

One of the nicest beaches, Lintou Beach (*líntóu gōngyúan*), is also on Penghu Island. Unfortunately, they charge NT$20 admission and there is a rather heavy military presence around the area. At the southwestern end of Penghu Island is Fengkuei Cave (*fēnggùi dòng*), a big attraction for Chinese tourists who want to see the 'dramatic coastal rock formations'. Personally, I didn't find them very dramatic and there was plenty of rubbish left behind by the tourists. However, the ride out there on a motorcycle is interesting, as there are views of small fishing villages.

**Places to Stay** Hotels are fairly easy to find in Makung and are rarely full. Budget travellers should try either the *Teachers' Hostel* (tel (06) 9273692) (*jiàoshī hùigǔan*), at 38 Shute Rd, where dormitories that sleep three people are NT$130 per person, or the *Youth Activity Center* (tel (06) 9271124) (*pénghú* *húodòng zhōngxīn*), 11 Chiehshou Rd, where dormitory accommodation costs from NT$150 to NT$250. Both are OK. The Teachers' Hostel is smaller and quieter, but the Youth Activity Center is a beautiful building by the sea. There are many other hotels across the street from where you get off the Kaohsiung ferry.

In the mid-price range is the *Hung An Hotel* (tel (06) 9273832), 16 Sanmin Rd, where doubles are NT$500.

Some of the more expensive hotels include the *Four Seas Hotel* (tel (06) 9272960) (*sìhǎi dàfàndiàn*), 3 Chienkuo Rd, where doubles cost NT$600 to NT$700; the *Pao Hua Hotel* (tel (06) 9274881) (*bǎohúa dàfàndiàn*), 2 Chungcheng Rd, which has doubles/twins for NT$1200/1600; and the *Hotel Chang Chun* (tel (06) 9273336) (*chángchūn dàfàndiàn*), 8 Chungcheng Rd, which has doubles that cost NT$900.

**Places to Eat** Seafood is the local speciality. Most of the seafood is not really cheap, but it's still about half the price of seafood in Taiwan. In Makung, the section of Sanmin Rd right near the fish market is wall-to-wall seafood restaurants. One place in this area that you can try is *xīn hǎiwángzǐ xiǎochībù* (tel (06) 9263188), 8 Sanmin Rd. A more classy place is *sìhǎi cāntīng* (tel (06) 9273335), in the basement of the Four Seas Hotel at 3 Chienkuo Rd.

If you don't want to limit yourself to seafood, some restaurants also have more traditional Chinese cuisine. A small and rather dumpy-looking place with excellent food is *zhēn hǎo wèi xiǎochībù* (tel (06) 9275575) at 57 Jenai Rd.

**Paisha & Hsiyu Islands**
There are two other large islands connected to Penghu by bridges, and both are interesting. They're called Paisha (*báishā*) (White Sand Island) and Hsiyu (*xīyǔ*) (West Island). Paisha's most famous attraction is a large banyan tree over 300 years old. Covering a huge area, the branches are supported by latticework. Walking under it is rather like walking through a cave. Paisha is connected

to Hsiyu by Taiwan's longest bridge, which is over 5 km in length.

Hsiyu is the most beautiful island, with many hidden coves. At the very southern tip of this island is the Hsitai Fort (*xītái gǔbǎo*), built in 1883 under the Ching (Manchu) Dynasty. It's well preserved and open to the public. It is claimed that on a clear day one can see the mountains of both Taiwan and mainland China from this fort. I couldn't see either, but that doesn't mean the mountains aren't there.

One of the best seafood restaurants in all the Penghu Islands is not in Makung but on Hsiyu. It's near the bus stop in the village of Hsiyu, which is right in the centre of the island, and is called *qīngxīn yǐnshídiàn* (tel (06) 9981128).

Connected to Hsiyu by a narrow bridge is the very tiny island of Hsiaomen (*xiǎomén yǔ*). Despite its small size, it's very scenic. There is a rugged natural stone arch carved by the sea on the north side of this islet.

**Outlying Islands**
For those who really want to get away from civilisation, there are boats and flights on propeller-driven aircraft to Chimei (*qīměi*) and Wang'an (*wàng'ān*), two islands to the south of Makung. There isn't much to do on these islands except admire the sea and surf. You can fly directly to Chimei or Wang'an from either Kaohsiung or Makung with Formosa Airlines or the Taiwan Aviation Company (TAC). A one-way Makung-Chimei ticket is NT$532; Kaohsiung-Chimei is NT$1180; Kaohsiung-Wang'an is NT$1204. The ferry boat from Makung to Wang'an costs NT$108 for an economy ticket and takes 1½ hours. The ferry from Wang'an to Chimei costs NT$145 and takes 3 hours.

Personally, I don't think that either of these two islands is worth the trouble. However, many Taiwanese go there – particularly to Chimei, where they take photographs of themselves standing in front of the Tomb of the Seven Virtuous Beauties. According to local legend, the 'seven virtuous beauties' were seven women who committed suicide when they saw pirate ships approaching because they thought they might be raped. While my sympathies go out to the unfortunate seven women, I've often wondered if the whole story wasn't conjured up by the Chamber of Commerce. It's certainly been a boon to the local tourist industry – you can buy Seven Virtuous Beauties ashtrays, postcards and teacups.

To the north of Penghu is Chipei Island (*jíbèi yǔ*), which is noted for its excellent beaches made out of a fine coral, not sand. It's great for swimming. There are no flights to Chipei, so you have to take a boat. Departures for Chipei are from Chihkan (*chìkǎn*), a village on the north shore of Paisha Island. From Makung, you can take a bus or taxi to Chihkan and then get the ferry to Chipei.

There are three companies operating boats to Chipei. These are: Hawaii Boat Company (tel (06) 9932237, 9932049) (*xiàwēiyí chúan gōngsī*); Paisha Boat Center (tel (06) 9931917, 9212609) (*báishā yóulè zhōngxīn*); and the Aimin Boat Company (tel (06) 9932232, 9911145) (*àimín chúan gōngsī*). They're all in Chihkan.

There is a resort area called *Chipei Sea Paradise* (*jíbèi hǎishàng lèyúan*) which charges a small admission fee; this is where most people stay. They have a dormitory for NT$200, while twins are NT$1000. Some people on the island rent out tatami dorms for NT$100 per person. You can camp inside the resort if you bring your own tent. Food is very expensive so bring your own. A wide-brimmed hat is essential, as there are no trees and the sun is powerful. At the resort you can rent sea scooters and other water toys.

## Things to Buy

Penghu is not an industrial place and therefore offers little that you couldn't buy more cheaply in Taiwan. One exception is the excellent peanut candy. There are many different varieties and they're all good. Since they usually all cost the same, you can mix many different kinds together. A Taiwanese kg (catty) of assorted peanut candy costs about NT$60. The flight back to Taiwan usually reeks of the dried fish and squid that

the local tourists take back with them. Thank goodness it's only a 30 minute flight.

## Getting There & Away

**Air** Although Penghu is a remote backwater, there are frequent flights by jet aircraft from Kaohsiung and Taipei, and somewhat fewer flights from Tainan or Chiayi. There is also a flight from Taichung, but on a small propeller aircraft rather than a jet. The fares are very reasonable: one way from Kaohsiung is only NT$570, and it's a few dollars cheaper from either Tainan or Chiayi. However, the airfare from Taipei is considerably more expensive at NT$967. Ditto for Taichung-Makung, which costs NT$919.

These flights are very popular and tend to be booked up a week or more in advance, especially during weekends and holidays. The flights from Kaohsiung seem to be the most heavily booked, so if you're travelling around Taiwan you might try to get on a flight from Tainan and Chiayi, where seat reservations are less competitive.

You have a wide choice of airlines. China Airlines (*húaháng*) and Far Eastern Air Transport (*yǔandōng*) have jet service to Makung. Other airlines with propeller-driven aircraft include Formosa Airlines (*yǒngxīng*), Great China Airlines (*dàhúa*), Foshing Airlines (*fùxīng*), Makung Airlines (*mǎgōng*) and Taiwan Aviation Company (*táiwán*).

**Sea** During the summer consider going to the islands by boat from Kaohsiung and returning by air. Boats depart from Pier No 1 in Kaohsiung every day at 9 am and arrive in Makung at 12.30 pm. Boats leave Makung at 3 pm and arrive back in Kaohsiung at 6.30 pm. Tickets should be purchased in advance from Southeast Travel Service (tel (07) 2312181, 5515823), 106 Chungcheng 4th Rd, Kaohsiung. Or you can buy the ticket in Penghu at Southeast Travel (tel (06) 9261210), 26 Chungshan Rd, Makung. A one-way ticket in economy class is NT$450.

If you go by boat, you can take a motorcycle or bicycle with you for little additional cost.

## Getting Around

**Airport Transport** The taxis waiting at the airport were asking NT$160 for the 9 km trip to Makung – not negotiable, since they line up for about an hour. I walked outside the airport and hailed a passing cab; the driver wanted NT$100 but I was able to negotiate it down to NT$50.

**Bus** Buses go along the main roads at an average rate of one per hour. The airport bus also runs only once an hour to Makung.

**Taxi** It is certainly possible to hire a taxi, but given the large distances between places this could be very expensive. Negotiate fares in advance.

**Motorcycle & Bicycle** Getting around Penghu by bus is possible, but given the rural nature of the place the best way to get around is to hire a motorcycle. Or you could bring one with you on the boat. A 10 speed bicycle is another possibility, but Penghu is large – Makung to Hsitai Fort is 35 km. There are no big hills, but remember that the sea breezes can be fierce, making it difficult for bicycles.

There are several places to rent a motorcycle. One of the best is *fēihóng zhū chē gōngsī* (tel (06) 9271616), 6 Chihping Rd. They also rent small cars. The cost for a 50cc bike is NT$300 per day.

## KINMEN & MATSU

*(jīnmén )* 金門
*(māzǔ)* 馬祖

Kinmen – formerly known as Quemoy – and Matsu are two obscure islands just off the coast of the Fujian province in mainland China. The islands became briefly famous in 1958 when communist troops started an artillery bombardment of them. At that time the USA had defence agreements with Taiwan, and for a while it looked as though the USA would get reluctantly dragged into yet another armed conflict with China, only 5 years after the Korean War had ended.

Taiwan's troops are well dug in now, having built huge concrete bunkers which are virtually bombproof. To everyone's relief the shelling eventually stopped, but the propaganda war continues. Gigantic loudspeakers, believed to be the largest in the world, broadcast opposing points of view across the narrow straits. Balloons containing pamphlets are launched from the islands and Taiwanese newspapers also find their way to the mainland.

Soldiers outnumber the civilian population on these islands. The islands remain under martial law, evening curfews are observed and lights cannot be used at night unless the windows are shuttered. Kinmen and Matsu even have their own currency to prevent capital flight. Nevertheless, these days life on the islands is not bad – at least that's what I'm told by former residents now working and studying in Taiwan. Unfortunately, I haven't been to either island and it's not likely that you will get to go there . Special permission is needed to visit and very few manage to get an invitation. Diplomats, dignitaries and a few journalists can usually get a pass, but most civilians cannot go there unless they have relatives on the islands. The islanders themselves are free to come and go, and there are regularly scheduled flights to Taipei. There has been a lot of talk about opening at least Kinmen to tourism, but so far it hasn't happened. Probably the easiest way for foreigners to get a look at Kinmen is from the other side – from the port of Xiamen in mainland China.

Besides feeding and entertaining the military, Kinmen has only one industry of any significance – the production of Kaoliang, Taiwan's strongest liquor.

## TAINAN

*(táinán)* 台南

Tainan is a stronghold of traditional Taiwanese culture. Tainan means 'south Taiwan', and it is the oldest city on the island. Tainan served as the capital for 222 years from 1663 to 1885. Today, it is the fourth largest city in Taiwan with a population of more than 650,000.

Tainan is a city with a long and interesting history. The Dutch invaded Taiwan in 1624

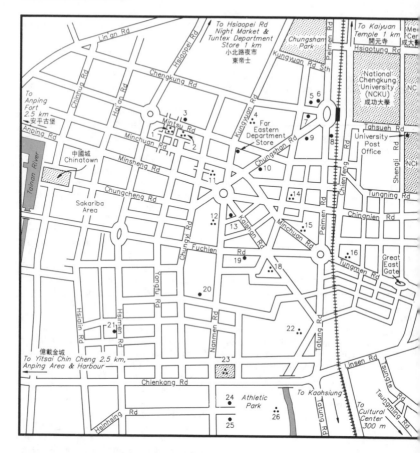

and set up their capital and military headquarters in Tainan. In 1661, 37 years later, the Dutch were successfully expelled by Cheng Chengkung, also known in the West as Koxinga. Koxinga was a Ming Dynasty loyalist who was forced to flee Taiwan from the mainland with 30,000 troops to escape the victorious Ching Dynasty (Manchu) armies. Only 1 year after ousting the Dutch, Koxinga died in 1662 at the age of 38. His supporters managed to maintain a Ming Dynasty stronghold in Taiwan until 1682, when the island was finally captured by the Manchus.

Tainan is the best place in Taiwan for temple viewing. There are over 200 temples in Tainan, though many are hard to find because they are tucked away in narrow side alleys, hidden by the new buildings sprouting up all over the city. While many are small neighbourhood temples, others are huge, including one in the suburb of Luerhmen which is claimed to be the largest temple in East Asia. If you simply stroll around Tainan you'll probably never see the best temples, since only a few are on the main boulevards. The map of Tainan shows where the most interesting temples are.

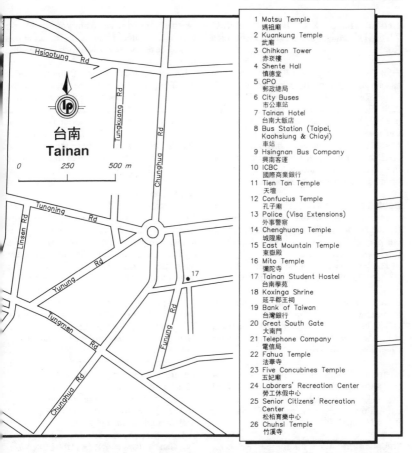

台南
**Tainan**

0    250    500 m

1  Matsu Temple
   媽祖廟
2  Kuankung Temple
   武廟
3  Chihkan Tower
   赤崁樓
4  Shente Hall
   慎德堂
5  GPO
   郵政總局
6  City Buses
   市公車站
7  Tainan Hotel
   台南大飯店
8  Bus Station (Taipei,
   Kaohsiung & Chiayi)
   車站
9  Hsingnan Bus Company
   興南客運
10 ICBC
   國際商業銀行
11 Tien Tan Temple
   天壇
12 Confucius Temple
   孔子廟
13 Police (Visa Extensions)
   外事警察
14 Chenghuang Temple
   城隍廟
15 East Mountain Temple
   東嶽殿
16 Mito Temple
   彌陀寺
17 Tainan Student Hostel
   台南學苑
18 Koxinga Shrine
   延平郡王祠
19 Bank of Taiwan
   台灣銀行
20 Great South Gate
   大南門
21 Telephone Company
   電信局
22 Fahua Temple
   法華寺
23 Five Concubines Temple
   五妃廟
24 Laborers' Recreation Center
   勞工休假中心
25 Senior Citizens' Recreation
   Center
   松柏育樂中心
26 Chuhsi Temple
   竹溪寺

Being a traditional city, there are frequent Buddhist parades and special temple worship ceremonies. At certain times specified in the lunar calendar, everyone performs a worship ceremony and at this time, the air is thick with smoke from the burning of 'ghost money' and incense. Tables are set out on the street, well endowed with scrumptious food meant as offerings to the gods. Ironically, Tainan also has the largest Christian population in Taiwan – it is claimed that Christians make up as much as 10% of the city's total population.

Temples and monuments are the main

attractions in this historical city. With a little effort you can see most of the really interesting ones in a day but you need to start early. Most of the sites are within walking distance of one another, but several will require a bus or taxi trip.

### Information

**Tourist Office** The Tourism Bureau (tel (06) 2265681) has a branch on the 2nd floor, 90 Chungshan 4th Rd.

**Money** ICBC (tel (06) 2231231) is at 90 Chungshan Rd, one long block from the train station. The Bank of Taiwan (tel (06) 2226181) is much farther out at 129 Fuchien Rd.

**Film** There is one place in Tainan where you can get good quality photofinishing on B&W film: Tai Chi Photo Supply (tel (06) 2286798, 2222234) (*tàijí zhàoxiàng cáiliào háng*), 11 Kungyuan Rd. It's right on the traffic circle where Kungyuan Rd intersects Minsheng Rd. I can recommend them only for B&W processing, because it's done on the premises by hand, while their colour printing is farmed out to another lab.

**Book & Music** Stores The best bookstore in town is Bookman Books (tel (06) 2754630) (*shūlín shūjú*), 99 Changjung Rd, Section 2, but overall Tainan has a poor selection of English-language books.

The best place for music tapes is Chiu's (tel (06) 2387924) at 135 Shengli Rd.

**Laundry** Don't hide your dirty laundry, get it washed cheaply at *bōbō zìzhù xǐyī zhōngxīn* (tel (06) 2384386), 20-1 Tahsueh Rd. It's next to the 89 restaurant, near Chengkung University.

**Hospital** Chengkung University Hospital (tel (06) 2353535) (*chéngdà yīyùan*) 成大醫院 is one of the most modern hospitals in Taiwan. It's on the corner of Hsiaotung Rd and Shengli Rd.

**Travel Agents** About the cheapest prices on international tickets can be obtained from Wing On Travel Service (tel (06) 2293141) (*yǒng'ān lüxíngshè*), 91 Minchuan Rd, Section 2. Also good is Southeast Travel Service (tel (06) 2234176), 149 Fuchien Rd, Section 1.

### Cofucius Temple
*(kǒngzǐ miào)* 孔子廟
Constructed in 1665 by General Chen Yunghua, a Ming Dynasty supporter, this is the oldest Confucian temple in Taiwan. On 28 September – the birthday of Confucius – a colourful dawn ceremony is held. You may

be able to get a ticket from your hotel or a tour agency should you be in Tainan at this time. The temple is at 2 Nanmen Rd, near the main police station.

Directly across the street from the Confucius Temple's main entrance is a small stone archway, which now forms the entrance of a busy alley. No one is certain when the archway was built, but historians estimate it was constructed in 1683 when the Confucius Temple was repaired. There are four stone archways remaining in Tainan and this is the oldest one.

### Great South Gate
*(dà nánmén)* 大南門
Tainan used to be a walled city. The walls were built in 1723 in response to an anti-Manchu rebellion. At one time there were eight gates leading into the city, but today only three remain. Of the three gates, the largest and best preserved is the Great South Gate.

The gate is in a small park, half a block south of Fuchien Rd and the Confucius Temple. When you leave the Confucius Temple, turn right and walk south along Nanmen Rd. Pass Fuchien Rd and you'll soon come to a little alley on the right side of the street. A white sign clearly says 'Ta Nan Men' and points into the alley. The fortresslike gate is so large you can't miss it. You're allowed to climb up into the gate and walk around on the top.

The other two gates in Tainan are the Great East Gate on Tungmen Rd and the Little West Gate, which is now relocated on the campus of National Chengkung University, east of Chengkung Lake.

### Chihkan Tower
*(chìkǎn lóu)* 赤崁樓
The Dutch built two forts in Tainan before Koxinga evicted them. One is the Chihkan Tower, also known as Fort Providentia, built in 1653. The other is Fort Zeelandia in Anping, a suburb to the west of Tainan, near the sea. Very little remains of the original Chihkan Tower as it was levelled by an earthquake in 1862. The two towers were rebuilt

in 1875. Inside there is a small museum. Chihkan Tower is at 212 Mintsu Rd, a short walk down the street from the Far Eastern Department Store.

### Kuankung Temple
(wǔ miào) 武廟

This old temple is dedicated to Kuankung (gūangōng), the saint of martial arts. He stands in contrast to Confucius, who is regarded as the saint of literature. Kuankung is known for his physical strength, while Confucius is revered for his wisdom.

The temple is on Mintsu Rd, directly opposite the Chihkan Tower. It looks unimpressive from the Mintsu Rd side where you first get a glimpse of it, but this is the back entrance to the temple. Walk down the narrow alley next to the temple and you'll soon find the front entrance.

### Matsu Temple
(māzǔ miào) 媽祖廟

As you face the Kuankung Temple, you will see an alley on your left. Walk down this alley for less than a minute and you'll come to the Matsu Temple. In contrast to the Kuankung Temple, which has a very simple, conservative look about it, the Matsu Temple is incredibly colourful. Go around the back and have a look at the temple artwork, all of which is original. Feel free to take photos.

### Tien Tan Temple
(tiān tán) 天壇

This temple is one of the most interesting places to visit in Tainan. It is more commonly known by its local name, tiān gōng. It is not very large but it is an extremely active Taoist temple, reminiscent of the Lungshan Temple in Taipei. A lot of incense and 'ghost money' is burnt here and plenty of food offerings are made to the ghosts. Occasionally, someone in a trance will be possessed by a ghost.

This temple is often packed with worshippers, but it is best to visit on the 1st and 16th days of the lunar month if you really want to see some activity. If you visit at the wrong time, it might be very quiet. Try to avoid dinner time, when everyone goes home,

unless of course you just want to photograph temple artefacts without being bothered by the crowd.

The temple is hidden away in an obscure alley just off Chungyi Rd (zhōngyì lù), near the intersection with Minchuan Rd.

### East Mountain Temple
(dōng yùe diàn) 東嶽殿

This is one temple that never gets mentioned in the tourist brochures and the locals seem reluctant to talk about it. I'm not sure why, but perhaps they associate it with superstition and witchcraft or perhaps they are just scared of the place. It certainly is morbid inside and it does give you the creeps. I too hesitate to write this place up, but not for the reasons already mentioned. My fear is that the temple's purpose could be misinterpreted. So if you go there behave in the same way you would in any other temple.

After this lengthy introduction, what am I talking about? The East Mountain Temple is like no other in Taiwan. It's a very small temple, but when you enter it you feel as though you've stepped into another world. The walls are blackened by over 300 years of burning incense and the air is often heavy with smoke. The murals on the wall depict Hell by showing horrifying scenes of torture.

I was fortunate on one visit to meet one of the temple custodians who explained in detail the history and purpose of the temple. He was an old man who couldn't speak Mandarin Chinese, only Taiwanese, so I had to use an interpreter. Among the things I learnt was that the temple was built in 1672 and that the terrifying murals are meant to warn people to lead a clean and moral life. Each torture shown is a punishment for a specific crime or evil deed.

This temple is often packed with people, many of whom wish to communicate with dead relatives or drive an evil ghost out of their homes. I've seen several old women in the temple, with their eyes closed, pounding their fists on the table, talking rapidly and surrounded by a crowd with tape recorders trying to record their words. These women are mediums who communicate with spirits. I also saw an exorcism ceremony. Scenes such as these are quite common.

You'll see some other interesting artefacts in this temple. The large statues staring down at you are those of General Hsieh and General Fan. General Hsieh is the short, fat one and General Fan is tall and thin. General Fan is often depicted with his tongue hanging out because he committed suicide by hanging himself. The story goes that General Fan and General Hsieh made an appointment to meet under a bridge by the river. General Hsieh arrived first and was drowned in a flash flood. General Fan arrived later and was so grieved to find his friend dead that he hanged himself. For this reason their statues are placed in many temples as a symbol of sincere loyalty.

The East Mountain Temple is at 110 Minchuan Rd, Section 1. They generally don't mind foreign visitors, but try to maintain a low profile. Please don't go flashing your camera in people's faces. There is no objection though to photographing the paintings, statues and other temple artefacts.

### Chenghuang Temple
(*chénghúang miào*) 城隍廟

The Chenghuang Temple is related to the East Mountain Temple, but it is not nearly so morbid or active. It is more like the other Taoist temples in Tainan. The figures of General Fan and General Hsieh can also be seen here. Chenghuang is the name of a god worshipped by the Hakka people, who make up some 5% of Taiwan's total population. Needless to say, many Hakka people come here. The temple is at 133 Chingnien Rd.

### Shente Hall
(*shèndé táng*) 慎德堂

This is not the best temple in Tainan, but it is very centrally located. It's on Kungyuan Rd just half a block from the Far Eastern Department Store. From the outside, this temple looks shiny and brand new. In fact, it's one of the oldest temples in Tainan. It was built during the Ming Dynasty and has recently had a facelift.

It's not a popular temple, so don't be surprised if you don't see anybody inside, but you are welcome to go in and look around. This temple is in reality a residence hall, occupied only by nuns. A woman who renounces her home can go there to live and cultivate her spiritual faith. Don't go upstairs, as that area is reserved for the nuns.

### Mito Temple
(*mítúo sì*) 彌陀寺

Constructed in 1718, this colourful temple has recently been restored. It's on Tungmen Rd just east of the railroad tracks.

On the 2nd floor of the Mito Temple is one of the most magnificent statues I've seen of the 1000-armed Kuanyin. This image indicates that the goddess is almighty. Eyes have been painted on her hands to demonstrate that she sees all, and she has several smaller heads attached to the top of her head – these many minds indicate her wisdom.

### Koxinga's Museum & Shrine
*(yánpíng jùnwáng cí)* 延平郡王祠

Koxinga is not a god, but a shrine has been built in his honour. He is the national hero who successfully expelled the Dutch from Taiwan. Koxinga and his troops landed in Taiwan in 1661 with the mission of freeing Taiwan from colonial rule and returning it to China. After a 6 month siege, the Dutch gave up and were allowed to leave Taiwan without any reprisals, thus ending their 37 year occupation of the island.

All this happened at a time of great upheaval in China. The Ming Dynasty, which was supported by Koxinga, was rapidly losing control of China to the Manchu invaders. Koxinga and his supporters moved to Taiwan with the hope of launching an invasion and destroying the

1000-armed Kuanyin, Mito Temple

Manchus. Instead, Taiwan fell to the Manchus in 1682. Koxinga never lived to see this. He died in 1663, just 1 year after his successful mission against the Dutch. The Manchus ruled China brutally until their overthrow in 1911.

Adjacent to the Koxinga Shrine is an interesting museum containing a large number of paintings, sculptures, a traditional Chinese sedan chair, costumes, and a model of the Dutch Fort Zeelandia. Unfortunately, only a few of the displays have English explanations.

The museum and shrine compound is open from 9 am to 6 pm. There is a NT$10 admission charge. Entrance is from Kaishan Rd. You can walk there from the Confucius Temple or take bus No 17.

### Fahua Temple
*(fǎhúa sì)* 法華寺

A short walk from the Koxinga Museum & Shrine, this temple is on Fahua St, an obscure narrow street connecting Kaishan Rd and Chienkang Rd. The Fahua Temple is over 300 years old and looks authentic and well preserved. The temple grounds are peaceful and contain many big, beautiful trees. There are some interesting murals on the walls and they're well worth photographing.

### Chuhsi Temple
*(zhúxī sì)* 竹溪寺

The Chuhsi Temple is one of the largest and most beautiful temples in the city. The temple is in a huge park complex called the Tainan Athletic Grounds *(tǐyù chǎng)*, just one block south of Chienkang Rd. It's a good area to go jogging, or play tennis and other outdoor sports, so of course the area is busy on weekends and holidays. However, the temple itself is rarely crowded in spite of its impressive size and beauty.

### Five Concubines Temple
*(wǔfēi miào)* 五妃廟

The Five Concubines Temple is actually not much of a temple and is only worth visiting if you are already at the Chuhsi Temple, a 5 minute walk away.

The Five Concubines Temple is more like an altar. It's very small and is dedicated to honour the five concubines of Ning Ching, who was a relative of the last Ming emperor. When Ning Ching died, it is said that his five concubines committed suicide. The temple sits in a pleasant park just north of Chienkang Rd. There is no entrance on Chienkang Rd, so you must walk one block further north and enter the park from the back.

### Kaiyuan Temple
*(kāiyúan sì)* 開元寺

One of the oldest and biggest temples in Tainan, the Kaiyuan Temple is a very pleasant classical Buddhist temple with spacious, peaceful grounds, gardens, trees and pagodas. The only problem with going there is that it is really too far to walk from the central area.

To reach the temple take bus Nos 1, 6 or 17 from the train station. The bus ride takes about 10 minutes and you get off near the intersection of Kaiyuan Rd and Peiyuan St *(běi yúan jiē)*. Kaiyuan Rd is the big, wide, busy road and Peiyuan St is a small side street. Walk down this street and you'll see the temple on your left. It takes about a minute to walk to from there. A taxi would cost around NT$50 or so from the city centre.

Don't confuse the adjacent hospital with the temple itself. The hospital is a beautiful example of traditional architecture and belongs to the temple.

### Anping Fort
*(ānpíng gǔbǎo)* 安平古堡

This is a place for history buffs. The Anping Fort is also known by its Dutch name, Fort Zeelandia. The Dutch built it in 1653 on what was then the coastline of Taiwan. Since then the coastline has extended several km westward due to siltation, and as a result, the fort no longer commands a sea view. This is one of two forts built in Tainan by the Dutch. The other is Fort Providentia (also called Chihkan Tower), which is right in the heart of Tainan.

Visiting Anping Fort would be more worthwhile if you could see the original, but

Temple art, Kaiyuan Temple

unfortunately it was levelled in the 1800s by a powerful typhoon. What you see today is a reconstructed fort and observation tower built in the 1970s. There is also a temple across the street. However, the site is a pleasant place and you could also take a taxi from there to Anping Beach *(ānpíng hǎishuǐ yùchǎng)*, a short ride away. Bus No 33 goes to the fort. Admission is NT$10.

### Yitsai Chin Cheng
*(yìzǎi jīn chéng)* 億載金城

The Yitsai Chin Cheng was at one time a small fortress with a moat. It was built by French engineers in 1875. Today, one of the original gates still remains in a 1 hectare park. Like the Anping Fort, it's mostly of interest to history buffs rather than sightseers. From Anping Fort, it's a very short taxi ride due south. You could also walk, though you might get lost. The address is 16 Nanwen Rd, Anping District. Bus Nos 15 and 33 go there.

## Cultural Center
*(wénhùa zhōngxīn)* 文化中心

The Cultural Center (tel (06) 2692864), at 375 Chunghua Rd, Section 1, is similar to othe cultural centres in Taipei, Taichung and Kaohsiung. Art exhibitions and live performances of opera and classical music are held here. If you'd like to find out the current schedule of events, drop by the centre or call – but it's unlikely that the person answering the phone will speak English.

## Places to Stay – bottom end

The cheaper hotels are found in the side streets in front of the train station. There are no hotels behind the train station.

There are three hostels in Tainan offering budget accommodation. The most popular is the *Laborers' Recreation Center* (tel (06) 2630174) *(láogōng xiūjià zhōngxīn)*. The address is 261 Nanmen Rd, but the entrance is actually quite a way back from Nanmen Rd on a long driveway. Immediately opposite it is the *Senior Citizens' Recreation Center* (tel (06) 2646974) *(sōngbó yùlè zhōngxīn)*. Both hostels charge the same rates: dormitories are NT$145 and double rooms are NT$430.

The *Tainan Student Hostel*, (tel (06) 2670526, 2689018) *(táinán xúeyùan)*, 1 Lane 300, Funung St, Section 1, charges NT$150 for dorm accommodation. This hostel is very clean and usually has empty beds, but for a while they were not accepting foreigners because they had a lot of trouble with Westerners taking drugs. The latest word is that they are now accepting foreigners again, but this could change. The hostel is a fine place to stay, but it's too far to walk to from the city centre. You can go there on bus Nos 7 or 19.

## Places to Stay – middle

A nice clean place is the *Asia Hotel* (tel (06) 2226171) *(dōngyǎ lóu dàfàndiàn)*, 100 Chungshan Rd, at the intersection with Mintsu Rd. Doubles are NT$500.

Somewhat more luxurious is the *Golden Hotel* (tel (06) 2203336) *(gāodēng jiǔdiàn)*, 111 Chengkung Rd, where doubles are NT$720. A good deal for the money is the *Oriental Hotel* (tel (06) 2221131) *(húaguāng dàfàndiàn)*, 143 Mintsu Rd, which has doubles from NT$600 to NT$800 and twins at NT$900.

## Places to Stay – top end

Hotels in Tainan out of the budget range are: the *Tainan Hotel* (tel (06) 2289101, fax (06) 2268502) *(táinán dàfàndiàn)* at 1 Chengkung Rd, which has doubles for NT$1600 to NT$2000; and *Redhill Hotel* (tel (06) 2258121, fax (06) 2216711) *(chíkǎn dàfàndiàn)*, 46 Chengkung Rd, which has doubles for NT$1250 to NT$1400 and twins for NT$1600 to NT$1800.

## Places to Eat

**Budget Eats** Like elsewhere in Taiwan, economically priced noodle shops occupy every street corner, but the area adjacent to National Chengkung University deserves special mention. Numerous cheap eating places catering to the student population surround the campus. Ironically, some of the classiest places in town are also in this area because it's considered a prestigious neighbourhood.

The line-up of eating establishments begins just opposite the main entrance gate of National Chengkung University and runs down the length of Tahsueh Rd *(dàxúe lù)*. Starting near the university post office, there are even more restaurants lining both sides of Shengli Rd.

For budget meals in spartan surroundings, a popular place is *shènglì fàndiàn*, at 110 Shengli Rd. I particularly like the hot spicy fried tofu *(mápó dòufú)*, liver-vegetable soup *(sānxiān tāng)*, boiled dumplings *(shǔijiǎo)* and fried dumplings *(gūotiē)*.

If you have a sweet tooth, just across the street is a sherbet store called *xiǎo máo wū mián mián bīng*. You'll see the sherbet on display, so just point to what you want. You can also order an ice-fruit salad *(mìdòu bīng)* or a papaya milkshake (*mùgūa niúnǎi*). They have a pool hall in the back room.

One of the best bargains in town can be found right inside the campus of National Chengkung University itself. There are several cafeterias on campus, but you'll have to ask a student where they are since they tend to change location periodically. Try to arrive a little early because it gets crowded and the food disappears quickly. University food isn't necessarily the best, but it's cheap.

A few blocks north of the university, you can find Tainan's best dumpling (*shǔijiǎo*) restaurant, *lǎo yǒu cāntīng* (tel (06) 2347057), 268 Shengli Rd. Prices are very low here.

You'll find plenty of good things to eat at the night market on Hsiaopei Rd. Chinatown also offers numerous foodstalls (see the Entertainment section). As you face the front entrance of Chinatown, off to the left (south) are narrow alleys. Go in there and you will find yourself in a night market area known as Sakariba (a Japanese word widely understood in Tainan). The streets here are extremely narrow and crowded with pedestrians and motorcycles. It's a great place to get something to eat, as one traveller wrote:

I recently ate from a pot which had been simmering sauce for 44 years (continuously) – they claim it's never been emptied and washed. My host seemed to know this – it's a local legend. Regardless, it was really delicious.

Jeanie Lin

One can only hope that they wash the bowls and chopsticks more frequently than the pot.

**Fast Food** If you want to do something depraved like eating hamburgers and drinking Coca-Cola, the place to head for is called *89* (tel (06) 2378838) (*bājiǔ měishí hànbǎo diàn*), 24 Tahsueh Rd. I don't care much for the hamburgers, but their fried chicken has kept me alive for years. This place has become something of a hang-out for Tainan's New Wave crowd. And if you don't like the hamburgers at 89, you can go right next door to *McDonald's*.

A good place for tasty fast food is *Tastee* (tel (06) 2245252) at 28 Kungyuan Rd, near the Far Eastern Department Store. The fried chicken is expensive if you order it à la carte, but cheap if ordered as part of a meal with rice (*jī kùai fàn*).

Just next to the Hsiaopei Rd night market is a huge shopping mall attached to the Tuntex Department Store (*dōngdìshì*), where you'll find a *Wendy's* fast-food restaurant.

**Tea House** An excellent teahouse is *táo hūa yúan* (tel (06) 2247123) at 18 Chienyeh St (*jiànyè jiē*), near the intersection of Kaishan Rd and Fuchien Rd.

**Restaurants** For a reasonably priced meal in very pleasant surroundings, a good place to try is *wǔkèlā* (tel (06) 2352867), 115 Shengli Rd. They have an English-language menu which is available on request. It is also near the university. Another pleasant place which has reasonably priced Western food is (*pú yúan xī cān*) (tel (06) 2341411), 163 Changjung Rd, Section 2, near the intersection with Tungning Rd. Yet another good place, but with higher prices, is *Zebra* (tel (06) 2365350) (*bānmǎ xī cāntīng*), 50 Shengli Rd, at the intersection with Chingnien Rd.

On Tahsueh Rd next to McDonald's is the *Vegetarian Restaurant* (*tiānrán sùshí gǔan*). The food is definitely vegetarian; it's a bit oily for my tastes, but 100% natural. They do make very good whole-wheat bread, a rare find in Taiwan. A more high-class vegetarian restaurant (with prices to match) is *tiān xīn yán sùshí cāntīng* (tel (06) 2201206), 31 Minsheng Rd, Section 1.

Good Mandarin-style Chinese food can be had at *běipíng yīmǔ yúan xiàn bǐng zhōu* (tel (06) 2388720), 135 Tungning Rd, near the intersection with Linsen Rd. Similar food, but with fancier decor and higher prices, can be had at *rú lín yī xiǎo gǔan* (tel (06) 2364650), 21 Changjung Rd, Section 3.

If fancy decor means a lot to you, you can enjoy a meal in air-conditioned comfort at the *Ambassador Restaurant* (tel (06) 2386666) (*dàshǐ cāntīng*), 8 Tahsueh Rd. I admire their interior decorating, but personally I find the food overrated. Just around the corner is an even more exclusive place, *My Steakhouse* (tel (06) 2381608) (*húa xīn xī cāntīng*), 123 Changjung Rd, Section 3.

Good Szechuan-style food is served at *yúyùan chūan cài cāntīng* (tel (06) 2285990), 117 Chungyi Rd, near Minchuan Rd. Another good place for Szechuan food is *Today's Restaurant* (tel (06) 2232881) (*jīnrì chūan cài cāntīng*), 62 Chungcheng Road. Two doors down is yet another excellent Szechuan restaurant, *róng xīng chūan cài cāntīng* (tel (06) 2213134), 56 Chungcheng Rd.

The best Western food in town can be found at the *Dragon Arch Restaurant* (tel (06) 2246332) (*lóngmén xī cāntīng*), 2nd floor, 215 Fuchien Rd, near the intersection of Fuchien Rd and Chungyi Rd.

Another place serving excellent Western and Chinese food is *Twin Oaks* (tel (06) 2267001) (*shūang xiàng yúan tíngyúan cāntīng*). It's at 146 Peimen Rd, Section 2, across the street from Chungshan Park. Prices are not exactly cheap. On the opposite side of the park is the similar but slightly less expensive *Old Place Restaurant* (tel (06) 2216761) (*lǎo dìfāng*), 317 Kungyuan Rd.

The *Redhill Hotel* (tel (06) 2258121) (*chìkǎn dàfàndiàn*), 46 Chengkung Rd, has several excellent restaurants on the 1st floor and in the basement, including a great Western buffet. Across the street from the Redhill is a good Szechuan restaurant, *júe sì chūan cài tīng* (tel (06) 2295133), at 111 Chengkung Rd.

The *Diamond Restaurant* (tel (06) 2253100) (*zhùan shí lóu cāntīng*) is famous for its dim sum. It's on the 5th floor of the Far Eastern Department Store; take the elevator because the stairs lead to the roof, bypassing the restaurant. The Far Eastern is on the corner of Mintsu Rd and Kungyuan Rd.

## Entertainment

There is an interesting outdoor night market on Hsiaopei Rd (*xiǎoběi lù yèshì*). It's most active during the summer months on a Saturday night. Unfortunately, it's a little far out of town so you'll probably have to take a taxi to get there – it's about a 10 minute ride from the city centre. You will find plenty of good things to eat and some good deals on clothing.

Just next to this night market is a huge shopping mall attached to the Tuntex Department Store (*dōngdìshì*). In addition to shopping, there is a movie theatre, swimming pool, rides for the children and a fast-food restaurant.

It might seem peculiar, but there is a Chinatown (*zhōngguó chéng*) in Tainan. Chinatown is contained within two large buildings and is a collection of movie theatres, a skating rink, shops where you can buy clothes, shoes and music cassettes, and about 100 hole-in-the-wall foodstalls. It's busiest at night, especially during the weekends.

**Cinemas** The cheapest movie house is in the basement of a Catholic church, the *húadēng yìshù zhōngxīn* (tel (06) 2358342). They have some really great classic movies for NT$30, but you have to call for the schedule.

The cheapest regular movie theatre in town is *qúanměi xìyùan* (tel (06) 2224726), 187 Yungfu Rd, Section 2. For only NT$60, you can see two films. Some other movie theatres in Tainan include:

*chénggōng xìyùan*
107 Hai'an Rd (tel (06) 2223700)
*wánghòu xìyùan*
6th floor, 323 Chungcheng Rd (tel (06) 2227761)
*wángzi xìyùan*
323 Chungcheng Rd (tel (06) 2225460)
*gúohúa xìyùan*
3rd floor, 118 Minchuan Rd, Section 2 (tel (06) 2261213)
*zhōngguó cheng xìyùan*
72 Huanho Rd (tel (06) 2215110)
*yánpíng xìyùan*
128 Hsimen Rd, Section 2 (tel (06) 2224282)
*dōng'ān xìyùan*
35 Lane 3, Tungmen Rd, Section 2 (tel (06) 2375650)
*mínzú xìyùan*
249 Mintsu Rd, Section 2 (tel (06) 2293528)

**MTV** There are a number of good MTV places

in Tainan. One popular place near Chinatown is called *Cash Box* (tel (06) 2264621) (*qián guì*), 5th floor, 322 Chungcheng Rd. Across from the north-east corner of Chungshan Park is *běijí gūang* (tel (06) 2212281) at 150 Peimen Rd, Section 2. Another popular MTV place is *Weekend Pie* (tel (06) 2384955) (*jiūmò pài*), 304 Changjung Rd, Section 2.

**Pubs** A very popular late-night hang-out for foreigners is *DJ Pub* (tel (06) 2378958), 22 Shengli Rd. Another hot spot is *Rock Station* (tel (06) 2378570), 8-2 Shengli Rd. Also popular with foreigners is *Dirty Roger* (tel (06) 2356527) at 104 Changjung Rd, Section 2. Another place to try is *Macanna Beer House* (tel (06) 2345882), 117 Shengli Rd.

## Things to Buy

There are two large department stores in Tainan. The more popular seems to be the Far Eastern Department Store (*yuǎndōng bǎihùo gōngsī*), on the corner of Mintsu Rd and Kungyuan Rd. The newest and largest shop in town is the Tuntex Department Store (*dōngdìshì bǎihùo*), which is just next to the Hsiaopei Rd night market.

Klin Supermarket (tel (06) 2222257) (*kèlín cāojí shìchǎng*) is a good place to pick up Western foods, liquor and other goods. It's at 83 Nanmen Rd, at the intersection with Fuchien Rd. A similar place, but with somewhat less to choose from, is *qiǎolì shēnghúo gǔan* (tel (06) 2239756), 25-2 Chengkung Rd.

Good buys in export-quality clothing can be had at Madame Fashion Company (tel (06) 2289466) (*zhúfù shāng chǎng*), 16 Fuchien Rd.

If you're in the market for a computer that's IBM-compatible, you'll find good service at Sunrise Computer Company (tel (06) 2344382) (*zǎoyáng*), 368 Chingnien Rd. They sell Asia-brand computers. There is an excellent Twinhead computer dealer called Hi-Tech Information Project Company (tel (06) 2206156) at 18 Mintsu Rd, Section 2. There is an Apple Macintosh dealer (tel (06) 2357979) at 16-2 Tahsueh Rd.

## Getting There & Away

There is no problem in reaching Tainan by public transport from all the other major centres in Taiwan. There are frequent buses and trains from Kaohsiung, Taipei, Taichung and Chiayi.

From Taipei, the train fare ranges from NT$366 to NT$504, depending on which class you travel. The bus fare from Taipei is NT$363.

From Tainan, China Airlines and Far Eastern Air Transport have flights to Taipei and the Penghu Islands. Wing On Travel Service (tel (06) 2293141) operates a bus direct to CKS airport.

## Getting Around

You can rent motorcycles from *yīliú jīchē* (tel (06) 2355023), 66 Tungping Rd. They only rent 50cc bikes and charge NT$700 per day.

## AROUND TAINAN
### Luerhmen
(*lùěrmén*) 鹿耳門

Luerhmen, which literally means 'Deer's Ear Gate', is the name of the site along the river where Cheng Chengkung (Koxinga) landed in Taiwan on 29 April 1661. However, the main attraction is not the historical site, but a huge temple which has been built nearby.

Actually, there are two temples and they're only a couple of km from each other. There is an interesting story which accompanies the construction of these two temples. Over the years the local people have been involved in a lot of heavy rivalry and nowadays two distinct groups have formed. They are in competition with each other as to who will end up building the largest temple in Taiwan. Thus the two temples have never really been finished, as they are in a state of constant expansion.

The only limiting factor is money, and so the temples have a nonstop campaign to raise funds for the never-ending construction. Should you decide that this is a worthy cause, you can donate money and have your name engraved on a marble slab, column or any other temple artefact of your choosing. All the artwork in the temple is engraved with

Heaven Holy Mother Temple, Luerhmen

One of Taiwan's popular TV shows is filmed here. Don't make a special trip out here just for this place, but if you're visiting the temple anyway and the weather is hot, the waterslides are a great way to cool off. Don't forget to bring a swimsuit and towel.

**Getting There & Away** The easiest way to get to Luerhmen is to take Bus No 29 from central Tainan. Else you could take bus No 34 to its terminus and then change to bus Nos 27, 28 or 29.

Tainan city bus No 27 goes to the Heaven Queen Mother Temple, which is adjacent to a tiny village called *māzŭ gōng*. There are plenty of shops selling food, souvenirs and other assorted goodies to pilgrims.

### Nankunshen
*(nánkūnshēn)* 南鯤鯓

Along with Peikang (discussed in the West-Central Taiwan chapter), Nankunshen is considered to be the most active, powerful, colourful and richest temple in Taiwan. Don't miss it! Although I repeatedly say throughout this book that you shouldn't visit tourist places on Sundays or holidays, I will make an exception for Nankunshen. This place is only really interesting on Sundays, especially if the weather is nice. At such times, thousands of enthusiastic worshippers descend on the temple and put on a sensational display of parades, fireworks, chanting, feasting and festivities. Bring lots of film and be prepared to move out of the way quickly when the firecrackers start exploding. However, if you visit on weekdays the place might be nearly deserted.

You may well see some devout worshippers practising a mild form of self-mutilation, where a macelike instrument is run across the back of the individual, tearing the skin and causing blood to flow. The cuts are not very deep but will usually leave scars. Only men participate in this particular form of worship. Those who do are presumed to be possessed by the gods and therefore immune to pain. The whole purpose of the self-mutilation is to demonstrate the gods' power.

Other worshippers paint their faces and

Chinese characters indicating who donated the cash to buy that particular item.

Of the two temples, the larger one by far is the Heaven Holy Mother Temple (*tiān shàng shèng mŭ*). It's adjacent to the village of Tucheng (*tŭchéng*).

The runner-up in the temple building competition is a Matsu temple called Heaven Queen Mother Temple (*tiānhòu gōng*). Personally, it looks to me like they've got a long way to go if they want to be number one.

If at all possible, try to visit Luerhmen on the 15th night of the 1st moon – the Lantern Festival. There are brilliant displays of fireworks. Protective clothing is a must; most people wear motorcycle helmets and faceshields.

Right near the Heaven Holy Mother Temple and the village of Tucheng is Woozland (tel (06) 2573811) (*wùzhì lèyùan*), a park known for its fancy waterslides. Popular with kids during the summer, it's a madhouse on weekends but isn't bad during the week.

At a worship festival in Nankunshen

dress up in costumes. They march in a procession, beating on gongs and drums, often carrying a Chinese-style sedan chair for a god to ride in. Meanwhile, firecrackers and skyrockets liven up the atmosphere.

Although the Nankunshen temple is old – it was built in 1662 – it has been kept in fine condition. Behind the temple is a garden area. As you approach Nankunshen on the bus, you'll notice that the surrounding countryside resembles pools of mud with nothing growing at all. In fact these are salt-evaporating ponds. This is about the sunniest place on the island and it's adjacent to the sea, so it is naturally Taiwan's major salt producing region.

**Getting There & Away** Getting to Nankunshen is easy. From Tainan, take a bus from the terminal of the Hsingnan Bus Company (*xīngnán kèyùn*). There are frequent departures and the ride takes about an hour and 15 minutes. If you take the bus, get off at the last stop. The terminal is about one block from the temple. To find the temple, just ask anybody where to find the *nánkūnshēn dàitiǎn fú*. There is also a bus from Kaohsiung.

### Hutoupei
(*hǔtóubēi*) 虎頭埤

About 12 km east of Tainan is Hutoupei, a small reservoir and park. It's basically a good picnic place. Swimming in the reservoir is not permitted, but it is possible to hire a rowboat and fishing is allowed. The Hsingnan Bus Company goes to Hutoupei from central Tainan. There is a youth hostel on the far side of the lake, though it's unlikely you'd really want to spend the night there.

### Wushantou Reservoir
(*wūshāntóu shǔikù*) 烏山頭水庫

Wushantou Reservoir is also known as Coral Lake (*shānhú tán*). Like Hutoupei, it attracts picnickers, fishermen and boaters. Wushantou is much larger and high-speed motorboats zip around the lake. A bus to Wushantou departs from the Hsingnan Bus Company (*xīngnán kèyùn*) terminal on Chungshan Rd in Tainan.

It's doubtful you'd want to spend the night there, but if you do the *Wushantou Guest House* (tel (06) 6983121) (*wūshāntóu gúomín lǚshè*) offers reasonable accommodation. They have doubles for NT$800 or you can stay in the dorm for NT$200.

### Tsengwen Dam & Reservoir
(*zēngwén shǔikù*) 曾文水庫

Tsengwen Dam & Reservoir are in the foothills of the Central Mountains. The reservoir is now the largest lake in Taiwan, though I feel that Sun Moon Lake is more beautiful. Nevertheless, Tsengwen Reservoir is a nice trip if you have the time. Swimming is not allowed, but boating is OK. If you want to, you can swim in the river just below the dam.

Although the view from the dam is scenic, a more interesting place to visit on the shore of the reservoir is Chiayi Farm (*jiāyì nóngchǎng*). Chiayi Farm has nice scenery and orchards, and the buildings are European in design. Chiayi Farm is reached by an entirely different route from Tsengwen Dam. See the Getting There & Away section for details.

The Tsengwen Dam area has a number of hiking trails – unfortunately, most of them are not marked. If you can find a Chinese person to guide you, try to do the hike from Tsengwen Reservoir to Little Switzerland (*xiǎo rùishì*). It doesn't really look like Switzerland, but it's still a nice walk.

Try not to visit Tsengwen Reservoir during the dry season, when the lake is low and has a 'bathtub ring' around it. The dry season is generally from October to April. When the lake is full it's very pretty and the water pouring from the dam's floodgates is impressive.

**Places to Stay** A couple of km below the dam is the *Tsengwen Youth Activity Center* (tel (06) 2234189) (*zēngwén húodòng zhōngxīn*), run by the China Youth Corps. They have dormitory accommodation for NT$100 and single rooms from NT$250 to NT$360. There is also a camping area and they rent out tents and quilts. It's a pleasant, quiet place to stay. You can swim in the nearby creek, just across the highway.

The *Chiayi Farm Guest House* (tel (05) 2521710) (*jiāyì nóngchǎng gúomín bīngǔan*) is a little more expensive but is right on the reservoir in pleasant surroundings. Doubles cost NT$880. This hostel is in the Chiayi Farm area of the lake.

**Getting There & Away** Buses depart for Tsengwen Dam from the Hsingnan Bus Company (*xīngnán kèyùn*) terminal on Chungshan Rd in Tainan. The trip takes about 1½ hours and, as usual, try to avoid going on Sundays.

If you want to go to Chiayi Farm (*jiāyì nóngchǎng*), take the same bus as for Tsengwen Dam, but get off in the village of Yuching (*yùjǐng*), which is several km before the reservoir. From Yuching you can get a bus to Chiayi Farm.

Another way to reach Chiayi Farm is to take the Tsengwen Dam bus to the last stop on the reservoir and then take a boat to Chiayi Farm.

## SOUTH CROSS-ISLAND HIGHWAY
*(nánbù hénggùan gōnglù)* 南部橫貫公路
Running between Tainan on the west coast and Taitung on the east coast, the South Cross-Island Highway climbs into the wilderness of Taiwan's mountains. Unlike the heavily used Central Cross-Island Highway, the South Cross-Island Highway is unpaved and has virtually no traffic. The area is blessed with spectacular scenery every km of the way. This route is closed occasionally because of landslides, especially during the rainy season around late May to early September, but despite this hazard, it is well worth making this trip if you want to see rural Taiwan at its best.

Most people do this trip going from west to east. This makes sense, especially if you decide to hike the middle section (highly recommended), as the west side is a gentle slope and the east side drops down steeply. The hike is popular with university students.

The trip can be made by car, bus or on foot. It can be done in a day if you simply want to rush through on a bus, but if you want to hike the central section, you should allow 3 days.

No matter which way you go, there is only one bus a day in either direction over this highway. From Tainan, buses depart at 7.30 am from the Hsingnan Bus Company (*xīngnán kèyùn*) terminal on Chungshan Rd. If you're going the other way, buses do not depart directly from Taitung, but from Kuanshan (*gūanshān*) at 8 am. Kuanshan is a short train ride north of Taitung.

### Mountain Permit
One hassle with this trip is that a mountain permit is required. Fortunately, it's a class B pass, an easy one to get. I would suggest getting it in advance from the Foreign Affairs Police if possible. Failing that, the permit can be obtained along the way. The bus from Tainan will stop in either the village of Paolai (*bǎolái*) or Chiahsien

(*jiǎxiān*). When coming from Kuanshan, it stops in Haituan (*hǎidūan*).

From both Tainan (west side) and Kuanshan (*gūanshǎn*) (east side) there is a bus, but neither make the trip all the way across the highway. Rather, the two buses meet midpoint on the highway at Tienchih (*tiānchí*), arriving just after noon. Passengers from one bus transfer to the other to complete the trip over the mountains. The bus drivers have lunch and a rest, then at about 2 pm they begin the trip down. Hikers coming from Tainan can get off the bus, have lunch and then start walking.

### Hiking from West to East
About 4 hours of walking from Tienchih takes you to the top of the highway at Yakou (*yǎkǒu*), at an elevation 2728 metres. There is a large tunnel, about half a km in length, and you have to walk through it. A flashlight is absolutely necessary as the tunnel is not lit and is totally dark in the centre – it's rather spooky in there.

Once you are out of the tunnel, walk downhill for a short distance and there are some buildings off to the right. This is the *Yakou Mountain Hostel* (*yǎkǒu shān zhūang*), where you can spend the night. It's best to have reserved a room in advance, but they won't turn anyone away. They will permit you either to sleep on the dining room floor for a small fee or to use the campground. You must visit the small police station next to the hostel and show your mountain pass if you stay there. It is *cold* at 2500 metres, so a sleeping bag and warm clothes are called for.

The hostel is the only place that has food and it is very poor food at that, so bring your own. If you want to eat at the hostel you have to reserve meals in advance, though they have a little kiosk selling cookies and other junk food.

If you get up early the next morning you can admire the extraordinary sunrise. As one traveller wrote:

Walk to the top of the pass at daybreak for lovely mountain vistas and, if conditions are good, for a beautiful display of the sea of clouds...I stayed there over an hour in extreme wind, some rain, some sun, and saw the most spectacular cloud show I have ever seen. The ever-changing patterns and colours raced over the summit at a speed I couldn't believe.

Ruthli F Kemmerer

Walk down the road past the beautiful waterfall. It's a full day's walk downhill to Litao (*lǐdào*), about 30 km or 7 hours by foot. Litao is an aboriginal village at 1070 metres elevation and there is a youth hostel. Remember to show your mountain pass to the police before settling in for the night. Good food is available in Litao from the little shop by the bus station.

A bus departs Litao twice daily at 8 am and 2.30 pm, heading down to Kuanshan on the east coast. If you still have the energy, you can get up early and walk for 2 hours from Litao to Wulu (*wùlù*); the 9 km walk takes you through a gorge that rivals Taroko Gorge in its beauty. The first bus stops in Wulu at 8.20 am, but unless you start out from Litao at 6 am you won't catch it. Of course, you can get the second bus in the afternoon.

After you reach Kuanshan, there are frequent trains heading both south to Taitung or north to Taipei.

### Side Trips
If you want a real challenge, you can climb Kuanshan (*gūanshǎn*), not to be confused with the small city of Kuanshan near Taitung. Kuanshan is a peak just to the south-west of the Yakou Youth Hostel. It's 3666 metres in elevation. You begin the climb from Yakou. A class A mountain pass is supposedly needed, but there is nobody up there to check. Not that I advocate you knowingly do anything illegal of course.

You can spend an extra night along this highway in Meishan on the west side. Meishan is a large aboriginal village and there is a youth hostel. There's nothing to do but relax and go for walks. There is a nice river nearby but the scenery is more exciting in Yakou, at the top of the highway.

## Places to Stay

You don't really have much choice, as there are only three youth hostels along this route. Camping is another possibility; although there aren't any real campgrounds, you are allowed to pitch a tent next to a youth hostel. If you desire luxury accommodation, you'd better stay in Tainan or Taitung.

*Meishan Mountain Hostel* (tel (07) 7470134) (*méishān shān zhuāng*), dormitory NT$100
*Yakou Mountain Hostel* (tel (089) 329891) (*yǎkǒu shān zhuāng*), dormitory NT$100
*Litao Mountain Hostel* (tel (089) 329891) (*lìdào shān zhuāng*), dormitory NT$100

## Places to Eat

Bring extra food along or you'll be sorry. All three youth hostels have meals, but only if they are booked in advance. Also the meals leave a lot to be desired – particularly at Yakou due to its remote location.

Some food is available from noodle stands near the bus terminals in Meishan and Litao, but nothing is available in Yakou except some biscuits.

# West-Central Taiwan 台灣中西部

If you have travelled down the east coast you would have already seen some of Taiwan's spectacular mountains, but the really big peaks are in this part of the country. It's here that you find Yushan, which at 3950 metres is the highest peak on the island. In just a few hours you can ascend by train or bus from coconut and banana groves to alpine forests.

This is where Taiwan's urban residents escape to when they have a holiday. The mountain resorts of Alishan, Tsaoling, Tungpu and Hsitou draw larger and larger crowds every year. In the foothills is Sun Moon Lake, a honeymoon resort which rivals Tienhsiang on the east coast.

The narrow coastal strip of west-central Taiwan is pancake-flat, agricultural land. A highly productive rice-growing region, this area is also rich in culture. It's here that you can see the enormous worship festivals at Peikang, and nearby Lukang is one of the most historical cities in Taiwan.

## YENSHUI
*(yánshǔi)* 鹽水

Yenshui is a fairly ordinary town between Tainan and Chiayi. However, the whole town collectively goes insane during the Lantern Festival on the 15th day of the 1st moon. It's the closest thing to a friendly riot. The real action occurs in the square at the intersection of Chungcheng Rd and Sanfu Rd. The activities start at 7 pm and continue past midnight.

It's the world's most spectacular display of fireworks. One after another, people ignite giant cardboard honeycombs stuffed with rockets; each one costs over NT$100,000. It's open warfare – the honeycombs are often aimed right into the crowd. There are similar fireworks displays in Luerhmen and Peikang, but nothing quite matches the grandeur of Yenshui. People from all over Taiwan converge on this town – the crowd is estimated at several hundred thousand.

As a veteran of Yenshui, I can say that the fireworks will be the least of the hazards you face. Much more dangerous are the spectators. With thousands of people standing shoulder to shoulder, the wild pushing and shoving becomes deadly. The sedan chairs charging through the crowd cause many injuries. The chance of being trampled should not be taken lightly. If you get up front, the safest thing to do is actually to run into the firecrackers, not away from them – this way you temporarily leave the crowd behind. There are always a few fistfights, usually resulting from arguments about whose firecracker hit whose girlfriend. Even though motor vehicles are supposedly banned during the festival, there are at least a few drunken birdbrains who enthusiastically drive their motorcycles right into the crowd at high speed. The ambulances do good business. So do the pickpockets.

Wear old clothing, since the sparks can burn little holes in cloth. A motorcycle helmet with faceshield is essential survival gear. An amazing number of people don't wear any protection at all – as any eye surgeon in the local hospitals can tell you. It is possible to carry a camera, but a large one dangling from your neck is certain to get broken. Much safer would be a small camera that fits in your pocket.

Down in the crowds it gets very hot, but you can expect the weather to be cold at this time of year. It's best to carry a couple of sweaters or jumpers and tie them securely around your waist when you get ready to plunge into the crowds. Wearing a small backpack or daypack would be very inconvenient. Those little packs that attach to your belt are much more secure in these crowds. Don't carry anything that you can't stuff into your pockets or beltpack, because you need both hands free to manoeuvre through the crowd and keep your balance.

The best location is on somebody's rooftop or terrace overlooking the square. This is where the TV cameras are set up. To

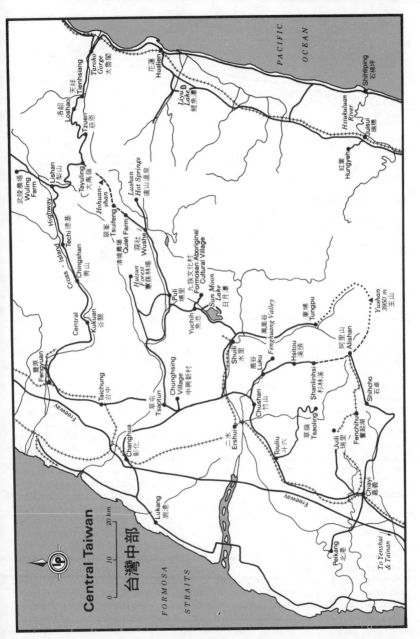

Central Taiwan
台灣中部

FORMOSA STRAITS

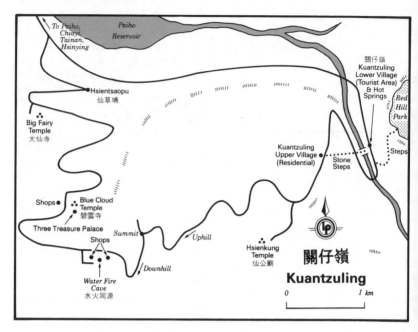

get these choice spots, you either have to know somebody or arrive early and expect to pay for the privilege. There are a few awnings that you might be able to climb onto (at your own risk), but it's not easy. Expect every square cm of space to be fully occupied.

Everything you need can be purchased in Yenshui. Street vendors capitalise on the situation and sell motorcycle helmets and face shields. Safety glasses are not widely available in Taiwan. There is no shortage of food and drinks.

A motorcycle or bicycle is the most practical way to get into and out of Yenshui during this festival. You can take the train to Hsinying and then walk 7 km or take a taxi to Yenshui, but start out early if you're going to depend on public transport.

Perhaps the best plan is to avoid Yenshui and instead visit the fireworks displays in Luerhmen and Peikang; your chances of injury are less in those places and you can watch the Yenshui display on TV. It's usually broadcast several weeks later.

## KUANTZULING
*(gūancǐlǐng)* 關仔嶺

Kuantzuling is an old hot springs resort which was popular in the times of the Japanese occupation. As hot springs go, these are rather unattractive because the water contains some clay, giving it the colour of milk. Ironically, real hot springs enthusiasts claim the mineral content is good for you and for this reason they still flock to Kuantzuling. During the occupation, the Japanese built their charming wooden inns with tatami mats. These days most of the Japanese inns have disappeared and given way to modern Chinese architecture – 'renaissance concrete box'.

Whether or not you care to soak in the mucky hot springs, this area in the foothills of Taiwan's mountains is pretty. However, the main attraction is the temples. Kuantzuling is one place that is best seen if you have your own vehicle.

If you have a couple of friends with you, the country roads around Kuantzuling are excellent for hiking, except on Sundays or holidays when the tourists in their cars flood into the area. Try to arrive early. When you get into town you will no doubt be greeted by a mass of wild chicken taxi drivers who will tell you that it is too far to walk anywhere and that there are snakes and tigers around, but that they will gladly give you a ride for NT$500 or so. It's up to you of course. Hiking will take the whole day, whereas a taxi tour of the area might last for 30 minutes. You can be sure that your driver will do his best to make the tour as short as possible – after all, once he dumps you off he can pick up another passenger. You might want to take a taxi to the Water Fire Cave and then walk from there. You can also reach the Water Fire Cave by bus from Paiho (*báihé*).

## Red Hill Park

The first place you should have a look at is Red Hill Park, up the stairs to your immediate left as you walk up the road out of town. It's a 10 minute climb to the park, which is not spectacular but nevertheless worth seeing.

## Hsienkung Temple
(*xiāngōng miào*) 仙公廟

After you've had a look at Red Hill Park, go back down to the road. Follow the road uphill. You can save some time by taking the stone steps (see map) but the road and the steps both go to the same place. The road loops around while the steps are more direct, but they will both bring you to upper Kuantzuling village. Continue along the road out of the village and into the countryside for several km. You'll eventually find a signposted turn-off on your left. This goes to the Hsienkung Temple, which is a pretty and peaceful temple sitting in the forest.

## Water Fire Cave
(*shǔihǔo dòng*) 水火洞

Back on the main road, continue uphill. It gets a bit steep but you'll soon reach the summit of the highway. It drops down and just about 100 metres away you'll find a bunch of tourist shops. It's a good place to have lunch. Just after the first tourist shops, you can walk down to your left and you'll find Water Fire Cave. The hot springs contain so much gas that it bubbles to the surface and ignites, giving the impression of burning water. I saw a picture taken in 1964 of this same place that showed the flame to be over 3 metres high; today it is much smaller, as the pressure of the gas is dropping.

## Blue Cloud Temple
(*bìyún sì*) 碧雲寺

If you are really tired of walking, there is a bus from the Water Fire Cave to the town of Paiho (*báihé*), but I really suggest you hang in a little bit longer. Just a 15 minute walk downhill will take you to a lovely temple, the Blue Cloud Temple, adjacent to the newer Three Treasure Palace (*sānbǎo diàn*). From there, you again have the option of taking the bus, but if you walk downhill some more you'll eventually come to Big Fairy Temple (*dàxiān sì*), which is an interesting place.

Just another 10 minute walk will take you to Hsientsaopu (*xiāncǎopú*). From here you can go by bus to Hsinying or Chiayi, but it may be easier to catch a bus first to Paiho (*báihé*). As it's a much larger town, there are numerous buses to Hsinying and Chiayi, and sometimes there are direct buses to Tainan as well. You could of course go back to Kuantzuling by bus if you want to spend the night there, though few people do that. Other than visiting the hot springs, there isn't much to do in the village of Kuantzuling.

## Getting There & Away

You can approach Kuantzuling from either Hsinying or Chiayi. If you are coming from the south, take a train to Hsinying (*xīnyíng*), then take a bus from the terminal directly across the street from the train station. Buses go direct to Kuantzuling.

If you're coming from the north, first go to Chiayi and then take a direct bus from the Chiayi Bus Company (*jiāyì kèyùn*) terminal at 501 Chungshan Rd. If you don't get a bus to Kuantzuling right away, take a bus to Paiho (*báihé*) and then another to Kuantzuling.

## CHIAYI
*(jiāyì)* 嘉義

A small city in the centre of Taiwan, Chiayi is the departure point for numerous journeys into Taiwan's high mountains. Travellers will probably be most interested in the trip to Alishan, Taiwan's leading mountain resort. It isn't likely you'll want to go out of your way to tour Chiayi itself, but you may elect to spend a night there on your way to or from the mountains. A nice side trip from Chiayi is to the temple city of Peikang.

### Information
**Money** ICBC (tel (05) 2241166) is at 259 Wenhua Rd near the Far Eastern Department Store. There is a Bank of Taiwan (tel (05) 2224471) at 306 Chungshan Rd.

**Travel Agents** A good travel agent for international tickets is Wing On Travel Service (tel (05) 2277001) (*yǒng'ān lüxíngshè*), 240 Linsen W Rd. Also recommended is Southeast Travel Service (tel (05) 2277025), 490 Chungshan Rd.

### Wufeng Temple
*(wúfèng miào)* 吳鳳廟

This temple is 12 km to the east of Chiayi. It was built in honour of a man named Wufeng. The circumstances of his death have become one of the most popular folk stories in Taiwan.

Wufeng was born in 1699 and lived in the Chiayi area. He worked as a liaison between the government and the aborigines. He became a good friend of the aborigines and learnt to speak their language.

At that time, the aborigines engaged in headhunting. Wufeng was unable to dissuade them from continuing this grisly practice. Then one day Wufeng summoned the aborigines to his office and told them that the next morning, a man on horseback, wearing a red robe and hat, would pass by his office. He

told the aborigines that they could decapitate this man, but that it would be the last head they would ever take.

Just as he said, a man in red robes did appear the next morning. The aborigines duly ambushed him and quickly cut off his head, only to discover shortly afterwards that it was Wufeng himself. Horrified at what they had done, the aborigines completely gave up the practice of headhunting.

Although this story is frequently told in Taiwan and is fully believed by the Chinese, many aborigines dispute it. It's been the source of bitter argument for years, but there is really no way to know the truth about Wufeng.

You can get to the temple by taking a bus from the Chiayi County Bus Terminal (*jiāyì xiàn gōngchē*), which is in front of the train station; there's a bus about every 70 minutes. There is a small museum in the temple that charges an outrageous NT$60 for admission.

### Places to Stay
The cheapest place in town is the *pénglái lüshè* (tel (05) 2272366), 534 Jenai Rd, where singles/doubles cost NT$120/200. The *Hotel North-west* (tel (05) 2223331) (*xīběi dàlüshè*), 192 Jenai Rd, has singles/doubles for NT$200/250. The hotel address will probably have changed by the time you read this because the street was being renumbered at the time I was there.

If you'd rather be a little closer to the centre of things, there are numerous moderately priced hotels on Chungshan Rd. A nice, clean-looking place is the *Hotel Shin Kao* (tel (05) 2272252) (*xīn gāo dàlüshè*), 581 Chungshan Rd, where doubles are NT$500. You can also try *tián yúan dàlüshè* (tel (05) 2222541), 434 Chungshan Rd, where doubles are NT$450.

Chungcheng Rd is also a rich hunting ground for hotels. About the cheapest is *Hotel I-Tong* (tel (05) 2272250) (*yī tóng dàfàndiàn*), 695 Chungcheng Rd, where doubles are NT$450. Next door is *jiā xīn dàfàndiàn* (tel (05) 2222280), 687 Chungcheng Rd, with doubles from NT$600 to NT$700. On the other side of the street is *tǒng yī dàfàndiàn* (tel (05) 2252685), 720 Chungcheng Rd, where doubles are NT$500 to NT$650. The *yì xīng lügǎan* (tel (05) 2279344), 739 Chungcheng Rd, has doubles for NT$500 to NT$700.

The *Yushan Hotel* (tel (05) 2224597) (*yùshān lüshè*), 410 Kungho Rd (*gònghé lù*), charges NT$250 for a double and is the most convenient place to stay if you want to take a bus to Fengshan the next morning, as the bus leaves from in front of the hotel. On the odd chance that they're full, you could stay at the *dōngshān lüshè* (tel (05) 2223857), 344 Kungho Rd, which also has doubles for NT$250.

The *Kowloon Hotel* (tel (05) 2254300) (*jiǔlóng dàfàndiàn*) on Kuangtsai St has doubles for NT$580. The *Hotel Country* (tel (05) 2236336) (*gúoyúan dàfàndiàn*), 678 Kuangtsai St, has doubles from NT$800 to NT$1100.

The *Wantai Hotel* (tel (05) 2275031) (*wàn tài dàfàndiàn*), 46 Hsinjung Rd, a km south of the train station, has doubles/twins for NT$855/1035. The most expensive place is the *Gallant Hotel* (tel (05) 2235366) (*jiānán dàfàndiàn*), 257 Wenhua Rd, with doubles for NT$1600 and twins for NT$1800.

## Places to Eat

As in most Chinese cities eating places are ubiquitous, but an area that deserves special mention is the night market on Wenhua Rd, near the Chungshan Rd traffic circle. The area is active in the daytime too, but at night it really comes to life.

Chungshan Rd is lined with restaurants on both sides, and various noodle and rice shops spill out into the side alleys. The little nameless hole-in-the-wall places are cheapest, but for nicer surroundings try *lǎotáng niúròu miàn* (tel (05) 2232662) at 504 Chungshan Rd. This place is famous for its beef noodles (*niúròu miàn*) and dumplings (*shǔijiǎo*).

Chiayi's best bakery is *xīn táiwān bǐngpù* (tel (05) 2222154), 294 Chungshan Rd, near the intersection with Wenhua Rd. Right across the street is *jī ròu fàn*, 325 Chungshan Rd, which is famous for its fried chicken.

If you're interested in hamburgers, fried chicken and milkshakes, you can enjoy these goodies in air-conditioned comfort at *Mikens* (*mài kěn bǎo*), 471 Chungshan Rd.

There is a top-notch seafood restaurant called *hǎi wèi zhēn* (tel (05) 2230722) at 335 Jenai Rd, about a km south of the train station.

Chuiyang Rd on the south side of town is Chiayi's new high-class district. Many of the city's best and most expensive restaurants are there. One place known for its seafood is *888* (tel (05) 2232888) (*bā bā bā hǎixiǎn*), 457 Chuiyang Rd. Just next door is an excellent Szechuan restaurant, *nǐ jiā wǒ jiā chūan cài gǔan* (tel (05) 2251871), 441 Chuiyang Rd. Continuing down the street on the same side is *Kobe* (tel (05) 2229626), 381 Chuiyang Rd, which is famous for steak dinners and other Western food.

## Entertainment

Chiayi doesn't have a particularly lively nightlife scene. Nevertheless, there are a few movie theatres and MTV places around. For MTV check out *láidiàn xiūxián gǔangchǎng* (tel (05) 2229288), 5th floor, 471 Chungshan Rd.

Several movie theatres exist right in the same building as the Far Eastern Department Store. Some other theatres include: *jiāyì xìyùan* (tel (05) 2222116), 155 Wenhua Rd; *hǔanán xìyùan* (tel (05) 2223236), 152 Hsinjung Rd; and *yǔandōng xìyùan* (tel (05) 2223312), 574 Chungcheng Rd.

## Getting There & Away

**Air** China Airlines has daily flights from Chiayi to the Penghu Islands. The China Airlines office is at 475 Chungshan Rd.

**Bus** The north-south freeway passes through Chiayi, and there are frequent transport services from all the major points to the north and south. The bus fare from Taipei is either NT$237 or NT$294 depending on which bus you take.

In Chiayi, there are two bus terminals in front of the train station. The terminal to your left as you leave the train station belongs to the Taiwan Bus Company (*táiqì kèyùn*).

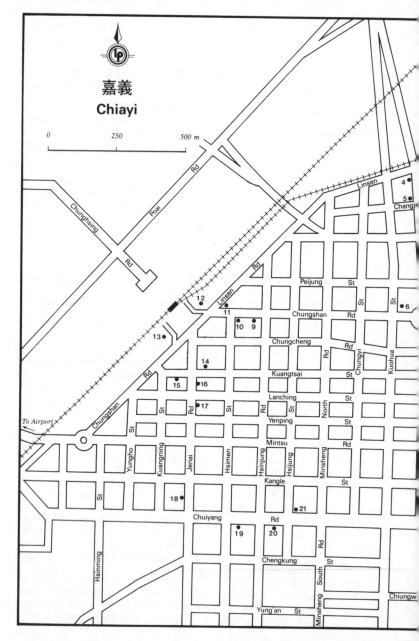

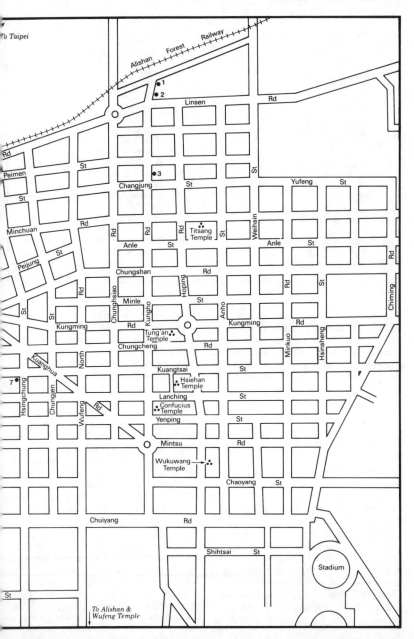

| | | | |
|---|---|---|---|
| 1 | Anhsing Bus Company<br>安興遊覽車 | 12 | Highway Buses (Taipei &<br>Kaohsiung) |
| 2 | Yushan Hotel<br>玉山旅社 | 13 | Chiayi County Buses<br>(Alishan & Mt Area)<br>嘉義客運 |
| 3 | Dongshan Lüshe<br>東山大旅社 | 14 | Hotel Country<br>國園大飯店 |
| 4 | ICBC<br>國際商業銀行 | 15 | Kowloon Hotel<br>九龍大飯店 |
| 5 | Far Eastern Department Store<br>遠東百貨公司 | 16 | Penglai Lüshe<br>蓬萊旅社 |
| 6 | Bank of Taiwan<br>台灣銀行 | 17 | Hotel North-West<br>西北大旅社 |
| 7 | Telephone Company<br>電信局 | 18 | Hai Wei Zhen Restaurant<br>海味珍活海鮮 |
| 8 | GPO<br>郵政總局 | 19 | 888 Restaurant<br>888 海鮮 |
| 9 | Chiayi Bus Company<br>(Peikang & Paiho)<br>嘉義客運 | 20 | Kobe Restaurant<br>神户西餐 |
| 10 | Police (Visa Extensions)<br>警察局外事課 | 21 | Wantai Hotel<br>萬泰大飯店 |
| 11 | Laotang Noodle Shop | | |

They run buses to major cities in Taiwan such as Taipei, Taichung, Tainan and Kaohsiung. The terminal to your right as you leave the train station is the Chiayi County Bus Company (jiāyì xiàn gōngchē), which serves nearby towns like Alishan, Peikang and Kuantzuling.

**Train** As it sits right on the north-south railway, Chiayi has train service to Taipei and Kaohsiung about once every 30 minutes.

## AROUND CHIAYI
### Peikang

*(běigǎng)* 北港

Only about 30 minutes by bus from Chiayi, the town of Peikang is the home of the beautiful Chaotien Temple (cháotiān gōng), the oldest and largest Matsu temple in Taiwan. True, you can get tired of temple viewing, but with the possible exception of Nankunshen, this temple is the most important in Taiwan. Chaotien Temple has the most activity, which includes parades and ceremonies, and the most money. If you find yourself in

Chiayi with a few extra hours on your hands, it's certainly worth the trip to Peikang.

Almost any time you visit this temple there is likely to be something going on, but the best time to visit is on Sundays or holidays, when things are really jumping. The bus will be crowded on those days, but it's worth it.

If you want to see a super-worship festival then try to visit on the birthday of Matsu, the goddess of the sea, which falls on the 23rd day of the 3rd moon in the lunar calendar. In the Western solar (Gregorian) calendar, that would fall sometime between the middle of April and the middle of May. Check with any local to get the exact date, as it varies from year to year. Many calendars sold in Taiwan also list the lunar dates.

I should warn you that attending a super-worship festival poses some tactical problems, especially getting there and back again. Every bus, taxi, car, motorcycle, bicycle, skateboard and ox-cart will be heading into Peikang at the same time. I don't know if anyone has done a count of the number of pilgrims who go there on Matsu's birthday, but it would be in the hundreds of thousands – 'people mountain people sea'. Actually, if you can't handle such crowds, you'd better visit Peikang at some other time.

Another huge celebration takes place in Peikang during the Lantern Festival, on the 15th day of the 1st moon, which is 2 weeks after the Chinese New Year – it's similar to the display at Yenshui.

**Getting There & Away** You can take a bus to Peikang from Chiayi. Buses operated by the Chiayi Bus Company (*jiāyì kèyùn*) at 501 Chungshan Rd depart every 10 minutes. The bus stops at the temple dormitory in Hsinkang (*xīngǎng*) first (the dorm looks like a temple, so don't get confused), then continues on to Peikang. The bus terminal in Peikang is several blocks from the temple. Just ask someone how to get to the Chaotien Temple (*cháotiān gōng*) and they'll point you in the right direction.

## ALISHAN
*(ālǐshān)* 阿里山

Ask any resident of Taiwan what is the most beautiful place on the island and the chances are high that he or she will say, Alishan. And no wonder! After the busy cities and the subtropical heat, Alishan is literally a breath of fresh air. At 2200 metres in elevation, the climate is cool and bracing. Climbing the mountains and breathing the cool air does wonders for your health. A trip to Alishan could restore a mummy to its former strength and vitality.

The views are impressive in any direction you'd care to look. In the morning, you can look out over the 'sea of clouds' with jagged peaks sticking out of the fog blanket. In the afternoon, when the fog usually rolls in and envelops Alishan, the forest has an eerie, timeless beauty of its own. There are plenty of magnificent old cedar trees and pines, a sharp contrast to the palms and banana plants on the plains below. Alishan attracts many tourists in the spring when the cherry trees are blossoming. Finally, there is Yushan (Jade Mountain) which at 3950 metres is Taiwan's highest mountain and one of the

Giant tree near Alishan

highest peaks in East Asia. Climbing Yushan is just one of the many interesting hikes in the Alishan area. To climb Yushan, a class A mountain permit is required.

If you come to Alishan, come prepared for the cold. Even in summer, it's certainly chilly at night. Many people don't seem to realise this and come unprepared. Fortunately, there is a way to survive. Several hotels rent out jackets for NT$50 a day. The jackets are usually coloured bright orange or fire-engine red, with the hotel's name in big letters on the back, lest somebody try to steal it.

The frequent afternoon thunderstorms, especially in the spring and summer, can also be a problem. If you get soaked you can freeze to death, so don't attempt any hiking in the area without proper waterproof clothing. Finally, one thing which must be organised in advance is money because there

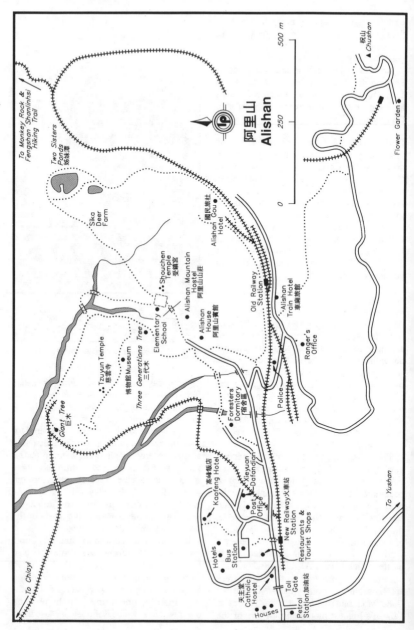

阿里山 Alishan

To Monkey Rock & Fengshan Shanlinhsi Hiking Trail

Two Sisters Ponds 姊妹潭

Sika Deer Farm

500 m

250

0

祝山 ▲Chushan

Flower Garden

國民旅社 Alishan Gou Hotel

Shouchen Temple 受鎮宮

Alishan Mountain Hostel 阿里山山莊

Alishan House 阿里山賓館

Old Railway Station

Alishan Train Hotel 車站旅館

Elementary School

Three Generations Tree 三代木

Tzuyun Temple 慈雲寺

博物館 Museum

Ranger's Office

Giant Tree 巨木

Foresters' Dormitory 宿舍區

Police

To Chiayi

To Yushan

高峰飯店 Kaofeng Hotel

Xieyuan Dafandian

Post Office

New Railway火車站 Station

Bus Station

Hotels

Restaurants & Tourist Shops

天主堂 Catholic Hostel

Houses

Toll Gate

Petrol Station 加油站

is no bank which changes travellers' cheques in Alishan.

Given all its charms, it's no wonder that Alishan is popular. Definitely avoid the weekends and holidays if you can. The transformation that takes place on weekends is truly amazing. On Saturday morning, it's so calm and peaceful you could hear a pin drop. Around 2 pm the first tourists start to arrive. By evening it's a bustling metropolis. Even the trees seem to wilt under the stress. Sunday is also busy, but around 3 or 4 pm the crowds vanish like magic. It's as if a tidal wave rolled in and rolled out again. Serenity returns and Alishan is just a sleepy mountain village once more, at least until the following weekend.

## Alishan Loop Hike

The most popular hike is an easy walk going in a loop past the Two Sisters Pond, an elementary school, the Alishan Giant Tree and a museum. You can also stroll up to the summit of Chushan, which is very peaceful and beautiful at any time other than the dawn rush hour.

You can also walk along the road leading to Yushan, but you cannot go further than the checkpoint without a mountain permit. The checkpoint is about a 2 hour hike from Alishan.

Highly recommended is the hike to Fengshan, a fantastic 10 hour or longer trek. Or you can walk to the resort area of Shanlinhsi. More details are provided further on.

## Sunrise at Chushan

The dawn trek to Celebration Mountain or Chushan (zhùshān) is religiously performed by virtually everybody who comes to Alishan. In fact, it's almost mandatory. Hotels typically wake up all their guests around 3 to 4 am (depending on what time the sun rises) so that they can stumble out of bed and begin the hour-long pilgrimage up the mountain. It's cold at this hour, so dress accordingly and bring a flashlight if you have one. There are minibuses and a train for those who can't handle the hike.

I personally feel that the walk is well worth the effort. You even see old ladies doing it barefoot because they soon discover their high-heeled shoes are a handicap. Finding your way is not difficult, and if it's a weekend or holiday you'll be swept along by the crowd.

If you're walking, you have the choice of two routes: the road or the stone steps. I prefer the steps as you can avoid the obnoxious smoke-spewing minibuses with their blaring horns. When you reach the summit, you can enjoy a nice cheap breakfast from any of the numerous vendors with their pushcarts. Or you can have a more expensive breakfast in heated comfort at *Sunrise House* on the summit.

Minibuses depart from the main parking area in Alishan and also from Alishan House, which is near the youth hostel further up the mountain. The buses are frequent and don't run to any particular schedule, but they'll probably leave at around 4.30 am during summer and a little later in winter (to coordinate with the sunrise).

The train departs from the main Alishan station and also makes a stop at the old station near Alishan House. The departure time is about 45 minutes before sunrise – in summer, I took the train at 4.30 am. Inquire the day before to be sure about the time. The round-trip fare is NT$100 and the trip takes 30 minutes.

If you go on a weekend you'll really understand what the Chinese mean by the saying 'people mountain people sea'. By the time the sun makes its debut, there will be 5000 or more people vying for space on the summit of the mountain. It seems to get more crowded all the time, and if this continues, they'll have to schedule *two* sunrises every morning. Just as the sun pops over the horizon, you'll hear the gentle roar of 5000-plus camera shutters going off simultaneously.

Then the mad stampede begins as everyone races to be the first one back to the minibus. My suggestion is to let them fight it out. The riot ends fairly quickly and in 45 minutes every last soul will have vacated the mountain, as if they had never been there. It's nice to linger on the summit for a while, to see the sun hanging over Yushan – Taiwan's highest peak – and to look down on the fog-filled valley below. You can then take a leisurely walk down to Alishan and you won't see anybody along the way if you wait long enough.

### Train Ride to Monkey Rock
*(shíhóu)* 石猴

After the sunrise, many of those racing back to Alishan want to get there in time for the morning train out to Monkey Rock, 8 km further into the mountains. The train goes there twice a day. The first departure is at 7.50 am, the second at 1.30 pm. The train leaves Monkey Rock at 9.55 am and 3.35 pm to return to Alishan.

Monkey Rock itself is just a rock, but the trip out there is nice and the views of the valleys below are impressive. The price is rather high for the short distance though – NT$120 one way, NT$200 for the round trip. When you buy the ticket, the clerk, who doesn't speak any English, will hand you an application for a mountain pass. Just write some English words in the spaces he points to and all will be well.

You can also walk this route. Along the way you will pass a sign in English saying that you need a mountain pass. Ignore it, everyone else does. Along the way, after the first bridge, you'll find a signposted trail on the right side of the tracks leading off to an aboriginal village. A little further on and you'll come to a tunnel. You should bring a flashlight as the tunnels are totally black inside and dangerously narrow. Don't linger in the tunnels – getting hit by a train could ruin your whole day.

At Monkey Rock train station, there is a trail that drops down steeply. This goes to Fengshan *(fēngshān)* and Shanlinhsi *(shānlínxī)*, two nice resort areas covered in detail further on in this book. This is a fantastic hike and can be done in 1 (very long) day. Start early.

The trail is signposted clearly enough, but all in Chinese characters. You might want to

do this with some Chinese hiking companions. During school holidays, if you catch the morning train to Monkey Rock with your gear, you will undoubtedly meet some student hikers heading out to Fengshan or Shanlinhsi.

### Places to Stay

Finding accommodation in Alishan is usually not a problem, except on the weekends when everything is full. When that happens you must resort to *mínfáng*, which means 'people's house'. In other words, you have to rent a room in someone's house, often a spare bedroom or attic they've set aside for just this purpose. There are a few people in Alishan who do this and the rates vary according to the facilities, but it's usually cheaper than a hotel; however, they do charge at least double on weekends and holidays. I did this once and paid NT$200 on a Saturday night for an attic I had to share with five people. The next day, the woman offered me the whole attic to myself for NT$100. To find *mínfáng*, simply ask around. Many of the vendors near the bus station and along the roadside can direct you to such a place. *Mínfáng* generally cost from NT$100 to NT$200 per person.

### Places to Stay – bottom end

The cheapest place in town is the *Alishan Mountain Hostel*, (tel (05) 2240132) *(ālǐshān shān zhuāng)*, where dorm accommodation is NT$100. Unfortunately it's often full. It's next to the expensive Alishan House.

The *Kaofeng Hotel* (tel (05) 2679739) *(gāofēng dàfàndiàn)* is a popular place with budget travellers. They have several standards of accommodation. Tatami singles/-doubles are NT$150/200; they are closet-size rooms but about the best deal you're going to find in expensive Alishan. Double rooms with shared bath cost from NT$400 to NT$800, or NT$800 to NT$1600 with private bath. It's just down the hill from the bus station, behind the tourist information office. You can also eat there for NT$100.

Many travellers like the *Catholic Hostel*

(tel (05) 2679602) (*tiānzhǔ jiào táng*), which has dorm beds for NT$200. It's at the lower end of the village, just past the entrance gate on the north side of the road.

The *Foresters' Dormitory* (*sùshè qū*) is not really a dormitory but rather a collection of houses which belong to those who work in government-related services in Alishan. They have rooms which they rent for around NT$150 per person. The standard of accommodation varies but is generally mediocre – it's usually a tatami attic and you'll have to share with several other people on weekends. To get into the Foresters' Dormitory, it's best to inquire first at the tourist information office near the bus station. This office is very helpful, but only a few of the staff speak English.

## Places to Stay – top end

Beyond the old train station is the *Alishan Gou Hotel* (tel (05) 2679611) (*gúomín lüshè*). A room which sleeps four people costs NT$1420 and doubles/twins cost NT$700/980. They also have some dormitory rooms for groups of six to eight people.

When you're facing the post office shown on the Alishan map, off to the left you'll see a small road going uphill. Follow that and you'll come to the *xiéyúan dàfàndiàn* (tel (05) 2679919). Double rooms are NT$900.

*Alishan House* (tel (05) 2679811) (*ālǐshān bīngǔan*) is considered the top place. Doubles/twins cost NT$1150/1300. Alishan House also operates the *Alishan Train Hotel* which, as the name implies, is a hotel built inside restored railroad cars; doubles/twins cost NT$800/1200. Both Alishan House and the Train Hotel are near the old railway station, at the upper end of the village.

Near the Kaofeng Hotel is the *gāo shān qīng bīngǔan* (tel (05) 2679716) where doubles cost NT$1200. Also nearby is the *yǒngfú biégǔan* (tel (05) 2679740), which also charges NT$1200 for doubles.

## Places to Eat

Almost every restaurant in Alishan is in the plaza near the bus terminal. Of course, some of the larger hotels also have a restaurant for their guests, but you'll find more variety in the plaza. All the restaurants are expensive and a few are dishonest. In particular, be careful of the restaurants serving 'fire pot' (*huǒguo*) – a stew where you throw everything into a pot of boiling water sitting on a burner in the centre of the table. What they often do is to throw a lot of things into the stew that you didn't order, and then charge you for them. How can you argue after you've eaten it?

The cheapest way to eat in Alishan is to buy food from the two grocery stores on the east side of the plaza (near the post office). You can buy instant noodles and just add hot water. Most hotels have hot water drinking fountains. You'll also need chopsticks and a spoon – many hotels will give you free disposable chopsticks from the hotel restaurant. The grocery stores also sell bread, fruit and other goodies, all reasonably priced.

Besides the restaurants in the plaza, you will see some occasional roadside vendors selling food from pushcarts near the Foresters' Dormitory.

## Things to Buy

There is plenty of the usual tourist junk for sale, but one thing worth buying is an Alishan bathrobe. Actually, I've seen identical bathrobes in other mountain resorts in Taiwan, so maybe I should call it a 'mountain bathrobe'. Whatever you want to call it, they are very warm, comfortable and durable – I've had one for years. A full-length bathrobe costs from around NT$160 to NT$200, subject to your bargaining abilities.

## Getting There & Away

**Bus** In 1982 the road to Alishan was paved and there is now a frequent, fast and cheap bus service to the village. It's not as exciting as the train, but it only costs NT$76 from Chiayi. The travelling time is 2½ hours going uphill, 2 hours coming down. Chiayi to Alishan by road is 79 km. The bus stops for a 10 minute break at the halfway point at Shihcho (*shízhōu*). As the bus approaches Shihcho, you can see many tea plantations. Departures from Chiayi are at 6.30, 8 and 9 am, and 12, 1 and 4 pm. On Sundays or holidays there are additional departures at 7 am and 2 pm.

From Taipei, there are 2 morning express buses to Alishan that depart at 8.30 and 9.30 am. Going the other way, the buses leave Alishan at 9 and 10 am. The fare is NT$321 and the trip takes 6 hours.

From Kaohsiung there is a daily bus that departs at 7.20 am. An additional bus departs at 11.10 am on weekends and holidays only. From Alishan, daily buses to Kaohsiung leave at 3.30 pm and the additional weekend bus leaves at 9.20 am. The fare is NT$196 and the travel time is 4 hours and 40 minutes.

From Taichung, daily departures are at 8 am. An additional bus departs at 11 am on holidays. From Alishan to Taichung, daily departures are at 1 pm and the holiday bus departs at 9.30 am. The fare is NT$174, and the travel time is 3 hours and 50 minutes.

There is a NT$65 charge to enter the Alishan Forest Recreation Area. You buy this ticket just before entering the village of Alishan.

**Train** Getting to Alishan can be half the fun. Until fairly recently there was no road at all, but one of the world's most beautiful railroads instead. This narrow-gauge railway was built by the Japanese during their occupation of Taiwan and the railway line came into use around 1912. It was built mainly to exploit the timber resources of the mountains, not to develop Alishan into a tourist resort.

Many forests were badly deplenished during the Japanese occupation, but reforestation has almost fully restored the area to its former beauty. Logging is still carried on in this area at a sustained rate, but it is only a minor industry nowadays.

Building the railroad was certainly a major engineering feat. The train passes through 50 tunnels, crosses 80 bridges, and climbs from the subtropics to the pine forests in just 72 km. It's a very scenic train ride if you have clear weather, but many travellers have been disappointed because fog in Taiwan's moun-

tains is so common. Your best defence is to get the earliest train, as the mornings are usually clear.

There are three trains daily in either direction. Two are 1st-class trains (*ālǐshān hào*) and one is 2nd class (*zhōngxīng hào*). The 2nd-class train is a local train and takes about 4 hours because it makes frequent stops.

If you arrive in Chiayi by train, you can get on the Alishan train and buy your ticket on board. You don't have to go into the station to buy a ticket, but doing so has an advantage – there is a better chance that you'll get a reserved seat and not have to stand. A 15% discount is offered on round-trip tickets, though it would be far cheaper to take the bus for the return trip. If you do buy a round-trip ticket, you book the return journey in Alishan.

The one-way fares are NT$373 for 1st class and NT$346 for 2nd class. When exiting the train station in Alishan you will be charged NT$65 for admission to the Alishan Forest Recreation Area. They charge half-price for people shorter than 145 cm (I'm not making this up).

The train schedule at the time of writing was:

### Chiayi to Alishan
|  | *depart* | *arrive* |
|---|---|---|
| 1st class | 8.25 am | 11.35 am |
| 2nd class | 9 am | 12.10 pm |
| 1st class | 12.50 pm | 4.03 pm |

### Alishan to Chiayi
|  | *depart* | *arrive* |
|---|---|---|
| 1st class | 8.40 am | 11.50 am |
| 1st class | 12.35 pm | 3.45 pm |
| 2nd class | 1.05 pm | 4.12 pm |

**Wild Chicken Taxi** Wild chicken taxi drivers hang around the Chiayi railway and bus station area and will approach any foreigner and yell, 'Alishan! Alishan!'. There is no reason to deal with them because the bus service is fine, unless of course you come in the evening after the last bus has departed. Expect to pay at least NT$1600 for a taxi. They are only legally permitted to carry a maximum of four passengers per taxi, so the trip would cost NT$400 each.

## AROUND ALISHAN
### Yushan
*(yùshān)* 玉山

Yushan, which translates as 'Jade Mountain', is Taiwan's highest peak. At an elevation of 3950 metres, it's higher than Japan's Mt Fuji and is one of the highest peaks in East Asia. Climbing it is certainly a beautiful trip and the only thing keeping most travellers from doing so is that a class A mountain pass is needed. You must get the pass through a licensed mountain club.

The highway leading up to Yushan begins at the petrol station just before the entrance to Alishan village. About 2 hours of walking will bring you to the gate where the mountain pass is checked. If you continue walking, you'll eventually come to the *Pierced Cloud Hut* *(páiyún shān zhuāng)*, where you can spend the night for NT$150. The next morning you can reach the summit.

There is an alternative route coming down that leads to Tungpu *(dōngpǔ)*. (Details about Tungpu are supplied further on in this chapter.) If you want to come down by way of Tungpu, be sure to get your mountain pass endorsed for it. If you take this route don't leave any luggage in Alishan, as you won't be going back that way.

During my last visit, a new highway was under construction from Alishan down to the east coast of Taiwan near Yuli. It promises to give access to some interesting scenic areas in Yushan National Park, but it's also an environmental disaster in the making. The fragile, high-elevation meadows and forests cannot withstand much impact from automobile exhaust, litter, sewage and other abuses of mass tourism. Construction of the highway itself will cause numerous landslides and soil erosion. The National Taiwan University Forestry Department, which has overall authority in this area, vehemently opposed construction of the road but the development interests proved to be more politically powerful. Other ecologically disastrous proposals have been made for Yushan National Car Park, so don't be surprised if someday there is a revolving restaurant on the summit of Taiwan's highest peak.

### Hike to Fengshan

The hike from Alishan to either Fengshan or Shanlinhsi follows the same trail for the first few km, after which there is a fork. Both hikes are great, though I personally prefer the one to Fengshan. If you have time, you can do both. The walk is almost entirely downhill – Alishan is 2190 metres, Shanlinhsi is 1600 metres, and Fengshan is 750 metres in elevation.

To reach Fengshan from Alishan, you can start by either taking the train to the end of the line at Monkey Rock or walking. If you walk, start out early because it's at least a 10 hour walk (28 km) from Monkey Rock and an additional 2 hours if you walk from Alishan. Monkey Rock to Shanlinhsi is about 8 hours.

Coming from Alishan, just off to the left of the tracks at Monkey Rock is a trail which drops steeply. If someone is around, ask them if this is the trail to Fengshan and Shanlinhsi since it's the same trail for the first few km. You go down, down and down. When you reach the bottom, turn right and walk along the dirt road. You eventually come to a signposted junction in the trail. The right fork goes to Shanlinhsi and Hsitou, the left fork goes to Fengshan. If you take the left fork you go downhill some more, eventually coming to Thousand People Cave *(qiān rén dòng)*. This is a magnificent overhanging cave: it's so large that it can supposedly hold 1000 people, though I think they'd have to be rather thin to fit in there. The cave is frequently used by hikers as shelter from the rain.

Continuing along, the trail makes another steep descent, eventually leading to Tzuyu Waterfall *(cíyù pùbù)*. When you reach the bottom of the falls, the path levels out and eventually becomes a dirt road. The obnoxious whine of motorcycles in the distance

# 阿里山健行區
# Alishan Hiking Region

To Chushan & Shuili

To Hsitou 溪頭 (Approximately 5 km)

Shanlinhsi 1600 m 杉林溪

0     5     10 km
*Approximate Scale*

Giant Tree 神木

Tsaoling 800 m 草嶺

*Shihpan Valley 石盤谷瀑布 Waterfall*

雌嶽瀑布 *Tzuyu Waterfall*

Clear Water River

Tea Plantation

Fengshan 豐山 750 m

千人洞 Thousand People Cave

石猴 Monkey Rock

Shimenggu 石夢谷

Alishan River

Taiho Hostel 太和山莊

Juili 1100 m 瑞里

太和 Taiho Village

▲ Big Buddha Mountain 大佛山

Distance Foreshortened

Alishan 2190 m 阿里山

奮起湖 Fenchihu 1400 m

Mountain Permit required for this road only.

To Chiayi

Shihtzulu 十字路

To Yushan

石卓 Shihcho

To Chiayi

reminds you that civilisation is not far off. After crossing the bridge over the river, you come to some farm houses and several hostels where you can spend the night.

The only bad thing about this hike is the possibility of getting lost. The trail is quite well marked in Chinese characters, but that isn't much use if you can't read them. If you hang around Monkey Rock in the morning, especially on the weekends, it's likely that you'll meet some university students doing either the hike to Fengshan or the hike to Shanlinhsi. They will often be happy to have you join their group. However, you should

be able to manage it yourself – just don't get off the main trail.

## FENGSHAN
*(fēngshān)* 豐山

You can walk to Fengshan from Alishan or you can take a bus from Chiayi. Either way, it's certainly worth visiting. However, it is a remote place so don't come here looking for nightlife. Hiking is the main activity and there isn't much else to do. However, tour buses do come up here on weekends – avoid the place at those times. The town is blissfully tranquil during the week and hasn't been ruined by commercialisation, at least not yet.

## Things to See

About an hour east of town on the trail leading towards Alishan is Tzuyu Waterfall (cíyù pùbù). About 2 hours east of town on another trail (further south) is shímènggǔ, an area known for its interesting slickrock formations. A 1 hour walk north of town takes you to Shihpan Valley Waterfall (shípángǔ pùbù), a series of six small waterfalls.

You can easily hike 5 km to the Taiho Hostel and from there do several other walks (see the Around Fengshan section further on in this chapter). It's even more interesting to walk to Tsaoling, one of Taiwan's biggest resorts, but the route follows the riverbed and is only feasible during the dry season. Again, see the Around Fengshan section for details.

## Places to Stay

There are five hotels in Fengshan with little to choose between them. However, the one I liked best was fēngjí shān zhuāng (tel (05) 2661363), where beautiful dorms go for NT$120. Doubles/twins are NT$500/1200 with private bath. The food is great – they grow it themselves. There is also a small grocery store in town where you can buy instant noodles and other packaged goodies.

## Getting There & Away

Buses depart Chiayi for Fengshan only once a day from approximately 7 to 7.30 am. The exact time varies so be there early, though the bus won't leave before 7 am. The fare is NT$180 and the trip takes 4 hours. The schedule is the same from Fengshan to Chiayi, with departures at about 7 am. If you want to take the bus from Chiayi to Fengshan, you should try to call the night before to let them know you are coming. That's because they have several vehicles and if they get enough passengers they will put on one of their larger buses. Otherwise, they will just use a minibus. If they get no passengers, they just won't go.

In Chiayi, the company to contact is the Anhsing Bus Company (tel (05) 2223527)

(ānxíng yóulǎnchē). The bus leaves from in front of the Yushan Hotel (see the Chiayi Places to Stay section).

If you want to hike to Fengshan from Alishan, see the Hike to Fengshan entry in the Around Alishan section.

## AROUND FENGSHAN
### Taiho Hostel Area
(tàihé shān zhuāng) 太和山莊
Just 5 km from Fengshan, the small lodge called Taiho Hostel can easily be reached on foot from Fengshan in less than 2 hours. Don't confuse the Taiho Mountain Hostel with the village of Taiho, which is several km further down the road. There are some nice hikes near the hostel, in particular the climb up Big Buddha Mountain (dàfóshān). Anyone can point you towards the peak, which takes about 3 hours to climb.

**Hike to Tsaoling** Unless it is very foggy, you can look out from the Taiho Mountain Hostel and clearly see the bustling tourist resort of Tsaoling perched on a neighbouring mountainside. Seeing it so close, you will undoubtedly be tempted to hike over there. I highly recommend doing so, as the scenery is spectacular and it's much easier to get buses out from Tsaoling than from Taiho – but there is one major obstacle.

Hiking from Taiho (or Fengshan) to Tsaoling requires crossing the Alishan River, which is only feasible during the dry season from October to about March or April. It is very dangerous during the wet season, which begins around April and continues until September. The river becomes a raging torrent at times. Even during the dry season, the fast-moving water can sometimes be thigh deep if it has rained recently. A rope or bamboo pole can be useful. Never attempt it during or after a thunderstorm. The walk only takes about 2½ hours in good conditions, but longer if the water is deep.

I did it in October with no equipment except for a bamboo pole. The fast-moving water was almost crotch deep and it was scary. I returned a month later and did the same walk – the water was only ankle deep.

If you want to do it after a typhoon, bring an inflatable raft, a pair of oars, a lifejacket, some prayer beads and incense. As the river meanders through a canyon, you have to cross it about five times. Start out early in the morning – if the river is impassable you can always just return to Taiho.

From either Fengshan or Taiho, the first 2 km of the hike involves walking down a footpath. When you reach a tea plantation, you have to drop down into the riverbed (see the Alishan Hiking Area map). As in many farming areas, there are some unfriendly dogs around the tea plantation – carrying a stick is advisable. I don't think they would bite, but who can be sure? As soon as I shook my stick at them, they ran away. The stick will come in handy anyway for fording the river. If you're a dedicated dog hater, you can avoid them completely by walking in the riverbed and bypassing the plantation. Walking in the riverbed is interesting, but slower and more difficult.

If the route to Tsaoling is impassable due to flooding, you could walk from Taiho to Fenchihu (*fènqǐhú*), about 25 km uphill on a narrow but paved road. From Fenchihu you can catch the Alishan to Chiayi train. Of course, you could take the once-a-day bus to Fenchihu, which is the same bus that goes to Chiayi, or you could hitch.

**Places to Stay** If you come here, you'll probably stay at the *Taiho Mountain Hostel* (tel (05) 2661222) (*tàihé shān zhuāng*). It costs NT$100 for a tatami, NT$600 for a double and NT$1200 for a four person room.

**Getting There & Away** The instructions for getting a bus to and from Taiho are the same as for Fengshan, so refer to the Fengshan Getting There & Away section.

## FENCHIHU
(*fènqǐhú*) 舊起湖
At 1400 metres above sea level, Fenchihu is a small town between Alishan and Chiayi, in a scenic, heavily forested area. If you took the train to Alishan, you would have passed right through it. Although most tourists head directly to Alishan, Fenchihu has begun to attract some of the overflow crowds. However, it's got a long way to go before it becomes an international resort.

Actually, I don't think Fenchihu will ever challenge Alishan because it doesn't have any really special scenery. There are a few nice hikes in the area and Fenchihu is pleasant, cool, forested and refreshing, but that's all. City-weary residents from Taipei like to go there to relax and it's certainly a good place for that. However, those looking for more spectacular vistas and steep hiking challenges should head directly for Tsaoling or Tungpu.

Apart from tourism, the other big industry in Fenchihu is horticulture. Greenhouses are everywhere and the owners won't object if you come in and have a look. Of course, they would be happier if you bought something. Prices are very reasonable. However, unless you'll be living in Taiwan for a while, I can only recommend that you browse. Travelling around Asia with a potted bamboo tree may be aesthetically pleasing but isn't exactly convenient.

### Big Frozen Mountain
(*dàdòng shān*) 大凍山
The Chinese certainly seem to like getting up at 4 am to climb a mountain and view the sunrise. If you are in Fenchihu on a weekend or holiday, you might as well get up with everyone else. The best view is from the summit of Big Frozen Mountain (*dàdòng shān*), where everyone goes to greet the morning sun. It's a 500 metre increase in elevation from Fenchihu and about a 2 hour walk one way from the hotel area. When there are lots of people some hotels run a minibus halfway up the mountain, so you only have a 1 hour walk.

On a clear morning you can see Chiayi. Of course, some people (I won't mention any names) are satisfied with getting up later and admiring the sunrise from the window of their hotel room.

### Other Hikes
If you want an easy hike, it's a short walk

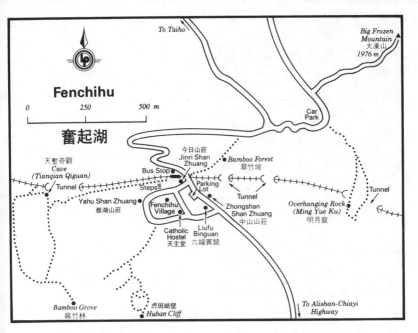

**Fenchihu**

奮起湖

0    250    500 m

To Taiho

Big Frozen Mountain
大凍山
1976 m

Car Park

天塹奇觀
Cave
(Tianqian Qiguan)

今日山莊
Jinri Shan Zhuang

竹竹坡
Bamboo Forest

Bus Stop

Tunnel

Steps

Parking Lot

Yahu Shan Zhuang
雅湖山莊

Fenchihu Village

Catholic Hostel
天主堂

Liufu Binguan
六福賓館

Zhongshan Shan Zhuang
中山山莊

Tunnel

Overhanging Rock
(Ming Yue Ku)
明月窟

Tunnel

Bamboo Grove
麻竹林

虎斑峭壁
Huban Cliff

To Alishan-Chiayi Highway

uphill from the train station area to the bamboo forest (*chùi zhúpō*). Here you can see some very rare square bamboo. Yes, the stem really is square.

Among the locals, the hike that's most popular is to a cave called *tiānqiàn qígǔan*, which is to the west (downhill) of Fenchihu. The hike takes about 3 hours for the round trip. The caves are small and they are definitely not suitable for claustrophobics. You've got to crawl through on your hands and knees and a flashlight is mandatory. But the walk leading down to the caves is nice, even if you decide not to crawl in.

The hike I like best is to *míng yùe kū*, an overhanging rock formation to the east (uphill) of the railway station. It's very interesting to walk through it – rather like a long cave with one wall removed.

Some hotels, such as the *jīnrì shān zhūang*, offer free, guided hiking tours of the area to all guests, but they require a group of at least 30 people. Most travellers will prob-

ably not be in Taiwan with 29 friends, but if you arrive on a weekend or holiday you can join any group of Chinese tourists. Of course, on weekends and holidays there is always the risk that the hotels will all be full.

### Places to Stay

Prices have risen almost to the ridiculous levels of Alishan. Fortunately, most places have tatami dormitories. Except on weekends, you can get into a dormitory by yourself without having a big group.

For foreigners, the best place to stay is the *Catholic Hostel* (*tiānzhǔ jiào táng*) (tel (05) 2561035). Dormitories cost NT$120 and the managers speak English.

The *jīnrì shān zhūang* (tel (05) 2561034) operates a good restaurant. They have dormitories for NT$180. Doubles/twins are NT$800/1200.

The *zhōngshān shān zhūang* (tel (05) 2561052) is a new, clean-looking hotel with very friendly management. The dormitories

Bamboo forest in Juili

cost NT$150. Doubles go for NT$800 to NT$1200. The *liùfú bīngǔan* (tel (05) 2561776) looks a bit shoddy on the outside but is OK inside. Doubles/twins are priced from NT$800/1200.

One more place to try is the *yǎhú shān zhǔang* (tel (05) 2561097), where dormitories are NT$120 and doubles are NT$800.

At least a 20% discount is available on weekdays.

### Getting There & Away

**Bus** If you're coming from Fengshan or Taiho by bus or foot, you have to pass through Fenchihu.

There are only three buses a day between Fenchihu and Chiayi. The 55 km trip takes at least 1 hour and costs NT$56 one way. Buses depart Chiayi at 9 am, 10 am and 3 pm. Buses depart Fenchihu for Chiayi at 9.15 am, 12.30 pm and 5.15 pm.

The Alishan to Chiayi bus does not pass through Fenchihu. If coming from Alishan by bus, you could get off at the rest stop

(*shízhōu*) and then walk or hitch 5 km to Fenchihu.

**Train** If you're coming by train from Alishan, it's convenient to stop off in Fenchihu. All trains make this stop, even the 1st-class express. The fare between Alishan and Fenchihu is NT$148 in 1st class and NT$138 in 2nd class. From Chiayi to Fenchihu, the 1st-class fare is NT$225 and 2nd class is NT$209. The train schedule at the time of writing was as follows:

### Alishan to Fenchihu

|  | depart | arrive |
|---|---|---|
| 1st class | 8.40 am | 9.52 am |
| 1st class | 12.35 pm | 1.48 pm |
| 2nd class | 1.05 pm | 2.21 pm |

### Fenchihu to Alishan

|  | depart | arrive |
|---|---|---|
| 1st class | 10.23 am | 11.35 am |
| 2nd class | 10.56 am | 12.10 pm |
| 1st class | 2.51 pm | 4.03 pm |

### Chiayi to Fenchihu

|  | depart | arrive |
|---|---|---|
| 1st class | 8.25 am | 10.23 am |
| 2nd class | 9 am | 10.56 pm |
| 1st class | 12.50 pm | 2.51 pm |

### Fenchihu to Chiayi

|  | depart | arrive |
|---|---|---|
| 1st class | 9.52 am | 11.50 am |
| 1st class | 1.48 pm | 3.45 pm |
| 2nd class | 2.21 pm | 4.12 pm |

### JUILI
*(rùilǐ)* 瑞里

Juili is a sleepy village consisting of just a few houses, an elementary school and some scattered hotels. Although the scenery isn't quite as spectacular as Alishan's, Juili has been barely touched by commercialism. There are pleasant hikes through bamboo forests, some nice waterfalls and a long narrow cave to crawl through. Basically, it's a fine place for hiking and relaxing, so if you need a few days of pleasant, peaceful surroundings, come to Juili. It is possible to hike from Juili to Taiho, Fengshan, Tsaoling or Fenchihu.

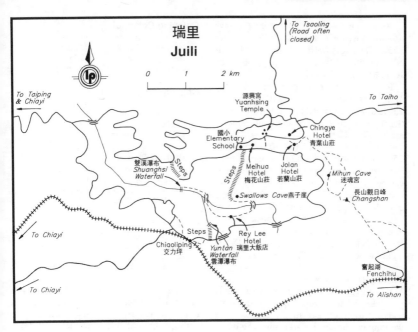

## Walks & Hikes

Among the things to see in Juili are the Yuntan (Deep Cloud) Waterfall (*yúntán pùbù*), the Shuanghsi (Twin River) Waterfall (*shūangxī pùbù*) and the Swallows Cave (*yànzǐyái*), which is actually an overhanging rock formation rather than a true cave.

Chinese hikers also like to visit the Mihun Cave (*míhún gōng*), but I didn't find it very interesting. It's just a long narrow hole to crawl through, with no stalactites or other formations inside – not really worth the trouble. However, the walk through the bamboo forest to get there is very pleasant.

As in Alishan, a crowd of people get up before dawn to hike up a mountain in order to view the sunrise. Juili's sunrise viewing spot is Changshan. From there it is possible to hike to Fenchihu.

You can hike from Juili to Taiho along a paved road. It is possible to hitch but traffic is very light, mostly farmers on motorcycles.

Hiking from Juili to Tsaoling is possible, but I can't recommend you do so because it involves crossing a dangerous river just before you reach Tsaoling. It's possible when the river is low, but you won't know whether it is until you're within sight of Tsaoling. If it turns out that the river is in the flood stage, you'll have to hike all the way back. Also, the trail is sometimes knocked out because of landslides.

## Places to Stay

I especially enjoyed my stay at the *Jolan Mountain Hostel* (tel (05) 2501210) (*rùolán shān zhūang*). The management was very friendly, the rooms were clean and the food was great. Dorm prices range from NT$120 to NT$150 and doubles/twins are NT$800/1200. The Jolan Mountain Hostel is not right on the main road, but the bus can let you off in front of the Chingye Mountain Hostel, from where you have to walk about 20 metres down a footpath. The hotel is perched on the steep side of a mountain.

Another place to consider is the *Chingye Mountain Hostel* (tel (05) 2501031) (*qīngyè shān zhūang*), with dorm/doubles at NT$120/600. This place is just above the Jolan Mountain Hostel.

Right near the elementary school is the *Meihua Mountain Hostel* (tel (05) 2501522, 2501222) (*méihūa shān zhūang*), where the dormitory costs NT$120 and doubles/twins are NT$700/1200.

The *Rey Lee Hotel* (tel (05) 2501310, 2501314) (*rùilǐ dàfàndiàn*) is the largest, fanciest and most expensive hotel in town. It can be busy even on weekdays, but on weekends it's a real circus. It's only real advantage over the competition is that it's much closer to the train station, a factor to consider when you're carrying a heavy backpack. Dormitories are NT$200, while doubles are NT$800 and twins cost from NT$1200 to NT$1600.

### Getting There & Away
You can get to Juili by either train or bus. If you take the train you'll have to do some walking to reach any of the hotels – but walking is what Juili is all about. The buses can drop you off right next to your hotel.

**Bus** The Chiayi County Bus Company (*jiāyì xiàn gōngchē*), which is right next to the train station, runs a bus to Juili once a day at 4.20 pm. Going the other way, they depart Juili at the ridiculous hour of 5.50 am. Since Juili is spread out over the mountainsides, tell the driver which hotel you want to get off at. Otherwise, get off at the elementary school and walk from there.

There is also a wild chicken bus company which departs Chiayi once a day at 1.30 pm from somebody's house at 111 Changjung St. From Juili, the bus departs at 7 am. This bus may be somewhat less reliable than the county bus, but the departure times are certainly more convenient.

**Train** Juili is about halfway between Alishan and Chiayi and can be reached by taking the Alishan train. You can get off the train in the tiny town of Chiaoliping (*jiǎolǐpíng*). The train schedule at the time of writing was:

**Chiayi to Chiaoliping**

|           | depart    | arrive    |
|-----------|-----------|-----------|
| 1st class | 8.25 am   | 9.52 am   |
| 2nd class | 9 am      | 10.25 am  |
| 1st class | 12.50 pm  | 2.18 pm   |

**Chiaoliping to Chiayi**

|           | depart    | arrive    |
|-----------|-----------|-----------|
| 1st class | 10.24 am  | 11.50 am  |
| 1st class | 2.19 pm   | 3.45 pm   |
| 2nd class | 2.50 pm   | 4.12 pm   |

**Alishan to Chiaoliping**

|           | depart    | arrive    |
|-----------|-----------|-----------|
| 1st class | 8.40 am   | 10.24 am  |
| 1st class | 12.35 pm  | 2.19 pm   |
| 2nd class | 1.05 pm   | 2.50 pm   |

**Chiaoliping to Alishan**

|           | depart    | arrive    |
|-----------|-----------|-----------|
| 1st class | 9.52 am   | 11.35 am  |
| 2nd class | 10.25 am  | 12.10 pm  |
| 1st class | 2.18 pm   | 4.03 pm   |

From Chiaoliping, get someone to point you in the right direction and walk on the paved trail that parallels the railway tracks. The path quickly cuts off to the left and drops downhill into the forest. A 5 minute walk along the trail leads you to a road and after another 40 minutes of hiking you come to the first hotel, the Rey Lee Hotel (*rùilǐ dàfàndiàn*). See the Juili map.

From this hotel, it takes over an hour to walk to the Juili Elementary School (*rùilǐ gúoxiǎo*), which is the centre of central Juili. The fastest route is to take the trail that drops steeply down to the river and the Swallows Cave, then uphill again. You have to climb hundreds of stone steps if you take this route; it's rather exhausting but much shorter than the road.

**Other** It is possible to walk from Juili to Taiho, a distance of 18 km. Hitching is a possibility but traffic on this road is very light. From Taiho you can reach Fengshan, Tsaoling or Fenchihu.

### TOULIU
(*dǒuliù*) 斗六
Touliu is a small city north of Chiayi.

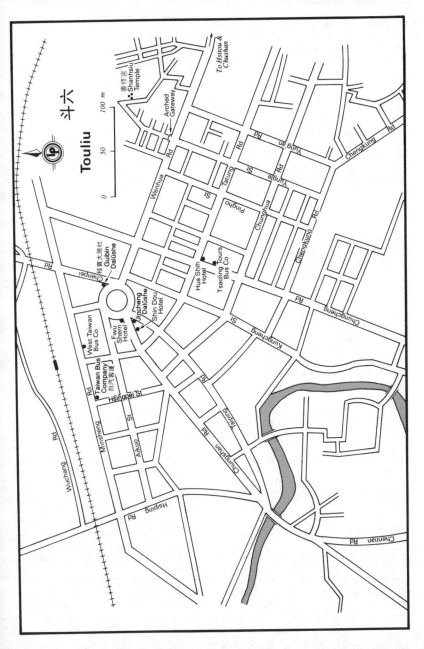

斗六

Touliu

100 m

50

0

To Hsitou & Chushan

華修宮
Shanhsiu Temple

Arched Gateway

Wenhua Rd

Pingho

15

Chunghua Rd

Tatung Rd

Yungan Rd

Yungle St

Chengkung Rd

Chenpei

桂賓大旅社
Guibin Dalüshe

Jincheng Dalüshe

Shin Dou Hotel

Hua Shih Hotel

Tsaoling Tours Bus Co

Chungcheng Rd

Fwu Shern Hotel

West Taiwan Bus Co

台灣客運
Taiwan Bus Company

Minsheng Rd

Hsingpei St

St

Aikuo

Taiping Rd

Kungcheng St

Rd

Chungshan Rd

Hsiping Rd

Chennan Rd

Wuchang Rd

Although the town itself is hardly a tourist attraction, it is an important transit point for travellers heading up to Tsaoling, one of Taiwan's premier mountain resorts.

## Shanhsiu Temple
*(shàn xiū gōng)* 善修宮

If you have an hour or 2 to spare in Touliu, there is a very interesting and beautiful temple called Shanhsiu Temple *(shàn xiū gōng)*. Locals also call it the Confucius Temple *(kǒngzǐ miào)*, though it's really not a true Confucian temple. Very few tourists go to this temple, but it's a lovely place and very well maintained. You can walk to the temple from the Touliu train station.

### Places to Stay

It's quite possible that you'll have to spend a night in Touliu. About the cheapest place in town is the *guìbīn dàlüshè* (tel (055) 324188), 1 Chenpei Rd, where doubles with private bath go for NT$260 to NT$350. Another good place with friendly management is the *Shin Dou Hotel* (tel (055) 323923) *(xīndū dàlüshè)*, 1 Chungshan Rd, where singles/doubles are NT$350/400. Right at the corner of Chungshan Rd and Taiping Rd is the *jīnchéng lüshè* (tel (055) 323954), where doubles go for NT$300 to NT$400.

Moving up in price, there is the *Hua Shih Hotel* (tel (055) 324178) *(húashì dàfàndiàn)*, 112 Tatung Rd, where doubles cost NT$520, twins NT$640.

For those who want to go luxury class, there is the *Fwu Shern Hotel* (tel (055) 341666) *(fúshén dàfàndiàn)*, where doubles/twins cost NT$1000/1600.

## TSAOLING
*(cǎolǐng)* 草嶺

In my opinion, Tsaoling (often misspelled 'Tsaolien') is one of the best mountain resorts in Taiwan, at least equal to Alishan. Although the mountains here are not terribly high, Tsaoling offers as many hiking opportunities as Alishan. Tsaoling is only about

| 1 | Aizilu |
| | 愛之旅 |
| 2 | Tsaoling Guest House |
| | 草嶺山莊賓館 |
| 3 | Green Mountain Hotel |
| | 高山青大飯店 |
| 4 | Jiaqi Dafandian |
| | 假期大飯店 |
| 5 | Yunglih Hotel |
| | 永利賓館 |
| 6 | Tsao Lien Hotel |
| | 草嶺大飯店 |
| 7 | Rainbow Vacation Hotel |
| | 踩虹大飯店 |
| 8 | Yunglih Hotel |
| 9 | Bee Farm |

800 metres above sea level, making it a good place to hike in winter while places like Alishan shiver. Nor is Tsaoling shrouded in the notorious 'Alishan fog'.

One of the nice things about Tsaoling is that it caters to both the windshield tourist who likes an organised bus tour as well as the rugged individualist who prefers to scramble up and down the mountains on foot. If you want a bus tour, it can be most easily arranged through the hotels.

## Penglai Waterfall
*(pénglái pùbù)* 蓬萊瀑布

The road that runs by the Green Mountain Hotel leads to this waterfall. Ask anybody and they'll point you in the right direction. Walk several km down the road and you will eventually reach a cable car. The operator will certainly try to persuade you to take the cable car, which costs NT$25 one way and NT$50 for the round trip. However, there is a trail just to the left of the cable car; the hike isn't difficult and it costs nothing.

Either way, you will come to the base of the waterfall, where there is yet another cable car, operated by a different owner. He also charges NT$25 one way and NT$50 for the round trip. Again, there is a trail just to the left which goes to the top of the waterfall –

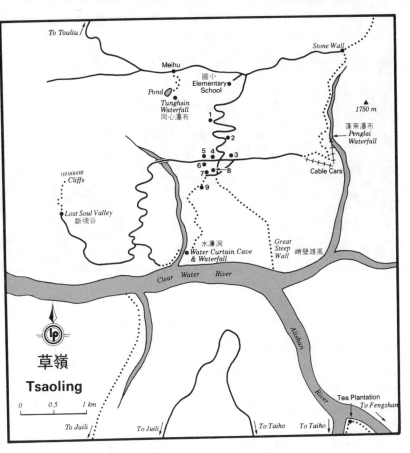

Map labels:
To Touliu
Stone Wall
Meihu
國小 Elementary School
Pond
Tunghsin Waterfall 同心瀑布
1750 m
蓬萊瀑布 Penglai Waterfall
1
2
5 4
3
6
7 8
Cable Cars
9
Cliffs
Lost Soul Valley 斷魂谷
水濂洞 Water Curtain Cave & Waterfall
Great Steep Wall 峭壁雄風
Clear Water River
lp
草嶺 Tsaoling
0    0.5    1 km
To Juili
To Juili
To Taiho
To Taiho
Aishan River
Tea Plantation To Fengshan

it's a steep, 15 minute walk. The cable car goes to the top of the waterfall, so it's your choice. It is definitely worth going up there as the view is great.

### Stone Wall
*(shíbì)* 石壁

From the top of Penglai Waterfall there is a hiking trail that goes several km upstream to the Stone Wall. It's not actually a wall, but a riverbed of slickrock – slippery as greasy noodles but very interesting. I walked on this thing during the rain – thank goodness for my lug-soled boots.

### Water Curtain Cave
*(shuǐlián dòng)* 水簾洞

To get to this cave from Tsaoling village, find the Rainbow Vacation Hotel *(cǎihóng dàfàndiàn)*, which is just below the main village area. Face the entrance of the hotel and just off to the left you'll see some stone steps which descend steeply. Follow these steps and you will soon reach a bee farm; continue down and you will eventually come to a waterfall and cave called Water Curtain Cave. From there you can descend to the river. There are some huts down there and people selling food and drinks.

Clear Water River in Tsaoling

### Lost Soul Valley
(*dùan hún gǔ*) 斷魂谷

From the riverside, there are two places you can go. The first place is called the Lost Soul Valley (*dùan hún gǔ*). As the name implies, it's a little hard to find. To reach it, head downstream along the river. On your right you'll find a road heading uphill. You walk uphill some way until the road forks. The left fork (lower fork) leads to the Lost Soul Valley. A bunch of food vendors have set up stalls near the base of the cliffs. The area is a series of cliffs with hiking trails and small waterfalls. There is some quicksand near one of the waterfalls, so watch out for it. The quicksand swallowed one of Meimei's shoes – perhaps they should call this Lost Sole Valley. Avoid this area during the rainy season (summer) as the cliffs are unstable. In one tragic incident in 1986, over 20 hikers were buried by a mudslide here. However, it's perfectly safe in the dry season.

### Great Steep Wall
(*chào bì xióng fēng*) 峭壁雄風

The second place is easy to find. Starting from Water Curtain Cave, head upstream along the river. On your left you'll eventually find a place where there are some ropes set up to climb the big rock face. This place is called the Great Steep Wall (*chào bì xióng fēng*). It's pretty safe and you can climb up. You'll come to an obvious trail at the top of the cliffs; just follow it and you'll get back to Tsaoling village.

If the river is in flood stage, you won't be able to walk from Water Curtain Cave to the Great Steep Wall, but you can reach the Great Steep Wall by a trail that descends from the Yunglih Hotel (*yǒnglì bīnguǎn*) area. You'll have a very full day of hiking if you go to all these places.

### Places to Stay
There are several good places to stay in the town itself and on the hillsides overlooking the village. On weekdays it's very easy to get into the dormitories and discounts of up to 50% are available. On weekends prices escalate dramatically.

I personally liked the *Yunglih Hotel* (tel (055) 831012) (*yǒnglì bīnguǎn*). On weekends, dorm accommodation costs NT$180 and doubles/twins go for NT$1000/1500. On weekdays, dorms cost NT$150 and there is a 50% discount on doubles and twins.

Another place that budget travellers should check out is the *Tsaoling Guest House* (tel (055) 831121) (*cǎolíng shān zhuāng*). Weekend rates for dorms are NT$180, while doubles/twins are NT$1000/1500. On weekdays, dorms are NT$150 and a 40% discount is offered on doubles and twins.

The *Sing Ming Hsiu Hotel* (tel (055) 831116) (*xīnmíngxiū dàfàndiàn*) has dorm accommodation for NT$180 and doubles/twins are NT$1000/1500. On weekdays, dorms cost NT$150 and there is a 25% discount on private rooms. *Aìzīlü* (tel (055) 831153) costs the same as the Sing Ming Hsiu Hotel, but the location way up on a hill makes it a poor choice. The view isn't especially good either.

The *Tsao Lien Hotel* (tel (055) 831228) (*cǎolíng dàfàndiàn*) costs NT$180 in the dorm, NT$1000 for a double and NT$1500 for a twin. The *Rainbow Vacation Hotel* (tel (055) 831218) (*cǎihóng dàfàndiàn*) is more expensive than most with doubles/twins at NT$1400/1700. The *jiàqí dàfàndiàn* (tel (055) 831389) is similarly pricey with doubles/twins for NT$1500/2000. However, they do offer a 50% discount on weekdays.

The most expensive hotel is the *Green Mountain Hotel* (tel (055) 831208) (*gāoshānqíng dàfàndiàn*), where doubles are NT$2000 and twins are NT$3000.

### Places to Eat

Surprisingly, there's not the assortment of restaurants in Tsaoling that you find in most of Taiwan's resorts. Perhaps this is due to the relative newness of the place. Most tourists eat in their hotels. If you don't want to do that, there are a couple of small noodle and rice shops along the main drag of Tsaoling. The *Yunglih Hotel* has a small restaurant on the 1st floor that's open to anyone who walks in, and the food is good.

### Getting There & Away

The easiest and most direct way to get to Tsaoling is from the small city of Touliu (*dǒuliù*), which is just north of Chiayi. There are plenty of buses and trains connecting Touliu with Chiayi.

There is only one small private bus company that makes the journey to Tsaoling. It serves as a good example of how Taiwan's car revolution has crippled bus service – a few years ago there were six buses daily to Tsaoling but now there are only two. The one-way fare is NT$100. The buses are run by Tsaoling Tours Bus Company (tel (055) 322388, 326788) (*cǎolíng yóulǎn gōngsī*), 47 Chungcheng Rd. Buses leave Touliu for Tsaoling at 8.30 am and 4 pm; they leave Tsaoling for Touliu at 7 am and 2 pm.

As already mentioned, you can hike from Alishan to Fengshan and then to Tsaoling. The last leg of the journey follows the Alishan River, and is beautiful but impossible during most of the wet season. If you find that the river is impassable you can still get to Tsaoling, but you will first have to get a bus down to Chiayi, a train or bus to Touliu, and then another bus up to Tsaoling.

## HSITOU
### (xītóu) 溪頭

Hsitou – commonly misspelled 'Chitou' or 'Shitou' – is a beautiful mountain park and forest reserve south of the Sun Moon Lake area. At an elevation of 1150 metres, the climate is perfect most of the year.

Like Sun Moon Lake, it's a prime spot for honeymooners. In Taiwan, couples on their honeymoon often dress very formally: the groom in a dark suit and tie, and the bride in a *qípáo*, a Chinese slit dress. Where else in the world can you see hikers dressed in a tuxedo, or in a slit dress, high heels and make-up? Of course you will also see plenty of young people in less formal attire, as the place is very popular with students. It's a zoo on weekends or holidays – seems like half the population of Taipei suddenly descends on Hsitou like vultures on a carcass.

The forest reserve was originally established by the Japanese during their occupation of Taiwan, but it is now run by the Forestry Department of National Taiwan

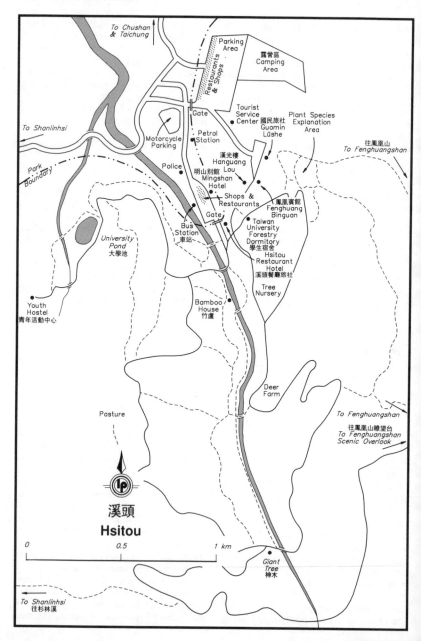

To Chushan & Taichung

Parking Area

露營區 Camping Area

Restaurants & Shops

To Shanlinhsi

Gate

Motorcycle Parking

Petrol Station

Tourist Service Center 國民旅社 Guomin Lüshe

Plant Species Explanation Area

往鳳凰山 To Fenghuangshan

Park Boundary

Police

漢光樓 Hanguang Lou

明山別館 Mingshan Hotel

Shops & Restaurants

Gate

鳳凰賓館 Fenghuang Binguan

Bus Station 車站

Taiwan University Forestry Dormitory 學生宿舍 Hsitou Restaurant Hotel 溪頭餐廳旅社

University Pond 大學池

Tree Nursery

Youth Hostel 青年活動中心

Bamboo House 竹廬

Deer Farm

To Fenghuangshan

Pasture

往鳳凰山瞭望台 To Fenghuangshan Scenic Overlook

溪頭 Hsitou

0          0.5          1 km

Giant Tree 神木

To Shanlinhsi 往杉林溪

University, in Taipei. Reforestation has been a major project, and a highly successful one at that. Unfortunately, the Forestry Department has been less successful at dissuading the central government from continuing with massive road building and hotel development projects in the mountains.

For tourists, the main attraction of the forest reserve is the opportunity to stroll through the thick groves of fir trees and bamboo. One of the great things about Hsitou is that it has a gate across the entrance which keeps most (but not all) cars and motorcycles out. However, you won't be disturbed by vehicles once you get onto the numerous hiking paths. Admission to the forest reserve costs NT$50.

From Hsitou, you can hike up to Fenghuangshan, a mountain 2 km to the north-east. At 1697 metres it's not extremely high, but the view is good.

On the way up to Hsitou the bus passes through Luku (lùgǔ), Taiwan's prime tea-growing region. If you have a window seat you'll get good views of the tea plantations. Just above the plantations are fantastic bamboo forests.

## Places to Stay

The main advantage of staying in the park is that there are fewer vehicles. Also, this is where you can find cheap dormitory accommodation. Just remember that if you go outside of the park, you'll have to pay another admission fee to get back in.

There is only one hotel outside the park gate, the *Mingshan Hotel* (tel (049) 612121) (míngshān biéguǎn). Actually, it's a collection of buildings with differing levels of accommodation. They have a 12 person dormitory for NT$120 per person; individual travellers may have trouble getting in. Otherwise, double rooms cost NT$500 and twins are NT$700 to NT$1200.

Everything else is inside the park gate and under the administration of the National Taiwan University Forestry Department. The *Hsitou Restaurant Hotel* (tel (049) 612111, 612345) (xītóu cāntīng lüshè) is where you should stop to find out about everything

inside the forest reserve. They book the rooms for the youth hostels as well as the pricey rooms and suites. Coming from the bus stop, it's immediately to your left as you go through the admission gate. They have doubles for NT$750 in the *fènghuáng bīnguǎn*; the *gúomín lüshè* costs NT$1100 to NT$1400; and the *hànguang lóu* is NT$1000.

Budget travellers should aim for the *Hsitou Youth Hostel* (xītóu húodòng zhōngxīn), where it costs NT$150 to stay in the dormitory and NT$500 for a double. Inquire at the Hsitou Restaurant Hotel.

*Taiwan University Forestry Dormitory* (táidà shǐyànlín xúeshēng sùshè) is meant primarily for the use of the forestry students from National Taiwan University. However, they have been known to allow travellers to stay there if they have plenty of extra room or want to practise their English. Dormitory accommodation costs NT$150. Once again, inquire at the Hsitou Restaurant Hotel.

## Places to Eat

Unless you're eating in the hotel you're staying at, the only other choice is a row of shops just outside the entrance gate near the bus station. The prices are a little high because you're paying for the pine trees and fresh air.

## Getting There & Away

The most frequent, direct buses are from Taichung, departing from the southbound bus terminal behind the train station. The trip takes 2 hours and the fare is NT$86. The bus is actually marked Shanlinhsi in Chinese, but it stops in Hsitou first before continuing up the mountain.

If you are coming from south Taiwan, you can get a bus directly from Chiayi (NT$90) or Touliu (NT$51) to Hsitou. No matter where you're coming from, you can always get a bus to Chushan (zhúshān) at the base of the mountain, and then a bus from Chushan up to Hsitou. Chushan to Hsitou costs NT$29.

From Sun Moon Lake, it's a little more complicated. You have to take a bus to Shuili,

To Hsitou

Entrance Gate

Green Dragon
Waterfall
青龍瀑布

Hotels

Bus
Station
車站

Hotel

Hotel

Camping 露營區
Area

Yen An
Waterfall

杉林溪
Shanlinhsi

0        0.5        1 km

Beginning
of trail

松瀧岩
Sunglungyen
Waterfall

To Alishan
27 km

reserve area which is called Hsitou and the Shanlinhsi area, some 20 km away and considerably higher at 1600 metres elevation. If you go to Hsitou also try to make it to Shanlinhsi, as it offers different scenery, some beautiful waterfalls and a cooler climate. There are plenty of hiking trails in Shanlinhsi and you can even hike to Alishan.

Brochures and advertisements for Shanlinhsi call it 'Sun Link Sea', a silly attempt to substitute an English rhyme for the Chinese words. If you ask anybody how to get to 'Sun Link Sea' they won't have the faintest idea of what you're talking about, so use the Chinese.

Entrance to Shanlinhsi now costs a heartstopping NT$100. Definitely avoid the place on weekends and holidays when it becomes standing room only.

**Hike to Alishan** People often hike from Shanlinhsi to Alishan or from Alishan to Shanlinhsi. From Shanlinhsi to Alishan it's uphill, so of course it's easier to begin the hike from Alishan. It's a long walk that takes a full day, so start at dawn.

From Shanlinhsi, the beginning of the trail is not very obvious, so ask people and check the map of Shanlinhsi in this book. You have to walk up an unpaved forestry road first, then climb a steep embankment and then you will suddenly find yourself on the trail. The trail is marked with a sign in Chinese pointing to Alishan. After 8 hours of walking you reach the railway tracks at Monkey Rock and then it's another 8 km on foot along these tracks through many tunnels and over numerous bridges to Alishan. A flashlight is needed for the tunnels. (Also refer to the Train Ride to Monkey Rock entry in the Alishan section earlier in this chapter.)

then a bus to Chushan (*zhúshān*) and then another bus to Hsitou. You can easily get a bus from Sun Moon Lake to Shuili, but it terminates at the bus terminal of the Taiwan Bus Company (*táiqì kèyùn*). To reach Chushan, you have to get a bus from the terminal of the Yuanlin Bus Company (*yúanlín kèyùn*). See the Shuili map for details.

### AROUND HSITOU
### Shanlinhsi
(*shānlínxī*) 杉林溪
Hsitou actually has two sections: the forest

**Places to Stay** Considering how much they are raking in from the admission fee, accommodation ought to be free. Unfortunately, that isn't the case. The *Sun Link Sea Hotel* (tel (049) 612211) (*shānlínxī dàfàndiàn*) is really a complex of hotels spread around the

Shanlinhsi area, near the bus terminal. If you can get into the dormitories, they cost NT$120 for a 10 person room. Doubles are NT$700 to NT$1200, twins NT$800 to NT$1500.

The best deal in Shanlinhsi is the campground, where you can set up your tent free of charge.

**Getting There & Away** The transport details are the same as for Hsitou. All buses going to Hsitou continue on to Shanlinhsi. There are buses connecting Hsitou and Shanlinhsi every 30 minutes. The last bus down is at 4.30 pm. Wild chicken taxis are also readily available.

### Fenghuang Valley Bird Park
*(fènghuáng gǔ niǎoyúan)* 鳳凰谷鳥園
Fenghuang Valley has an aviary (tel (049) 753100) which you can enter and watch some 280 species of birds fly around. It's nice, but touristy – not so great that you'll want to go out of your way to come here unless you're a dedicated bird-watcher. It's too bad that the aviary isn't in Hsitou so visitors can see both the forest reserve and aviary at the same time. As it is, you'll have to spend a lot of time and money on buses to get from Hsitou to Fenghuang Valley. Most travellers don't bother.

Admission to the bird park is NT$80 and it's open from 7 am to 5 pm daily.

If you want to see Fenghuang Valley, you can get a bus from Chushan (*zhúshān*), a large town at the base of the mountain below Hsitou. If you're already in Hsitou, you have to go back down to Chushan and then get a bus back up to Fenghuang. There are a few buses direct from Taichung.

Finding your way is easy if you're driving your own car or motorcycle, because there are many English signs pointing the way – apparently, the Tourism Bureau is heavily promoting the place. Don't confuse Fenghuang Valley with Fenghuangshan. Fenghuangshan is a mountain next to Hsitou and is approached by a slightly different route.

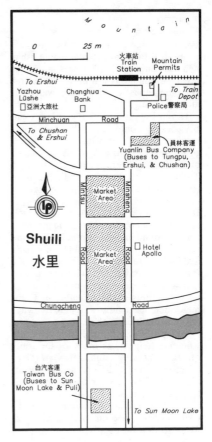

### SHUILI
*(shuǐlǐ)* 水里
Shuili is not a tourist attraction – it's an essential transit point to the south end of Sun Moon Lake. If you are travelling between Sun Moon Lake and Tungpu or Hsitou, you must go through Shuili. It's possible you'll even spend the night there.

There are many hotels clustered around the train station, though most have signs only in Chinese. An economical and reasonably clean hotel is *yǎzhōu lǚshè* (tel (049) 772151), 266 Minchuan Rd. A double room with shared bath is NT$250.

## TUNGPU
*(dōngpǔ)* 東埔

For me, Tungpu is it – the best mountain resort in Taiwan, even better than Alishan and Tsaoling. At 1120 metres above sea level the climate is just perfect. The area is mountainous, with abundant waterfalls and hot springs.

If you love hiking, Tungpu is a treat: the scenery could hardly be more spectacular. Tungpu even has a 'back door' route for climbing Yushan, Taiwan's highest peak. There is little else to do in Tungpu but hike all day and soak those tired muscles at night in the hot springs. If this appeals to you, then visit Tungpu. If you're not a hiker, you might as well skip Tungpu because there is no place for riding around in a car or tour bus. All the scenic attractions are outside the village and must be reached by walking on some fairly steep trails. My great fear is that this will change – let us only hope that no evil genius at the Chamber of Commerce decides to build a 'scenic freeway' to the summit of Yushan.

Tungpu is also not a place for people who fear heights, as many of the trails offer breathtaking, panoramic views from the edges of sheer cliffs. That said, try not to miss Tungpu. It's one of the most challenging hiking spots in Taiwan.

You need a class B mountain pass to visit Tungpu – see the Getting There & Away section for details.

## Rainbow Waterfall
*(cǎihóng pùbù)* 彩虹瀑布

If you want to take a short walk on your first day, you can hike up to Rainbow Waterfall. The path is easy to find. Just walk up the main street of Tungpu, going uphill, and when you reach the Shenghua Hotel take the trail to the left. The way is fairly obvious. The walk up to the falls takes about 30 minutes; 20 minutes to come back down.

Take a nice soak in the hot springs and get a good rest for the next day's hike, because it's a long, uphill trail.

## Father & Son Cliff
*(fùzǐ dùanyaī)* 父子斷崖

Starting from Tungpu, take the dirt road that drops slightly downhill and winds around the mountain. Before long you will come to a path on the left that goes steeply uphill. The path is well marked and has a sign in Chinese characters. If you miss the path, you'll soon come to a village, in which case you have come too far (see the Tungpu Hiking Area map). Following the path uphill, you'll soon reach Father & Son Cliff. The path looks unstable and is not for the chicken-hearted. I predict that at some point in the future, this part of the trail will collapse and it will be necessary to carve a new route. Anyway, don't linger here too long, in case it decides to collapse whilst you're standing on it.

## Happy Happy Hot Springs
*(lè lè wēnqúan)* 樂樂溫泉

Continuing past Father & Son Cliff, you'll eventually reach a fork in the trail. The right fork drops steeply downhill to the river below and is well marked with a large sign in Chinese, which is an advertisement. The name of this place is Happy Happy Hot Springs. Although it's a beautiful place, I can't recommend that you go there – it has been commercialised in rather poor taste. If you do go, you will find a small cable car operated by an electric winch for crossing the river. There is a sign telling you to help yourself. You get in the cable car, push a button and before long you're on the other side of the river. Just as you step out, somebody jumps out of the bushes and demands NT$60 per person for crossing the river.

If that doesn't make you Happy Happy, continue down the trail and you'll find a restaurant. The food is OK but the prices are double those in Tungpu. There is also a hotel charging NT$350 per person for a tatami. Just across the river, via another cable car, are the hot springs. They are beautiful, with many natural rock formations. To help you enjoy the scenery, the management has spray-painted cute names in Chinese characters right next to each formation. Some of the

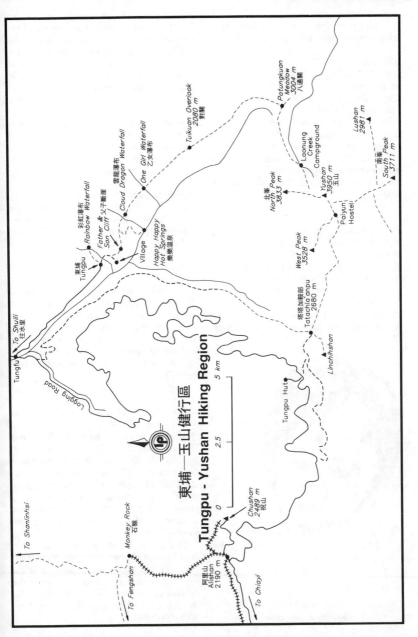

東埔－玉山健行區
**Tungpu - Yushan Hiking Region**

To Shuili 往水里

Tungfu

Logging Road

To Shanlinhsi

To Fengshan

Monkey Rock 石猴

Alishan 阿里山 2190 m

To Chiayi

Chushan 祝山 2489 m

0    2.5    5 km

Tungpu Hut

Tungpu 東埔 Village

Rainbow Waterfall 彩虹瀑布

Father & Son Cliff 父子斷崖

Cloud Dragon Waterfall 雲龍瀑布

One Girl Waterfall 乙女瀑布

Happy Happy Hot Springs 樂樂溫泉

Tuikuan Overlook 對關 2080 m

Tatochiampu 塔塔加鞍部 2680 m

Linchihshan

Patungkuan Meadow 八通關 3004 m

Laonung Creek Campground

Yushan 玉山 3950 m

North Peak 北峰 3833 m

West Peak 3528 m

Paiyun Hostel

Lushan 2981 m

South Peak 南峰 3711 m

rock formations look like they've been modified to make them more exotic.

## Waterfalls

If you bypass Happy Happy, take the left fork of the trail going uphill and you'll reach Cloud Dragon Waterfall (*yúnlóng pùbù*). Further on is One Girl Waterfall (*yì nǚ pùbù*).

It's unlikely that you'll have the time to do much more hiking in one day. Day hikers return to Tungpu along the same route. When you reach Tungpu you can soak those tired muscles in the hot springs before falling into an exhausted and satisfied sleep. Happy Happy.

## Patungkuan & Yushan

If you want to continue along the trail it leads to Patungkuan (*bātōngguān*), a lush, green alpine meadow. You'll need camping equipment if you want to stay up there. From there you can climb Yushan, Taiwan's tallest peak. However, if you plan to go higher than Patungkuan you need a mountain pass and it's not the same pass you got for visiting

Yami (aboriginal) child

Tungpu. It is possible to sneak in, but if you run into the Yushan National Park Police you'll have some explaining to do. I understand there is a steep fine if you get caught.

Alternatively, you could take the easier route and climb Yushan from Alishan, then descend through Patungkuan and wind up in Tungpu. It's an exciting trip, but any such expedition is for experienced hikers only, with a mountain pass and the necessary equipment such as heavy-duty rain gear and a sleeping bag.

## Places to Stay

The *Aboriginal Youth Activity Center* (tel (049) 701515) (*shāndì húodòng zhōngxīn*) has dormitory accommodation for NT$140 and doubles for NT$480 to NT$600. It's at the high end of town, a short but steep uphill walk. The baths use hot spring water, a real treat.

The next best deal for budget accommodation is *cùilúan shān zhūang* (tel (049) 701818), with doubles at NT$300 without bath. Actually, if you don't mind sharing your bed, you can squeeze four people in here for the same price, making it the cheapest place in town. Doubles with private bath cost NT$500.

Right next to the Aboriginal Youth Activity Center is the *Shenghua Hotel* (tel (049) 701511) (*shènghúa dàfàndiàn*), where doubles cost NT$540.

Slightly downhill from the Shenghua Hotel is the *Hong Lin Hotel* (tel (049) 701569, 791326) (*hónglín biéguǎn*), where doubles are NT$500 and a four person room is NT$800. I rather like this place because of the fine wooden interior decorating, a pleasant break from the usual concrete box architecture of youth hostels. The management is friendly.

The *dōngpǔ shān zhūang* (tel (049) 701090) has doubles/twins for NT$1000/-1200. The fanciest place in town is at the lower end of the village near the bus stop, the *Ti Lun Hotel* (tel (049) 701616) (*dìlún dàfàndiàn*) where doubles/twins are NT$1000/1500.

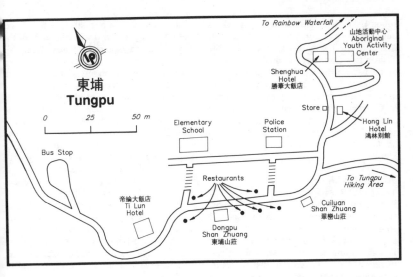

## Places to Eat

A lot of people eat in their hotels, which is fine except that you usually have to order the meal at least a few hours in advance and be there when it is served. If you'd rather just eat when you feel like it, there are several little restaurants at the lower end of town near the Ti Lun Hotel.

The cheapest way to eat dinner is to buy instant noodles (styrofoam bowl included) from the several grocery stores in town. You'll need chopsticks and a spoon. Most hotels have drinking fountains that can supply boiling hot water as well as cold.

## Getting There & Away

Getting to Tungpu is not especially difficult, but you need a mountain pass. Fortunately, it's a class B pass. In fact, there is no need to get the pass in Taipei as it can be obtained easily in Shuili (*shúilí*), a town at the bottom of the mountain where you catch the bus to Tungpu. You get the pass in the Shuili police station for NT$10. The police station is just to your right as you face the train station. They are closed from noon to 1 pm for lunch. Don't expect the police to speak any English. You must fill out the application form, which

is written in Chinese. They basically want to know your name, passport number and birth date. All you have to do is write (in English if you can't write in Chinese) in the spaces that the policeman points to and all should be OK. The whole procedure takes less than 5 minutes.

On your way up the mountain, the bus will stop and you have to go inside the police station and have your pass stamped. Save your mountain pass; you must return it to the policeman who will board the bus on your way back to Shuili.

With pass in hand, you can take a bus directly from Shuili to Tungpu. There are two bus companies with separate terminals in Tungpu, so make sure you get the right one. The bus terminal you want is operated by the Yuanlin Bus Company (*yúanlín kèyùn*). There are seven buses per day on weekdays and 10 buses daily on weekends and holidays.

The first bus departs Shuili at 7 am and the last bus at 5 pm. I won't give the schedule, as it changes often. The trip takes about 1½ hours going uphill, or 1 hour going down.

Before you get to Tungpu, you must first get to Shuili. If you are coming from Sun

Moon Lake, that's easy enough: just take a bus directly to Shuili, which takes about 30 minutes. The bus will drop you off at the Taiwan Bus Company terminal – walk over to the Yuanlin Bus Company terminal.

If you're coming from Hsitou, first go to the bottom of the mountain by taking a bus to Chushan (*zhúshān*), and then a bus to Shuili. If you're coming from either north or south Taiwan, take the train to Ershui (*èrshuǐ*), then the bus or shuttle train to Shuili.

## SUN MOON LAKE
### (*rì yùe tán*) 日月潭

Sun Moon Lake is one of Taiwan's most popular resort areas for both tourists and young couples on their honeymoon. It's popular for a good reason. It's easily Taiwan's most beautiful lake – the clear, sparkling blue waters set against the magnificent mountain backdrop is a wonderful sight to behold. The elevation is 760 metres, giving the area a pleasant climate most of the year. Naturally, it's best to visit during weekdays to avoid the large crowds that often descend on the place. Even on weekdays expect to see many tour buses, often carrying groups of visiting dignitaries, overseas Chinese and tourists from Japan and elsewhere.

Sun Moon Lake is a natural lake, but during the Japanese occupation a dam was built to raise the lake's level and generate hydroelectric power. At that time, the electric power generated was sufficient to supply all of Taiwan's needs. This dam still generates power, but with the island's heavily industrialised economy and rising standard of living, hydroelectricity can now supply only a fraction of the total demand. Today Taiwan depends on nuclear power and coal-fired plants for most of the island's electricity.

### Things to See
There are many things to see around the lake and it takes at least a full day to have a good look at this place. If you are a hiker, you could walk from Sun Moon Lake village to

Tzuen Pagoda at the opposite side of the lake, but it's a long way and will take most of the day. Fortunately, there are buses plying this route at the rate of about one an hour between 8 am and 5 pm. If you miss the last bus back you can take a taxi or hitch.

You can rent a rowboat and visit Kuanghua Island (*gūanghúa dǎo*) in the middle of the lake. If rowing is too much exercise for you, there are motorised boats that offer tours around the lake. Fishing is popular but I was told that swimming isn't permitted. Furthermore, the locals say the lake has piranhas! I have my doubts about that, though I concede it's possible.

Another thing to see is the Wenwu Temple (*wénwǔ miào*), a large, beautiful structure very close to the Sun Moon Lake Hotel. There is also a phony aboriginal village that draws a lot of tourists, and the Hsuanchuang Temple (*xúanzhùang sì*) is at the far end of the lake.

A short distance from Sun Moon Lake is the Formosan Aboriginal Cultural Village (*jiǔ zhú wénhùa cūn*). If you have any real interest in Taiwan's aboriginal culture, you should definitely try to make it there. More details are provided in the section on the village, further on in this chapter.

### Places to Stay
This is a popular area and accommodation can be tight on weekends, but on weekdays you'll always be able to find something.

The *Sun Moon Lake Hotel* (tel (049) 855911) (*rì yùe tán dàfàndiàn*), 23 Chungcheng Rd, has doubles/twins for NT$1890/2100. It's not in the village, but near the Wenwu Temple.

The *Sun Moon Lake Youth Activity Center* (fancy name for a youth hostel) (tel (049) 855811) (*rì yùe tán húodòng zhōngxīn*) is also away from the town, near the 'aboriginal village' on the other side of the lake. They have doubles for NT$1000 and a dormitory for NT$150. To get to either of these places, take the local bus from Sun Moon Lake village. It will drop you off right in front of the youth hostel or the Sun Moon Lake Hotel if you tell the driver where you are going.

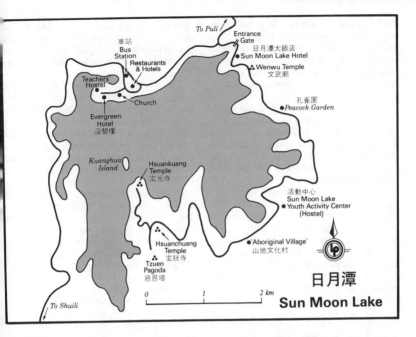

日月潭
**Sun Moon Lake**

*Evergreen Hotel* (tel (049) 855311) (*hánbì lóu*), Sun Moon Lake village, has doubles for NT$800 and twins from NT$700 to NT$1200. The *Teachers' Hostel* (tel (049) 855315) (*jiàoshī húiguǎn*), Sun Moon Lake village, has doubles/twins for NT$814/1155.

If all the places mentioned are full, check around Sun Moon Lake village. There are so many hotels you can't help but fall over them. A fairly typical one is the *Ming Shin Hotel* (tel (049) 855357) (*míngshèng dàfàndiàn*), where a double with shared bath is NT$300, or NT$550 with private bath. This is the rate on weekdays – on the weekends, it's a seller's market and the sky is the limit.

### Places to Eat

Sun Moon Lake is one of the most expensive resort areas in Taiwan. There are plenty of places to eat, but nothing is very cheap at Sun Moon Lake. For about three times the usual price, you can get noodle or rice dishes in the numerous restaurants lining the street near the bus terminal in Sun Moon Lake village. Ditto for the 'aboriginal village'. If you are staying at the *Youth Activity Center*, your best bet is to eat there.

### Getting There & Away

There are several directions you can approach from, but it's easiest to get to Sun Moon Lake from Taichung.

**To/From Taichung** As you leave the Taichung train station, turn right and walk one block until you come to a large bus depot (*gānchéng chēzhàn*). There are plenty of wild chicken taxi drivers who will grab any Westerner by the arm and yell in his/her face, 'Sun Moon Lake'. Ignore them and buy a bus ticket for NT$74. The buses go directly to the lake in 2 hours. If you've just missed the bus and don't want to wait for the next one, first take a bus to Puli, then get another bus to Sun Moon Lake.

**To/From Taipei** There is a direct bus departing from the north bus terminal. The travelling time is slightly more than 4 hours and the fare is NT$234. An alternative would be to take a bus or train to Taichung first, and then transfer to the Sun Moon Lake bus.

**To/From South Taiwan** You can go to Taichung first, but Sun Moon Lake can be reached by a shorter and cheaper route if you are willing to make a couple of transfers. There are frequent buses between Sun Moon Lake and the town of Shuili (*shǔilǐ*), which is just south of the lake.

To reach Shuili from south Taiwan, first take a train to either Touliu (*dǒuliù*) or Ershui (*èrshǔi*). Ershui is closer and I recommend doing it that way. From both Ershui and Touliu there are buses to Shuili.

Also, there is a very interesting small train that runs between Ershui and Shuili. It's a little bit slower than the bus, but more fun. Anyway, once you get to Shuili, you'll find plenty of buses heading up to the lake. Unfortunately, the main bus terminal in central Shuili is not the terminal from where the Sun Moon Lake bus departs. You must get to the terminal of the Taiwan Bus Company (*táiqì kèyùn shǔilǐ zhàn*), a short walk away (see the Shuili map).

### Getting Around

Sun Moon Lake looks like an excellent place to ride a bicycle – unfortunately, I couldn't find anybody hiring out bikes. Buses go around the lake and stop at all the major points of interest. Taking a tour by taxi is not unreasonable if you can organise a group to share the cost. The easiest way to do this is to form a group while on the bus going to the lake and include some Chinese tourists. Let them do the bargaining and don't pay until the tour is finished.

### FORMOSAN ABORIGINAL CULTURAL VILLAGE

(*jiǔ zhú wénhùa cūn*) 九族文化村
A very short distance from the north-east of Sun Moon Lake is the Formosan Aboriginal Cultural Village. For those with an interest in

Taiwan's aboriginal culture, this is a worthwhile trip. Although commercialised, the reproductions of aboriginal dwellings, arts and crafts are realistic and quite tastefully done.

There is a NT$200 entrance fee to this area, but it's not too unreasonable since you can easily spend half a day there. The 'tribal villages' are spread out over a large area, so you need to do a lot of walking or take the tourist minibus. On weekends and holidays there are continuous aboriginal song and dance shows, all free of charge.

When you first enter the grounds, you come into a large European-style garden and château – about as appropriate as an igloo in the Sahara Desert. They seem to have been thrown in as an added tourist attraction for locals, who don't get many opportunities to see the palaces of Europe. On the other hand, the gardens are very beautiful and save you the cost of a trip to France in case you haven't been there.

Just up the hill from the gardens, there is a small plaza where the aboriginal song and dance shows are performed. Just adjacent to the plaza is a museum housing aboriginal artefacts, both original and reproductions.

You can follow either the footpath or the road up the mountainside. There are nine villages in all. Each one represents a separate tribe, except for the Tsou-Shao village which represents two tribes. There are a total of 10 aboriginal tribes in Taiwan and they are the Ami, Atayal, Bunum, Paiwan, Puyuma, Rukai, Shao, Saisiat, Tsou and Yami.

For additional information about the Formosan Aboriginal Cultural Village, you can phone their office on (049) 895361. It's open daily from 7 am to 5.30 pm.

### Getting There & Away

Although it's very close to Sun Moon Lake, there are no direct buses to the village. You have to take a bus from Sun Moon Lake village to Yuchih (*yúchí*), and then another bus to the Formosan Aboriginal Cultural Village. The buses depart Yuchih at 7.30, 9.20 and 11.05 am, and 1, 2.35, 3.30 and 5 pm.

There are direct buses from the town of

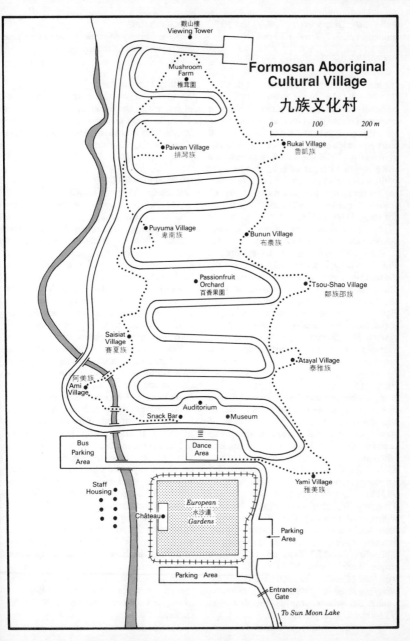

Formosan Aboriginal Cultural Village
九族文化村

観山樓 Viewing Tower
Mushroom Farm 椎茸園
Paiwan Village 排灣族
Rukai Village 魯凱族
Puyuma Village 卑南族
Bunun Village 布農族
Passionfruit Orchard 百香果園
Tsou-Shao Village 鄒族邵族
Saisiat Village 賽夏族
Atayal Village 泰雅族
阿美族 Ami Village
Snack Bar
Auditorium
Museum
Bus Parking Area
Dance Area
Yami Village 雅美族
Staff Housing
Château
European 水沙連 Gardens
Parking Area
Parking Area
Entrance Gate
To Sun Moon Lake

0    100    200 m

Puli (*pǔlǐ*). They leave at 7, 8.40 and 10.30 am, and 12.20, 2, 3 and 4.30 pm.

## PULI
*(pǔlǐ)* 埔里

Right in the centre of Taiwan, just north of Sun Moon Lake, is the town of Puli. It is definitely not a tourist attraction, but it is an important transit point for many scenic areas. Puli does have an active and interesting night market, but it's also a very noisy and traffic-choked town. The streets are so narrow that there is a real danger of being hit by a car while walking, as I discovered when a speeding car broke its mirror against my backpack frame. It's unlikely you'll want to stay in Puli for long. About the best I can say about the place is that the Chenghuang Temple (*chénghúang miào*) is very pretty.

There are two important bus terminals in Puli. The large bus terminal belongs to the Taiwan Bus Company (*táiwān qìchē kèyùn*). Down the street, about half a block away, is the Nantou Bus Company (*nántóu kèyùn*) East Station. If you're going to Wushe, you leave from this terminal. There is also a Nantou Bus Company station on the other side of town. Buses to Wushe stop at both stations.

### Places to Stay
It is possible you may have to spend a night in Puli if you arrive late and need to catch a bus the next morning. One advantage of staying in Puli is that it is easy to find cheap accommodation and food, even on holidays when nearby expensive resorts like Sun Moon Lake are packed out. About the cheapest place in town is the *Tokyo Hotel* (tel (049) 982556, 983256) (*dōngjīng dàlüshè*), 113 Tungjung Rd, where doubles cost NT$200 with shared bath and NT$400 with private bath. Right next door is the slightly pricier *Jinshan Hotel* (tel (049) 982311) (*jīnshān dàfàndiàn*), at 127 Tungjung St, where singles/doubles cost NT$400/500. In the west part of town near the post office is the *yǒngfēng lüshè* (tel (049) 982304), 280 Nanchang St, where singles/doubles cost NT$400/450 with private bath.

### Places to Eat
There are plenty of cheap places to eat near the Taiwan Bus Company terminal.

### Getting There & Away
For details of how to get from Puli to places of interest in the area, refer to the Getting There & Away sections for Huisun Forest, Wushe, the Formosan Aboriginal Cultural Village and Quiet Farm.

## HUISUN FOREST
*(hùisūn lín chǎng)* 惠蓀林場

To the north of Puli in a mountain valley, the Huisun Forest area is fast becoming a popular picnic, camping and hiking spot for residents from the Taichung area. Although not as spectacular as Alishan, Tungpu, Hohuanshan and other high mountain resorts in Taiwan, some consider Huisun a better place to go in the winter because it is warmer. At 1000 metres above sea level, the climate is milder than the higher mountains. Furthermore, Huisun has not been ruined by commercialisation, at least not yet.

The valley is heavily forested with pines and there are a number of hiking trails. There is a white-water river rushing through a canyon and you can camp nearby. There is also a lodge with economically priced rooms.

All things considered, if you are on a hurried trip through Taiwan, you could bypass Huisun without feeling you've missed something big. On the other hand, if you have the time and desire to spend a couple of days in a beautiful, pine-scented valley with nice hiking trails, it's worth the trip. I feel it is too hot in summer, but pleasant during autumn, winter and spring.

Hiking is the main activity in Huisun. Refer to the Huisun Forest map for the main trails. The hike to Frog Rock is steep but one of the best in the valley. During the week, walking along the main road through the valley is pleasant, but on weekends and holidays the traffic can be too heavy. Admission to Huisun Forest costs NT$50, or NT$30 for students.

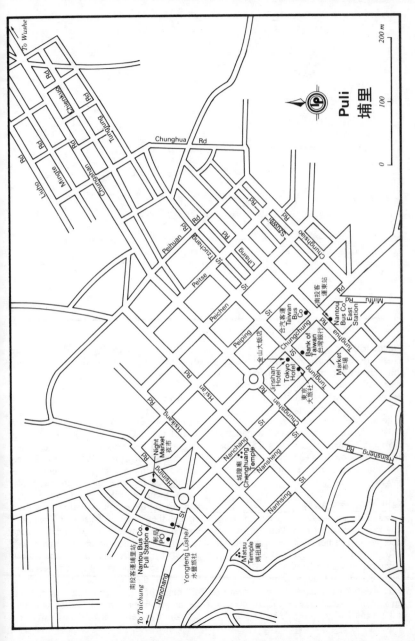

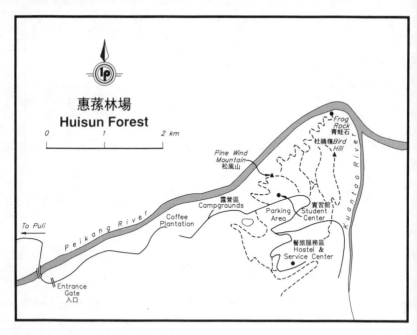

惠蓀林場
**Huisun Forest**

0    1    2 km

Frog
Rock
青蛙石
杜鵑嶺 *Bird Hill*

*Pine Wind Mountain*
松風山

露營區
Campgrounds

青習館
Student Center

Parking Area

To Puli

Coffee Plantation

*Peikang River*

*Kuantao River*

餐旅服務區
Hostel & Service Center

Entrance Gate
入口

## Places to Stay

There are several places to stay and everything is under the same management. Reservations are a good idea on weekends and holidays; call (049) 941041. If you arrive without a reservation, go to the service centre to book a place for the night.

There is a wide range of accommodation available. Dormitories cost NT$120 per person while doubles go for NT$900. There are four person rooms for NT$250 per person.

## Getting There & Away

Buses to Huisun are not frequent. There are only two buses daily from Puli and the trip takes about 1½ hours. Buses leave Puli at 8.40 am and 2.15 pm; going the other way, they leave Huisun at 10.30 am and 3.55 pm. On weekends and holidays only, there are two buses from Tsaotun (*cǎotún*), a town 17 km south of Taichung. Buses leave Tsaotun at 8 am and 2.45 pm; they leave Huisun for

Tsaotun at 10 am and 4.40 pm. The buses are operated by the Nantou Bus Company (*nántóu kèyùn*).

## WUSHE

*(wùshè)* 霧社

At 1148 metres above sea level, Wushe offers a cool mountain retreat with magnificent scenery. The town sits on the mountain ridge, and in the valley just below there is a large reservoir. Although many tour buses come through on the weekends, you can easily escape them by walking down to the reservoir. To get there, just walk down the road through the village by the school. The reservoir, named Green Lake (*bì hú*), is most beautiful during the spring and summer wet season. In the dry season the water level drops and a great deal of mud is revealed. Even then, the surrounding countryside is still magnificent, the peaceful surroundings are invigorating and the air is fresh and cool.

If you'd prefer a less strenuous activity to

hiking down to the lake, walk down the street leading out of town. On the left side of the road there is a 'moon gate'. Walk through it, heading uphill, and you will soon come to a peaceful temple, surrounded by trees. A perfect place to sit and contemplate the meaning of life, the universe and other such things that need contemplating.

In 1930, Wushe was the scene of a violent uprising of the local aboriginal population against the Japanese occupation forces. The Japanese, with their usual efficiency, quickly crushed the rebellion and left over 1000 dead. There is a mural in the youth hostel depicting this battle and there is a plaque by the temple to honour those who died.

## Places to Stay

If you want to stay in Wushe, the main street is lined with several reasonably priced hotels. The cheapest place is the youth hostel operated by the China Youth Corps. It's right at the end of the main street on the hill. It's called the *Wushe Mountain Hostel* (tel (049) 802611) (*wùshè shān zhūang*) and costs NT$100 for dorm accommodation.

The *Wuying Hotel* (tel (049) 802360) (*wùyīng dàlüshè*), 59 Jenho Rd (the main street of town), charges NT$600 for a double.

## Getting There & Away

Getting to Wushe is not difficult. There are a few direct buses a day from Taichung – if you catch one, fine, but if not just take a bus to Puli. If you are coming from Sun Moon Lake, also take a bus to Puli. The bus will drop you off by the large bus terminal in Puli, which belongs to the Taiwan Bus Company (*táiwān qìchē kèyùn*). From there walk down the street about half a block to a tiny hole-in-the-wall bus terminal operated by the Nantou Bus Company (*nántóu kèyùn*) to buy a ticket to Wushe. Puli to Wushe is 24 km up a steep highway through a scenic gorge.

## AROUND WUSHE
### Lushan Hot Springs
(*lúshān wēnquán*) 蘆山温泉

At 1200 metres elevation and 9 km east of Wushe, Lushan offers hot springs and delightful mountain scenery. Actually, most of the hot springs aren't particularly natural because they have been taken over by hotels and are simply indoor bathtubs. You don't have to stay in the hotel to use the hot baths, but then you have to pay an entrance fee if you want to 'take a rest' (*xiūxí*) – not always cheap either. After you've had a nice soak in the hot water, go outside and admire the view.

Lushan is a village perched precariously on both sides of a steep gorge with a river rushing through the centre of town. The two sides of the town are connected by a foot suspension bridge. This feature gives the town a unique advantage as no cars can cross the bridge, therefore making one side of town almost traffic-free. I do say almost because there is always some moral cripple who doesn't want to walk and instead takes a motorcycle across the footbridge. But not many people do that, so you can easily escape the whining sound of the infernal combustion engine. For dedicated car haters, this is obviously the side of town to look for a hotel room.

There is a pleasant short hike from the village along the gorge. Going upstream, you will soon find a little restaurant perched on the cliffs. There is a man there selling eggs which you can cook in the hot springs. He also sells oolong tea by the pot, so you can sit and drink tea and watch the river rush by. If you need some more exercise, I found a path that seems to go on forever – where it ends I do not know. To find it, go up the hill just behind the police station, passing a small hotel. You will see the powerline towers. Follow them for a while and the service road narrows into a path going up, up and up.

**Places to Stay** The cheapest place in town is the *Policemen's Hostel* (tel (049) 802529) (*jǐngguāng shān zhūang*). As the name implies, it is indeed for policemen, but they allow others to stay there if they have space – usually no problem on weekdays. Of course, if you're planning to break the law, you'd best do it in another hotel. Double rooms with shared bath are NT$180, or NT$400 with private bath. Six person dormitories are NT$60 per person. The hostel has hot spring baths.

Moving upmarket, there is the *Skyline Inn* (tel (049) 802675) (*tiānlú dàfàndiàn*), where doubles cost a breathtaking NT$1200. The *Honeymoon Hotel* (tel (049) 802355) (*mìyùe gǔan dàfàndiàn*) has doubles for NT$1000.

**Getting There & Away** Buses to the hot springs run about once an hour from nearby Wushe. There are occasional direct buses from Taichung.

## QUIET FARM
*(qīngjìng nóngchǎng)* 清境農場

Perched 1700 metres above sea level, Quiet Farm is undergoing a transformation from an agricultural region into a tourist resort. And as one old farmer told me, it's not so quiet anymore, at least not on weekends when the tour buses, cars and motorcycles roll in. During the week it's still very quiet and that's the time to visit if you wish to see this farming area famous for its orchards. However, nearby Hohuanshan is more scenic and offers better hiking opportunities.

Quiet Farm is not actually one farm, but a group of farms along the highway that runs from Wushe to the top of Hohuanshan. In addition to the orchards, where you can pick your own fruit for a small fee, they also raise cows. There aren't many places in Taiwan where you can see cows and this is one of the main reasons why Quiet Farm is so popular with the city folk. Also, the Chinese have a real affection for grass – not the kind you can smoke, but the kind that cows munch on. Quiet Farm has one very large pasture, and Chinese tourists flock there to take endless photos of each other standing in the grass and cow manure.

When going up the mountain, sit on the right side of the bus for the best view.

### Places to Stay

I personally prefer to stay in Wushe because it feels more like a real town than a tourist resort. If you stay in Quiet Farm, let price be your guide.

There are several campgrounds in Quiet

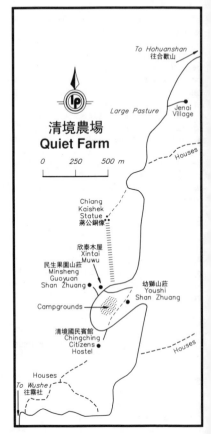

Farm which also rent out camping equipment. On weekends the tents may all be in use, so you would be better off bringing your own gear at these times. Most of the hostels fill up quickly on weekends and holidays.

The *yòushī shān zhūang* (tel (049) 802533) charges NT$100 to sleep in the dormitory and NT$350 for doubles. The *mínshēng gǔoyúan shān zhūang* (tel (049) 802533) has singles/doubles at NT$400/500 and the dormitory price is NT$100. The *xīntài mùwū* (tel (049) 993392) has singles/doubles for NT$400/600. At the *Chingching Citizens' Hostel* (tel (049)

802748) (*qīngjìng nóngchǎng gúomín lüshè*), the dormitory costs NT$250 and doubles/twins are NT$700/900.

### Getting There & Away

To reach Quiet Farm, take a bus from Puli or Wushe. It's an 8 km ride from Wushe. The same bus goes higher up the mountain to the tiny village of Tsuifeng, where you begin the 6 hour hike to Hohuanshan. You could stay at Quiet Farm and get this bus to Tsuifeng the next morning if you wish to do the Hohuanshan hike. Of course, you could also stay in Wushe. Due to the isolated location and tourist traffic, food is quite expensive at Quiet Farm – except of course for fruit.

### CHANGHUA

*(zhānghùa)* 彰化

There is little reason to make a special trip to Changhua. The town has a notable temple, but for most travellers Changhua will be a brief stopover on the way to or from Lukang.

### Information

**Tourist Office** There is an obscure branch of

the Tourism Bureau (tel (047) 232111) on the 3rd floor, 39 Kuangfu Rd.

**Money** ICBC (tel (047) 2321111) has a branch at 39 Kuangfu Rd.

### Pakuashan
*(bāguàshān)* 八卦山
If you do get off the bus or train in Changhua, the main attraction is Pakuashan *(bāguàshān)*, a small mountain park in the city topped with a very large Buddha, 22 metres tall. You can go inside and look out of various windows which have been made where his eyes, ears, etc are. Adjacent to the Buddha are some colourful pagodas and a temple. It's certainly touristy on weekends but tranquil enough at other times.

### Places to Stay
Taichung is a more interesting city to spend the night in, but if you decide to stay in Changhua, consider the following places. All of them are near the train station.

The *hóngyè dàlüshè* (tel (047) 222667), 5 Lane 100, Chang'an St, has singles/doubles with shared bath for NT$200/250. Right next door is the *jīnchéng lüshè* (tel (047) 225379), which charges NT$300 for a single and NT$350 to NT$450 for a double. The *Sanhuo Hotel* (tel (047) 224646) *(sānhé dàlüshè)*, 31 Lane 96, Yunghsing St, has doubles for NT$250 to NT$550.

*Lees Hotel* (tel (047) 236164) *(yúnhé bīngǔan)*, 566 Chungcheng Rd, Section 1, is a relatively plush place where singles/doubles are NT$490/590. At the *Taiwan Hotel* (tel (047) 224681) *(táiwān dàfàndiàn)*, 48 Chungcheng Rd, Section 2, doubles are NT$840 to NT$1050 and twins range from NT$1050 to NT$1260.

### LUKANG
*(lùgǎng)* 鹿港
Lukang, which means 'Deer Harbour', is mainly of interest to the historian. Lukang was a thriving port in the 1600s and remained so until it was closed in 1895 by the Japanese. Unlike in other parts of Taiwan, there are many original buildings still standing, but

the effect of modernisation is beginning to show. Lukang is still worth a visit if historical things interest you, but don't expect to find a perfectly preserved ancient Chinese village. Wander through the narrow alleys for some interesting photographs.

### Lukang Folk Arts Museum
*(lùgǎng mínsú wénwù gǔan)*
鹿港民俗文物館
Probably the best sight in Lukang is the Lukang Folk Arts Museum (tel (047) 772019) *(lùgǎng mínsú wénwù gǔan)*, at 152 Chungshan Rd. The museum contains a large collection of porcelain, furniture, lacquerware, musical instruments, a bridal sedan chair and other interesting artefacts. The entrance fee is a rather steep NT$60, or NT$40 for students. The entrance to the museum is not obvious from Chungshan Rd. You first must find the police station, just to the left of which is a narrow alley. Follow the alley to the end, then turn left and you'll see the museum about 100 metres in front of you.

### Temples
Lukang has two notable old temples, both of which are undergoing restoration. The Lungshan Temple *(lóngshān sì)* is dedicated to Kuanyin, the goddess of mercy, and the Matsu Temple *(māzǔ miào)* is dedicated of course to Matsu.

### Places to Stay
Although many tourists visit Lukang, very few spend the night there. As a result there are only a few old hotels in town, some of which double as brothels. Many people stay in nearby Changhua where there is a wider selection of hotels.

The *Peace Hotel* (tel (047) 772600) *(hépíng lüshè)*, 230 Chungshan Rd, has singles/doubles for NT$350/400 with private bath. It looks rather tattered around the edges, but I suppose it would do for the night. Nearby is the *wànchūn lüshè*, 255 Chungshan Rd, where singles/doubles are NT$350/400. Right next door is another hotel charging the same: the *měihúa lüshè* (tel (047) 772072) is at 253 Chungshan Rd.

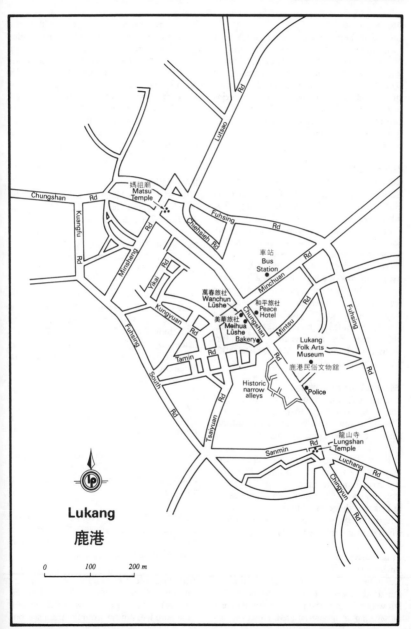

媽祖廟
Matsu Temple

Chungshan Rd

Kuangfu Rd

Lutsao Rd

Fuhsing Rd

Chiehsieh Rd

Minsheng Rd

Yikai Rd

車站
Bus Station

Minchuan Rd

Fuhsing Rd

萬春旅社
Wanchun Lüshe

和平旅社
Peace Hotel

Kungyuan Rd

美華旅社
Meihua Lüshe Bakery

Mintsu Rd

Lukang Folk Arts Museum

鹿港民俗文物館

Tamin Rd

Fuhsing South Rd

Historic narrow alleys

Police

Tsaiyuan Rd

Chungshan Rd

龍山寺
Lungshan Temple

Sanmin Rd

Luchang Rd

Chungyun Rd

**Lukang**

鹿港

0        100        200 m

## Places to Eat

Lukang is famous for its good food. A local speciality is 'cow's tongue cake' (*niú shé bǐng*). It's not really made out of a cow's tongue, but it resembles one in shape and size. It's best eaten hot. It's available from street vendors or from the numerous bakeries that line the streets. In front of the Matsu Temple are about five stores all selling delicious oyster omelettes and oyster soup for around NT$30 a serving.

## Things to Buy

Lukang is famous for its handicraft shops. Those wanting to take home Oriental arts and crafts will be in ecstasy. In the factories, which are easy enough to find along Chungshan Rd in Lukang, you can buy statues, monuments, wood carvings, tables, paintings, embroidery and pottery.

You can negotiate with the artisan who made the goods, which theoretically means you should get them cheaper. Lukang may well be one of the best places in the world to buy such things. If you're planning on buying something heavy, like furniture, you'll need the services of a freight forwarder such as Jacky Maeder (tel (02) 5624225) in Taipei.

## Getting There & Away

Lukang is 21 km south-west of Taichung. If you come from the south, get off the train in Changhua and take a bus from the terminal across the street from the station. The trip only takes 15 minutes.

From Taichung, there are some buses leaving from a small terminal (*zhānghùa kèyùn*) behind the train station. The buses stop briefly in Changhua, then continue on to Lukang; the journey takes about an hour. Alternatively, you could take a train to Changhua and then get a bus to Lukang.

## TAICHUNG

*(táizhōng)* 台中

Taichung, which means 'central Taiwan', is the third largest city on the island and is known as an educational and cultural centre rather than an industrial area. However, it's increasingly becoming a big city, with all the urban headaches of crime, traffic and pollution. There are many universities and it's a good place to study Chinese if you'd rather not be in Taipei. For tourists, the city itself is not a big attraction, but Taichung is a major jumping-off point for trips into the spectacular Central Mountain Range. If you're touring Taiwan's mountains you are almost certain to stop off in Taichung, and it's also quite likely that you'll have to spend at least 1 night there.

## Information

**Tourist Office** There is a branch of the Tourism Bureau (tel (04) 2270421) on the 4th floor, 216 Minchuan Rd.

**Money** ICBC (tel (04) 2281171) is at 216 Minchuan Rd. The Bank of Taiwan (tel (04) 2224001) is at 140 Tzuyu Rd, Section 1.

**Bookstores** Check out the Central Bookstore (*zhōngyāng shūjú*) at 125 Chungcheng Rd. The English-language books are on the 2nd floor. Caves Books (tel 04 2216602) (*dūnhúang shūjú*), one of Taiwan's best bookstores, now has a small store in Taichung in an obscure location at Room 11, 8th floor, 185 Minchuan Rd.

**Laundry** If you need fast laundry service, the place to go is *sùbìlì* (tel (04) 2266906), 421 Fuhsing Rd, Section 3, on the south side of railroad tracks. For NT$100 minimum, they'll give you a whole machine to yourself and have your clothes done in 1 hour. They can have them ready in about 5 hours at a cheaper rate.

**Hospital** Taichung Hospital (tel (04) 2222506) (*táizhōng yīyùan*) 台中醫院 is at 199 Sanmin Rd, Section 1, at the intersection with Minchuan Rd.

**Travel Agents** A good travel agent for international tickets is Wing On Travel Service (tel (04) 2251191) (*yǒng'ān lüxíngshè*), 91 Chienkuo Rd, not far from the train station.

Also good is Southeast Travel Service (tel (04) 2261171), 218 Chienkuo Rd.

## Science Museum
*(kēxúe bówùgǔan)* 科學博物館

This is one of Taichung's biggest attractions. Adjoining the museum is the Space Theater *(tàikōng jùchǎng)*. The whole complex is constructed in an ultra-modern style, but is very tastefully done and worth a visit. The address is 1 Kuanchien Rd, which is near the Hotel National in Taichung's most prestigious neighbourhood. It's only 10 minutes by bus from the centre. To get there take green bus Nos 22, 46, 47 or 48.

## Taichung Park
*(táizhōng gōngyúan)* 台中公園

This is a pleasant park with a lake where boating is permitted. It's just off Kungyuan Rd.

## Confucius Temple
*(kǒngzǐ miào)* 孔子廟

Though not as old and rustic-looking as the one in Tainan, this temple is larger and more colourful. Like other Confucius temples, it has a dawn ceremony on 28 September, the birthday of Confucius. The temple is on Shuangshih Rd, about a 20 minute walk from the train station, or you can take red bus Nos 10, 11, 40 or 46. It's closed on Monday.

## Martyrs' Shrine
*(zhōngliè cí)* 忠烈祠

If you visit the Confucius Temple, it's very convenient to visit the Martyrs' Shrine, as the two are adjacent to each other. The shrine is in honour of those who died fighting for their country. On 29 March (Youth Day) a ceremony is held here.

## Paochueh Temple
*(bǎojúe sì)* 寶覺寺

A few blocks beyond the Confucius Temple is the Paochueh Temple at 140 Chienhsing Rd. This temple features a huge Buddha, 31 metres tall. The Chinese call him Milefou, a derivation of the original Indian name Maitreya. Services are held at 5 am and 7 pm

and they can last for several hours. You can take green bus Nos 6, 14, 16 or 17 to get there.

## Universities

Taichung has four well-known universities. As a tourist you may not have a big interest in universities, but one worth seeing is Tunghai University *(dōnghǎi dàxúe)*, a private co-ed school with a beautiful campus and innovative architecture. It's a long way from the centre so you must take a bus or taxi. You can get there by taking either red bus No 38 or green bus No 22 to the last stop, which is on the university campus.

The largest university in Taichung is Chunghsing *(zhōngxīng dàxúe)*, a public co-educational institution. Fengchia University *(féngjiǎ dàxúe)* is a private co-ed school, and Chingyi University *(jìngyí xúeyùan)* is a private women's college.

## Cultural Center
*(wénhùa zhōngxīn)* 文化中心

The Cultural Center (tel (04) 2257311) is similar to the ones in Kaohsiung and Tainan. Featuring opera, art exhibits and concerts, the Cultural Center will probably be of more interest to residents than travellers. To get the current schedule of events, drop by the centre or call. The address is 600 Yingtsai Rd, near Wuchuan Rd. Take red bus No 3 or green bus No 20.

## Taiwan Museum of Art
*(měi shù gǔan)* 美術館

This is one of Taiwan's best art museums. The exhibits are rotated, so you'll need to call or pick up a schedule of events if you want to find out what's on.

The museum (tel (04) 3723552) is at 2 Wuchuan W Rd, right next to the Cultural Center. It's open Tuesday to Saturday from 9 am to 5 pm, and on Sunday from 9 am to 8 pm. Closed on Monday. Admission is NT$10.

## Places to Stay – bottom end

It's much easier to find good budget accommodation if you are travelling with

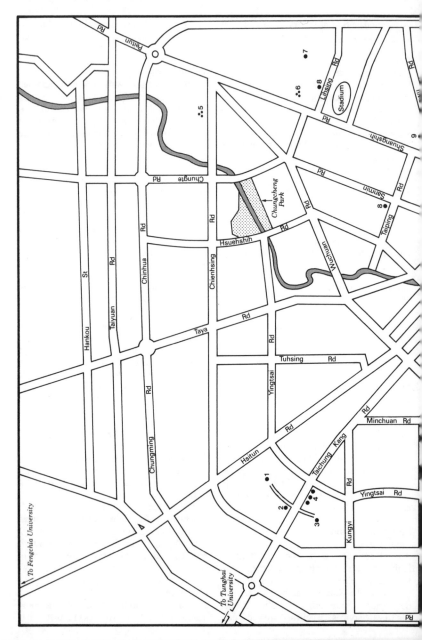

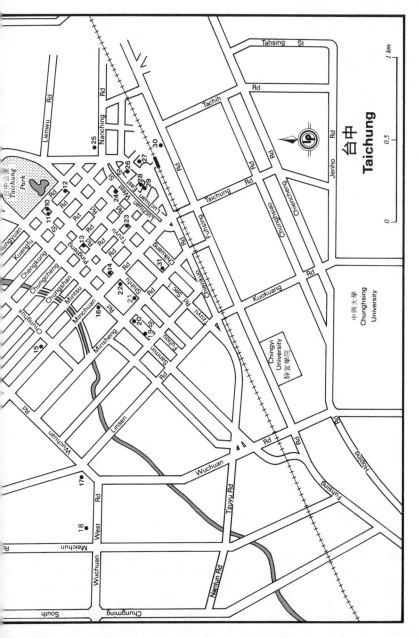

Taichung
台中

| 1 | Science Museum 科學博物館 |
| 2 | McDonald's 麥當勞 |
| 3 | Hotel National 全國大飯店 |
| 4 | Pubs |
| 5 | Paochueh Temple 寶覺寺 |
| 6 | Confucius Temple 孔廟 |
| 7 | Martyrs' Shrine 忠烈祠 |
| 8 | Lai Lai Department Store 來來百貨 |
| 9 | Swimming Pool 游泳池 |
| 10 | YMCA 青年會 |
| 11 | Haohua Movie Theater 豪華戲院 |
| 12 | McDonald's 麥當勞 |
| 13 | Central Bookstore 中央書局 |
| 14 | GPO 郵政總局 |
| 15 | ICBC |
| 16 | Taichung Hospital |
| 17 | Cultural Center 文化中心 |
| 18 | Taiwan Museum of Art |
| 19 | YMCA 青年會 |
| 20 | Police Station (Visa Extensions) 外事警察 |
| 21 | Telecommunications 電信局 |
| 22 | Municipal Government 市政府 |
| 23 | First Hotel 第一旅社 |
| 24 | Shopping Mall 第一廣場 |
| 25 | Buses to Sun Moon Lake, Lishan & Hualien 干城車站 |
| 26 | Fengzhong Movie Theater 豐中戲院 |
| 27 | Taipei Buses 台汽總站 |
| 28 | Jiancheng Lüshe 建成旅社 |
| 29 | Dongcheng Dalüshe 東城大旅社 |
| 30 | Buses to Hsitou, Chiayi & Kaohsiung 南站 |
| 31 | Bank of Taiwan |

somebody. There are several hotels with rooms for NT$300 or less. Taichung is difficult for a single budget traveller wanting to pay less than NT$200. The only youth hostel in this city provides accommodation for female students on a monthly basis, which is not much use to travellers.

One of the cheapest places in town is *zhōngzōu lüshè* (tel (04) 2222711), on the 2nd floor at 129 Chienkuo Rd. They have singles/doubles for NT$200/250. It's on the circle just opposite the train station behind the bus stop, between Chungcheng Rd and Chungshan Rd. Just to the left of this place is a narrow alley called Lane 125. On this lane you will find the *jiànchéng lüshè* (tel (04) 2222497), 10 Lane 125, Chienkuo Rd. They have singles/doubles for NT$200/250 with shared bath, or NT$350 with private

bath. The *dōngchéng dàlüshè* (tel (04) 2225001), 14 Chungshan Rd, has doubles starting at NT$250 with shared bath, NT$350 with private bath.

A few blocks from the central area is the *First Hotel* (tel (04) 2222205) (*dìyī lüshè*), 51 Chikuang St (*jìguāng jiē*), where singles start at NT$300. It's very close to the classy Taichung Hotel.

### Places to Stay – middle

*Fuh Chun Hotel* (tel (04) 283181) (*fùqūn dàfàndiàn*), 1 Chungshan Rd, doubles from NT$380 to NT$430; on the traffic circle opposite the train station

*Fuhsing Hotel* (tel (04) 2225005) (*fùxīng dàfàndiàn*), 3-1 Chungshan Rd, doubles with private bath for NT$470 to NT$700; just off the traffic circle opposite the train station

*Plaza Hotel* (tel (04) 2293191) (*dáxīn dàfàndiàn*), 180 Chienkuo Rd, has doubles for NT$525 to NT$650;

immediately to your right as you exit the train station *Crown Hotel* (tel (04) 2292175) *(wáng guàn dàfàndiàn)*, 184 Chienkuo Rd, doubles for NT$500 to NT$650; to the right as you exit the train station *Hotel Chance* (tel (04) 2297161) *(qiǎohé dàfàndiàn)*, 163 Chienkuo Rd, doubles for NT$770 to NT$910; to the right and across street when exiting the train station *Ming King Hotel* (tel (04) 2245577) *(míngjūn dàfàndiàn)*, 11 Chungcheng Rd, doubles/twins NT$980/1560

*Lucky Hotel* (tel (04) 2295191, telex 51321 TCLUCKYH) *(jíxiáng dàfàndiàn)*, 68 Minchuan Rd, doubles from NT$880

### Places to Stay – top end

*Hotel National* (tel (04) 3213111, fax 3213124) *(quánguó dàfàndiàn)*, 257 Taichung Kang Rd, Section 1, doubles for NT$2380 to NT$2580, twins NT$2580 to NT$2800

*Park Hotel* (tel (04) 2205181, fax 2225757) *(jìnghúa dàfàndiàn)*, 17 Kungyuan Rd, doubles from NT$1210 to NT$1730, twins from NT$1420 to NT$1940

*Plaza International Hotel* (tel (04) 2956780, fax 2930066) *(tōnghǎo dàfàndiàn)*, 431 Taya Rd, doubles/twins are NT$2900/3200

*Taichung Hotel* (tel (04) 2242121, fax 2249946) *(táizhōng dàfàndiàn)*, 152 Tzuyu Rd, Section 1, doubles from NT$1155 to NT$1785, twins for NT$1890

*Twinstar Hotel* (tel (04) 2261811) *(shūangxīng dàfàndiàn)*, 158 Fuhsing Rd, Section 4 (behind railway station), doubles/twins for NT$1200/1500

### Places to Eat

The best night market stretches out along the length of Chunghua Rd. The local speciality is seafood but you can buy just about anything.

There is a cheap cafeteria called *táizhōng páigǔ* (tel (04) 2249905) at 20 Minchuan Rd, near the train station.

Nice big roasted chickens can be had at *míngzhì hànbǎo zhájī* (tel (04) 2206726), opposite the Far Eastern Department Store, at the corner of Tzuyu and Chungcheng Rd. Along similar lines is *Mikens* (*mài kěn bǎo*), 152 Chengkung Rd, at the corner of Tzuyu Rd.

You can get good Western food at the *Sun Moon Restaurant* (tel (04) 2265528), 8 Taiping Rd. They feature steaks, pizzas and chicken. Prices are moderate.

If pizza is on your mind, check out *Boston Pizza* (tel (04) 2206285), 2nd floor, 131 Tzuyu Rd, Section 2. It's near the Park Hotel.

The ritzy part of Taichung is not in the centre but out on Taichung Kang Rd on the way to Tunghai University. A prominent landmark in this area is (brace yourself) *McDonald's* (tel (04) 2296111), 306 Taichung Kang Rd, Section 1, near the luxurious Hotel National. The locals claim that this particular McDonald's makes more money than any other in the world. I don't know if that's true, but they certainly have plenty of business.

In the same neighbourhood is a great Mongolian barbecue place called *Ta Han* (tel (04) 2206446) *(dàhàn mónggǔ kǎoròu)*, 13 Lane 79, Taichung Kang Rd, Section 1. Lane 79 is near the intersection of Taichung Kang Rd and Minchuan Rd.

Just opposite McDonald's is an excellent French-style restaurant called the *Fontainebleau* (tel (04) 2227777) *(fēngdān báilù)*, 35 Kuanchien Rd, at the intersection with Taichung Kang Rd. It's one of Taichung's most elegant restaurants and prices are not cheap.

At 27 Kuanchien Rd, just down the street from the Fontainebleau, is a good place serving Cantonese food, the *King Jade Restaurant* (tel (04) 2287777) *(jīnbì yúan)* – it's expensive like everything else in this neighbourhood.

Right next to the Hotel National is the *Beautiful Garden Restaurant* (tel (04) 3217711) *(liányúan cāntīng)*, 261 Taichung Kang Rd, Section 1. They specialise in seafood, but are not cheap.

### Entertainment

**Cinemas** Some of the more popular movie theatres in town include the *háohúa dàxìyùan* (tel (04) 2225020), 62 Kuangfu Rd; *fēngzhōng xìyùan* (tel (04) 2221879), 25 Chengkung Rd; *nánhúa xìyùan* (tel (04) 2257008), 4th floor, 2 Lane 2, Chungyi Rd; and the *sēnyù xìyùan* (tel (04) 2223170), 15 Hsingmin St.

**Pubs** Most pubs are either closed or empty during the day, but things get moving around

7 pm. If pub-crawling interests you, the area near the Hotel National is the place to go. All the pubs cater to Westerners and have beer, food and music. Among the places to try are the *Bali Hai* (tel (04) 3210080), 225 Taichung Kang Rd, Section 1; *Sam's Place* (tel (04) 2278143), 156-5 Taichung Kang Rd, Section 1; and the *Wagon Wheel* (tel (04) 3211339), 229 Taichung Kang Rd, Section 1.

Moving upmarket, there's *Blue Bay* (tel (04) 3259488), in the basement at 247 Taichung Kang Rd, Section 1, right next to the Hotel National. It's an exclusive place – it's lively and has good food, but prices are on the high side of the spectrum.

You can enjoy good snacks and German beer at *Alt Heidelberg* (tel (04) 2266453), 13 Kuanchien Rd.

**Beer Halls** Wenhsin Rd in the north part of the city is Taichung's kinky neighbourhood, filled with 'love motels' and the biggest 'barbershops' I've ever seen. Nevertheless, it's also the location of gigantic beer gardens, most of which are respectable places. They cater to a mostly upper-class Chinese clientele, serve good food and are not exactly cheap. About the largest is *Beer City* (tel (04) 2917788) (*qīngmài dàcāntīng*), 199 Wenhsin Rd, Section 4.

**Activities**
**Swimming** There is a public swimming pool on the north-east corner of Shuangshih Rd and Chingwu Rd, opposite the rear entrance of Taichung Park. It is only open in summer.

**Bowling** If you like bowling and billiards, visit the New Taichung Bowling Center (tel (04) 2228041) (*xīn táizhōng bǎolíng qiúgǔan*), 14 Shihfu Rd. Another place to try is Amber Lanes (tel (04) 2321177) (*hǔpò bǎolíng qiúgǔan*), 111 Taya Rd.

**Miscellaneous** A building at 115 Luchuan West St houses Taichung's most popular discos. On the 9th floor is *DD*. Admission is NT$200 for men, NT$100 for women. It's very popular with students. On the 10th floor

is *Telstar Disco* (*tiān wáng xīng*); the 7th floor is occupied by the *Golden Butterfly Dance Hall* (*jīn húdié*); the 4th floor is home for a dance hall called *háokè*. Although the 2nd floor doesn't have a disco, it does have *Kiss MTV*. And down in the basement is a skating rink.

**Things to Buy**
The cheapest large store in Taichung is Da Da Department Store, at 32 Luchuan E St. Better quality at higher prices can be found at the Far Eastern Department Store, 48 Tzuyu Rd, Section 2. Just around the corner is the Evergreen Department Store, at 63 Tzuyu Rd, Section 2; this is probably the most expensive store in Taichung. The Lai Lai Department Store (*lái lái bǎihùo gōngsī*) is at 125 Sanmin Rd.

Taiwan's biggest shopping mall (*dìyī gǔangchǎng*) was being constructed at the corner of Chungcheng Rd and Luchuan West Rd at the time of writing. It should be open by the time you read this.

Good deals on export-quality clothing can be had at Madame Fashion Company (tel (04) 2214952) (*zhǔfù shāng chǎng*), 357 Chengkung Rd.

DTK-brand computers can be bought from Asia Pacific Computer (*yàtài*) (tel (04) 2261961), 18 Lane 49, Chungshan Rd. Computers carrying the Asia label can be bought from *rìchéng* (tel (04) 2228725), 196 Sanmin Rd, Section 3.

**Getting There & Away**
As it's located 105 km south of Taipei on the major north-south freeway and railway line, you won't have trouble getting to Taichung. In addition to the north-south freeway buses, there are also buses coming over the mountains from Hualien on the east coast, via the scenic Central Cross-Island Highway. There are direct buses to many scenic areas in central Taiwan, such as Sun Moon Lake, Hsitou, Alishan, and Wushe (via Puli).

From Taipei the bus fare to Taichung is NT$156 and the train fare ranges from NT$188 to NT$259.

When leaving Taichung, it's helpful to

know that there are three major bus terminals. The one in front of the railway station is for buses heading for Taipei and other places in the north. The bus terminal behind the train station (*nán zhàn*) is for southbound buses (Kaohsiung, Hsitou, Chiayi). For country buses (Sun Moon Lake, Wushe, Lishan, Hualien, but not Hsitou) the bus terminal (*gānchéng chēzhàn*) is two blocks north of the train station.

### Getting Around

**Bus** If you have a day to spend in Taichung, there are a few interesting things to see and do. If you decide to get around on the city bus, a special note is in order. Taichung has two bus companies. One company (*táizhōng kèyùn*) operates green buses, and the other (*rényǒu kèyùn*) operates red buses. This can create a bit of confusion for the uninitiated. For example, a green bus No 22 goes to different places from a red bus No 22.

The fare is NT$7 on ordinary buses and NT$9 for air-conditioned buses – even in winter when you don't want air-con. The exact change is required. You can buy a bus card valid for 10 rides, but a green bus card cannot be used on a red bus and vice versa.

**Motorcycle** You might consider renting a motorcycle for taking some trips into the mountains. The best place I could find for 125cc bikes was *nántún chēháng* (tel (04) 3821509, 3898083) at 58 Nantun Rd, Section 2. It's somewhat far out from the centre and you'll probably need a taxi to get there. Have a Chinese person ring them up to get directions. Sorry I couldn't find anything more central, but places renting bikes in Taichung are not numerous.

### CHUNGHSING VILLAGE

(*zhōngxīng xīn cūn*) 中興新村

I wouldn't call this a tourist attraction. However, many of the English-language tourist maps published in Taiwan mark Chunghsing Village with a star, circle or something else to show that it is a special place, but then offer no explanation why it is

so. I finally went there to find out what makes it so notable.

Chunghsing Village is a model city built for Taiwan's government workers. In appearance it vaguely resembles an American-style suburb. In addition to being a model city, it has an important administrative function as the seat of the Taiwan Provincial Government.

Most tourists probably wouldn't want to spend their time there, but foreign residents of Taichung may want to have a look as it is only a short distance away. Frequent highway buses heading south of Taichung stop there, including the Sun Moon Lake bus.

### CENTRAL CROSS-ISLAND HIGHWAY

(*zhōngbù hénggùan gōnglù*)

中部橫貫公路

This spectacular highway connects Taroko Gorge on the east side of Taiwan with the city of Taichung on the west, a distance of 195 km. Virtually every km of this highway offers a stunning view of lush forests and towering mountain peaks, and should not be missed if you have the time. The road is occasionally closed due to landslides, especially after a typhoon – which is not surprising considering that in many places the road is carved out of sheer cliffs.

### Places to Stay

Assuming you travel from west to east, you will come across youth hostels in the following order. Refer to the Youth Hostels map in the Facts for the Visitor chapter for addresses.

*Chingshan Mountain Hostel* (tel (045) 244103) (*qīngshān shān zhuāng*), dormitory is NT$100 and triples are NT$500
*Techi Mountain Hostel* (tel (045) 981592) (*déjī shān zhuāng*), dormitory/doubles cost NT$100/500
*Tayuling Mountain Hostel* (tel (038) 691111) (*dàyǔlíng shān zhuāng*), dormitory costs NT$100
*Tzuen Mountain Hostel* (tel (038) 691111) (*cīēn shān zhuāng*), dormitory costs NT$100
*Loshao Mountain Hostel* (tel (038) 691111) (*luòshào shān zhuāng*), dormitory/double NT$100/360
*Tienhsiang Youth Activity Center* (tel (038) 691111) (*tiānxiáng húodòng zhōngxīn*), dormitory/double NT$100/500

## Getting Around

It takes slightly more than 8 hours by bus to travel across the island on this highway. From Hualien, buses depart for Taichung at 7.30, 8 and 11 am. Going in the other direction, buses depart Taichung for Hualien at 7.15, 7.50 and 9.30 am. The fare is NT$300. You can also catch the bus in Tienhsiang. Although the trip can be done in 1 day, I recommend taking at least 3 days because there is plenty to see along the way. The side trips to Wuling Farm and Hohuanshan are particularly outstanding.

For those with even more time, energy and ambition, it is possible to do this journey by foot, or bicycle if you're really fit. I know it sounds crazy, but there are actually quite a few hikers who walk nearly the entire length of the Central Cross-Island Highway. It's best to do it on weekdays, when traffic is minimal. To do the journey by foot takes at least 5 days and life is made easier by the fact that you can always change your mind and catch a bus. The highest region, near Tayuling, is particularly scenic, and from there you can walk to Hohuanshan, one of Taiwan's most beautiful mountains.

There are convenient youth hostels all along the route. Reservations are advisable, especially during the summer school vacation. It's probably a good idea to find a few people to go along with you. Otherwise, after 5 days of walking alone along this road, you're liable to find yourself talking to the trees and squirrels. Don't forget to take some waterproof clothing with you.

If you'd prefer to walk down rather than up, you could take a bus to the summit of the highway at Tayuling and then walk downhill all the way, either towards Hualien (east) or Taichung (west). During the cold months (November to May), I suggest you walk from Tayuling towards Taichung (west) because the east side of the island gets locked in by cold rain and fog. The west side is usually sunny – in fact, winter is the dry season.

If you're not headed to south Taiwan, then Fengyuan is an important transit point at the western end of the highway. It's about an hour north of Taichung (see the Central Taiwan map). You can get a train from Taipei to Fengyuan and bypass Taichung completely. This saves nearly 2 hours on a trip from Taipei to the Central Cross-Island Highway.

## KUKUAN
*(gŭgŭan)* 谷關

Kukuan is a small town and hot spring resort at the western end of the Central Cross-Island Highway, about 1½ hours by bus from Taichung. Being rather close to the city, it gets crowded on weekends, but it is OK at other times. The scenery is certainly good, though not as spectacular as higher up in the mountains. Kukuan has an elevation of 750 metres.

The hot springs are piped into hotel baths; unfortunately there are no outdoor pools. In addition to the hot springs, another attraction is the hike up to Dragon Valley Waterfall (*lónggŭ pùbù*). It's an easy hike – only 3⅓ km for the round trip. However, it's in a park and they charge a steep NT$80 admission. Within the park is a zoo and botanical garden. To find the park, cross the footbridge near the Dragon Valley Hotel and just follow the trail. Bring some junk food to feed the monkeys.

### Orientation

The town is divided into two – one half is next to the highway and the other on the north bank of the river. You get to the north side by crossing a footbridge on the eastern (upper) part of the village. The north side is definitely the nicer part of town, since it has no whining motorcycles or cars.

### Places to Stay

Kukuan is overrun with tourists on weekends and holidays, but on weekdays business is very slow and most hotels offer a 20% discount off the rates quoted here.

Many of the hotels have tatami dormitories. If you're a single traveller, you can't be certain that you can stay in them. If the hotel is empty – as it often is on a weekday – they'll usually let you stay by yourself in the dorm.

Across the footbridge on the north bank is the *gŭgŭan shān zhŭang* (tel (045) 951126),

Hsuehshan (Snow Mountain)

which costs NT$100 for the dorm and NT$350 for a double. The *dōngguān wēnquán dàfàndiàn* (tel (045) 951111) has doubles/twins for NT$800/1000. The *dōnggǔ fàndiàn* (tel (045) 951236) has dorms for NT$150 and doubles for NT$800.

*Utopia Holiday Hotel* (tel (045) 951511/5) (*jiàqí dàfàndiàn*) is a great place to stay, and it ought to be for the price – doubles/twins cost NT$1200/1800. It's also on the quiet north bank of the river.

On the busy side of town, the *Dragon Valley Hotel* (tel (045) 951325, 951365) (*lónggǔ dàfàndiàn*) has doubles/twins for NT$1350/1550.

### Getting There & Away

Buses from Taichung are frequent, starting at 6 am. All buses running between Taichung and Lishan stop in Kukuan.

In Kukuan the bus stop is at the east end of town, right in front of the Kukuan Hotel. The buses do not stop in the centre of town.

### LISHAN 梨山

(*líshān*) 梨山

Lishan, or 'Pear Mountain', is a small farming community along the Central Cross-Island Highway. Some 1900 metres above

sea level, the area is famous for growing cold-weather fruits like apples, peaches and pears, which cannot grow in the subtropical lowlands of Taiwan. It has also become popular recently with tourists from the city seeking refuge from the summer heat. There really isn't that much to do in Lishan itself, but it is a transit point for the trip to Wuling Farm and Snow Mountain.

There is a big fruit market in Lishan. However, the prices aren't really a bargain, although you can be sure that the fruit is fresh off the tree. The dried fruits are a much better deal and they make good lightweight snacks for travelling.

Hiking opportunities are limited in Lishan because most of the land is occupied by orchards. However, if you don't mind strolling down a quiet country road, you can hike to Lucky Life Mountain Farm (*fúshòushān nóngchǎng*). Along the way you pass a small villa which once served as a mountain retreat for Chiang Kaishek. The whole hike is only about 10 km. To find the road leading up there, walk out of town on the highway going east (towards Hualien). Less than a km of walking brings you to a church on the left side of the road. On the right side is the road you want. The road passes the elementary

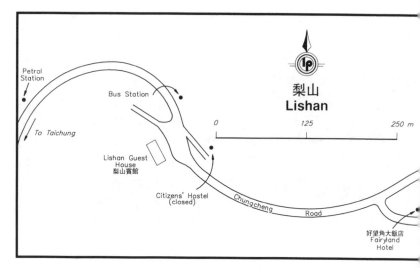

梨山
Lishan

Petrol Station

Bus Station

To Taichung

Lishan Guest House
梨山賓館

Citizens' Hostel (closed)

Chungcheng Road

好望角大飯店
Fairyland Hotel

0    125    250 m

school, Chiang Kaishek's villa and the Lishan Culture Museum (*líshān wénwù gǔan*). The museum is good, and the views from the back porch of the surrounding mountains are fantastic.

## Places to Stay

So many tour buses arrive in Lishan on weekends and holidays that it's a wonder the mountain doesn't collapse. Accommodation is very tight at these times, so you're definitely better off arriving on a weekday. Just opposite the bus station is the *Lishan Guest House* (tel (045) 989501) (*líshān bīngǔan*). It is one of the most beautiful luxury hotels in Taiwan and not outrageously expensive for the level of accommodation provided: doubles are NT$750 to NT$900 and twins are NT$1000 to NT$1350. It's very popular and it's difficult to get in during a weekend.

The following rates are for weekdays. Try to avoid Saturday night, when the rates will be about 50% higher if you can find a room at all!

Chungcheng Rd is the main road in town; it's actually part of the Cross-Island Highway. It's mostly lined with restaurants, but there are a few hotels including the *líshān*

*lüshè* (tel (045) 989261), which charges NT$300 for a double. *Fu Chung Hotel* (tel (045) 989506) (*fúzhōng dàfàndiàn*), 61 Chungcheng Rd, has singles/doubles for NT$500/600.

One block south of Chungcheng Rd and running parallel to it is Mintsu Rd, which is where most of the hotels are. The cheapest is *gǔangdá dàlüshè* (tel (045) 989216), 21 Mintsu Rd (next to the fire station), which has doubles with private bath for NT$200. The *yànhúa lóu dàlüshè* (tel (045) 989615, 989511) has doubles for NT$300. The *shèngxīn fàndiàn* (tel (045) 989577) has singles/doubles for NT$400/500. The *Li Tu Hotel* (tel (045) 989256, 989512) (*lìdū dàlüshè*) has singles/doubles for NT$400/500. *Fairyland Hotel* (tel (045) 989256, 989512) (*hǎowàngjiǎo dàfàndiàn*), 52 Mintsu Rd, charges NT$600 for doubles.

## Getting There & Away

Lishan is easily reached by any bus going along the Cross-Island Highway between Hualien and Taichung.

From Taichung there are 13 buses daily, with the last bus leaving at 2.30 pm. Most of the buses from Taichung terminate the trip in

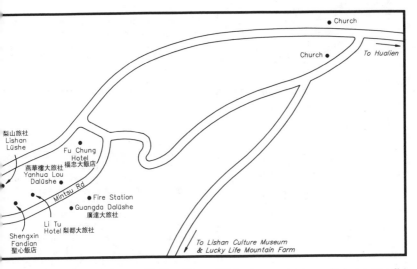

Lishan but a few continue to Hualien. The fare is NT\$140 and the trip takes 3½ hours. From Hualien, the buses leave at 7.30, 8 and 11 am and take 4½ hours to reach Lishan. The Hualien to Lishan fare ranges from NT\$134 to NT\$161, depending on which bus you take.

There are three buses daily going to Lishan from the east coast city of Ilan.

## AROUND LISHAN
### Wuling Farm
*(wǔlíng nóngchǎng)* 武陵農場

Wuling Farm was originally conceived as a government-sponsored agricultural project to grow fruit and to resettle retired servicemen who fought for the Republic of China on the mainland. Increasingly the area is attracting tourists, especially young hikers who want to challenge Taiwan's second highest peak, Hsuehshan *(xǔeshān)*, or 'Snow Mountain', which is 3884 metres in elevation.

Whether you climb this peak or not, the whole area around Wuling Farm is beautiful, and so far it has not been heavily commercialised. On weekends it may get crowded, so come during the week if you can.

**Hikes** A mountain permit is supposedly required for Hsuehshan, but there is no one around to check it. It's a 10 to 12 hour climb to the summit. There are two huts along the way where you can spend the night. The first one, Chika Hut *(qīkǎ shān zhūang)*, is a 2 hour hike from the trailhead and has water. The second one, Three Six Nine Hut *(sān liù jiǔ shān zhūang)*, is an additional 6 hour climb and has no water. There are no facilities at the huts, so you'll need a sleeping bag, food, stove and other backpacking paraphernalia.

A much easier hike would be to Yensheng Waterfall *(yānshēng pùbù)*. It's at the top end of the valley past the Youth Activity Center. From there you could also climb Peach Mountain *(táoshān)*, which has an elevation of 3324 metres.

**Places to Stay** There are three places to stay in Wuling. The *Wuling Guest House* (tel (045) 901183) *(wǔlíng gúomín lǚshè)* is the classiest, with doubles/triples at NT\$1000/1200. The *Wuling Rest House* (tel (045) 901259) *(róngmín xiūxí zhōngxīn)* is much cheaper and is right near the bus stop; the dormitory costs NT\$120 and doubles are NT\$400.

The *Wuling Youth Activity Center* (tel (045) 901020) (*qīngnián húodòng zhōngxīn*) is a 5 km hike up the valley road from the last bus stop. The dormitory costs NT$132 and doubles are NT$1100.

All these places are practically empty during the week but can fill up on weekends and holidays. Camping is not permitted next to the hostels or in the farming area of the valley. If you want to camp, you'll have to do it in back country.

**Getting There & Away** Wuling Farm is 25 km north-east of Lishan, just off the branch

highway leading down to the coast at Ilan. It's most easily reached by bus from Lishan. There are six buses daily, departing from Lishan at 8 and 10.10 am, noon, and 1, 3 and 4.50 pm.

The buses going from Ilan to Lishan also stop at Wuling Farm.

### HOHUANSHAN 合歡山
*(héhūanshān)* 合歡山

No doubt many visitors to Taiwan will be surprised to learn that in this subtropical island there is a ski resort. Mt Hohuan (which means 'Harmonious Happiness') reaches an elevation of 3416 metres and the summit is above the tree line. At this height it is cool even in summer, but in winter the night temperatures can dip well below freezing and there is sufficient snowfall in January and February to permit skiing. However, the skiing isn't very good – the ski lift broke down years ago and hasn't been repaired. So 'skiing' consists of walking up the hill yourself and sliding back down. Admittedly, it's good exercise.

During the rest of the year it is certainly worth visiting Hohuanshan for the magnificent views. In the morning, you can usually witness that beautiful Taiwanese phenomenon, the 'sea of clouds'.

Hohuanshan is reached by an unpaved branch highway that runs off the Central Cross-Island Highway. This narrow road runs between Tayuling and Wushe and it is the highest road in Taiwan.

Hohuanshan is peaceful during the off season, but when it snows everybody converges on the mountain. People in Taiwan have few opportunities to see snow, so when it falls on Hohuanshan everyone who can makes the pilgrimage there to see the white stuff. I personally prefer the mountain when there is no snow and it is quieter and warmer.

If you survive the cold night, the next morning you may encounter hikers heading off to climb Mt Chilai (*qíláishān*). If you are invited to go, I recommend you politely decline unless you want to die young. Chilai is notorious in Taiwan as the site of many fatal accidents, due to the severe weather changes and a vertical, crumbly, rocky face. The mountain is dominated by a tremendous jagged, sawtooth ridge. The 'trail' follows this ridge line and offers numerous opportunities for hang-gliding and skydiving.

## Places to Stay

There is a youth hostel near where the bus drops you off in Tayuling. Take the switchback trail up the hill to reach the hostel. Otherwise, you'll have to walk up a long dirt driveway. Reservations for this hostel are usually made from the Tienhsiang Youth Hostel (tel (038) 691111/3). The local hostel is called *Tayuling Youth Hostel* (*dàyǔlǐng shān zhūang*).

At Hohuanshan there is only one place to stay, *Sung Hsueh Lou* (*sōng xǔe lóu*) (tel (049) 802732). In English, Sung Hsueh Lou means 'Pine Snow Hostel'. The tatami dormitory costs NT$130, and doubles are NT$1200 during the peak season (winter) and NT$900 during the off season. There are no stores in or near the hostel, so bring food, film, toilet paper, a flashlight and plenty of warm clothes. If you don't have a reservation, bring a sleeping bag because there is only one quilt for every guest and there probably will be no extras. If all the beds are taken, it's almost certain they will allow you to roll out a sleeping bag on the dining room floor when it's time for lights out.

In any event, be prepared for a cold night. At 3400 metres you are no longer in the tropics, so be sure to bring your winter woollies. No matter how nice the weather might be it can change in minutes during the day, and at night the temperature absolutely plummets.

## Places to Eat

*Sung Hsueh Lou* is the only place that has food or anything else. Prepared meals are available but only if you made a reservation in advance. Otherwise, they probably won't even have enough leftovers for you. You are

therefore strongly advised to bring extra food unless you want to forage for nuts and berries.

## Getting There & Away

One major tactical problem with visiting Hohuanshan is that there is no bus service along the dirt road that leads to the top of the mountain and the lodge. You have two options, either to go by wild chicken taxi or to walk. Opportunities for hitching are limited because traffic is almost nil. There are two routes, and ideally you should go up one way and down the other. Most people approach from the north side because it's shorter. Either route may be closed occasionally due to landslides.

**North Side** Wild chicken taxis from the base of the mountain will be waiting for you near the bus stop in Tayuling. They charge about NT$250 to NT$400, subject to bargaining. The best way to arrange this is to round up a group of Chinese tourists on the bus to Tayuling so you can split the cost. Let them handle the bargaining.

If you walk from Tayuling, it's a steep but breathtakingly beautiful walk of 9 km – 4 hours uphill or 3 hours downhill. Certainly the best way to appreciate the scenery is on foot.

**South Side** From Puli, you can get a bus to Tsuifeng (*cùifēng*) (elevation 2375 metres) and from there it's 15 km, or about 6½ hours of walking. The bus departs Puli from the Nantou Bus Company Station (*nántóu kèyùn zhàn*). There are no taxis in Tsuifeng, nor is there a place to stay unless you camp out. The nearest place that has accommodation is Quiet Farm, but Wushe has a youth hostel and is a better option for budget travellers. The bus from Puli passes through Wushe and Quiet Farm, and terminates in Tsuifeng. Start early because the weather is usually clearest in the morning.

# North-West Taiwan 台灣西北部

## HSINCHU
*(xīnzhú)* 新竹

Hsinchu is a moderate-size city and is known mainly for its windy winter weather and Science-Industrial Park. The Science-Industrial Park is where most of Taiwan's high-technology companies are located, but it's not a place for tourists. Likewise, the city itself is not of special interest to most travellers, other than as a transit point on the way to Shihtoushan or Tapachienshan.

### Information

**Tourist Office** The Tourism Bureau (tel (035) 217171) has a branch on the 3rd floor, 115 Chungcheng Rd.

**Money** ICBC (tel (035) 217171) is at 129 Chungcheng Rd. The Bank of Taiwan (tel (035) 266161) is at 29 Linsen Rd.

### Things to See

The main attraction in Hsinchu is the Hsinchu Zoo (*xīnzhú dòngwù yúan*). As zoos go, it is quite small. You can find it in Chungshan Park, behind the train station, just near the Confucius Temple (*kǒngzǐ miào*).

Also worth visiting is the Chenghuang Temple (*chénghúang miào*), near the intersection of Chungshan Rd and Tungmen St.

There are two national universities in Hsinchu, specialising in science and technology. You could check out the bookstores and perhaps meet some students. The two universities are Tsinghua University (*qīnghúa dàxúe*), 855 Kuangfu Rd, and Chiaotung University (*jiāotōng dàxúe*), 100 Tahsueh Rd.

### Places to Stay

There is no need to look any further than the area near the train station. I like the *Golden Swallow Hotel* (tel (035) 227151) (*jīnyàn dàfàndiàn*), 11-1 Mintsu Rd. They even have waterbeds! However, at NT$500 for a double, it's one of the more expensive places, though in this case you're really getting what you pay for.

The *dōngbīn dàlüshè* (tel (035) 223162), 14 Linsen Rd, has doubles for NT$400 and serves a good breakfast. The *zhōngyáng lüshè* (tel (035) 224126), 30-1 Chungcheng Rd, has singles for NT$320 and the manager speaks some English. The *dōngbǎo dàlüshè* (tel (035) 234177), 9 Mintsu Rd, has doubles for NT$400. The *yínchŭan dàlüshè* (tel (035) 224135), 5 Chungcheng Rd, has friendly management and doubles cost NT$350. The *bīnchéng dàfàndiàn* (tel (035) 269255), 15 Chungcheng Rd, has doubles for NT$550 to NT$850.

Top of the line is the *CITC Hsinchu Hotel* (tel (035) 263181, fax 269244) (*zhōngxìn xīnzhú dàfàndiàn*). Doubles are NT$1995 to NT$2210, twins are NT$2310 to NT$2520.

### Entertainment

One movie theatre, *zhōngyáng xìyùan* (tel (035) 222655), 27 Chang'an St, shows two films for only NT$50. Some of the other theatres include the *húayáng xìyùan* (tel (035) 222335), 181 Chungcheng Rd; *jiāhúa xìyùan* (tel (035) 213131), 240 Chungcheng Rd; and *gúomín dàxìyùan* (tel (035) 222833), 65 Chungcheng Rd.

### Activities

If bowling alleys interest you, check out the Hsinchu Bowling Center (tel (035) 224128), 240 Peimen St.

### Things to Buy

The Far Eastern Department Store is at 110 Chungcheng Rd, less than a block from the Tungmen Circle.

### Getting There & Away

Hsinchu is some 70 km south-west of Taipei and sits right on the major west coast rail line. Buses run by the Taiwan Bus Company run frequently from Hsinchu to Taipei and

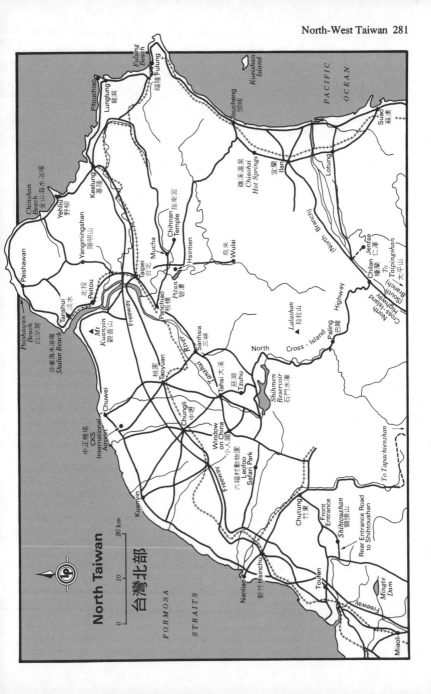

| | | | |
|---|---|---|---|
| 1 | City Government Building<br>市政府 | 9 | Dongbao Dalüshe<br>東寶大旅社 |
| 2 | Police (Visa Extensions)<br>外事警察 | 10 | Yinchuan Dalüshe<br>銀川大旅社 |
| 3 | Chenghuang Temple<br>城隍廟 | 11 | Xingao Lüshe<br>新高旅社 |
| 4 | Far Eastern Department Store<br>遠東百貨 | 12 | Dongbin Dalüshe<br>東寶大旅社 |
| 5 | GPO<br>郵政總局 | 13 | Hsinchu Bus Company<br>新竹客運 |
| 6 | Bincheng Dafandian<br>賓城大飯店 | 14 | Bus Station<br>車站 |
| 7 | Zhongyang Lüshe<br>中央旅社 | 15 | Swimming Pool<br>游泳池 |
| 8 | Golden Swallow Hotel<br>金燕大飯店 | 16 | Confucius Temple<br>孔子廟 |

Taichung. There are less frequent bus services to smaller cities such as Tainan and Chiayi.

## SHIHTOUSHAN
*(shītóushān)* 獅頭山

Shihtoushan, or 'Lion's Head Mountain', is a leading Buddhist centre in Taiwan. The name derives from the fact that the mountain vaguely resembles the head of a lion when viewed from a distance. For foreign visitors, the main attraction is the chance to visit temples and the opportunity to stay in a Buddhist monastery with beautiful natural surroundings.

The temples are not very old, and indeed there were some new ones under construction when I first visited, but they are all very nice.

Spending the night in one of the monasteries can be interesting, but this is not the place for nightlife. Shitoushan is a very restful place and draws a steady stream of pilgrims from all over Taiwan. You can watch the morning services at the crack of dawn.

Monks and nuns lead a spartan lifestyle and follow a rigid daily routine. They go to bed early and get up early. In a monastery you must bathe daily, not in the morning but always in the evening or late afternoon when hot water is available; expect to bathe between 3 and 6 pm, which is early by Chinese standards. This is because the monks and nuns go to bed at 8 pm. You can stay up later if you like so long as you don't disturb those who are sleeping.

Since the monks and nuns get up at the crack of dawn, you will have to as well. Expect breakfast to be served at about 5.30 am, lunch at noon and dinner at 5.30 pm. The food is good and vegetarian. Strict silence is observed while eating. Don't waste your rice! If you throw any away the monks are liable to get upset, as they believe in wasting nothing. If you need additional snacks, you can buy them from some of the vendors at the foot of the hill.

During the day, you are free to come and go as you like. You only need to be on your best behaviour in the temple grounds. The monks and nuns realise that Westerners have their own peculiar customs and they are reasonably tolerant, but when you're on their turf they also want you to be tolerant and respect their religion and lifestyle. After all, you're living in their temple. Men and women cannot sleep together, even if they're married. Kissing and caressing in public is a big no-no. You may take photographs in the temple but don't disturb the worshippers. If the daily routine and social practices of a monastery are too confining for you, it's better not to stay there.

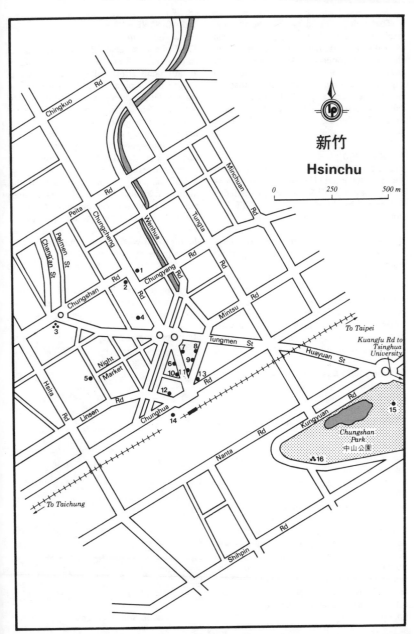

新竹

Hsinchu

The Hsinchu area is very windy, especially in winter, so bring a jacket as it can be really chilly at night. From the bus stop to the top of the mountain takes over an hour of hiking up a steep incline, so try to keep luggage to a minimum. If your backpack is overloaded, you can put the heavy items in a box and stash it in the luggage storage room at the Hsinchu train station for NT$12 per day.

### Places to Stay

Staying at a monastery is a major attraction for many travellers. The more or less mandatory donation is NT$300 and this includes dinner and breakfast. It's another NT$50 if you stay for lunch. In keeping with Buddhist custom, all the meals are vegetarian. If you don't think you want to stay in a monastery, then visit Shihtoushan as a day trip from Hsinchu.

The most popular monastery is the *Yuankuang Temple*. It's near the top of the mountain, offers the best scenery and there is a caretaker who can speak English. The other monasteries which offer accommodation are *Linghsia Cave* (*língxiá dòng*); and *Chuanhua Hall* (*qùanhùa táng*).

### Getting There & Away

From Hsinchu, you cannot go directly to Shihtoushan – you must transfer buses. First take a bus to Chutung (*zhúdōng*), which is a 25 minute trip. Buses run about once every 10 minutes from the terminal of the Hsinchu Bus Company (*xīnzhú kèyùn*), which is on the traffic circle in front of the Hsinchu railway station.

From Chutung there are buses to Shihtoushan, a 40 minute trip. They are not frequent. As always, the schedule is subject to change, but at the time of writing departures from Chutung were at 6.40 and 10.40 am, and at 1.55 and 5 pm. The first bus does not run on Sundays or holidays because it's used primarily to shuttle schoolchildren. On weekends, there are additional buses at 8.30 and 9.15 am, and at 3.30 pm. The bus lets you off at the last stop and from there you walk up, up, up.

### TAPACHIENSHAN

*(dà bà jiān shān)* 大霸尖山

This is the most beautiful peak in Taiwan. At an elevation of 3505 metres, it's not exactly an afternoon stroll either. The summit is shaped like a pyramid and is sheer on all sides, but it is possible to reach the top, partly thanks to some metal railings that were installed by the government. The railings do impinge slightly on the natural setting, but not too much, and they are probably necessary to keep the fatality rate down to a reasonable level.

Unfortunately, the situation here is the same as at Yushan – the whole area requires a class A mountain pass, and individual travellers cannot get one unless accompanied by a licensed guide. The most practical way to do this trip is with a mountain club. Contact the Alpine Association ROC (tel (02) 5911498), 10th floor, 185 Chungshan N Rd, Section 2, Taipei.

The peak is not actually near Hsinchu, but that's more or less the starting point. Take a bus from the terminal of the Hsinchu Bus

The summit of Tapachienshan

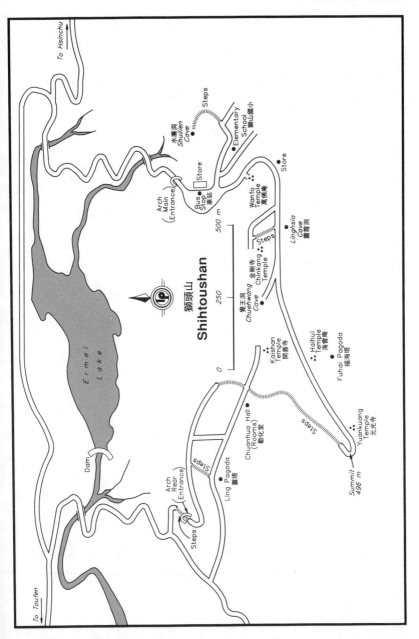

獅頭山
Shihtoushan

To Hsinchu

To Toufen

Ermei Lake

Dam

水濂洞 Shuilien Cave

Steps

Elementary School 獅山國小

Store

Arch Main (Entrance)

Bus Stop 車站

500 m

250

0

Wanfo Temple 萬佛庵

Store

Chinkang Temple 金剛寺 Chinkang Temple

Steps

Linghsia Cave 靈霞洞

覺王洞 Chuehwang Cave

Kaishan Temple 開善寺

Haihui Temple 海會庵

Fuhai Pagoda 福海塔

Yuankuang Temple 元光寺

Summit 496 m

Steps

Chuanhua Hall (Rooms) 勸化堂

Ling Pagoda 靈塔

Arch Rear (Entrance)

Steps

Steps

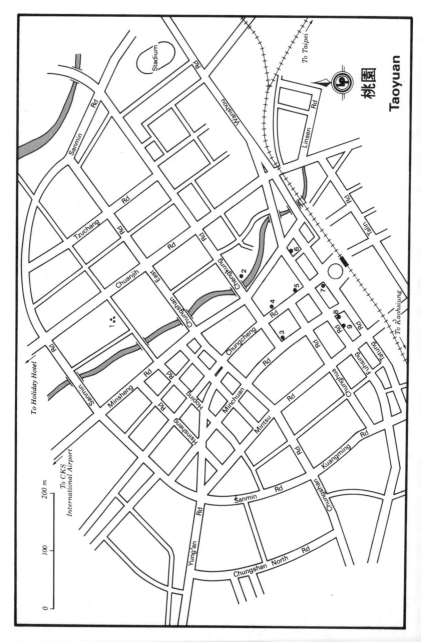

Taoyuan

桃園

| | |
|---|---|
| 1 | Paoan Temple<br>寶安寺 |
| 2 | ICBC<br>國際商業銀行 |
| 3 | GPO<br>郵政總局 |
| 4 | Far Eastern Department Store<br>遠東百貨 |
| 5 | McDonalds<br>麥當勞 |
| 6 | Hotel Today<br>今日飯店 |
| 7 | Taoyuan Bus Company<br>桃園客運 |
| 8 | Taiwan Bus Company<br>台汽客運 |
| 9 | Taoyuan Plaza Hotel<br>南華大飯店 |

Company (*xīnzhú kèyùn*) to the town of Chutung (*zhúdōng*). From there you can get a bus to the base of Tapachienshan.

## TAOYUAN
*(táoyúan)* 桃園

If you have been travelling around Taiwan in a clockwise direction, it is not necessary to return to Taipei if you are leaving from CKS International Airport. Of course many people do like to stay in Taipei for the nightlife, but there is another alternative.

The airport is adjacent to the city of Taoyuan, south-west of Taipei. You should certainly stay in Taoyuan rather than Taipei if your flight departs at 4 am or some other ungodly hour. There are no buses at this time of the morning, but a taxi from Taoyuan to the airport will be cheaper and faster than from Taipei. Negotiate the fare in advance. Last time I was there, drivers were asking NT$300 to NT$400.

### Information
**Tourist Office** The Tourism Bureau (tel (033) 376611) maintains an office on the 2nd floor, 2 Chengkung Rd, Section 2.

**Money** You can easily change money at the airport. However, if you prefer to do it in the city, ICBC (tel (03) 3376611) has a branch at 2 Chengkung Rd, Section 2.

**Travel Agent** If you still haven't bought an air ticket to leave Taiwan, you can get one at Southeast Travel Service (tel (03) 3354677), 244 Fuhsing Rd.

### Places to Stay
Not surprisingly, hotels are abundant in Taoyuan. You can find them in the train station area, and there is also one adjacent to the airport. If you are a budget traveller it might be better to stay in Taipei, as there are no youth hostels or dirt cheap hotels in Taoyuan.

One of the best deals is *Hotel Today* (tel (03) 3324162) (*jīnrì fàndiàn*), 81 Fuhsing Rd, where singles/doubles are NT$735/840. The *tiān wáng xīng bīngǔan* (tel (03) 3364135), 7th floor, 60 Chungcheng Rd (same building as the Far Eastern Department Store), has doubles for NT$700.

Some more expensive places are: *Taoyuan Plaza Hotel* (tel (03) 3379222, fax 3379250) (*nánhúa dàfàndiàn*), 151 Fuhsing Rd, where doubles/twins are NT$1260/1575; and *Holiday Hotel* (tel (03) 3254021) (*táoyúan jiàrì dàfàndiàn*), 269 Tahsing Rd, where doubles are NT$1800 and twins are NT$2000.

There is also the *CKS Airport Hotel* (tel (03) 3833666, fax 3833546) (*zhōngzhèng gúojì jīchǎng lügǔan*), PO Box 66, CKS Airport, Taoyuan. Singles are NT$1785 and twins range from NT$1890 to NT$2100. The hotel is right in the airport area, about 2 km from the terminal building, and not close to anything else. Most of the guests are either flight crews or transit passengers whose departing flight was unexpectedly delayed.

### Getting There & Away
If you are coming from Hsinchu, Taichung, Chiayi or other places in the south, you could take a train or bus to Taoyuan. The train is usually more convenient because most highway buses bypass Taoyuan and head directly to Taipei. All north-south trains on the west coast stop in Taoyuan.

## AROUND TAOYUAN
### CKS Airport
*(táoyúan zhōngzhèng jīchǎng)*
桃園中正機場

During the day and in the early evening, there is a direct bus running from the Taoyuan train station area to the airport. Don't forget to save NT$300 for the departure tax. You must have receipts if you want to change NT$ back into US$ or other foreign currency. The bank in the airport stays open until 7.30 pm. They are also meant to open if there is a late departure, although once when I needed to change money at 8 pm the bank wasn't open. To be on the safe side, don't have excessive NT$ if you are departing late at night. It is very difficult to exchange NT$ outside Taiwan, except in Hong Kong, but even there the exchange rate is not as good. Only in Taiwan will you get the official rate.

If you've been reading the pamphlets put out by the Tourism Bureau, you might have heard of the Chiang Kaishek Aviation Museum (tel (03) 3832677) *(zhōngzhèng hángkōng kēxúe gǔan)*. It's not a bad museum, but most travellers will find it inaccessible. It is right next to the CKS Airport Hotel, a full 2 km from the airline terminal building. You might think that you could walk there, but you would have to walk on a freewaylike road with no pedestrian footpaths. Nor is there a regular shuttle bus. About the only people who get to see the museum are guests at the CKS Airport Hotel. It's open from 9 am to 4.30 pm every day except Monday, and admission is NT$30.

# Index

## Maps

## THANKS

Thanks must go to the following readers who wrote into us with information about Taiwan:

Michael Bauer (HK), Eric Bouteiller (Tai), Gordon Boyce (Tai), Jeff Brauer (USA), Sandy Brauer (USA), Lawrence Brown (Tai), David L Burdette (Tai), Andrew Burgin (Chi), I Ming Chan (Aus), Joanna Cheung (HK), William Combs, Anthony Coogan (UK), John Coomber, Richard Cox (HK), Dr Diana Crampton (It), Kayla Dakota (Tai), Jack Dempsie (Tai), Terry Desjarlais (USA), Doug Dewar (C), Julian Di Bez (Aus), Lynne Doole (J), Ira S Drucker (USA), Nancy Eng (Tai), Dag Fritzson (Sw), Tara Gallagher (USA), Laure Gilbert (Tai), Wolf Gotthilf (D), Mark Graham, Jan Hader (USA), Harald Hagg (Nl), Mary Ann Hales (USA), Stephanie Haudtmann (D), David Hobbs (USA), Amigo Hostel (Tai), David & Greba Hughes (UK), Peter Hutcheson (USA), Dianne Ingram, V A A Jacobsen (Dk), Steffan Jonsson (Sw), Ruthil F Kemmerer (USA), Andreas Kiefer (CH), Yoni Kuperman (Thai), Monika Landolt (CH), John Lee (Tai), Efrat & Ran Lilach (Isr), Jeanie Lin (Tai), Des McKenna (Aus), J Miller (Tai), Jane Moore (CH), Dan O'Brien (USA), Judy Perry, Philip Rees (UK), Lis Reichhoff (D), Sonia Salah (C), Bill Sander (USA), Allan Scarff (UK), Michael Schur, Frank Shelton, J M Shotwell (USA), J P Siau (F), John Singleton (USA), Wolfgang Spude (D), Carl Stevenage (Aus), Lester Stoller (USA), Jenny Su (Tai), I J Swift (UK), Neil Taylor (UK), A H Tellier (USA) Jean-François Tremblay (C), Dean Vandenbrink (C), Lucia Vigil (USA), Nick Vivian (UK), Ian Walter (Aus), Cal Warnecke (USA), Thomas Weiss (D), Michael William (J), Joseph C Williams (J), Yew Ho Yong (S).

Aus – Australia, C – Canada, CH – Switzerland, Chi – China, D – Germany, Dk – Denmark, F – France, HK – Hong Kong, Isr – Israel, It – Italy, J – Japan, Nl – Netherlands, S – Singapore, Sw – Sweden, Tai – Taiwan, Thai – Thailand, UK – United Kingdom, USA – United States of America.

| cm | in |
|----|-----|
| 0 | 0 |
| 1 | |
| 2 | |
| | 1 |
| 3 | |
| 4 | |
| 5 | 2 |
| 6 | |
| 7 | |
| | 3 |
| 8 | |
| 9 | |
| 10 | 4 |
| 11 | |
| 12 | |
| 13 | 5 |
| 14 | |
| 15 | 6 |
| 16 | |

## Temperature

To convert °C to °F multiply by 1.8 and add 32
To convert °F to °C subtract 32 and multiply by .55

## Length, Distance & Area

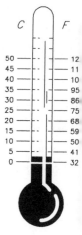

|  | *multiply by* |
|---|---|
| inches to centimetres | 2.54 |
| centimetres to inches | 0.39 |
| feet to metres | 0.30 |
| metres to feet | 3.28 |
| yards to metres | 0.91 |
| metres to yards | 1.09 |
| miles to kilometres | 1.61 |
| kilometres to miles | 0.62 |
| acres to hectares | 0.40 |
| hectares to acres | 2.47 |

## Weight

|  | *multiply by* |
|---|---|
| ounces to grams | 28.35 |
| grams to ounces | 0.035 |
| pounds to kilograms | 0.45 |
| kilograms to pounds | 2.21 |
| British tons to kilograms | 1016 |
| US tons to kilograms | 907 |

A British ton is 2240 lbs, a US ton is 2000 lbs

## Volume

|  | *multiply by* |
|---|---|
| imperial gallons to litres | 4.55 |
| litres to imperial gallons | 0.22 |
| US gallons to litres | 3.79 |
| litres to US gallons | 0.26 |

5 imperial gallons equals 6 US gallons
a litre is slightly more than a US quart, slightly less than a
British one

# Guides to North-East Asia

*North-East Asia on a shoestring*
Concise information for independent low-budget travel in China, Hong Kong, Japan, Macau, South Korea and Taiwan, plus short notes on North Korea.

*Hong Kong, Macau & Canton - a travel survival kit*
This practical guide had all the travel facts on these three diverse cities, linked by history, culture and geography.

*China - a travel survival kit*
This book is the recognised authority for independent travellers in the People's Republic. With essential tips for avoiding pitfalls, and comprehensive practical information, it will help you to discover the real China.

*Tibet - a travel survival kit*
The fabled mountain-land of Tibet was one of the last areas of China to become accessible to travellers. This guide has full details on this remote and fascinating region, including the border crossing to Nepal.

*Japan - a travel survival kit*
Japan is a unique contrast of modern cities and remote wilderness areas, of sophisticated technology and ancient tradition. This guide tells you how to find the Japan that many visitors never see.

*Korea - a travel survival kit*
The second edition of this comprehensive guide includes an exclusive chapter on North Korea, one of the world's most reclusive countries – finally opening its doors to independent travellers.

*Also available:*
*China* phrasebook, *Korean* phrasebook, *Tibet* phrasebook, and *Japanese* phrasebook.

# Lonely Planet Guidebooks

Lonely Planet guidebooks cover every accessible part of Asia as well as Australia, the Pacific, Central and South America, Africa, Eastern Europe, the Middle East and parts of North America. There are four main series: *travel survival kits*, covering a single country for a range of budgets; *shoestring* guides with compact information for low-budget travel in a major region; *walking* guides ; and *phrasebooks*.

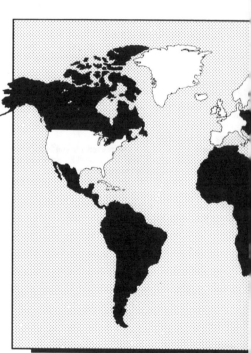

# Mail Order

Lonely Planet guidebooks are distributed worldwide and are sold by good bookshops everywhere. They are also available by mail order from Lonely Planet, so if you have difficulty finding a title please write to us. US and Canadian residents should write to Embarcadero West, 112 Linden St, Oakland CA 94607, USA and residents of other countries to PO Box 617, Hawthorn, Victoria 3122, Australia.

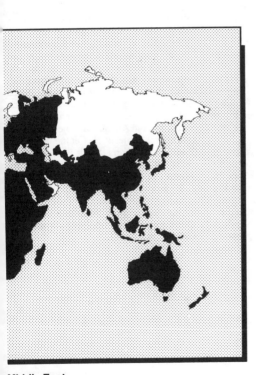

## Eastern Europe
Eastern Europe

## Indian Subcontinent
Bangladesh
India
Hindi/Urdu phrasebook
Karakoram Highway
Kashmir, Kadakh & Zanskar
Nepal
Nepal phrasebook
Pakistan
Sri Lanka
Sri Lanka phrasebook
Trekking in the Indian Himalaya
Trekking in the Nepal Himalaya

## Africa
Africa on a shoestring
Central Africa
East Africa
Swahili phrasebook
Morocco, Algeria & Tunisia
West Africa

## North America
Alaska
Canada
Hawaii

## Mexico
Baja California
Mexico

## South America
Argentina
Bolivia
Brazil
Brazilian phrasebook
Chile & Easter Island
Colombia
Ecuador & the Galapagos Islands
Peru
Quechua phrasebook
South America on a shoestring

## Middle East
Egypt & the Sudan
Egyptian Arabic phrasebook
Israel
Jordan & Syria
Yemen

## The Lonely Planet Story

Lonely Planet published its first book in 1973 in response to the numerous 'How did you do it?' questions Maureen and Tony Wheeler were asked after driving, bussing, hitching, sailing and railing their way from England to Australia.

Written at a kitchen table and hand collated, trimmed and stapled, *Across Asia on the Cheap* became an instant local bestseller, inspiring thoughts of another book.

Eighteen months in Southeast Asia resulted in their second guide, *South-East Asia on a shoestring*, which they put together in a backstreet Chinese hotel in Singapore in 1975. The 'yellow bible' as it quickly became known to backpackers around the world, soon became *the* guide to the region. It has sold well over 1/2 a million copies and is now in its sixth edition, still retaining its familiar yellow cover.

Today there are over 80 Lonely Planet titles – books that have that same adventurous approach to travel as those early guides; books that 'assume you know how to get your luggage off the carousel' as one reviewer put it.

Although Lonely Planet initially specialised in guides to Asia, they now cover most regions of the world, including the Pacific, South America, Africa, the Middle East and Eastern Europe. The list of *walking guides* and *phrasebooks* (for 'unusual' languages such as Quechua, Swahili, Nepalese and Egyptian Arabic) is also growing rapidly.

The emphasis continues to be on travel for independent travellers. Tony and Maureen still travel for several months of each year and play an active part in the writing, updating and quality control of Lonely Planet's guides.

They have been joined by over 50 authors, 40 staff – mainly editors, cartographers, & designers – at our office in Melbourne, Australia, and another 10 at our US office in Oakland, California. Travellers themselves also make a valuable contribution to the guides through the feedback we receive in thousands of letters each year.

The people at Lonely Planet strongly believe that travellers can make a positive contribution to the countries they visit, both through their appreciation of the countries' culture, wildlife and natural features, and through the money they spend. In addition, the company makes a direct contribution to the countries and regions it covers. Since 1986 a percentage of the income from each book has been donated to ventures such as famine relief in Africa; aid projects in India; agricultural projects in Central America; Greenpeace's efforts to halt French nuclear testing in the Pacific and Amnesty International. In 1990 $60,000 was donated to these causes.

Lonely Planet's basic travel philosophy is summed up in Tony Wheeler's comment, 'Don't worry about whether your trip will work out. Just go!'